THE WILDLIFE STORIES OF FAITH McNULTY

THE WILDLIFE STORIES OF

by Faith McNulty

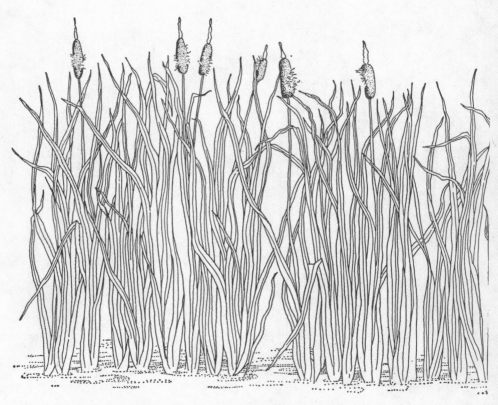

DOUBLEDAY & COMPANY, INC.

FAITH McNULTY

illustrated by Robin Brickman

GARDEN CITY, NEW YORK 1980

Books by Faith McNulty

THE GREAT WHALES
MUST THEY DIE?
THE WHOOPING CRANE
THE BURNING BED
THE WILDLIFE STORIES OF FAITH MCNULTY

To Richard Martin
Who Took Part in Everything

CONTENTS

Prologue: BECOMING AN ANIMAL REPORTER   1
  1. MOUSE   11
  2. BRITISH MICE   23
  3. A SWIM WITH A MANATEE   47
  4. SOUTH COUNTY NOTES   61
  5. KOKO KISSED ME   97
  6. THE WHOOPING CRANE   121
  7. THE EVER HUNGRY JAY   311
  8. AND THE INDRI SANG   319
  9. WOODCHUCK   371
 10. THE FALCONS OF MORRO ROCK   383
 11. A DESERT FISH   397
 12. THE GREAT WHALES   413
Epilogue: AND THE SONG ENDS   467

THE WILDLIFE STORIES OF FAITH McNULTY

Prologue
BECOMING AN ANIMAL REPORTER

I don't really know why I like animals so much, any more than I know why some people don't. I was brought up in a family in which animals played a large part. Our circle included dogs, cats, horses, and whatever stray wild things I was able to find on a New England farm—snakes, toads, woodchucks, rabbits, robins, turtles. But neither exposure nor heredity guarantees a rapport with animals. My mother and father loved animals. My aunt, who lived with us and was constantly exposed to them, did not. I think she tried but failed. She wished them all well and wished they would stay out of the house and especially out of her bathtub. They simply had no message for her.

Perhaps "message" is the key word in describing the attraction of animals—at least for me. The message is a cryptic one, but I feel a certainty it is there.

Many lucky people find all their questions answered by Scripture. Others orient themselves in time and space by their relation to their own species. Neither has helped me very much in fixing my position in creation. But when I watch a bird fly, or hold a mouse in my hand, I feel something drawing me as hidden water draws a forked stick held in the hands of a dowser. It is a sensation of intense curiosity; a feeling of messages written there if only I could read them. If answers to the central mysteries are spelled out anywhere, I believe it is in the pyramid of life, and any mouse might be a Rosetta Stone.

Of course, I haven't had such heavy thoughts on my mind as I've gone about my business of meeting animals and reporting what I've learned. In fact, I never defined these feelings until a little while ago, when I began to put down notes seeking to explain why I chose this rather peculiar line of research.

My interest began, I'm sure, in childhood when I wanted so much to know what it is like to be an animal; how it would feel to be part of their world, to see *our* world through their eyes. This is a primitive question, ages old, that possibly dates back to whenever it was that man stopped talking to animals or lost the ability to read their minds by reading his own. I believe the question still occurs anew to any child who has the opportunity to watch birds fly, to stroke a purring cat, or exchange kisses with a loving dog. Unhappily, however, more and more modern children are denied contact with nonhuman creatures and their curiosity and intuitive feeling of kinship wither away. I say "unhappily" because I believe it is a vital experience to do as I did long ago; catch a frog and discover that it has bony fingers and golden eyes; dig up an earthworm and feel its slithery vitality as it squirms on your palm, watch cows graze and calves nurse. People who grow up ignorant of the 99 percent of creation that is nonhuman have, it seems to me, a sadly limited idea of where they are.

There are many aspects to the mystery that draws me to animals. Animals make their living in such extraordinary ways. For any species to be here it must find food and shelter and evade death long enough to mate and bring forth viable young. I think of the difficulty I have in doing these things even though I have great stored resources to draw on. My shelter and other needs are supplied by specialists. Without this help I would quickly die. The little red fox out in my woods fends for herself and saves her own life anew each day. If I were her size, without hands, without companions (and perhaps with four kids), I feel sure I wouldn't make it. But the fox does it all with what seems like ease and grace and has time left over for sunbathing on the sandbank down by the pond.

Again we come back to the question of mind. We know that the fox is guided by a mind just as we are, but there our knowledge stops short. What kind of mind is unknown. We know that the physical components of her brain are simpler, but not radically different from our own. We know that the fox has memory, that she makes choices, and shows some emotions comparable to human emotions—fear, anger, pleasure, devotion to offspring. Along with such similarities there are very large differences. Some are differences in the development of the five senses. Imagine what it would be like to be able to smell what a fox can smell —the footprint of a rabbit in the grass, for instance—or to "feel" one's way in the dark by echolocation like bats and dolphins.

How a fox or a dolphin or any other animal perceives its world and makes its choices, to what extent it "thinks" in the sense that we think, is a question that several generations of scientists have refused to deal with, regarding it as unanswerable, anthropomorphic, and foolishly unscientific. Dr. Donald R. Griffin of Rockefeller University, in a critical review of the dominant attitudes of twentieth-century behavioral science, published in 1976, noted that many scientists would clearly prefer to pack such questions as I have mentioned back into the "secure Pandora's Box where they have quietly rested for so many years." "Others," Griffin wrote, "appear simply to prefer statements of faith that man is radically different in kind from all other animals and, furthermore, is intrinsically superior, not only mentally but in fundamental moral values." Currently a new wave of investigators of animal behavior are beginning to pick at the lock of Pandora's Box, and already one or two disconcerting secrets have slipped out. The idea that animals may use both tools and language, for instance, can cause much mischief to the belief that man is unique in his possession of mental experience.

I do not pretend to be a student of the new ethology or capable of interpreting it in serious depth, since I am a writer, not a scientist, but I have learned of the new trend in the scientific study of animals with a great deal of pleasure, since it grapples with some of the ideas that intrigue me most.

When I was a child we had a big telescope on the porch. One clear night my father pointed it at the moon. I saw the silver sphere transformed into a pale, stony desert marked with craters. Some mystery, at least, was dispelled. "But," said my father, "what is on the *other* side? That is something no one will ever know." He was proved wrong in my lifetime. I wish I could live long enough for further answers about the hidden side of animal life to be similarly revealed.

Another aspect of animals that attracts me is quite simply their beauty. To my mind it is hard to find an ugly animal. When I do find one ugly it is usually because it reminds me of some unattractive quality of my own species. The rhino has a mean squint. Hippos are obese, like cartoon fat ladies. Male elephant seals have swollen noses that look as though they had been caught in a slammed door. A while ago I visited an island off Lower California where elephant seals haul up on the beach. Watching the massive, lumpy bull seals humping about, I felt as though some mischievous person had tied their hind legs together—or that perhaps they were contestants in a sack race. I'm sure their way of getting around doesn't bother elephant seals, but it bothered anthropomorphic me.

Primates, apes and monkeys, of course arouse the most anthropomorphic feelings of all. To my mind, there are more species that could be considered ugly among our cousins than in any other family. Blue-nosed baboons and whoever those fellows are whose bright red behinds look too sore to sit down on make me grateful that evolution didn't bestow those attributes on me, as it possibly could have.

But ugly animals seem to me to be rare, while many are so beautiful; unexpectedly and ravishingly beautiful. My lovely cat now and then brings in a newly dead chipmunk. I take it from her and hold it limp and still warm in my hand while I admire it. I feel a bit sad because it is dead, but after all it was a quick and natural death. Close at hand, I can see all the complex shadings of color of the chipmunk's coat: russet, fawn, white, and sharp fine lines of black. I marvel at the design; a unique design belonging to chipmunks only. I wonder: Why? Why does it have perfect, pencil stripes of black? Something to do with camouflage, I suppose, but if so, why don't other rodents who share their habitat have the same markings? Even the beauty of animals stirs curiosity and poses questions.

I feel this curiosity all over again each time I have a chance to see and learn about a species that is new to me. My first such chance came to me quite accidentally about fifteen years ago, when my husband found a baby mouse on the doorstep of the barn. We raised her, and for the first time since I grew up I had an opportunity to observe a wild animal—if not in the wild, at least close at hand and undisturbed by my presence. The mouse fascinated me. I went to the library to read up on mice and underwent my first experience in groping, untrained, through biological literature. I found it difficult, but not impossible.

Perhaps I should explain, going back a bit biographically, that until the time of the mouse I had spent my adult years working in New York, surrounded by cement and engrossed in human affairs. In the 1940's, when I began to work as a writer, articles on wildlife were comparatively rare. I always read whatever animal stories I came across with particular interest, but it did not occur to me that writing them could become a specialty. In 1958, my husband and I moved to a farm in Wakefield, Rhode Island, only a mile or two from the one where I summered as a child. I wrote a piece about the mouse for *Audubon Magazine,* and then, casting about for a subject for a long piece for *The New Yorker* (where, I am proud to say, I have been employed for some years), I became involved with whooping cranes. What, I wondered, *is* a whooping crane, and why should it become extinct? I began my research from a platform of total ignorance. This can be very helpful when you start to learn about a subject, because it means your curiosity is intact. You haven't lost your virginity, so to speak.

One animal led to another; cranes to black-footed ferrets, to whales, and so on. I began to learn the ropes; how to find experts on whatever animal I was interested in at the moment and pick out from their store of knowledge the pieces that were of use to me. I'm particularly inclined to like people who like animals, and meeting them has been an extra reward of my work. On the darker side is what I have learned about the ever-widening conflict between the needs and desires of the human race and the needs of animals. I was once so naïve I didn't know that animals are a source of much controversy, bitterness, and conflict among humans. Most of it stems from competition between man and animal for food and land. I found that animals often share the same fate as other inarticulate minorities—they are cheated, exploited, and abused. Laws designed to protect them are flouted and immediate human gain or gratification put above long-term benefits for all. A need for living space compels human beings as it does animals, and all over the world, people are taking over forests, deserts, mountains, and seas that once belonged to animals. This force is so huge and of such complex components that no one can suggest a solution or foresee the outcome. This aspect of animal affairs was not known to me when I started reporting. Learning of it, and finding that the best-informed people have the least hope of an outcome favorable to animals, has been very sad.

My sorrow and anger over this has, I am sure, influenced a great deal of what I have written, but it is not what I want to dwell on in this book. Here I want to pass along what I have learned about the animals I've met; to tell as nearly as possible what they are like, and how it has felt to see them at close hand. Above all I would like to convey, if I can, the great pleasure some of these experiences have brought me.

Once I found myself in the cockpit of a sailboat in the Atlantic off Bermuda listening through earphones to the sound of whales singing underwater as they glided invisibly somewhere below the surface like living submarines. For me it was an extraordinary moment, and I felt incomparably fortunate and grateful to fate for giving it to me. In a closer encounter, I paid a visit to a gorilla. I had always been curious about how it would feel to be close to a great ape without bars and without fear. We met and after an exchange of gifts Koko, the gorilla, kissed me. She smelled sweet, like new-mown hay, and we looked into each other's eyes with almost equal curiosity. My attention span, however, was longer. While I remained fascinated she dismissed me in favor of a peanut-butter sandwich.

To see another primate I went as far as Madagascar, where lemurs, the most primitive member of our family, are found. The largest lemur now living is the indri. They are beautiful black and white animals, without tails and with huge golden eyes, that sometimes walk erect but spend most of their lives in the tree-tops. One morning I found myself on a path in a Madagascar forest as the sun was coming up, turning the dew into soft mist and sending golden shafts through the forest. I knew that somewhere high in the treetops, warmed by those golden shafts, indris were rising from their leafy beds and preparing to meet the dawn in a fashion that went back through uncountable years to the beginning of their time. At dawn, and at some other times too, indris raise their voices in what might be called song. I waited, and the song came. It was so beautiful and strange that I was unprepared and overwhelmed. Thinking of it now, and of how little time is left in which there will be indris to sing, makes me want to cry. But as I stood in the forest, listening, it was a moment of great wonder and happiness.

1

MOUSE

On a sunny morning in early September my husband called me out to the barn of our Rhode Island farm. I found him holding a tin can and peering into it with an expression of foolish pleasure. He handed me the can as though it contained something he had just picked up at Tiffany's. Crouched at the bottom was a young mouse, not much bigger than a bumblebee. It stared up with eyes like polished seeds. Its long whiskers vibrated like a hummingbird's wings. It was a beautiful little creature and clearly still too small to cope with a wide and dangerous world.

I don't know how old Mouse was when Richard found her, but I doubt it was a fortnight. She was not only tiny, but weak. He told me he had found her on the doorstep and that when he picked her up he thought she was done for. By chance he had a gumdrop in his pocket. He placed it on his palm beside the limp mouse. The smell acted as a quick stimulant. She struggled to her feet and flung herself upon the gumdrop, ate voraciously, and was almost instantly restored to health.

Richard made a wire cage for Mouse (we never found a name more fitting), and we made a place for it on a table in the kitchen. Here I could watch her while I was peeling vegetables but I found that I often simply watched while uncounted minutes went by. I had had no idea that there were so many things to notice about a mouse.

For the first few days Mouse had the gawkiness of a puppy. Her head and feet looked too big. Her hind legs had a tendency to spraddle. But she had fine sharp teeth and a striking air of manful competence. She cleaned herself, all over, with serious pride. Her method was oddly catlike. Sitting on her small behind (she could have sat on a postage stamp without spilling over), she licked her flanks, then moistened her paws to go over her ears, neck, and face. She would grasp a hind leg with suddenly simian hands while she licked the extended toes. For the finale she would pick up her tail, and as though eating corn on the cob, wash its inch and a half of threadlike length with her tongue.

Mouse's baby coat was dull gunmetal gray. It soon changed to a bright reddish brown. Her belly remained white. She had dark gray anklets and white feet. I had thought of mouse tails as hairless and limp. Not so. Mouse's tail was furred, and rather than trailing it behind her like a piece of string, she held it quite stiffly. Sometimes it rose over her back like a quivering question mark.

When Mouse's coat turned red I was able to identify her from a book—*The Mammals of Rhode Island*—which said that although *leucopus,* or white-footed mice, are easily confused with *maniculatus,* or deer mice, there are only *leucopus* in Rhode Island. The book also said that white-footed mice are found everywhere, from hollow trees to bureau drawers; that they are nocturnal and a favorite food of owls. Judging by Mouse's enthusiasm for chicken, owl, if she could get it, would be one of *her* favorite foods. Her range of taste was wide. Though grains were a staple, she liked meat, fruit, and vegetables. I usually offered her a tiny bit of whatever was on the chopping board. She tasted and considered each item, rejecting some and seizing others with delight. A melon seed was a great prize. To this day, when I throw melon seeds in the garbage I feel sad to waste them and wish I had a mouse to give them to.

Mouse became tame within a few days of her capture. She nibbled my fingers and batted them with her paws like a playful puppy. She liked to be stroked. If I held her in my hand and rubbed gently with a forefinger, she would raise her chin, the way a cat will, to be stroked along the jawbone, then raise a foreleg and wind up lying flat on her back in the palm of my hand, eyes closed, paws hanging limp, and nose pointed upward in apparent bliss.

Mouse could distinguish people. If, when she was asleep, I poked my finger into her nest, she licked and nibbled it as though grooming it. If my husband offered his finger, she would

sniff it and then give it a firm little bite accompanied by an indignant chirp. When, for a time, she was in my sister's care, she accepted my sister but bit anyone else. In one respect, however, she never trusted even me. She suspected me of intending to steal her food. If I approached while she was eating she assumed a protective crouch. I think she was uttering tiny ultrasonic growls.

When I looked up scientific studies of mice I was disappointed to find that most investigators had been interested, not in the mice, but in using them as a tool to study something related to human physiology. In one paper, however, I read that "in mice the rate of defecation and urination is an index of emotionality." Dedicated scientists had spent days harassing mice and counting the resultant hail of tiny turds. I had assumed that mice have no control over these functions; an inference based on the careless behavior of certain anonymous mice that sometimes visited my kitchen shelves. When I handled Mouse, however, nothing of the sort ever happened. It could not have been sheer luck. She must have exercised some restraint.

I was surprised by still other aspects of Mouse's behavior. She was a heavy sleeper. She slept in a plastic cup from a thermos, covering herself with a bedding of rags that she shredded into fluff as soft as a down quilt. If I pushed aside the covers I would find her curled up on her side like a doughnut, dead to the world. As I touched her, her eyes would open. Then she would raise her chin, stretch herself, and yawn enormously, showing four wicked front teeth and a red tongue that curled like a wolf's. She would rise slowly, carefully stretching her hind legs and long toes, then suddenly pull herself together, fan out her whiskers, and be ready for anything. Her athletic ability was astounding. As she climbed around her cage she became incredibly flexible, stretching this way and that like a rubber band. She could easily stand on her hind legs to reach something dangled above her. Her jumping power was tremendous. Once I put her in an empty garbage pail while I cleaned her cage. She made a straight-upward leap of fifteen inches and neatly cleared the rim.

Mouse's cage was equipped with an exercise wheel, on which she traveled many a league to nowhere. Richard and I racked our brains for a way to utilize "one mouse-power." Her cage was also furnished with twigs that served as a perch. After a while I replaced her plastic cup with half a coconut shell, inverted and with a door cut in the lower edge. It made a most attractive mouse house; quite tropical in feeling. She stuffed her house from floor to ceiling with fluff. She kept some food in the house, but her major storehouse was a small aluminum can screwed to the wall of the cage. We called it (and beg the generous reader to forgive the cuteness), the First Mouse National Bank. If I sprinkled birdseed on the floor of her cage, Mouse would work diligently to transport it, stuffed in her cheeks, for deposit in her bank.

Mouse was full of curiosity and eager to explore. When I opened the door of her cage she ran about the tabletop in short bursts of motion, looking, somehow, as though she were on roller skates. I feared she might skate right over the edge of the table, but she always managed to stop in time. All objects she met— books, pencils, ashtrays, rubber bands, and such odds and ends— were subjected to a taste test. If a thing was portable, a pencil for instance, she might haul it a short way. Her attention was brief; a quick nibble and on to the next. One day she encoun- tered a chicken bone. She grabbed it in her teeth and began to tug. As she danced around, pulling and hauling, she looked like a terrier struggling to retrieve the thighbone of an elephant. Alas, the task was too great. She had to settle for a fragment of meat and leave the bone behind.

What fascinated me most was Mouse's manual dexterity. Her front paws had four long fingers and a rudimentary thumb. She used them to hold, to manipulate, and to stuff things into her mouth for carrying. Her paws were equally equipped for climb- ing. They had small projections, like the calluses inside a man's hand, that helped her to cling, fly fashion, to vertical surfaces.

Though Mouse kept busy, I feared her life might be warped by loneliness and asked a biologist I knew for help. He not only determined Mouse's sex (this is not easy; to the layman the rear end of a mouse is quite enigmatic) but provided a laboratory mouse as a companion.

I found the new mouse unattractive. He had a mousy smell, whereas Mouse was odorless; I named him Stinky. His coat was like dusty black felt. He was careless about grooming. He had small, squinty eyes, a Roman nose, a fat-hipped, lumpy shape, and a ratty, hairless tail. Nature would not have been likely to create such a mouse without the help of man. With some misgiv- ings I put him in Mouse's cage. She mounted to the top of her perch and sat shivering and staring, ears cocked so that her face looked like that of a little red fox.

Stinky lumbered about the cage, squinting at nothing in par- ticular. Stumbling over some of Mouse's seeds, he made an en- thusiastic buck-toothed attack on these goodies. This stirred Mouse to action. She flashed down the branch and, cautiously approaching from the rear, nibbled Stinky's tail. He paid no heed, but continued to gobble up whatever he found. Mouse nibbled him more boldly, working up from his tail to the fur of his back. I began to fear she would depilate him before he realized it. Finally she climbed on his back and nibbled his ears. He showed a certain baffled resistance, but made no other response. Disgusted, Mouse ate a few seeds and went to bed.

From this unpromising start a warm attachment bloomed. The two mice slept curled up together. Mouse spent a great deal of time licking Stinky, holding him down and kneading him with her paws. He returned her caresses, but with less ardor, reserving his more passionate interest for food. Food was a source of strife. In a contest Stinky was domineering but dumb. Mouse was quick and clever.

Stinky's greed prompted Richard to fashion Mouse's bank, tailoring the opening to fit her slim figure and exclude Stinky's chubby one—or at least most of it. He could get his head and shoulders inside, but not his fat belly. Richard fastened the bank near the top of the cage. When Stinky got his head in, his hind part was left dangling helplessly, and he soon gave up attempts at robbery.

One day, as an experiment, I put the bank down on the floor of the cage. Stinky sniffed at the opening. Mouse watched, whiskers quivering, and I had the distinct impression of consternation on her face. With a quickness of decision that amazed me, she seized a wad of bedding, dragged it across the floor of the cage, and stuffed it into the door of the bank, effectively corking up her treasure. It was a brilliant move. Baffled, Stinky lumbered away.

In spite of their ungenerous behavior toward each other, I felt that Stinky made a real contribution to Mouse's happiness. Once or twice I separated them for a day or so. Their reunions were joyous, with Mouse scrambling all over Stinky and just about licking him to pieces, and even stolid Stinky showing excitement. They lived together for about a year. I wasn't aware that Stinky was ill, but one day I saw Mouse sitting trembling on her branch when she should have been asleep. I looked in the cup and found Stinky stone-cold dead. "Mouse will miss you," I thought as I heaved his crummy little body into the weeds. I got another laboratory mouse called Pinky to take Stinky's place, but he bullied Mouse so relentlessly that I sent him back. Mouse lived alone for the rest of her days.

Before closing Mouse's story I would like to tell about an episode that took place in Mouse's first weeks with me. After I had had her about ten days I found a lump on her belly near the hind leg. I first noticed it as she lay on her back in my palm while I stroked her. The lump grew larger each day and I feared she had some fatal disease—a tumor of some sort. During the ensuing search for help for Mouse I discovered a peculiar fact about human nature; for some reason people laugh at a mouse.

I live near the University of Rhode Island. I phoned and said I wanted to talk to an expert on mice. The response was laughter. I said my mouse had a mysterious ailment. More laughter, but I was given the name of a woman, Dr. C., I'll call her. Carrying Mouse in her cage, I found the professor in her office. I explained my trouble. When Dr. C. stopped laughing she said she couldn't touch my mouse lest it have germs that would contaminate her laboratory mice. She suggested I ask Dr. H. to examine Mouse. We went to his office. Dr. H. chuckled patronizingly and agreed to look at Mouse's lump. I took her out of her cage and held her belly up for inspection. Both professors gasped at the sight of the lump. Both were baffled.

Dr. H. offered a shot of penicillin, but admitted he had no idea how to measure a dose for a patient weighing half an ounce. Dr. C. forthrightly suggested autopsy. I thanked them and left. Crossing the campus, I passed the library. On an impulse I borrowed a manual of veterinary medicine and took it home.

That evening I skimmed through descriptions of disease after disease looking for symptoms that might fit. Nothing sounded similar to Mouse's trouble until I came to "Cuterebra Infestation" on page 929 and knew I had found the answer. The larva of the botfly, the manual said, lives in a pocket that it forms under the skin of its host, which may be any mammal, most often young. When the parasite reaches full size it emerges through the skin. The manual said that the cure was a simple matter of opening the lump and removing the larva. I hurried to the telephone and dialed a local veterinarian. His wife answered and insisted that I give her the message. Foreseeing difficulty, I replied evasively, "I have an animal that needs a slight operation."

"What kind of animal?" persisted Mrs. Vet.

"A mouse."

There was a long, cold silence. Then the woman asked, in icy tones, "Is it a *white* mouse?"

"No," I admitted. "It is brown."

Mrs. Vet said that her husband did not include mice in his practice and hung up.

The next day my young son hit his toe a glancing blow with an ax while chopping wood, inflicting a wound that needed stitches. As it happened, I had been just about to take Mouse to our local animal shelter for further consultation. She and her cage were in the car as I drove my son to the emergency room at the hospital. While he was being stitched a plan formed in my mind.

The moment John limped out of the operating room I button-holed the young doctor, a nice soap opera type. I told him I had a mouse that needed surgery. He laughed. With his eye on some pretty nurses standing nearby, he made jokes about calling in the anesthetist, scrubbing up, and so on. The nurses giggled and my cause was won. "Don't go away," I cried, and ran out to get Mouse.

When I got back the doctor had the sheepish look of a man who has been trapped by his own jest, but when he saw Mouse's problem his eyes widened with pure scientific amazement. He studied the lump. We gravely discussed the operating procedure. I held Mouse tightly, on her back, in the palm of my hand. A nurse applied a dab of antiseptic. The doctor made a small incision. Mouse squeaked, but there was no blood. The doctor called for forceps and pulled forth a big, horrible, wiggling grub. There was a babble of astonishment, congratulations, and, inevitably, laughter from the crowd that had gathered around us. The doctor looked pleased and put the grub in a bottle of alcohol as a medical curiosity.

I put Mouse in her cage. She ran about lightly, showing no ill effects. I took her and my limping son home. Both patients healed quickly. I paid a large bill for John's toe, but there was no charge for the mouse.

Mouse lived with me for over three years, which is, I believe, a good deal beyond the span usually allotted to mice. She showed no sign of growing old or feeble, but one day I found her dead. As I took her almost weightless body in my hand and carried it out to the meadow, I felt a genuine sadness. In a serious sense she had given me so much. She had stirred my imagination and opened a window on a Lilliputian world no less real than my world for all its miniature dimensions. By watching her I had learned and changed. Beyond that there had been moments, elusive of description, when I had felt a contact between her tiny being and my own. Sometimes when I touched her lovingly and she nibbled my fingers in return, I felt as though an affectionate message were passing between us. The enormous distance between us seemed to be bridged momentarily by faint but perceptible signals.

I put Mouse's body down in the grass and walked back to the house. I knew that there may be as many mice as there are visible stars. They are given life and extinguished as prodigally as leaves unfolding and falling from trees. I was not sad for Mouse because of her death, but sad for me because I knew I would miss her.

2

BRITISH MICE

During the time I had Mouse I found that when I told people about her they tended to be bewildered or incredulous. Most of them felt that mousekeeping was for children and must involve a smelly little fish tank full of white scurrying things, forever reproducing and forever in need of housecleaning. There was an inference that any adult who enjoyed such pets must be daft. I would insist that Mouse was neat and clean and odorless and smart. I showed her off to guests, pointing out her grace and describing her clever feats. Few friends shared my enthusiasm. As a mousekeeper I felt isolated.

A clue that perhaps the British have a warmer understanding of mice came to me in an obituary that I chanced to find in the New York *Times:*

> Lord Wrottesley, the peer who once said, "I prefer my animals to politics," died recently at 88. The Associated Press reported that he had devoted his life to a vain effort to breed the perfect spotted mouse.

I studied this with regret. Here was someone who had shared my feeling that a mouse is capable of perfection. It was frustrating to hear of him only after his death. The news item also raised questions. What, I wondered, is an *imperfect* spotted mouse? Why had Lord Wrottesley's lifelong effort to obtain a perfect one been in vain? And what, for that matter, *is* a spotted mouse? White mice, black mice, and brownish wild mice like mine were the only mice I had ever seen. A little later a British friend who knew of Mouse sent me a handful of pamphlets. "Did you know," she wrote, "that there is a British National Mouse Club? They have been working to improve the breed of what they call 'Fancy Mice' and show them at county fairs."

As a rule, I'm not much interested in "improving" breeds of animals. The results are so often the reverse. I'm not keen on animal beauty contests either; cat and dog shows leave me cold. But there was something about a mouse club that I found irresistible.

I began to look through the pamphlets. It was quickly apparent that the club represented a small band of people who took mice seriously and were proud to carry the banner of the Fancy Mouse. The club's list of members showed a total of about three hundred names. Judging by my own experience, I felt they must be valiant indeed to carry on in the face of public indifference if not derision.

In one of the pamphlets I found a paragraph by C. H. Johnson, a former president of the National Mouse Club, that let me know I had found kindred spirits at last. Johnson wrote:

> I have kept mice for over twenty years and, believe it or not, so great is the beauty, charm and fascination of the Fancy Mouse that my interest never ebbs. I have decided that it is most unkind of us, as Mouse Fanciers, to keep such a good thing to ourselves and that in all fairness our fascinating hobby should be widely known.

Delighted, I read on. Another authority on Fancy Mice, Mr. A. C. Jude, had this to say:

> The ideal mouse is a mouse in its most attractive form . . . graceful in outline, pleasing in color, and of perfect proportions; an animal that would impress by its beauty. Try to visualize such a mouse! . . . The body is long, slim, a trifle arched over loin, and racy looking. The tail is quite as long as the body, and comes out of the body gradually, thick first and then tapering to a fine end. The head of the mouse will draw particular attention. It will be seen that the head is carried without suspicion of neck. It seems to fit straight on to the shoulders, keeping a clean, unbroken line with the chest and back. The width between the ears gives a strong and massive effect. The eyes are large, bold and bright, sometimes black, pink or occasionally ruby, like balls of falling sunlight.

The romance of Mr. Jude's imagery quite overwhelmed me as I followed his instructions to visualize such a mouse. In the next paragraph he pointed out that perfection is never easily attained:

> Much of the pleasing effect gained by good type will be lost unless the coat quality is of high standard. It should be short,

flat to the body, smooth and glossy, and sleek to the hand. This quality must be bred for, and the whole is the outcome of dry, warm housing and correct feeding.

The author then turned to the technical details of breeding:

Mice reach their adult period in roughly three months, and are then ready to mate. . . . The doe carries her young from eighteen to twenty-one days. As soon as a doe is in kindle the buck should be removed. He must on no account be put with other bucks as severe fighting may occur.

I knew that male mice fight, but not that a pregnant mouse is "in kindle." I consulted the Oxford English Dictionary and found that "kindle," a Middle English verb, now dialect, means to bring forth young, with particular reference to hares and rabbits, and was used by Shakespeare in the line "As the Conie that you see dwell where she is kindled." I felt that the use of Shakespearean English gave the subject even greater dignity, and I liked that.

I have long been fascinated by the ingenuity with which people find ways to gratify the aesthetic longing that is born in everyone. Breeding special and beautiful mice seemed to me not only ingenious but to express especially fine perception as well. It also struck me as concentrating within a small compass a number of those traits that we think of as coming to fullest flower in the British character. My husband and I were just then planning a summer trip to England. On an impulse, I decided to look up the British mouse fanciers. I felt sure I would like a mouse show better than a cricket match and even though the mouse fanciers and I might differ in our approach we both belong to the brotherhood of "animal people." Accordingly, I wrote to Mr. Percy Ashley, listed in my pamphlets as "Hon. Secretary, Treasurer and Press Representative" of the National Mouse Club, at 214 Fog Lane, Manchester.

Mr. Ashley's reply was prompt and his stationery was almost as informative as his letter. Beneath his name, printed in big bold type, were the words "Dreamholm Stud" and beneath his address the line "A Craftsman Cabinet Maker" and the further message

"Maker of Maxey Cages—Also Travelling Boxes for Rabbits and Cavies. My boxes are the lightest made, yet strong, saving pounds in Carriage." In another column were the statements:

Life Member and Life Judge of the
National Mouse Club

———

Winner of More Trophies and Prizes
than any other fancier

———

Over 60 Years' Experience

———

Visits by Appointment

The letter itself was brief. "When you are in England I could arrange to meet you at my house," Mr. Ashley wrote. "I could tell you more in five minutes than I could write in hours. I have over sixty years' experience. I await further letter from you."

I wrote back that I would surely visit him.

With my husband, I approached Manchester, and my rendez-vous with Mr. Ashley, by car, in the gloom of a chill, gray summer evening. Manchester is a city of soot-stained brick walls, towers, turrets, gables, and wrought-iron ornaments that make it a museum of Victoriana; fitting headquarters for what I felt must be a somewhat old-fashioned sport.

In the morning, I took a taxi over to Mr. Ashley's house while my husband set off sightseeing in another direction. As I drove through Manchester's cramped and gloomy streets, I reflected that if I lived here I might be more than glad to lose myself in the cultivation of little animals sleek to the hand and with ruby eyes, "like balls of falling sunlight," as Mr. Jude had described the ideal mouse.

Fog Lane, Mr. Ashley's street, was in a district of neat, cottagy brick houses, most of them with a bit of grass or garden. The district spoke neither of richness nor of poverty but of small, snug rooms with fireplaces, pet parakeets, flowery wallpaper, and elderly couples. In front of Mr. Ashley's house was a small yard planted with nasturtiums, and on the gravel walk leading to his door stood a motor scooter. My knock was answered promptly by a short, stocky man, indeterminately elderly, with a pink, round, smiling face. This was Mr. Ashley, who seized my hand and with brisk cordiality ushered me into his study. The room was as snug as I'd expected, but I was unprepared for the array of cups and trophies that crowded every table and shelf, and the banners, ribbons, and plaques that covered most of its wall space.

Mr. Ashley settled me in a chair by his crowded desk, seated himself, and beamed as I stared about the room at the incredible clutter. "I've won more prizes," he announced, in a rich North of England accent, "than any other person living or dead. I have over twenty-five thousand awards—many more than I can display here, of course. Some of the mouse awards and ribbons are on the sideboard over there." He indicated a small, trophy-laden piece of furniture. "The mouse scrolls and certificates are in the drawers. I have lots of rabbit trophies, too. Most of the other trophies were won by my football teams." Mr. Ashley explained that a few years earlier he had founded a ladies' football club with himself as manager. The club was so successful and its travel schedule kept him so busy that he had been forced, after some sixty years of mousekeeping, to liquidate his mousery.

"I gave them up last year," he said regretfully. "All I have at present is some rabbits. You see, my wife wasn't too keen on my mice, but she liked the rabbits. Finally, she put her foot down. She said she'd feed the rabbits while I was away, but not the mice, and so they had to go—nearly sixty of them, and they were beauties. In the last three years that I exhibited I won thirty-nine championships. *Championships*, mind you. *Four* would be considered good. I won the highest award in mice—the Woodiwiss Bowl—over thirty years ago, and I've won the Mendel Gold Cup four times."

I must have looked disappointed at finding that he had no mice, and Mr. Ashley, sensing this, hastened to say, "I keep on with mice as secretary of the club, of course. It's a big job; correspondence, keeping records, writing a weekly article for *Fur and Feather*, a journal that reports our activities."

Mr. Ashley joined the club way back in 1910, but the organization had its beginnings before his time. According to the records, the first mouse competition in Britain, and perhaps anywhere, was held at Oxford in 1892 and was won by a gentleman named William Wild with a Cinnamon Red mouse. Just how Wild and other pioneer mouse fanciers, presumably scattered around the countryside, first got in touch with one another to arrange a competition is not recorded. Perhaps a handful of them were already friends, and from a casual comparison of their pets a spirit of rivalry evolved.

I picture a meeting of these men, mustached and bowler-hatted Victorians, during which one of them takes from his pocket a Cinnamon Red mouse. The others admire its perfection. "I say, that's a winner, that mouse!" one of them exclaims. "Think so?" says the owner modestly. "He's not a bad mouse, at that." From that moment, of course, the owner is on the lookout wherever he goes for other fanciers of mice against which to pit his beautiful mouse, and then it is only a short step to the setting up of classes.

The National Mouse Club, Mr. Ashley told me, was formally organized in 1895. "Actually, it was the Mouse and *Rat* Club then," he went on, as if making a distasteful admission. "But rats don't really fit in, so the mouse fanciers threw the rats out. Now they're trying to get back in, but we won't have 'em."

The Mouse Club's first president was a Mr. S. Woodiwiss, and serving under him was a committee of a dozen members, including three ladies—Miss Grimston, Miss Dickenson, and Mrs. Welburn—as well as Walter Maxey, of London, who became its secretary in 1897 and who invented the Maxey Mouse Cage, a neat little box, with a conveniently easy-to-open wire-mesh front, now widely used for exhibiting mice. "Walter Maxey was the club's real founder," Mr. Ashley said. "He was its secretary from 1897 to 1909, and he was active in it until he died, about fifteen years ago. He was a fine man and a great mouse fancier. Many's the time I pedaled all the way to London on my push bike just to see Walter Maxey."

Mr. Ashley rummaged among his souvenirs and found a pamphlet containing a rather shadowy picture of Maxey. It showed a long-legged man standing against a bush, with a walking stick in one hand and a bowler hat in the other. A drooping mustache gave him the dolorous expression frequently found in portraits of Victorian males, but the features above it were boyish and cheerful. "Walter Maxey put terrific devotion into mice," Mr. Ashley said solemnly as he closed the pamphlet.

In 1896, a year after its formation, the club was included in a dog, cat, and rabbit show. Seventy mice were entered, and the Woodiwiss Bowl, now so highly coveted, was presented for the first time. As I learned this, my thoughts flashed back to Lord Wrottesley. In 1896 he was twenty-two. Perhaps he attended this show and his longing for the perfect spotted mouse may have originated then. The next year a mice-only show in London brought together a hundred and seventy-two mice competing in fourteen classes. Since then enthusiasm for mice has grown steadily, Mr. Ashley told me, though the club had difficult times during each of the world wars.

"It was nip and tuck for a while," Mr. Ashley said, "but we pulled through, and we've grown steadily since. Now we have over three hundred members and a hundred and ninety pounds in the bank from membership fees. Another victory for mice is that we're now included in livestock shows. It took years to get mice admitted. The horsemen scorned them. I said to the horsemen, 'A mouse is worth more by weight than a horse is.' They couldn't refute that, so they had to let us in!"

There are thirty-six varieties of Fancy Mice, Mr. Ashley explained, the differences being all a matter of coloration. Each variety is placed in one of four categories—Self, Tan, Marked, and A.O.V., or Any Other Variety. From the club's manual, *Rules & Standards,* I learned that the Self category (mice of a single overall color) embraces ten varieties—White, Red, Fawn, Black, Blue, Dove, Silver ("as near as possible to an old silver coin"),

Chocolate ("plain, not milk chocolate"), Champagne ("pinkish, free from mealiness"), and Cream ("very pale, not to be confused with ivory, stone, or very dilute champagne"). The Tan category accounts for another ten varieties, which bear the same names as the Selfs—White, Red, Fawn, and so on—but in their case the color refers only to the color of their upper sides; their bellies must be "a rich, golden hue that extends to the feet." The smallest category is the Marked Varieties, of which there are only four—all piebalds, with any of the ten basic colors occurring in patterns referred to as Dutch, Even Marked, Broken Marked, and Variegated or Spotted. The remaining twelve varieties, most of them distinguished by concentric bands of two or more contrasting colors, are lumped together in the A.O.V. catchall category.

National Mouse Club members compete for thirty-eight trophies, as well as a multitude of lesser prizes, each carrying with it a certain number of the points by which a mouse may make the climb to Single Champion and thence to Double Champion, Treble Champion, Quadruple Champion, and so to the final pinnacle of Supreme Champion. As a rule, superior coloring is half the battle for a mouse on its way up the championship ladder, but it must also excel in several other characteristics—Condition (not fat, glossy coat), Shape and Carriage, Ears (large and tulip-shaped, free from creases, carried erect with plenty of width between them), Eyes (large, bold, and prominent), Muzzle (long, strength carried out to end), Tail (long and uniform, no kinks)—and, as if that were not enough, it must be "perfectly tractable and free from any vice."

I asked Mr. Ashley how the Fancy Mouse differs from the house mouse. "Ah," he said, "the Fancy Mouse and the house house are fields apart. *Fields* apart! Of course, the Fancy is a mutation of the house mouse, but that was donkey's years ago. The Fancy is bigger, has a longer tail. It is a bolder, *slicker* animal in every way—and more tractable. Very individual, our mice are—each of them has a different way about it. I think they know their owners by feel and smell. At a show a novice mouse is all atremble, like a two-year-old horse in the starting gate, while an older mouse takes it in his stride."

I asked Mr. Ashley how he had happened to go in for mice, and he willingly plunged in. "I got my first mouse when I was five years old, and by the time I was twelve I was in it seriously," he said. "My father was in the fruit business. He kept a few cab horses and I sold fruit from a horse-drawn cart when I was only a little lad. In the evening, it was my job to groom the horses, and when that was done I could spend some time with my mice, which I kept, along with some lop-eared rabbits, in the loft over the stable." As he thought back Mr. Ashley's expression became tinged with sheepishness. "I fed the horse corn to the mice and rabbits without my father's knowledge," he confessed. "He'd have thought we couldn't afford it. There was little money in those days. I got my first mice for sixpence that I'd worked and saved for."

At the age of twelve, Mr. Ashley continued, he went to work as an apprentice to a cabinetmaker. At eighteen, when he was earning eighteen shillings ninepence a week, he married and joined his father's fruit business. When World War I broke out, he served overseas and afterward went into business for himself as a dealer in surplus goods of all kinds, retiring at the age of seventy.

"Even in the early days when money was short, I was never without animals," Mr. Ashley said. "I had a passion for them. Once, I swapped my wife's dolly tub and peg-a-leg—her washing machine, you'd call it—for a dog. Another time, I sold our sideboard to buy a rabbit. My wife understood, and she didn't fuss."

Mr. Ashley looked at his watch and asked me to excuse him while he went into the next room to watch a horse show that was being broadcast on television. But, he hastened to add, he hoped I would stay and look over the minutes of past meetings of the National Mouse Club. He further suggested that I call on a local breeder named John Hartley, who had a collection of first-rate Fancy Mice, and follow this up by attending a mouse show at the Didsbury Fair Grounds, a few miles from Manchester, during a forthcoming Bank Holiday. Ashley pulled a large, battered ledger out of a bookcase, placed it on the desk for me, and, after shaking hands, hurried off to his rendezvous with the telly.

When Mr. Ashley had shut the door, I seated myself at his desk and turned the leaves of the ledger. It covered the period from 1933 to 1962, and I soon found myself marveling at the meticulous care with which the affairs of the Mouse Club had been set down by its devoted secretaries and with what pride its members had noted their achievements. Now and then, however, a jarring note had intruded on the placid tempo of the proceedings, such as this one, during a meeting in 1935: "Mr. Clark read a serious report handed to him by one of the judges, Mr. W. Turton, saying that in his opinion a Red Mouse belonging to Mr. L. Madeley had been tampered with in such a way as to alter the natural coloring of the mouse. Mr. Madeley was asked to explain and he readily gave his explanation, saying that the cage had been sprayed with permanganate of potash whilst the mouse was in the cage. The chemical had dyed the fur of the mouse, but it was purely with the idea of disinfecting that Mr. Madeley had instructed his son to spray the cage and not with any intent of gaining prizes under false pretences. Mr. Turton then proposed that the matter be left for the discussion of the Executive Committee at a later date." After this, the members had turned—gratefully, I presumed—to a consideration of the question "whether a judge was in order in passing a mouse with no whiskers and it was proposed by Mr. Horton that a mouse with no whiskers was not a complete mouse and therefore a judge had no power to pass such an exhibit." Reasonable enough, but I suspected that even the diversion of debating the status of a whiskerless mouse could not have allayed the dismay of the members over the affair of the dyed Red Mouse. According to a subsequent entry, the executive committee, despite Mr. Madeley's ingenious explanation, had seen to it that "Mr. Madeley was reprimanded for exhibiting the stained mouse and warned to discontinue."

By 1940, the impact of war on the world of mice was discernible. At the meeting of the club that year, "Mr. Johnson spoke of the difficulties of the times, but urged that as far as possible matters pertaining to mice be carried on as usual." The members settled down to a discussion of a new variety of pink-eyed mouse whose fur was described as "a delicately blended shade of light fawn and silver, the two colors so evenly intermingled as to give the appearance of shot silk." In 1941, German bombing raids made it impossible to hold meetings in London, but the members got together elsewhere. At a meeting in 1942, "the question of the safety of the National Mouse Club trophies was raised and the President said precautions were being considered. Later that year, owing to the paper shortage, the club was having a hard time persuading the editors of *Fur and Feather* to continue carrying its column, "Mouse Notes." "I am compelled to take a very serious view of the matter," Mr. Jude, the late author–connoisseur of Fancy Mice, wrote to the membership. But somehow the club managed to keep afloat, and by 1951, as I could see by the installments of "Mouse Notes" filed in the ledger, it was once again sailing on serenely. "Welcomed the Cotswold Mouse Club . . . ," "Extended thanks to . . . ," "Discussed lilac mice . . ." On this cheerful note, I closed the ledger.

A few days later I found Mr. Hartley, the mouse breeder whom Mr. Ashley had recommended, on Chatsworth Road, in an area where plain little brick houses lined the streets row on row. They were workingmen's houses, of a previous era, but in Mr. Hartley's row they were not as drab as they might be, for Chatsworth Road is wide, with an ample view of the sky, and each house has a bit of garden in front of it. At the time of my visit the gardens were wildly abloom with the roses that flourish in Manchester's damp climate.

Mr. Hartley wore a questioning expression when he opened the door in answer to my knock, but as soon as I explained that my errand was to visit his mice, this changed to delighted surprise. "Why, I just this minute finished cleaning up me mice!" he exclaimed, his eyes widening behind his dark-rimmed round spectacles as if this was the greatest of all possible coincidences.

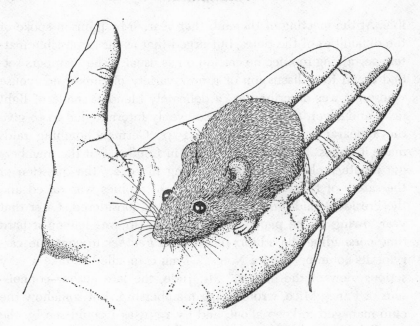

Nervously running his hands through his mop of dark hair, he apologized for the old clothes he was wearing, and drew me into his small living room, where, just as in Mr. Ashley's home, the most conspicuous aspect of the decor was a display of mouse trophies. Proudly he called my attention to two silver cups that he and his fifteen-year-old daughter, Jacqueline—his partner in mouse breeding—had jointly won while exhibiting as a team. When I had admired the cups, he bounded over to a bookcase and pulled out a cardboard filing box, from which he poured a torrent of show ribbons and prize certificates onto the floor. Then, kneeling beside them, he sorted them out lovingly.

"I've got three championships!" Mr. Hartley told me, as though still marveling at the accomplishment. "Here's a certificate I won last week in Liverpool with a White! This big green Special is from the Airedale Mouse Club! Here's a championship made out to Snowball! He's me big White buck. He's a Double Champion now! Here's one for me Tan—a Silver Tan buck—the best Tan at the Summer Cup Show! All the best mice in the country are at the Summer Cup Show, and he beat the whole lot! Forty-eight firsts this year!" he went on, his face alight with pleasure. "I've won so many with me Whites that a lot of chaps are bashin' at me now. Out to get me, you might say."

Mr. Hartley leaned back on his heels amidst the splendor of ribbons and certificates spilled on the floor and went on talking with earnest excitement. "I've got about two hundred and fifty mice out in the backyard. It's a big job, that many mice. It takes me whole Saturday to keep them shipshape. Even on me holidays I come back every few days to tend them. I've got a record of every mouse—how it's bred and all that. There's a lot of science in winning—you've got to study the judges as well as the mice. For instance, some like a dark shade and some a light. Ashley, now, he's a terrific judge of mice. A few weeks ago, he was standing by me while another chap was judging. Ashley bet me he could pick the winners in order—first, second, third, and fourth—out of seven mice on the table, and sure as apples is apples he was right! He's especially good with Self mice. That's what he always bred. I've got some Creams he bred and sold to somebody else and the other chap let them go to pot. Didn't weed them out properly. Now I've started to bring them back. You have to be a bit ruthless with mice. That's the only sad part. Jacqueline is sympathetic and can't do it."

A medium-sized man of forty-two, who was captured at Dunkirk, spent the rest of the war in German prison camps, and was presently employed as a clerk by the Northwestern Gas Board, Mr. Hartley told me that he had acquired his first mice at the age of ten. "Then I went to pigeons and later to rabbits," he said. "But then Jacqueline came home with some mice one day, and I got interested in them all over again. I wish you could meet her, by the way, but she's having a bit of a holiday with some relatives in Blackpool. Anyhow, thanks to Jacqueline, I'm back to mice, and I like them best. They're economical, they're clean, they're lovely little animals if you handle them right. They cost me about ten bob a week—for food, entry fees, and so on—and I make a little bit up with selling a few now and then. Five bob is a reasonable price for a mouse, though there's some fanciers might charge you fifteen. I've got one I refused three pounds for. I give a lot of mice away to youngsters who can't afford to buy them." He began stuffing the prizes back into the box. "Aye," he said, looking up at me intensely. "If somebody is hard up for mice, I'll help 'em out. I don't believe in being tightfisted with mice." Those words have remained with me ever since as a delightful and generous sentiment.

"Come on now!" Mr. Hartley said, springing to his feet. "Let's go out in the back and have a look at the mice." He led me through the kitchen, where his blond wife was frying sausages and potatoes for supper, and we paused while I was introduced. "She didn't think she'd get used to the mice at first," Mr. Hartley told me, "but now she knows them and they know her." His wife smiled, and he and I went on out the back door into a yard.

In one corner, beside a patch of leeks and lettuce, was a neatly constructed shed, painted green. Mr. Hartley propped open the door and we entered. Inside, stacked on shelves, were rows of wooden boxes covered with wire mesh. Rustling and squeaking could be heard from within. "Let's see," said Mr. Hartley. "What'll I show you first?" He moved a stool to the doorway. "I think I'll start with me Tans." He selected a box, placed it on the stool, and lifted the cover. "Cream and Tan, these are," he said. "This is a good litter." I peered in and saw two long, slim, cream-colored mice and a number of young, all agitatedly running about on a bed of sawdust. Their whiskers and ears were aquiver and, I must say, I felt sorry about their confined lives.

"This is the dam," Mr. Hartley told me as he picked up one of the adults by the tail. I noticed that her red eyes did indeed gleam "like rubies in the sunshine" as she dangled momentarily from his fingers. Then he placed her on his arm, where she remained quiet but quivering while he stroked her fine, shiny fur. "She's a good mouse, this one," he went on. "A breeder. She's given me two litters already." He dangled another mouse so that I might examine the distinctive tan fur on her belly. It was a strange, bright, orangy brown. "See how perfectly the tan breaks at the feet," Mr. Hartley said. "The line there has to be absolutely clear-cut." He gave a knowing look. "There's even been breeders known to trim it a bit with a scissors, but that sort of thing doesn't happen often."

Mr. Hartley replaced the mouse, shelved the box, and brought out another. In it was half a coconut shell, turned end up, with a small aperture cut in its base, making it look like a miniature tropical hut. It was both charming and practical, and it gave me the idea for a coconut-shell house for my own mouse. He picked up the shell, and a handful of sinuous, shiny black mice—one adult and the others half grown—scattered from beneath it. "My Blacks have gone to pieces," he said sadly. I said they looked quite perfect to me, as, indeed, they did. "No, no," Hartley insisted. "They've all sorts of faults, but I may get some good ones out of them yet." With a sigh, he put the Blacks back on their shelf, and then instantly regained his high spirits as he reached for still another box, saying, "Here! I'll show you old Snowball, the Double Champion." Snowball, the sole occupant of the box, backed off and peered up with red eyes while Mr. Hartley poked him in gingerly fashion. "I only have to touch him to get bit," he said. "That is, unless I'm careful. But once he's in your hand he's all right." With a quick dart, he had Snowball by the tail and then in his palm. "That's how a buck should be!" Mr. Hartley said with admiration, bouncing the mouse in his palm. "Weight to him! Sturdy!"

I could see that Snowball was a bit larger than the others, and I decided not to confess that otherwise I found him no more and no less beautiful.

After returning Snowball to his solitary abode, Mr. Hartley showed me a succession of mice in the whole gamut of recognized colors, commenting all the while on their good and bad points. To wind up the session, he brought out the Whites that he was grooming for the Didsbury show. His manner took on a new intensity as he examined them, stroking their coats anxiously. "A mouse can lose condition overnight, and there you are with all your hopes shot right out from under you," he said. "You know what I do to give 'em sleekness? A drop of port for a day or two before a show. They call me crackers, but it works!"

Picking up a handsome snow-white animal, Mr. Hartley said, "Here, this is the one for Didsbury. Look at 'im. Big. Solid. Fine ears. Good tail." After studying the mouse for a long, long time, he replaced it with a worried frown, then turned and gazed at me solemnly. "I honestly think," he said finally, "that with this mouse I have a chance to win at Didsbury."

Early on the morning of the Bank Holiday, I made my way to the Didsbury Fair Grounds, where long white tents had been set up on the perimeter of a large meadow surrounded by tall and ancient trees. The grass was fresh and green, and the sun, for a change, was bright. A loudspeaker mounted on a van crackled out exciting music, pennants fluttered in a brisk breeze, exhibitors and white-smocked officials hurried about importantly, vendors were converting vans into booths from which to sell tea and sandwiches and beer, and the entire scene was bustling with busyness and expectancy. I saw a whole family walking gravely along, like a guard of honor, beside a great, pompous, brown-and-white cow that obviously had been sudsed and brushed within an inch of her life. A man hurried by, cradling one enormous cucumber, on his way to the Produce Tent. Well-shined dogs on leashes and youngsters on horses were everywhere.

A tent with a signboard outside reading "Rabbits, Cavies, Mice" was my goal, and on entering it and looking around, I experienced a moment of disappointment, for all I could see were ranks of cages full of rabbits and cavies set up on long tables arranged to form a hollow square. But then I caught sight of Mr. Ashley's cheery pink face *within* the square and saw that the mouse arena had been set up there. I pushed through the rabbit-and-cavy crowd and joined the mouse people—perhaps half a dozen of them—in their snug enclosure, where they were hard at work unpacking traveling cases in which absentee contestants in other parts of the country had sent cages containing mice. Mr.

Ashley, of course, was in the thick of things, setting out Maxey cages in rows on a long table. The mice inside them pressed quivering whiskers through the mesh and scurried in their sawdust bedding.

"Some good mice here today," Mr. Ashley said when we had greeted each other. "Looks like about two hundred entries." He paused in his work to introduce me to some of the others, among them a tall, casual young man of twenty or so, Ken Ramsden, a fancier of Dutch and Silver Fox mice, who was to serve with him during the judging as one of the show's two stewards. "There's one prize Ken always gets," somebody remarked. "His Silvers always bite the judge."

"Only *certain* judges," Mr. Ramsden said. "I know how to train 'em."

While I was peering into the cages, Mr. Hartley arrived, breathlessly lugging two big traveling boxes and followed by his family, including Jacqueline, who had come back from her holiday in Blackpool with, naturally, a terrible cold in the head. "Three of me best Agoutis started in to molt overnight," Hartley told me apprehensively. "I've had to throw in some others at the last minute. In this game you never know. I've still got me Whites, though." He gave an excited wink and a grin as he and Mrs. Hartley and the two youngsters started unpacking.

Since it would be a while before the mouse judging began, I left the arena to tour the other exhibits. The Fair Grounds were gayer and busier than ever now, and the air was sweet with the smell of trampled grass. I jostled my way through tents containing needlework, potted plants, cacti, statuesque layer cakes, mounds of vegetables, tiers of flower arrangements, fat hens with fantails and roosters the size of eagles, looking proud and confused as they bumped their heads against the tops of their cages. At last, I walked back across the Fair Grounds to the tent I had started from, but before rejoining the mice, I paused to watch a man tenderly combing an enormous and featureless mound of white fluff. As he smoothed out tiny tangles in the fur with a patient and delicate touch, only a faint quivering of the mound made me realize that it was a live Angora rabbit, though which end was which it was quite impossible to tell.

When I returned to the mouse enclave, I found it crowded with mice and fanciers. Hartley introduced me to the judge who would officiate that day, Dan Taylor, a well-set-up, competent-looking man in his early thirties, with a handsome, clean-cut face. He was a shipping clerk in a mail-order house, but with his businesslike air and in his white judging smock he looked the part of a young doctor in a television serial. Presently, he sat down at the judging table, ready for action, and a hush came over our small group. Mr. Hartley, who had been pressed into service to record the decisions, sat down at the far end with a ledger and a stack of prize cards, and I took a seat beside him.

The first class was for White, Cream, Champagne, or Fawn Self Adults and in it Mr. Hartley's big White, the one on which all his hopes were riding, would meet its initial test. At ten o'clock, with the cages of the entries ranked in front of him—ten in all—the judge took a deep breath and then, frowning intently, opened the first cage, from which he extracted a shining, cream-colored mouse by the tail. While every fancier present watched attentively, he held it up, examined it swiftly as it paddled its feet in the air, and popped it back into its cage. He reached for the next cage and withdrew a beige-colored mouse, and in a moment it, too, was hanging, head down, from his fingers.

"That's the one to beat, that Champagne," Mr. Hartley whispered to me tensely. He pulled a nylon stocking out of his pocket and rubbed his hands on it. "You can spoil a mouse if your palm is damp. I keep this in my pocket to rub 'em down. No lint," he explained.

The judge continued his work, swift and intent, dangling each mouse by the tail, peering at its feet, expertly turning it upside down to inspect its underside, and sometimes measuring the length of a tail against that of a body. Now and then, he would place a mouse on his forearm and blow on the fur to part it. The mice seemed resigned to these indignities and made no great effort to resist them or to escape.

Mr. Hartley nudged me gently. "Number fourteen," he whispered, indicating a mouse just then swinging from the judge's fingers. "That's me big White." His expression, I noticed, was strained but controlled.

The judge flipped Mr. Hartley's White onto his arm, stroked it, and blew gently into its fur. Then, holding it by the tail with his left hand, he reached for another White with his right—one that he had examined previously—and swung the two mice side by side. He frowned and narrowed his eyes as he peered at the swinging pair. Finally, with terrible but enigmatic decisiveness, he popped both mice back into their cages and reached for another entry.

Mr. Hartley fingered the record book before him. "I've brought along a good Cinnamon—a baby," he whispered, as if he'd already given up on his White's chances. "And me *baby* White isn't bad either. But I *could* lose with all of them."

After several minutes of diligent comparison, the judge had pushed five of the ten cages to the rear rank. Now, once again, Mr. Hartley's big White dangled in the air, this time beside the Champagne. The judge squinted at the two mice for what seemed an age. Then suddenly he returned them to their boxes, swiftly wrote some numbers on a card, handed the card to Mr. Hartley, and leaned back in his chair.

Mr. Hartley's big White was the winner. The Champagne was second. Mr. Hartley allowed himself a happy sigh and then quickly got to work, entering the decision in the record book. "Well, I'm glad we made it," he said finally, and added, with a wink, "I've had 'im in bed with me for a week for fear something would happen to 'im."

There was a momentary hum of talk around the table as the stewards removed the cages of the retiring contestants and substituted those of the entries in the next class. Again the judge went earnestly to work. By noon he had disposed of eight of the twenty classes, in the course of which he had been bitten by Mr. Ramsden's choicest Silver Fox (but had magnanimously given it a first, anyway), and had taken to sucking his injured thumb reflectively between rounds. Mr. Hartley's big White had triumphed again—in a Challenge class (against other winners)— and his baby White had won a first. Mr. Hartley's nerves seemed to have steadied a good bit, but he was now sweating out the possibilities for his Agoutis in the afternoon classes. Agouti mice have brown fur with silvery tips to the hairs and are very pretty indeed. "I've a sneaking feeling the adult might do it," he confided to me at one point while sipping a cup of tea fetched by his wife. After mulling over the matter a minute or two longer, he said abruptly, "If I don't win with me adult Agouti, I'll commit hara-kiri right outside this tent!"

I felt that I needed a break, so, leaving the mouse people still hard at it, I went outside and joined the many who, with never a thought of mice, were now having sandwiches and tea as they sat on the sun-warmed grass enjoying an enormous impromptu mass picnic. A horse show was in progress in a ring in the center of the grounds. I walked over and sat in the grandstand and watched a class for Ladies' Hunters. This was the big-time stuff of the fair, and the stand was packed and tense. As the hunters galloped past, beautiful and breedy, with thudding feet and creaking leather, I thought I'd never before seen animals so huge. Disloyal though I knew it was to mice, I stayed on for the Grand Parade of the winners of previous classes. The band music was brassy and grand, and in the lead was a magnificent pair of bay Clydesdales hitched to a shining red brewery wagon. They smacked the ground smartly with their great feather-duster feet.

Suddenly, as it often does in Britain, the sky became overcast. I walked back to the mouse tent through a light, misty rain. When I rejoined Mr. Hartley he nudged me jubilantly, and whispered, "The Agouti did it! Got a first, 'e did! That's five wins today! The Grand Challenge is next, and that'll be it!"

We watched in silence for some time and then, while the stewards were changing the cages in front of the judge, Mr. Hartley turned to me with a modest disclaimer. "You know, I'm not sure the Agouti is really as good as all that," he said. "The light is failing a bit. In this light it's hard to judge."

At last, it was time for the Grand Challenge class, and though Mr. Hartley didn't let on, I think he was pretty certain that he had it in the bag with his big White. Nevertheless, he flushed with pleasure as he read his number on the winner's slip. The surprise came a few minutes later when the judge called for Mr. Hartley's Agouti, and after a long, tense comparison of the Agouti with both the big White and a snappy-looking Red mouse, gave the Agouti the Best in Show. Mr. Hartley squeezed my arm, and then, all business, solemnly recorded his triumph in the ledger. Looking exhausted, the judge leaned back in his chair and lit a cigarette. "I'll have mice before me eyes when I go to sleep tonight," he said, rubbing his face with his hands. He had been judging steadily for six hours. Mr. Hartley stood up, frankly beaming. He opened the big White's cage and stroked the animal, prompting it to make a halfhearted effort to escape. "Get back in there, love," Mr. Hartley murmured, easing it gently toward the rear of the cage with his finger.

As I said goodbye to my newfound friends, all hands were at work, packing the mouse cages into the traveling cases. Jacqueline was standing by, holding a silver cup—the Agouti's trophy—on which were inscribed the words "BEST MOUSE."

Outside, the drizzle had become a downpour and the Fair Grounds looked bleak and trampled under the dark sky, but the horse show was still going on in the center ring. A dauntless rider came pounding along through the drenching rain, with water running down his back in broad streaks and the hoofs of his mount squelching in the sodden turf. As I hurried on, I reflected that however much the dripping horseman might scorn the mouse-fancying Mr. Hartley, the latter at least was in out of the rain and his mice—their laurels already won, their feet both warm and dry—were resting cozily in their cages.

3

A SWIM WITH A
MANATEE

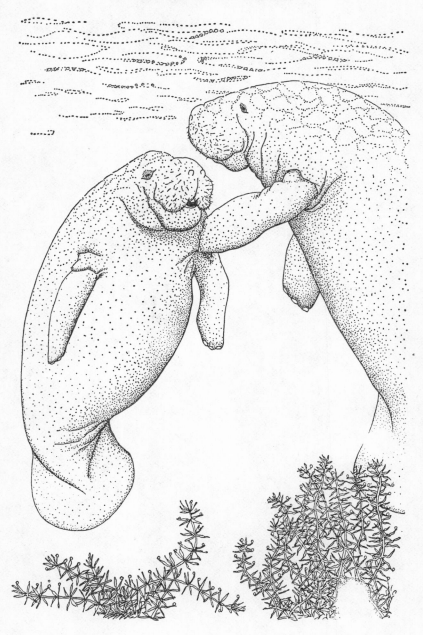

Whenever I undertake a new animal assignment I look forward tremendously to meeting a wild species I have never met before. I find it wonderful to go behind the scene with biologists and glimpse, however briefly, the animals they are studying. I had my first taste of this excitement when I was ten years old and my father took me on a privileged visit to the Bronx Zoo. One of the curators was his friend. I was allowed to sit on the back of a Galápagos tortoise as it was lured by a receding banana to move ponderous step by ponderous step. It gave me a sense of tortoise time. At such a rate it is no wonder it takes a tortoise two hundred years and more to reach the end of his road. When I had dismounted, the keeper lifted up a huge, gentle black snake and draped it like a Hawaiian lei around my neck. Warned not to be afraid, I stood and felt its living weight move across my shoulders; watched its tongue flicker as it explored my arm and looked into its impersonal reptile eye. I still remember the thrill of thus receiving at first hand an impression of "snakeness"; a being neither cold nor warm, hostile nor friendly, and supple from tip of tongue to tip of tail.

A good many years have passed since then. Nevertheless, I recaptured some of the same feeling of delighted learning when I was able to meet, briefly but pleasurably, what may be the gentlest creature on earth—the manatee.

I floated face down on the water of the Crystal River, in Florida, looking through a mask into a shadowy world through which sunbeams cut bright pathways and clouds of silt swirled like smoke. Beside me I could see the shiny black frog feet of a biologist named Daniel Hartman and of his assistant, James Powell, Jr. Hartman was trailing a white belt of foam rubber, to which an ultrasonic transmitter, or pinger, had been attached, and which he hoped to fasten around a manatee's tail. Beneath us, gliding in and out of the darkness, were two manatees—long, gray shapes that looked as big as one-man submarines. I had a good view of the manatee directly beneath me. It glided easily, stroking the water with a tail flattened horizontally, like a beaver's, but shaped more like a Ping-Pong paddle. Its hide had a mottled look, and etched on its back, like graffiti scratched on stone, was a series of white lines—healed scars of wounds inflicted during an encounter with a motorboat propeller. Nearly every manatee Hartman has encountered in his study of the species is thus marked; besides making clear the danger that boats pose to manatees, the scars have incidentally served as indentifying symbols, enabling Hartman to distinguish fifty individual manatees, give them names, and chart their coming and going.

One manatee slipped away into the gloom, but the other turned and hung in the water facing Hartman, swaying gently, its flippers held out like arms akimbo, and looking disarmingly like a captive balloon. Seen full-face, the manatee is so homely of visage, its expression one of such innocence as to be utterly beguiling. Its head is small compared with the inflated bulk of its great round body; there is no neck to speak of and no external ears. This manatee's small, deep-set eyes stared steadily at the swimmers with an expression of simpleminded curiosity mixed with surprise, while its long, bristly muzzle had a despondent, hound-dog droop. Hartman swam closer to the manatee, and still she didn't flee. (I say "she" because Hartman later told me that he recognized this manatee as a female he had named Piety, one of the half dozen or so with whom he has been able to make particular friends.) For an instant, the man and the manatee hung face to face. Piety stared steadily and then, with what can only be described as a look of tender affection, swam forward, reached out with her flippers as though to embrace Hartman, and bestowed a bristly, nuzzling kiss full upon Hartman's face mask. Hartman reached out and stroked Piety's huge, rubbery back. Piety revolved, presenting her round flanks and even rounder underside. For the next three or four minutes, I watched a slow-motion ballet as Hartman, assisted now by young Powell, tried to slip the belt around Piety's ever-waving tail. Powell took over rubbing the front end of Piety, holding her attention, while

Hartman maneuvered for position at the tail end. The belt was bulky, and he found it difficult to move it quickly through the water. To fasten it, it would be necessary to encircle the narrow part of Piety's tail (the handle of the Ping-Pong paddle) and press together the two ends of the belt, which were covered with self-gripping fabric. Several times he came tantalizingly close to success, but Piety invariably swished out of reach at the crucial moment. Then, suddenly, he came closer than ever. Piety must have felt the belt grip her tail. She gave a great, convulsive, indignant flap and shot out of sight in the dark water, leaving Hartman and Powell and me in the swirling silt stirred by her abrupt departure. We were not able to find Piety again, or another approachable manatee, that day. That night, the weather turned warm and the manatees disappeared from the area, riding down the river and out into wider waters at the river's mouth, in the Gulf of Mexico, where it would be impossible to find them. Hartman retired to think about ways of designing a belt that could be more easily attached to a manatee.

The manatee is, of course, one of that curious group, the water mammals. It is a large beast, shaped like a tapered balloon, weighing around a thousand pounds, and ten feet or so in length. Like the whale and the seal, the manatee is a creature whose ancestors moved from land back to a life in the sea. Its years in the sea have not altered it as much as the whale has been altered, but more than the seal, which still spends some time on land. The manatee never leaves the water, but it is not equipped, as whales are, for life in the open ocean. It spends its time in rivers and estuaries and offshore along the fringes of the land. Despite their similarities, whales, seals, and manatees are not close cousins but the descendants of different beasts that took to the water at different times. Improbable as it sounds, the nearest relative of the manatee is thought to be the elephant. Like the elephant, the manatee is completely herbivorous, grazing on river and sea grasses. Like the elephant's, the manatee's mammary glands are pectoral. The manatee's teeth resemble the elephant's. It has no incisors or canines, only molars. When in old age an elephant's teeth wear out, the elephant dies of starvation, and the same may be true of manatees; no one knows. Lacking front teeth to crop its food, the manatee uses its long, muscular upper lip, which is cleft in the middle and equipped with stout bristles, to grasp food and push it into its mouth. The manatee has lost its hind legs (though vestigial bones remain), and its forelegs have become flippers. Though the finger bones are hidden within the flipper, the Florida manatee still has three fingernails at the end of the flippers, reminders of its terrestrial existence. Manatees use the flippers not for fast swimming but for close maneuvering, for support when they rest on the bottom, and for embracing each other.

In technical classification, the manatee belongs to a small and select group. It is a member of the order Sirenia—so named in honor of the mythical mermaid for which manatees are said to have sometimes been mistaken. Other Sirenia are the dugong, a somewhat similar marine creature found off the shores of East Africa, southern Asia, and Australia, and the enormous and defenseless sea cow, which was discovered in the Bering Sea in 1742 and exterminated by ruthless slaughter within twenty-seven years. There are three species of manatee; one lives in the rivers of central West Africa, another in the Amazon basin, and the third on the shores of the Caribbean, including both the east and the west coast of Florida. All manatees have the misfortune to be delicious eating. Men have preyed on them since primitive times, and still do. No one knows how numerous manatees once were, but they are now rare everywhere, and probably diminishing each year. The only exception to this appears to be in Florida, where Hartman has made the happy discovery that the creatures are holding their own and that a few local populations may even be increasing.

It has come to me lately as a matter of some surprise that scientists really know very little about a great number of animals. This seems strange in a time when biologists can explain the most intricate workings of single cells. The reason for this lack of knowledge is that until recently few scientists bothered to study in depth creatures whose lives appeared to have no direct relation to human welfare. Now, suddenly, with the interrelatedness of life becoming more apparent and more significant for our own future, there is an urgency to catch up.

Until Hartman undertook his study, very little was known about the manatee. Dead manatees had been dissected and their bones and organs described, but, scientifically speaking, that was about it. Early Floridians had enjoyed eating manatees and presumably slaughtered them in great numbers. There are no figures on their onetime abundance. Manatee steaks were popular in Florida until the 1900's. By then, the creatures had become very scarce, but they were saved from extinction by a state law, passed around 1905, that banned further killing. The manatee is an elusive animal, hard to see unless you're looking for it. Occasionally its back glides out of the water like a whale's, but usually nothing more than its nostrils appears above the surface. Consequently, until recently the small surviving population was hardly noticed except by a few fishermen and guides. In the 1950's, a biologist employed at Everglades National Park, J. C. Moore, did some manatee studies. Among other things, he found that manatees congregated in the warm water discharged from a power plant in downtown Miami, where he was able to watch them from a bridge. His observations were the first important contribution to knowledge of the manatee, but the water in which the manatees swam was so dirty that Moore was able to see only a small part of what they did.

In 1967, Hartman, then a graduate student at Cornell, chose the manatee as the subject for his doctoral dissertation. Exploring the west coast of Florida, he came to the Crystal River and found that he had stumbled on an ideal place to study manatees. At certain times, they congregated around springs whose water was so clear that every detail of their submarine lives could be observed. Hartman had gotten there in the nick of time, as it turned out. In the years since he came to Crystal River, pollution and the growth of waterweeds have so darkened the water that visibility is now only a few feet. A river that was one of the most beautiful in the world has been converted into just another thoroughfare for fishermen in powerboats and a wastebasket for human debris. The Crystal River that Hartman found in 1967 was an extraordinary place. A great number of springs—the largest sixty feet deep and thirty feet across—pour out six hundred million gallons of crystalline water a day at the delightful temperature of seventy-four degrees winter and summer, forming a large bay and a wide river flowing seven miles to the shores of the Gulf of Mexico. The river teems with fish. There are crabs and oysters to be taken at its mouth and shrimp farther out in the Gulf. There had been some commercial fishing in the river, and logging nearby, for a hundred years, but the lovely wooded shores of the bay were not seriously disturbed until about fifteen years ago. Then the developers arrived. Year by year, they have fought the jungle with chain saws and bulldozers to provide flat, barren building lots; have dug dank, stagnant canals to make each lot a "waterfront" site; buried the sandy shoreline of the bay under cement seawalls, and erected hundreds of suburban homes, whose septic tanks leach nutrients into the water. While these changes were underway, some unrecorded ecological accident introduced two exotic plants into the river. One was *Hydrilla verticillata,* native to China, and very like a water plant commonly used in the aquariums of fish fanciers, and the other was *Myriophyllum spicatum,* or water milfoil, native to Eurasia. These plants thrived in the nutrients the new homeowners were pouring into the water. The once clean, sandy bottom of the entire bay is now covered with weeds and the silt of their decay. The river is crystal no longer, and there is no way that it can ever be restored to its former beauty.

To study the manatees, Hartman got into the water with them, wearing mask and flippers, and spent three or four hours a day swimming among them and noting their behavior. He gave the females southern names in keeping with the surroundings: Miss Molly, Flora Merry Lee, Pearly Mae, and his favorite of all, Lavaliere. He found that the manatees had vastly differing personalities; some fled; some were wary but curious; some, particularly Lavaliere, not only were unafraid but sought his attention. Lavaliere loved to be rubbed and in return would try to enfold him in her rubbery arms.

The life of the manatee, Hartman discovered, is as simple, as peaceful, and possibly, were it not for motorboats and divers, as blissful as life can be. The central rhythm of its life seems to be dictated by the weather and consequent water temperature. When the weather cooled, in October, Hartman found that the manatees came upriver from the Gulf and congregated in the warmer waters of the springs. With the return of warm weather in March or April, they dispersed again. But even during the winter they came and went quite often, according to the temperature, cruising back and forth from the Gulf and sometimes into an adjacent estuary. During the summer, they disappeared, presumably into the deeper waters where tracking them is difficult. Essentially, manatees lead their lives quite independent of each other. They do not have a herd in the sense that some animals do —no leaders and no lasting attachments except between mother and calf—but when they meet in the close confines of the river they enjoy each other's company, playing and cavorting underwater like frolicsome blimps.

Here are some of the things that Hartman observed underwater:

The manatees' main business in life is peaceful browsing, cowlike, on underwater pastures. Usually they simply graze, but sometimes they use their flippers to pull food into their mouths.

Manatees nap with closed eyes, sometimes near the surface but more often on the bottom, from which they slowly, sleepily rise every few minutes for a breath of air and then sink again. Sometimes they are pestered by fish that peck at their hides searching for microorganisms. The manatees flinch and slap ineffectually with their flippers like a man bothered by mosquitoes.

Manatees are remarkably supple. Waking from a nap, they

may close their eyes and arch their backs, or curl forward like a shrimp, emitting a lengthy groan. This stretching may be followed by a back dive to the bottom and a headstand in the sand.

Manatees rub themselves with their flippers as far as they can reach. They also use their flippers to clean their teeth. Apparently food trapped in their mouths is irritating, and Hartman saw manatees become almost frantic as they attempted to get rid of it. They also rub their bodies, with apparent pleasure, against such things as rocks and poles and lobster traps.

Manatees emit squeals, chirps, squeaks, and screams, which Hartman could hear plainly underwater. He saw no air bubbles accompany these sounds and has no idea how they are produced. Manatees seem to use their voices less to communicate than to express emotion, as in moments of fear, internal conflict, sexual arousal, protest, or play. One manatee squeaked, as though with pleasure, when Hartman scratched its back, and he heard others squealing and chirping as they rubbed themselves on rocks and logs. Sex is accompanied by a medley of sounds, and fright evokes a high-pitched scream. Calves answer the alarm calls of their dams.

Manatees are inquisitive. They investigate oddities encountered in the water by nudging, licking, or taking them in their mouths. Hartman saw one manatee chewing on a Coke bottle, another carrying a beer can around, another nudging a log, and so on. Manatees nibbled his flippers, munched on his anchor rope, and tried to carry off his underwater thermometer.

Perhaps the greatest flaw in what is otherwise a design for an idyllic life is in the sex lives of manatees. Male manatees are very sexy and female manatees are not. As a cow comes into estrus, there is a long period during which she is intensely attractive to males but is quite uninclined to mate. Consequently, she collects a train of increasingly frantic suitors, who pester her relentlessly. Hartman guesses that things are arranged this way so that a herd will gather and there can be selective competition for the privilege of mating. This is the only time there is anything like aggression between manatees. The males jockey for position near

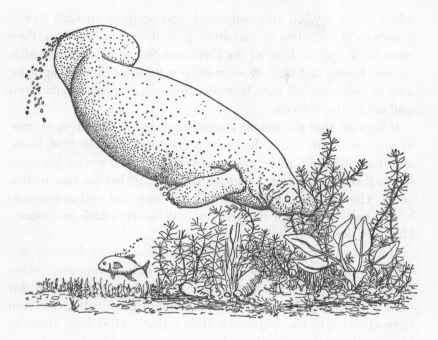

the female, colliding and bouncing off each other like living beach balls. The males probably enjoy the chase, and from time to time relieve their feelings with homosexual embraces, but the female shows no pleasure as she flees, dodges, and as a last resort rolls on her back to frustrate their advances. Hartman saw one female followed for days by a herd of amorous males—almost the whole male population of the bay at that time. They gave her no peace until at last some mysterious clock within her ticked to the right second and she decided to submit, allowing herself to be embraced, with the male lying on his back beneath her, and accepting one lover after another. Even when there is no cow in estrus, male manatees are always hopeful, constantly searching for sexual possibilities, and easily excited. If there is nothing better around, they engage in homosexual play. Females never do.

Play is an important part of manatee social life; the young, especially, do a great deal of kissing, caressing, and cavorting that is not sexual in intent. Females happily join in, allowing themselves to be nibbled and embraced, and seeming to bask in enjoyment. The kissing of manatees is odd and interesting: they press their lips to those of another manatee as in a human kiss. No one knows just why. One scientist suggested that it might be a bit of behavior left over from life on land, where animals often sniff each other's faces.

It appears that the female manatee produces her calves at two-to three-year intervals. She seeks a sheltered spot to give birth, and then, it is said, raises the newborn to the surface on her back for its first breath. The young manatee is suckled for one to two years. The mother is solicitous of her young and will attempt to lead a calf away from danger, but will never attack an enemy. Her only defense is flight.

Hartman believes that manatees have very acute hearing and depend on their vision only for close inspection, since they often frequent murky water. They probably smell little underwater, for their nostrils are closed most of the time, but possibly they can taste changes in the water—an ability that would help them to identify their whereabouts and recognize other manatees.

Hartman found it easier to spy on the intimate behavior of manatees than to make accurate population counts or to assess their future. He feels that in the local area of the study—that is, the river estuaries from the Chassahowitzka to the Withlacoochee—the population of manatees is healthier than it was a few years ago, though there are still probably not much more than a thousand in all. Hartman suspects that for manatees a bit of pollution has a silver lining; increased waterweeds provide more food, and the dredging of canals extends their habitat.

On the other hand, the incessant small-boat traffic on every navigable waterway is a serious menace to manatees. Fishing in Florida is no longer a peaceful pastime. A ride on a river is almost like rush hour on the freeway, with equally reckless speeders at the wheel. Many manatees are hit and survive their wounds, but there is no way of telling how many die of them. Their bodies sink at first; later, afloat, they could easily be carried into hidden nooks in the river or to the marshy, inacces-

sible shores of the Gulf and never be found. Manatees are
protected by law, but they are harassed by divers, hooked by
bored fishermen, and shot at by vandals. Scuba diving is a
standard sport at Crystal River. Hartman found that the manatees that gathered to rest or play in the warm waters of the
spring were forced to flee when divers arrived, for almost
invariably the divers teased and plagued them unmercifully.
However, as the waters darken more and more this is one
harassment that may come to an end.

There are limits to the pollution and disturbance manatees can
stand. The great estuary of Old Tampa Bay, for instance, was
once a natural gathering place but is now barely habitable for
them. Farther south, however, there is sanctuary in the Everglades, and this area probably has a substantial manatee population. There are few manatees around the Keys—perhaps because
of a lack of fresh water—but they can be found on the entire east
coast of Florida, and they occasionally migrate as far north as
North Carolina.

On a worldwide scale, the future of the Sirenia is probably far
less rosy than it is in Florida. The manatee's cousin, the dugong,
has disappeared from wide areas of its Indo-Pacific range. The
African and Amazonian manatees are protected but nevertheless
they are often harpooned and netted wherever human beings can
find them. Today the powerboat is spreading along remote shores
as waterweeds are in the Crystal River, and this means that there
can be few manatee sanctuaries left.

Practical-minded biologists have tried to devise a use for
manatees. Manatee steaks for the gourmet market? Manatees as
aquatic lawn mowers, chewing their way through weed-choked
waterways? There are several problems in the way of such
schemes. One is the very slow birthrate. It would take six or
seven years to raise a manatee from conception to maturity. Outside of the tropics there would be the problem of protecting
them from cold spells, which can be fatal. Still another problem
is finding ponds big enough to hold a large population of manatees.

It is probable that for as long as we allow manatees to survive they will go on leading utterly useless lives. Useless to people, that is. There is a large school of thought, among both laymen and professionals, that finds uselessness in animals intolerable. People who hold this view believe that every animal must serve a human purpose—that to justify its existence it is obligated to satisfy one human appetite or another. They ask of every animal, "What good is it?" and if it is "no good" they see no "sense" in letting it survive. To those who ask this about the manatee it can be answered that the manatee serves a very high purpose indeed, although it is an abstract one. The manatee is, as far as I know at the moment, the only example of a higher mammal that lives its life virtually without aggression toward its own species or any other species. Perhaps some obscure member of our group—such as the sloth or the platypus—is equally peaceful, but I doubt it. The manatee is a mammal like us. It has a brain and a nervous system much like ours, but one characteristic so fatally pervasive in the rest of the animal world has somehow been bred out of it. The manatee will not fight, even to protect itself or save its young. It injures no other vertebrate creature. Surely there is some use in contemplating this uniquely blameless life.

SOUTH COUNTY
NOTES

Rhode Island license plates carry the legend "Discover Rhode Island." I can't help wanting to erase that message and keep secret the place that I find more beautiful than anywhere else in the world. Perhaps part of the reason I find it so is that I remember so well how it looked when I was a child, before development transformed country stores into supermarkets and quiet pastures into half-acre lots dotted with ranches and Capes and split-levels. In a way I remember even before my childhood and back into my mother's. There was a great deal of talk at the dinner table dealing with recollections of a few decades past and these became part of my own. The house in which we spent every summer was a Victorian house built in 1883 by my grandparents, and all during my youth it remained intact. The same pieces of furniture stood where they had always stood. The tall clock that was ceremoniously wound up with a big brass key every Sunday ticked as it always had.

Its slow, sure tick-tock was like the heartbeat of a living being, a reassurance that within the house all was well. Outdoors also everything seemed to remain the same year after year. I wasn't aware that the trees were getting taller and that the serene vistas of shrubbery and lawn and garden remained unchanged only because of the daily work of Percy Blanchard, our "man on the place," who, armed with mowers and shears, devoted a summer-long struggle to holding back the disorderly, aggressive forces of growth.

When I have known someone when young and beautiful, I tend to see them as beautiful after they have aged. I may concede slight alterations in their former perfection, but I'm sure I do not see them with the same eye as someone who never knew them in youth. Perhaps there is something of this in my view of the corner of Rhode Island, known as South County, in which I live.

Unfortunately for me I can't ignore what is happening here. A jungle of growth is overwhelming this county and there is no way to hold it back. Not many people want to. Newcomers, never having seen South County in youth, are not aware of the changes they bring with them. All they know is that it is much more beautiful here than wherever it was they came from. If I were to tell them how I feel about the houses and highways covering the landscape like a strangling vine, not many people would sympathize with me and all could say with justice that I am selfish in my regrets.

Some of these thoughts were in the back of my mind one early-summer day when I happened to find myself briefly back in New York. I picked up a copy of the New York *Times* and noticed an ad that set off a bit of wishful thinking mixed with nostalgia.

In the first days of June, when I was a child, we went from our winter home in New York to my grandmother's in Rhode Island for the summer. Even now, long afterward, when the sun heats the pavements in the city and the breeze is warm, I feel that it is time to go, and I think of The Place in Rhode Island as though it must still be there. I think of wading through meadow grass suddenly grown up as high as my waist and of warm sun above me and cool green dampness under my bare feet. The Place supported five red-and-white cows, a workhorse, a hen yard, and a huge vegetable garden. This was all tended by Blanchard, our gardener, and I spent much of my time following him around. I especially remember milking—the cow chewing and the milk zipping into the pail. If Blanchard was in a good mood, he would squirt some milk into my mouth or onto my bare foot, and squirt the cat for good measure. The milk was delivered to the cook, who took some of it and poured it into a funnel on top of a large contraption called a separator.

The machine made gurgling, revolving noises and then miraculously poured, out of two spouts, a jet of skim milk and a jet of cream. From the cream the cook made butter in a large wooden churn. A couple of times, she let me make my own butter. To do this, you put the cream in a jar, screwed on the lid, and shook it and shook it for a long time. Eventually, little golden balls would show up, and then lumps of real sweet butter, floating in milk. It was quite interesting and instructive. This all came back to me when I saw an ad in the *Times* for a new contraption at a fancy hardware store named Hammacher Schlemmer. "Now make your own fresh cream," it said. "It's all so easy and so inexpensive. Simple, quick. Our Cream Maker also makes pouring cream for coffee and cereals, whipped cream . . ." What made me rub my eyes was reading what the Cream Maker uses to make cream out of: butter and milk! What a marvelous idea! The principle here is the thing. It could improve this country enormously—a machine that works backward. Maybe someday, if this idea catches on, someone will invent a really big, powerful Reverse Machine. The first thing I would like to put in it is the four-lane highway that runs over The Place, through the pasture where the cows used to be. Then I would like to feed it the shopping center. As all the flat-roofed, horrid buildings went in, there would be gurgling, revolving noises inside. Then out would come cool, dark earth and green grass. Soon there would be a pasture with five red-and-white cows ready to give milk from which we could make cream and butter.

Oiled Bird

In January a couple of years ago there was a tragedy at sea somewhere off our shores. It would have seemed remote, no more than a few words on the evening news broadcast, had I not had an encounter that brought it to my doorstep. Just after the episode I put down some notes:

It was a bright, sunny day. Snowy fields glittering outside my window. Lots of birds in the bird feeder. The sky perfectly blue, and the air as cold and clear as water in a mountain brook. A lovely interval between the storms we've been having this January. My phone rang. A friend said she'd heard that a man fishing

down at the Pier had seen a penguin sitting on a rock. I doubted
it was a penguin, but I was curious. I got in the car with my dog
and drove the four or five miles from my farm to the Pier. On the
stone fishing jetty, I parked beside a van. A tall young man—mustache, watch cap, denim jacket, blue jeans, binoculars—was looking out at something in the water. He said that it wasn't a penguin—that it was an oil-covered seabird, probably a murre.
Standing on a rock with its wings stuck to its sides, it had looked
like a penguin. Now it was back in the water. He couldn't figure
out any way to catch it. He had no boat, and even if he did have
one the bird could dive and get away. The young man said that
his name was Jim Herrmann and that he was a biologist. We
watched the bird bobbing on the water. There was almost no
surf. Sometimes waves roll in here and crash against the seawall,
but on this summer day of winter there were only shiny wavelets
lapping the rocks. Herrmann said that the bird wouldn't last
long. Another storm was due, and anyway the bird would starve
in a few days. The little waves were washing it closer to us. It
looked serene and graceful. No distress. It was eerie to see it float
without complaint—or any sign that it was doomed. Herrmann
felt bad about leaving it there, he said, but he guessed there was
nothing he could do. He turned to go. I couldn't leave quite yet.
Suddenly, a series of larger waves came along. They washed the
bird toward the rocky shore. I called to Herrmann, and he came
back. The bird was at the edge of the rocks. A bigger wave came.
I don't know if the bird scrambled ashore or was tossed, but it
disappeared among the boulders. Herrmann's hopes revived. He
said that maybe the bird was wedged in a crevice. If so, he
might be able to get it. He climbed down among the boulders
and along the shore. I followed. Then the bird reappeared—it
had got up on a rock about fifty feet ahead of Herrmann and just
a few feet from the water's edge. It stood up straight on the rock
with its wings hanging down, looking very much like a penguin.
It seemed to be trying to soak up warmth, but, even in the bright
sun, the air was icy. Herrmann dropped behind a rock, so as not
to startle the bird back into the water. Then he crept along—

slowly, cautiously—stalking it. I followed. It was exciting. Like a kid's game. When the bird turned our way, we stopped dead and waited. The bird hopped and struggled up to a higher rock. That was good. Now there was room for Herrmann to get between it and the water. He took off his jacket and balled it up under one arm. The bird was looking nervous now. Turning its head this way and that. Herrmann moved fast. He reached his goal—the narrow space between the bird and the slippery, weed-covered rocks where the sea lapped. Then he threw his jacket over the bird and dived after it, like a football player covering a ball. He shouted in triumph, and got to his feet, holding the bird bagged inside his jacket. When I got to him, he was grinning. "Gee whiz!" he said. "I did it. At last, I saved something." The bird was a quiet lump inside his jacket. We picked our way back to smooth ground. Herrmann stopped and opened the jacket a little. I saw the bird's dark gray head and pale breast, its slender bill. Its bright bird eye closed and opened, closed and opened. Herrmann said he would take the bird to the Norman Bird Sanctuary, in Middletown, to be cleaned. I congratulated him, and went back to the car.

Since it was such a lovely day, I decided to take my dog for a walk on the beach at the other end of Ocean Road. I drove under the arch between the Towers, designed by Stanford White, which are all that remains of Narragansett's heyday as a watering place. In the nineties, it had a casino and a bathing pavilion. My grandmother used to come here in a horse-drawn carriage. The casino and the pavilion have been replaced by what our town officials consider suitable for a seaside "playground"—parking lots and an apartment-and-shopping "complex." However, the beach is still one of the most beautiful beaches in the world. I parked and walked along the sand, and my dog dashed about in great joy. On the mile-long stretch of beach, half a dozen other people were walking, with children and dogs racing around them. A flock of sandpipers mined the sand at the water's edge. No oil on them, apparently. They flew easily when I approached. I looked out at the far-stretching flatness of the sea, which ended in a sharp line at the horizon. It was totally empty out there. I wondered how far out it was to the place where a tanker with thirty-eight sailors from Taiwan and eight million gallons of oil sank recently. I had heard someone on television surmise that most of the oil would stay solid in the cold depths, like a giant glob of Silly Putty, and roll around for years on the ocean floor. The Chinese sailors, floating peacefully dead, wouldn't last nearly so long. Sailors are more biodegradable. I thought of the rescued bird. It linked me to that scene more compellingly than any of the words I'd read or heard spoken about the disaster. I wondered how many days the bird had swum and floated and endured to reach our shore with its message from way out there. As I was walking along thinking about this, I heard a roar, and a blue sports car carrying three young men whipped through the gate opening onto the beach. The car zoomed across the frozen sand and roared along, swaying and sashaying. As it passed me, scattering snow and sand, smashing down small dunes, just missing a dog, I saw the young men's faces. They were having a wonderful time. That glimpse told me that the bird had brought its message in vain.

Smew

That winter there was another bird visitor to our county. A friend, Aliça Waterston, called me and asked, "Have you seen the smew?" Aliça often asks startling questions and so I wasn't surprised—merely puzzled. "What is a smew?" I had to ask. She told me that it was a Russian bird and that I must not miss its unprecedented visit here. Thanks to Aliça's timely tip I put together an account of this tiny, feathered *tovarich*.

Smews are waterfowl that nest in northern Europe and Asia from Sweden to Siberia. Never before in recorded history had a smew visited our East Coast under its own steam. At 9:35 A.M. on January 3, 1976, two bird-watchers were on the shore of

Green End Pond, just off First Beach, on the border between
Newport and Middletown, Rhode Island. They were Hugh
Willoughby, forty-four, a real estate man from Riverside, Rhode
Island, and Robert Bushnell, of North Providence, who is a
production controller in a manufacturing plant. Willoughby had
been bird-watching for fifteen years. His life list of species
observed is close to six hundred, which puts him in the
top ranks of bird-watchers. Bushnell, twenty-nine, had been
bird-watching for only four years, but had a commendable life
list of three hundred and twenty-three. The scene at the pond
that morning was icy but peaceful. Numbers of water birds—
green-winged teal, common mergansers, canvasbacks, and various gulls—were riding on the open water of the partly frozen
pond. They were all familiar species and easily identified. Then,
momentously, Bushnell saw bobbing on the wavelets a bird that
looked like a little white diving duck with a crested head. Since
there is no such thing as a little white diving duck with a crested
head among North American birds, Bushnell exclaimed, "What
the hell is *that?*" Willoughby looked, and agreed that it was not
an American bird. Finally, he said, "Damned if it doesn't look
like a smew!" For this inspired conjecture Willoughby is generally credited with the discovery of the Newport smew, but he
quickly and modestly points out that it was Bushnell who first
spotted it.

Both men were excited, but their emotion was tempered by
the possibility that it was a tame bird that had escaped from an
aviary. Willoughby hurried home to consult his bird books,
which confirmed that the bird was a smew. He called Charles
Wood, the co-editor of *Rhode Island Field Notes*, with the news.
From that moment, word of the smew sped along the intricate
communications network that links bird-watchers all over the
country. The Massachusetts Audubon Society maintains a telephone service called the Voice of Audubon. Anyone dialing
(617) 259-8805 hears a recorded message giving an up-to-date
report of interesting bird sightings. There are similar rare-bird-
alert systems in the New York and Washington areas. In addi-

tion, bird-watchers are quick to phone colleagues and friends. Thus, within a day hundreds of people were aware of the little white bird on Green End Pond. For several days, however, the question of its origin remained unsettled. At first, few people believed that the smew could be a bona fide wild bird. Audubon people called all the waterfowl fanciers who might have lost a smew. Smews are difficult to keep in captivity. It turned out that there were only eleven smews in captivity in the United States, and they were all accounted for. European weather patterns were examined. A storm with hundred-mile-an-hour winds had swept into northern Europe just before the smew arrived, and people speculated that as a result the bird could have been carried across the Atlantic by freakish air currents. Watchers also noted that the smew had no band and was as wary as any wild bird. By the end of the week, doubts about its authenticity as a far-flung smew had vanished.

I learned all this when Aliça and I visited the smew, a week after the first sighting. We drove along the beach road, where a grassy embankment encloses one end of a large reservoir adjacent to Green End Pond. A dozen or more cars were parked beside the embankment, and the edge of the reservoir was lined with people looking through telescopes set on tripods. We scrambled up the bank, and a Siberian wind hit us in the face. A man muffled in a parka pointed out a distant white speck and invited me to look through his telescope. I saw the smew. It was the cutest little duck I'd ever seen—white, with a large black eye spot, a crested head, and two black crescent bars on each side of its breast. Its outline was plump. Its neck arched in a graceful curve. The man said that the smew, a male, was only sixteen inches long and weighed less than two pounds. It is a merganser —specifically, *Mergus albellus*. The species is quite uncommon even in its home range. Suddenly, the smew ducked its head and vanished, reappearing a moment later. There was a murmur of pleasure from the bird-watchers. Mergansers feed on small fish caught underwater. The smew resumed floating. Watching, I was reminded of Dorothy, swept by a cyclone into the Land of Oz, and wondered if the smew was aware of its enormous journey. Its small form riding serenely on the bright water gave no clue. Shortly, when icy tears blurred my sight, Aliça and I slid down the bank, returned to our car, and drove a couple of miles to the office of the Norman Bird Sanctuary to talk with its director—Lee Gardner, an ornithologist with a beard that looked enviably warm that day. Gardner said he had spotted the smew a few hours after Willoughby and Bushnell saw it, and had recognized it immediately, since he had seen smews on the Black Sea (where migrating smews appear in winter) when he was a professor in Istanbul some years ago. He, too, had called the Audubon people, in some excitement, and he had been a little disappointed to find that they already knew.

Gardner had his own theory of how the smew got here. He doubts that it was blown over from Europe, and thinks it was a bird that had migrated eastward, as Siberian smews do, into China. Thence it could have wandered on to Japan and to the Aleutians, and finally reached Alaska. Each year, a handful of smews show up in the Aleutians, and they have been seen as far east as British Columbia. On the Alaskan coast, the weather is relatively mild, but inland there are fierce storms. If the smew had been caught in one of these, prevailing winds would have carried it southwest into Canada and diagonally across the United States to Newport. The past autumn was exceptionally mild, Gardner points out, and the smew would have found open water in which to feed along the way. A smew must eat every thirty-six hours or it dies. "Other birds have crossed the continent from Alaska," Gardner said. "Some experts don't agree, but my theory is much more plausible."

What lies ahead for the wandering smew? Will he ever return home? Gardner thinks not. The cues that trigger migration in birds—hormones, day length, and weather patterns—would not induce him to fly either west to Siberia or east to Europe. Therefore, his exile is permanent. How long can he survive? Surprisingly, his new environment is not radically different from his home range. Newport is at the same latitude as portions of the smew's normal wintering ground. His problem is isolation from his own species in unfamiliar territory during weeks of freezing temperature. If the reservoir freezes over, as it may any day, all the birds must leave for open water. Some species can find food at sea, but common mergansers and smews prefer to feed in fresh water. The smew's survival will depend on his finding unfrozen estuaries and ponds farther south. Ducks often find food by following old-timers who know the way. Fortunately for the smew, there are other mergansers on the pond—both the American, or common, merganser and the red-breasted merganser. (The third native species, the hooded merganser, is as rare here as the smew is in its home range.) Perhaps the smew will recognize his American kin and follow them to new feeding grounds. Then, if he survives the winter, he will migrate north in the spring and find the marshes and bogs of Canada, which are much like those of Siberia. But he will find no other smews. We asked Gardner if this meant that the smew is doomed to solitude as long as he lives. "Perhaps not," Gardner said. "I am a romantic. I see an outside chance that our mergansers will tolerate him. He is the wrong color, but he is still a merganser and speaks essentially the same language they do. Who knows? He might even find an American mate. Meanwhile, he is settling down very well. Eating frequently. Preening himself. Today, there was a very good sign —he disappeared and came back. That means he is scouting and remembering."

Snow in Rhode Island

One reason I am still able to see South County as beautiful is that after the war I was lucky enough to buy a farm that has taken the place in my life of the one on which I spent my youth. I am too far from the road to be aware of traffic and no other houses are visible from mine. I have a dog, two horses, and two cats. There are a lot of wild animals around, too. One winter my husband and I had our own private version of "Treetops," the place in Africa where tourists used to go to watch wild animals come to a water hole. Each evening we put a dish of food scraps on the lawn beneath our bedroom window and shone a spotlight on it. Then we would darken the room and watch. Quite soon the local population of skunks, raccoons, foxes, and opossums accepted our invitation to dine.

They seemed unaware of the spotlight and we could watch at close range as the raccoon elbowed the opossum aside, the fox waited warily at the edge of the pool of light, and the skunk, moving with the self-assurance that comes from superior armament, unhurriedly took possession of the dish and ate his fill. This winter pastime ended when our dog came to live with us, but I remember it with pleasure and retain the feeling it gave me that this farm is home not just for me but for a lot of other beings who enjoy it so unobtrusively that I am happy to pay their taxes for them as long as I am able.

One recent winter there was a dramatic snowstorm that undoubtedly brought a lot of people a lot of trouble, but we were lucky enough to have plenty of food and fuel and the storm caused us no problems. In fact, we enjoyed it. What follows is a report written just after the storm.

We don't often have deep snow here, and when it comes, it changes everyone's life, but it is hard for me to think of it as a disaster. Difficult, perhaps, but not a disaster. Nevertheless, whenever two or three more snowflakes than usual fall on our little state the politicians get on the phone to Washington asking for Emergency Aid, and for several evenings the news is full of talk about our being a "disaster area." The words are delivered in solemn, almost reverent tones. The reverence may be induced by the thought of all the money that will fall on us like warm, green snowflakes if Washington decides to designate our condition disastrous. The day after the recent big snowstorm, while Washington was trying to make up its mind on this point, I conducted my own survey of the effects of the heavy snow. I covered a limited area, bounded by the shopping center, the post office, the Atlantic Ocean, and my snow-covered orchard and barnyard.

I began at the shopping center, and, for what it's worth, I can report that the place looked absolutely normal. The bleak expanses of parking lots were just as bleak and grimy as on any other day, and only a bit slushier. Within the supermarket, the shelves and aisles were crammed with things and people, as they always are. Under the fluorescent lights, the fruits and vegetables shone with strange, unnatural colors, as they always do. As far as I'm concerned, the only disaster is that the shopping center is there at all, in place of the general stores of yesteryear. Anyway, Washington, I don't think you need send help to the shopping center. I found the post office also looking normal. The flag was flying. A man was hacking ice off the steps. There was, as usual, no place to park, and I had to leave my car a block away. However, when I went in I learned that the New York *Times* had been delayed. Whether this rates as a disaster depends on what is in the *Times,* and I will have to postpone judgment until my copy finally comes.

I visited the ocean by driving south a few miles on Route 1 and turning off on the Moonstone Beach Road, which comes to a dead end beside one of a series of salt ponds with which our area is blessed. The ponds are wonderful winter havens for water birds. As usual, I found several bird-watchers scanning the frozen distances with field glasses. I stopped to talk with a man wearing a blue cap and a plaid lumber jacket, who gave me the exciting news that the smew had returned.

The smew I'd seen in Newport two years before had flown off in April and hadn't been reported since. Well, the man told me, just two weeks before the recent big storm a smew was spotted on Quonochontaug Pond, a bit southwest of Moonstone Beach. It was hardly possible that it was a new and different smew. It was like hearing good news about an old friend and I found something wonderfully cheering in the fact that this tiny individual had found our shores hospitable and survived. The news of the

smew's return had spread on the bird circuit and joyous birders have flocked to welcome it back; its return is considered a fine testimonial to our neighborhood.

The smew must have found the great snowfall delightfully homelike, and after the storm passed it was seen bobbing happily on the icy waters. I thanked the man for telling me all this, and crossed the dunes to have a look at the ocean. The ocean was looking wonderful. The water was as clear and as green as bottle glass. The beach was as neat as a pin, the sand smooth and clean. Every beer can had been swept away, every old bathing cap and Clorox bottle buried or carried out to sea. In their place was some interesting driftwood. I hope Washington will note that the ocean in our area has never been better.

Back home I found my first evidence of disaster: a dead blue jay lying stiff under a big tree. I picked him up and examined him for cause of death. I could find no sign, and put the body back on the snow. His surviving companions, clustered at the bird feeder, all looked strong and healthy. At the front door, I found a second disaster—the oil bill that the deliveryman had left tucked into the doorjamb while I was out. I put it on my desk. Early the next morning, in bright sunshine, I resumed my survey. I found that the snow around the house was of a tricky and difficult depth. If I could ski, it would have been perfect. But since I can't I had to be content with a less glamorous sport called floundering. I started floundering out to the stable, breaking through the thin crust. Looking down at the glittering whiteness beneath my feet, I could see that I was not the first abroad. Where the wind had blown the snow to lesser depths, the roofs of mouse-made tunnels were visible, forming wandering patterns like veins. I paused to wonder about the vista inside the tunnels from the point of view of the mice. Is there icy-blue light when the sun shines through, or is the light golden? I imagine that the walls of the snow tunnels look a bit like the white tile in the Holland Tunnel, but that, unlike the Holland Tunnel, a mouse tunnel is filled with clean, white air. There is no engine roar, and only an occasional squeak at traffic intersections. One of the ways mice survive in snow is to eat bark from young trees—especially from expensive fruit trees. I noted that several tunnels led in the direction of apple trees I'd planted the previous spring. Burpee sells plastic collars to put around trunks to fend off mice. I ordered several and forgot to put them on. I am chalking up the probable apple-tree disaster to my own carelessness, and am not asking for help from Washington. Floundering on to the stable, I rounded a corner and surprised a fox snoozing on the manure pile. This, I realized, must be the warmest spot in town. Its internal heat, plus its steep slope and the sun on its dark surface, had melted the snow, creating a sort of Red Fox Riviera. It seems foxes have known about alternate energy sources all along. Reluctantly, the fox got up, shook himself, and trotted off lightly on the delicate crust of the snow. No floundering for him. His coat was a lovely shade of orange. He was beautifully made: long, slender legs, slender body, elegant brush. He paused behind a bush to stare at me and then moved on. I hoped he had found the dead blue jay and had it for breakfast.

That evening I was pleased when the findings of my survey

were confirmed by the TV newscast. The governor, it said, had withdrawn his request for federal aid, and Rhode Island wasn't a disaster area after all.

Here is another winter event, less cheerful I'm afraid, that I felt compelled to record:

Early on a snowy morning just a day or two before Christmas my phone rang and a neighbor told me that my horses had gotten loose and were over on the Curtis Corner Road. I put some oats and a saddle and bridle in the back of the car and my husband and I started out to fetch them. As we drove along Ministerial Road, I thought how lovely and rural our dear South County looked; for this and other reasons I felt full of warm Christmas feelings and gratitude for the blessings of life here.

Making the scene even prettier, bringing it to life, were two little boys walking along the road toward the woods by the brook. They seemed part of the native fauna, like rabbits or deer, and I was happy to share this morning with them. My husband stopped the car and I lowered the window and hailed them, asking if they'd seen any loose horses.

They were appealing kids; their faces flushed with the clean, cold air and their eyes bright. One was carrying a big Havahart trap, a kind of trap made of wire mesh that imprisons an animal without killing it, and the other boy held a leg-hold trap. They hadn't seen any horses. I asked what they were planning to catch.

"Oh, anything!" one boy answered, and then, impatient to get on with their project, they turned and hurried on. We drove on, too. Since then I've been thinking about what happened, or may have happened, after that. I have no way of knowing, but these are my imaginings.

I suppose the boys put the traps down somewhere in the woods on the edge of the swamp where the low ground has so far held off developers and where the small native animals still find seclusion—a wild world in miniature. During the day it got colder and windier and that night there was a heavy snow.

Maybe no animals moved around during the storm and so the traps waited, jaws open, perhaps for a day, or several days.

If the boys caught nothing in the first few days probably their interest waned and the excitement of other Christmas diversions absorbed their thoughts so that they didn't come back to the traps for quite a while. Or maybe they caught something right away. I can't tell which way it worked out.

If they did catch an animal, what kind was it? As they said, it might have been anything; a rabbit, a wandering cat, a raccoon, an opossum, or perhaps even a stray fox or a rare and remarkable weasel. The kind of animal makes no difference really. Whatever it was, it was searching for food, which animals, unlike modern children, do not find in supermarkets, and it was having tough going in the icy weather. Then suddenly it was caught.

If it was caught in the leg-hold trap, it was terrified and agonized. If it was caught in the Havahart trap, it was terrified and, unless released fairly soon, quietly froze to death. In either case the animal was quite possibly dead when the boys got back to the traps. But if the animal wasn't dead, what then? What did they do with it? Kill it? How? Play with it? How, without being bitten? Take it home and try to "tame" it? If its leg was broken or dislocated, what did they do about it?

After I thought about these various possibilities I thought about where the boys had gotten the traps. Trapping for fur was once considered a legitimate way to make a living and trapping to get rid of "vermin" an acceptable way for a farmer to protect his chickens and his stores of food. Those days are past in our region of New England, and even when it was sanctified by need trapping wasn't a nice death for an animal. But traps are still legal and they can be sold or given to any kid to use as a toy. I don't blame the kids. Trapping an animal is an exciting idea to a boy and no twelve-year-old can be expected to imagine how it will be for the animal.

I caught up with my horses and rode home on Maisie, the mare, while the pony trotted sociably beside us. I rode through the open meadows that lie between my house and the road and where, miraculously, there are still a couple of hundred acres with no house in sight. The snow hadn't been marked by any human footsteps. A few birds flew across the gray sky. It was peaceful and lovely.

I wondered how many small creatures I was passing without seeing clues to their presence; mice, snug in some well-provisioned den, rabbits crouching in sheltered hollows deep in the briar patches, maybe a deer over there in the woods, and somewhere, the fox that I have heard yapping on still, cold nights.

It was a lovely ride. Just the right thing to do at Christmas-time. But unfortunately I was thinking about the traps that the boys were probably just then putting down in some strategic place. I wondered if the trapped animal would die on Christmas morning, just as the kids were opening their newer toys.

Coal from the Sea

The winter of '79 was a terribly cold one and I put down some thoughts on the topic of keeping warm, beginning with coal given back to us by the sea. It seems that from time to time lumps of anthracite coal, presumably spilled from cargo vessels that sank many years ago off our treacherous coast, come up in the nets of fishermen. If the fishermen are thrifty, they bring the coal home. It burns beautifully, with a flickering blue-green flame, and makes a slow, steady fire that keeps a stove warm all through the night. To me there is something wonderful and a bit eerie about this coal—coal that was mined such a long time back and intended for burning in nineteenth-century furnaces, and is now warming twentieth-century houses. A hundred years and more ago, before railroads took over, coal and other cargo came to New England in coastal schooners. The schooners carrying the coal that is now being netted off our shores might have been bound for Newport or Providence or Boston and come to grief off Point Judith, which was once notorious for the number of wrecks it caused. I've been thinking of the spilled coal waiting on the timeless bottom of the ocean while eventful generations went by on land. Perhaps some of these pieces of coal were mined at the beginning of the great revolution brought on by the fossil fuels and are finally being consumed in its twilight.

I heard about the coal from the sea in what seemed an unlikely place. I was having a haircut in Sue's Beauty Cottage, on Main Street. Sue was born a Browning, and a lot of past and present Brownings were, or are, fishermen. Sue has had two husbands, also fishermen, and has three sons who are fishermen. She is an attractive, dark-eyed woman with a keen business mind and old-fashioned thrifty ways. When she told me about her sons bringing home coal, I realized that a surprising number of things in the town are tied together by fuel. They include Main Street, the Beauty Cottage, Sue's Yankee business skill, and a new way of life—as far as heating goes—that has been sweeping New England in the wake of a new phenomenon: the rediscovery of the parlor stove. Sue's Beauty Cottage is on Main Street because of fuel. Main Street used to be the business center of our town. After the war, automobiles strangled it and left it for dead. One by one, the stores closed; Steadman's market, Palmer's men's furnishings, Clarke's shoe store, and a number of others disappeared, while chain stores sprang up out along the highway. Main Street's empty stores became available at low rents for small businesses like Sue's. A couple of years ago, when the oil crisis hit, Sue was one of the first people in town to realize which way the wind would blow. She became a dealer in wood-burning stoves. She rented premises next door to the Beauty Cottage to display them in, sharing the space with Gladys Watson's antiques. The stoves looked much at home surrounded by Mrs. Watson's old rockers, patchwork quilts, and pine chests. The stove business took off beyond Sue's most optimistic dreams.

Even in August, she would have to drop her scissors a dozen times a day and dash from the Beauty Cottage to the stove display to talk to a customer. Last autumn, she told me she was making three times as much out of stoves as out of beauty.

I have ordered a stove and am looking forward to it eagerly, like a birthday present. At twilight, when the windows turn a cold, dead gray, I would love to light a fire, but I don't start one in the fireplace, because I know that it would suck expensive oil-produced heat up the chimney. Instead, I reach for a sweater and think how cozy it will be when I put wood in my parlor stove, and draw my chair close. From talking with owners of stoves, I've found that installing parlor stoves is not a matter of grudgingly giving in to necessity. It is something that is being done with real enthusiasm. Stove owners love their stoves. They like to compare notes on money saved, on how to keep a stove burning all night, on how pleasant it is to have a warm stove as the focus of a room. There is also pleasure in freeing yourself from the system. When you light your parlor stove, you throw off the shackles that held you captive to the fuel dealer, the repairman, OPEC, and Sheik Yamani. You can thumb your nose at Sheik Yamani. You feel you are dependent on no one—except, perhaps, the person you bought the wood from.

That, of course, is the rub. All these new stoves are going to require a lot of wood. Fortunately, there is a lot of wood in New England. For decades, it has gone unused; fallen trees have been left to rot or have been carted to the dump. Now such wood will be gathered for burning, as it was generations ago. The same is true of coal from the sea. Sue says that until lately fishermen would throw back any coal they found in the nets, along with seaweed and trash fish. Now they carefully collect it, piece by piece, and most voyages produce a respectable heap. She estimates that her sons have brought her a full ton of coal this winter. At night, when she stokes her stove, she puts one or two big lumps in with the glowing wood, and the fire lasts until morning. Of course, I know that coal salvaged from the sea hardly pro-

56040

vides an answer to our energy problem. Nevertheless, I find it a delightful circumstance that something our great-grandfathers left behind accidentally is being discovered just at the moment of need.

Spring on Main Street

The sap is rising in the merchants in our town. They aren't turning green in person, but their establishments are putting out new shoots and displaying goods in all sorts of enticing colors and shapes, like blossoms. Damon's hardware was the first to catch my eye, with a row of garden carts—red and green—and big wicker baskets on the sidewalk. The Base Camp has a stack of canoes, and to me nothing is more exciting, more alluring than a canoe. This is a bouquet of canoes in beautiful colors. One is daffodil yellow. Two are deep-water green, to glide on a mountain lake shadowed by pines. Two are light blue, for clear, cold northern streams. One is red; it will look marvelous in dark water anywhere—perhaps idling among pickerelweed and water lilies— or overturned on a grassy shore at evening. In the window of our department store there are blue and white skirts and blouses suggesting tennis, and yellow espadrilles. Boy and girl mannequins are dressed for play on a lawn, so neat and clean that they may be going to a birthday party or to visit a fussy grandmother. In New York, summer clothes have doubtless been on display for months, but here we mostly go by the *real* season.

As I walk along Main Street, I discover one spring thing after another. Dove & Distaff Antiques has already filled its window box with pansies. Sherwin Williams is having a terrific paint sale. Handmade posters tucked into the corners of store windows offer invitations. There will be a May Breakfast at the Elks Hall, $3.00 for adults, $1.50 for children, and a Country Dance at the Westerly Center for the Arts, admission $3.00. The Baha'i Coffee House offers a Free Evening of Music and Refreshments, All

Welcome. The Snug Harbor Volunteer Fire Department is also having a May Breakfast, and, unlike the Elks, the firemen disclose their menu: ham, eggs, coffee, toast, doughnuts, johnnycakes, cereal, home fries, milk, juice. All this for $2.50. If I go to a May Breakfast, I'll go to theirs. There will be a rummage sale at the Grange and an auction of dahlia tubers at which the Dahlia Society will serve free refreshments. The Peace Dale Congregational Church is having a Handbell Concert. I am not sure how this is connected with spring, but it adds to the profusion of possibilities.

At the shopping center I stop by Woolworth's, which, in our town, has mysteriously metamorphosed from dime store to department store. As usual, I find something to disapprove of. Because Woolworth's is an alien plant without roots in our soil, it responds not to local weather but to instructions from some distant computer, or so I presume. In any case, it has burst into full bloom too early. In addition to hardy perennials such as barbecues, lawn mowers, redwood tables, and plastic chairs, it has unwisely put out flats full of tender annual plants: tomatoes, petunias, marigolds. The wind still has a sharp bite to it and the plants look chilled and miserable. Some are outright dead. No local person in his right mind would put out tomatoes so early. I am sorry for the plants, but not for Woolworth's. It serves them right.

On my way home, I step into the hardware store. Here I find the true pulse of spring, and it is throbbing. There is an electronic device that dings each time a customer walks through the door; the dings come in rapid succession. I contemplate a display of roots and dormant plants—begonia, clematis, and so on—pictures on their packages show them flowering in vivid colors. A rack of seed packets offers ravishing possibilities—from ageratum to zinnia. Here before me is the heart of the matter of spring. Ranged around the plants and seeds are a multitude of implements designed for nurture, for defense, or for aggressive action. Spring in the country is not, as some suppose, calm and gentle. It is a time of competition and striving, with fierce struggles for possession taking place in and above every inch of ground. The tools displayed urge me to enter the fray. For nurture, there are lawn foods, tree foods, bags of peat moss and mulch, hoses coiled like benign green serpents. For defense, there is Rabbit Gard Wire, labeled with a picture of a hungry, frustrated rabbit peering through it at luxuriant lettuce. For active warfare, there are bags and bottles of herbicides, and insecticides, and ranks of hoes, rakes, snippers, clippers, weeders, and cutters. Mr. Damon, the proprietor, steps over for a word with me. The door dings constantly while we talk. He says that the rush of customers began a couple of weeks ago, with the first warm days. "It escalates every day," he says. "In spring, time is of the essence." He is right. I feel almost overwhelmed with urgency.

A Summer Bird

That year the urgency never seemed to let up. There was quite a bit of rain and things grew madly. No sooner was the garden under control than it was time to do the hay. "Doing the hay" entails assembling, all at one time, the man who mows and bales, four strong boys, to pick up the bales and stack them in the barn, and four days of good weather. None of these is any good without the other. It takes four clear days to dry the hay after it is cut. Incompletely dry hay goes moldy and at worst can catch fire through spontaneous combustion and burn up the barn. Sometime in June when the grass looks ready I begin anxious conferences about the weather with my neighbor Harrie Davenport, who does the mowing and baling. As soon as the die is cast and the cut grass is lying on the ground, I begin trying to line up the boys to work four days hence. Without their muscle we are helpless. The boys are apt to be evasive or unreliable. They are not sure where they will be four days from any given day. There is a better job in the offing or a trip somewhere. They offer the phone number of a friend of a friend whose last name they can't remember. I have to tell them that if the weather looks threatening we may bale a day early. Davenport always wants to bale as soon as possible. I, full of anxiety about mold and fire, want to put it off to the last moment. We usually compromise. All in all, when you bring in hay you are flirting with disaster all through the procedure and my nerves are stretched like rubber bands. This year was no exception as far as tension goes, but we succeeded in bringing in a fine crop of hay. While all this was going on there was another event, of which the following is an account.

We have a lot of starlings living around our farmhouse and nesting in our barn. I have ambivalent feelings about them. I know I am supposed to dislike starlings, because they are interlopers rather than native birds, and because there are too many of them. They evict other, gentler birds from nesting places. They flock together, making mess and noise that greatly annoy some people. On the other hand, I like to see them walking across my lawn in phalanxes with a busy, businesslike stride, as they search for Japanese beetle grubs that I am glad to get rid of. Also, in the spring, when I go out to the barn and hear their nuptial songs, I find them varied and beautiful. This year, the nuptial songs were followed by the cheeping of a multitude of baby starlings—perhaps actually only a dozen, since that's all it takes for baby starlings to sound like a multitude. They are very vocal, and their voices rose and fell in excited choruses, first from one corner of the barn, then from another, as the parents came in with food. One of the nests was on a beam high over the doorway. Just when my husband and I were busiest, getting in hay, I happened to glance down as I went through the door, and saw, sitting solemnly on the concrete, an ugly, half-feathered little starling. He must have only just fallen, or one of my voracious cats would have got him. I actually groaned. I looked at him with real chagrin, recognizing him as a gratuitous and unwelcome burden. "I *don't want* a baby starling," I said to myself. "I really don't." Just then, my black panther of a house cat glided innocently out of the shadows. I picked up the starling impatiently—the way a housewife picks up another dirty dish—and carried him into the house and put him in a box in the bathroom. I have a book that gives advice on caring for wild orphans. Its main recommendation for young birds is a diet of dog food. I fed the bird easily enough, but I was so cross about the whole thing that I would barely look at him. Besides, I didn't want him to be, as the ethologists put it, imprinted by me. I wanted him to grow up as a wild starling, with no illusions that I was his mother, so I barely let him glimpse me at each feeding.

For two days, all through the frantic business of getting the hay baled and into the barn, I stopped whatever I was doing every hour or so and went and fed the damned bird. On the third day, when the rush was over, I realized that the stack of baled hay had brought the nest from which the bird had fallen within reach of a ladder. I persuaded my husband to climb up and put him back. When my husband climbed down, he reported that the bird had settled in beside his single nestmate with no fuss. That, I thought with relief, is that. Two more days passed. I crossed the threshold of the barn and chanced to glance down, and there on the concrete waiting for me was my damned bird. The sequence of events was as before: the bird stowed in a box in the bathroom; the hourly duty grudgingly performed. This time, I knew I was stuck with him until he fledged, so I grudgingly gave him a name—Albert Ross, to be pronounced rapidly. Like most of us, I had read about imprinting and how by early experience birds learn to behave in a way appropriate to their species. It occurred to me that there was no use in saving the bird's life if he grew up without knowing how to be a starling, and this he could hardly do shut up in a cardboard box in a silent bathroom. I made a nest of hay inside a birdcage, carried the cage to the barn, and hung it from a rafter—safe from the cats—so that the bird could see and hear the noisy comings and goings of the other starlings. I noticed that between feedings baby starlings, unless they are asleep, keep up a sort of whirring, purring sound, like a human baby crooning in its crib. I guessed that it is designed to remind the mother of her duty.

My bird did it, too, of course. When I approached, I could tell by the intensity of the sound how hungry he was. When I kept him waiting too long, the crooning turned to a loud, eloquent, insistent whir.

I took Albert's cage to the barn each morning and brought it into the bathroom each night. During the day, I made five or six visits to feed him. When I walked into the barn, filled with the crooning of many little birds—a sound that seemed full of confidence that satisfaction would always come—it struck me that the barn was a happy place. It had good vibes, as they used to say. I usually knew when it was feeding time without looking at my watch. This phase lasted about a week. By then, Albert was hopping restlessly around his cage, and I realized that it was time to think about launching him. I called a biologist I know. I opened by saying that what I had was only a rotten starling, but nevertheless I would appreciate instructions on preparing him for release. The biologist said that first the bird should be allowed to flutter around some safe enclosure and practice flying. A screened porch would be ideal. I have a screened porch, so that was O.K. Then I should teach him to eat by himself instead of from my fingers. Then I should put him outdoors for trial flights, allowing him to return to the porch for reassurance and refuge when he wished. When he was ready, he would leave for good. I explained that Albert was hardly tame, since I hadn't allowed him to be imprinted by me. I wondered if I should continue to be careful about this. "Don't worry," the biologist said. "They forget very quickly and go wild." He also said I needn't apologize for raising a starling. "They're great birds," he said. "Good bug catchers, very smart, beautiful song. That's why they were brought here in the first place." Then he added a bit teasingly, "I bet you love that bird." This suggested to me an image of a sappy woman murmuring baby talk with each offering of dog food, so I said coldly that I found Albert "interesting" and that I was grateful for the advice.

Now I had more contact with Albert. He soon flew around the screened porch competently, but he would eat only from my hand. He quickly became very tame. He spent most of his time perched on a bamboo blind waiting for me. Whenever I appeared, he launched himself at me, to land, chirping and begging, on my arm. I tried every strategy to get him to peck at food. I scattered it at his feet on a bench. I held it before his beak. I secreted it. No dice. This went on for several days. I worried. I called the biologist, who said to let him go hungry all day and then put food before him. That day was hell. Albert was desperate, and I felt awful. At twilight, he still had not pecked a single crumb, so I fed him and, with relief, watched him go contentedly to bed on a perch I had fixed for him in a sheltered corner. The next day, there was a partial breakthrough. I put down a big ashtray full of water. Albert hopped in and took a vigorous bath, during which he sipped some water. I felt like cheering.

By now, I had had Albert about two weeks. He looked quite adult, but not like a starling. He was a soft gray color, with a pale spot on his chest. His outline was graceful. He was a nice-looking bird. When I went out to the barn, I realized that his class had graduated. The barn was silent, but the lawn was busy. Where the lawn mower had recently passed, I saw mother starlings working intently, followed by gray juveniles who seemed to watch the mother bird and emulate her movements as she probed the sod for grubs. It was clear what I had to do next. Albert and I went outside. I put him on the ground, and squatting down, scratched up the earth with a trowel. Albert watched, whirring insistently for food. A worm appeared. Quick as a flash, Albert seized it. I continued scrabbling, hopping to a new location when the previous one was exhausted. We found all sorts of insects: wireworms, grubs, beetles. Albert was enthusiastic. Finally, he was full, and flew to a tree. I felt relief that another hurdle was behind us, but when I returned to the porch Albert cried out and flew in with me. It was just as well. At that moment, one of my cats passed by.

Now we were on the homestretch, but new worries seized me.

I was teaching Albert to find food by hunting on the ground, as a starling must, but I was unable to give the warning cry that would teach him to beware of predators. He was foolishly trusting of my dog and would land on the ground right under her nose. I couldn't be with Albert every minute he was outside; besides, he needed to learn to do his own hunting. For two days, I shut up my cats and left Albert outdoors. It didn't work. In the first place, he did very little searching on his own. He spent most of his time in the tree by the porch door waiting for me to come out, so that we could search for food together. Every time I went out, he would fly down to the ground and hop along after me wherever I went. I usually responded by getting down on all fours and scrabbling through the grass with my fingers while Albert stood by to grab whatever little scurrying things I scared up; then, when I left Albert, he always flew back to his perch in the tree. Inside the house, the cats were furious and frustrated. Maneuvering to get in or out without letting one of them escape was nerve-racking. They waited by the door. I swore and kicked them back. It was all too easy to visualize what would happen if one should get out: my two weeks of hard labor going down the drain as Albert flew trustingly into the jaws of death.

When nothing had changed by the evening of the third day, I knew that the impasse must be broken. I was under too much stress. "I've got to get rid of the damned bird," I told myself. I recalled that there is a bird sanctuary twenty miles from my house. I found that it had a phone number. I asked the man who answered if I could lay a partly fledged starling on him. He said he didn't know much about the job but was willing to try. I put Albert in his cage, covered it with a towel, and drove to the sanctuary. Even muffled by the towel, the bird's voice was penetrating. Albert chirped all the way in apparent bewilderment and alarm. I said, "It's going to be all right, Albert. I promise you it will be all right."

I found the sanctuary headquarters and the caretaker, a friendly young man in jeans with a red beard. He told me he had a degree in invertebrate biology. That was reassuring. He should be good at finding insects. I let Albert out of the cage and he sat on my arm. We both admired him. Then I got down on the grass and showed the young man how to rummage about so that Albert could find food. I told him that Albert liked a nice, deep bath. I told the young man that if he would just look after Albert for a few days, helping him to find food and learn his way around, the bird would probably go wild after that. I picked up the towel and cage, and left. As I drove out, I was reassured by the sight of the young man on all fours progressing slowly across the lawn with Albert hopping along beside him. During the silent drive home, I felt relief that anxiety over Albert's safety had been removed. I congratulated myself on such a fine solution. I looked forward to a leisurely drink, with no bird-nurturing duties to perform. A drink would cheer me up.

Around noon the following day, I called the sanctuary. The young man said that when darkness came Albert had split. He had disappeared into the trees and hadn't been seen since. The young man said that he was sorry and hoped the bird would be O.K. As soon as I hung up, I realized my mistake. At home, I had put Albert on the porch each night while the cats were let out. Naturally, at bedtime he had gone to look for his accustomed sleeping place. He had probably fluttered in confusion through the dark woods. At daylight, I imagined, he had started out again for home. He would probably stop at the first house he came to. If a person appeared, Albert would land at that startled person's feet and beg. I prayed there would be no cats in the house that Albert found.

I went out to tidy up the porch. I took down Albert's perch and picked up the food dishes and the ashtray bathtub. Outside, the lawn was dotted with starling parents guiding and instructing their young with an air of busy competence. They were a noisy bunch. Each time one of the young birds spoke in a voice like Albert's, there was an involuntary response inside me. I wondered how long it takes for a person who has become imprinted by a bird to get over the illusion that she is its mother.

Autumn Storm

Late August and early September are the season of hurricanes, and though most of them turn harmlessly out to sea, now and then one of them roars across our shores. In 1938 I experienced the first in several generations to hit South County. I was staying with my mother and aunt in our old home. Like everyone else in Rhode Island, we had no warning of what was in store for us. We had made no preparations and by the time we realized that this was no ordinary September line storm it was too late to board up windows or fill the bathtubs with water.

The hurricane's moment of greatest fury came during the night and I will never forget lying in bed in the dark (there was no electricity of course), listening to the terrifying roar of the storm. During gusts the house shivered and creaked in distress and the roof seemed to tug at its moorings. The sounds of wind and rain and multitudes of flying leaves were so loud that it was impossible to distinguish the crashings of individual trees from the general chaos of noise. When, in the morning, I woke and looked out the window to a clear, smiling dawn, the first thing I saw was that our great linden tree had fallen. It had sheltered me since childhood and I must have had the unrealistic expectation that it always would. At the sight of it torn down, roots ignominiously bare and broken, I burst into tears. I was quite young then and hadn't learned to accept any loss.

A couple of years ago, on a day in early September, there was again the threat that a hurricane might come our way. By now I have been living at the farm for twenty years. Like my first home, it too has lovely trees and one special one, a huge ash tree, has taken the place in my feelings of the linden of long ago. On the eve of the expected hurricane I wrote down a log of how I had spent the day:

I am writing this before the hurricane, on an electric type-

writer. After the storm, this typewriter won't work. It is 9:30
P.M., the six o'clock news said the storm was coming straight at
us. My husband and I have spent all day on the storm. By about
six o'clock, we had done everything we could, and were very
tired. In the morning, when we first heard that the storm was
coming our way, we thought about food and light and fuel, but
without any sense of real urgency. Then we drove to town
around noon and found that our gas station had a queue of cars,
stretching out into the highway. In an instant, the psychology of
shortage beset us. We drew up at the end of the line, wondering
if the gas would hold out until we got to it. It did. We drove on,
and found, to our surprise, that the hardware store was open,
though today is a legal holiday here—V-J Day. Al Damon, the
proprietor, had opened the store because of the storm, and was
alone behind the counter in semi-darkness. We joined a huddle
of people waiting to ask for hurricane lanterns, fuel, charcoal,
candles. Damon handed out the supplies on his shelves and then
went down into the basement and brought up all he had. With
his permission, we telephoned a couple of friends and told them
of the opportunity. When our turn came, we asked for four lanterns—the extra lanterns were for our friends. Next, we picked up
the mail, and I was struck by how faithfully we performed this
habitual errand, which could not possibly have anything to do
with the coming night—the night the big ash tree might fall.

The big ash tree. That is at the heart of my foreboding. From
the moment I remembered the tree—while we waited for our loot
of lamps and charcoal—I have been aware of how terrible it will
be if the ash tree falls. The ash tree is about ninety feet tall and
about ninety feet wide. A tree man came by once and said that it
must be at least two hundred years old. It is so big you can't see
how big it is until you get right up to the trunk and imagine
climbing into the lowest branches. They are as high above you as
the second story of a house and are as big around as ordinary
tree trunks. A few years ago, one branch fell. It was just a small
part of the tree, but it lay spread out on the ground like a dead
whale. My husband spent days cutting it up. The ash tree is be-

tween our house and our barn. If it falls westward, it will crash into our roof. If it falls toward the northeast, it could crush the barn. But it is not these dire possibilities that bother me. It is the thought that it might fall at all that I cannot bear.

We made a list of things to do. Draw water in bathtubs, fill gallon jugs with drinking water, check window latches, and so on. Our sins of omission have all been uncovered—the unfixed leaks, the unhinged screens. All day long, I have been conscious of using things that perhaps will not be here, or usable, tomorrow. Hot water from the faucet. The electric stove, on which I boiled a dozen eggs. The electric clock. I stifled an impulse to vacuum the floors—for me, an unprecedented desire. When the kitchen was tidy, we worked outdoors, dragging in the porch furniture and picking up every odd tool or object that might hurtle through a window. Most of the day, rain fell straight down— warm and needle-fine or warm and in fat streams, as though from an adjustable shower head. I often looked at the sky, where I supposed the sword of Damocles hung concealed in the wads of dark gray cloud folded over us. There was almost no wind— strangely little wind for such a lot of rain. Between showers, a great many swallows appeared and swooped and dived and rose again, as though very excited.

The pleasantest thing I did all day was to prepare our two horses for the night ahead. I cleaned the stalls, brought in fresh bedding and buckets of clean water, and filled the racks with hay. The horses were probably amazed, because in summer I don't usually do anything like this for them but leave them out to take care of themselves. They were very wet, and entered the stalls willingly and ate the hay with a look of gratification. When I closed the doors of their stable, the small dwelling looked quite secure. It was the only thing I had done all day that I felt might really turn out all right.

By six o'clock, everything was done, everything outside was quiet. Inside, there was the TV—the news programs full of alarms, and charts showing the storm coming, and pictures of people hauling in their boats and leaving their homes. A sudden lonesomeness assailed me. Earlier in the day, I had made one or two essential phone calls, but I hadn't had time for anything else. Now I began to call friends. A number of lines were busy. We were establishing communications. Tomorrow, phoning will probably be impossible. Like us, several friends live at the end of long, tree-lined roads and very likely will not get their cars out for days, until the debris of fallen trees is cleared. We decided to leave our car out on the highway, a quarter of a mile from the house. I called my friends and arranged to go by tomorrow morning and look in their mailboxes, which are on the highway, so that if they have needs or messages for the outside world they can walk down their driveways and leave a note. I was quite pleased at having thought of this simple way to survive the loss of the telephone. We exchanged hurricane lore. The heavy rain, we agree, increases the danger that trees will fall, because their roots can be more easily wrenched out of the softened earth. We discussed our nerves. We all hate waiting. "Are you nervous?" someone asks. "I've been nervous as a cat all day."

Just before dark, I went out and picked all the flowers— begonias, nicotiana, zinnias, well washed but still intact. I gathered an armful, in profusion. I looked at my dozen of green tomatoes and wondered if they would survive. There was still no wind.

Now we're battened down. There is no one else to call. We've had supper. The TV news says the storm is coming, but here inside the lighted house there is no sign of anything unusual, except the sound of leaves. A few minutes ago, I stepped outside and found that it was still warm—seventy-two degrees on the porch thermometer. The air was very soft, but there was no rain. The wind felt gentle and smelled sweet and tropical, alien to New England. Whereas all day we'd had the sound of dripping rain, now we had the sound of leaves stirring. The vanguard of the storm has arrived. I looked up into the branches of the monumental ash tree. They were moving restlessly, as though the tree were coming to life to meet the imminent struggle. It must have lived through many hurricanes, but now, in its great age, it is more vulnerable than ever before. There was nothing else I could do for it, so I pronounced a blessing on it, as though it were going into battle. Its multitude of leaves reminded me of a medieval host. Its lashing arms seemed full of life and strength, and I returned to the house with new hope that the great ash would be there in the morning.

During the night the storm veered away from us and blew out to sea. We had heavy rain and a high wind and fallen electric wires, but that was all. The ash tree was unharmed; hardly a branch fell. Now it seems not unrealistic to hope that it will indeed be there, to shelter me, for the rest of my days.

5
KOKO KISSED ME

Koko is a gorilla. She is hairy and black, agile and strong. When I met her she was living in a trailer parked in a yard behind the Leland Stanford Junior Museum on the Stanford campus in California. Since Koko was six months old she had been almost exclusively among humans, listening to their speech and observing their behavior. At one year she began learning to "speak" by making signs with her hands. At five she had progressed to a sign vocabulary of over two hundred words and, though she could not utter any of them, seemed to understand their spoken equivalents and many other English words as well. On intelligence tests designed for human children she scored about six months below the average child of the same age. Were she human her intellect would be classified as "low-normal" and her accomplishments would be of little interest. But because Koko is a gorilla she has hidden within her, somewhere behind her dark, sloping brow and under her cap of bristly black hair, all the secrets of the mental life of the subhuman primate. This makes whatever she has to say of unusual interest.

Koko lives with a young woman named Penny Patterson (christened Francine), who loves Koko and hopes to devote her life to studying her, and perhaps Koko's children and grand-children. What Penny wants to explore is the barely known world of the minds and feelings of animals. Penny grew up in Urbana, Illinois, the daughter of a psychology professor, and came to Stanford in 1971 to study for a doctorate in psychology. At that time the results of a brilliant, innovative experiment by Drs. Beatrice and Allen Gardner, of the University of Nevada, who taught sign language to a now famous chimpanzee named Washoe, were being debated in scientific circles. Other re-searchers had tried to teach chimpanzees to speak vocally and failed. It was widely assumed that apes lack some mysterious neural or intellectual attribute granted solely to *Homo sapiens*. In the 1950's a chimp named Vicki was raised as a human child might be, but remained dismally inarticulate. This experiment was generally considered definitive proof of the inability of apes to speak. But the Gardners watched movies of Vicki and noticed that though she was mute her gestures were subtle and eloquent. Jane Goodall had watched wild chimpanzees and also noticed that they made meaningful gestures. Putting the two observations together, it occurred to the Gardners that sign language might be a lingua franca for communication between apes and men. They chose a system of hand signals known as American Sign Language, widely used by the deaf, in which each distinct gesture conveys a different word. In 1966 the Gardners began to teach signs to Washoe, who was then a year old. Her first word was "more," spoken by touching the fingertips together. At two she was combining signs in phrases such as "give me sweet." It seemed to many people that for the first time since St. Francis a human-animal dialogue had occurred. Others scoffed at the inference that what Washoe was using was "language," which for centuries man has claimed as his unique accomplishment, separating him from all other animals. The scientific press was full of articles attacking Washoe's achievement and comparing it to the performance of a rat that has learned to press a lever. Nevertheless, experiments with human-animal communication continued. Dr. David Premack taught a chimpanzee named Sarah to use plastic tokens as language symbols. At the Yerkes laboratory another chimp named Lana learned to "read" and "write" on the keys of a computer.

The Gardners' ideas and techniques fascinated Penny Patterson and she wondered how a similar experiment with a gorilla rather than a chimpanzee might turn out. Because of their size, scarcity, and a reputation for ferocity, gorillas have seldom been studied. Fifty years ago Dr. Robert Yerkes, pioneer primatologist, described gorillas as "aloof, obstinate and negativistic . . . resistant to imitation." As recently as 1959 two experimenters named Knoblock and Passaminick concluded that gorillas are much stupider than chimpanzees.

Penny wondered if they were right. Visiting the San Francisco

Zoo, she discovered a baby gorilla in the zoo nursery. An infectious disease had hit the zoo's gorilla group, and Koko, tiny, malnourished, and ill, had been taken from her mother for nursing care when she was six months old. When Penny found her she was a year old. She was affectionate with men, cold to strange women. She bit Penny at their first meeting. Penny was undaunted and in the summer of 1972 arranged to work with Koko in the zoo nursery.

The baby gorilla soon formed a deep attachment to Penny; she cried so desperately when Penny left her that at night Penny generally sat by Koko's crib until she fell asleep. Since she was also attending classes, Penny found this stage of her life with Koko extremely demanding, but her great reward was that Koko began to learn. She learned some signs by imitating Penny; others when Penny guided her hands, shaping them in the proper gesture until Koko got the idea. As she matured, and learned how to learn, the process speeded up until Koko was learning as rapidly as Washoe had, thus putting to rest the idea that gorillas are stupider or more resistant than chimpanzees. Although Washoe was shielded from spoken language in order not to confuse her training, Penny talked to Koko and Koko often seemed to understand spoken language as well as signs.

As Koko grew she became too active for the zoo nursery and she and Penny moved to a trailer on the Stanford campus. When I learned of Penny and Koko, through a newspaper story, I felt a tremendous tug of interest and curiosity. The gorilla is a collateral relative of ours; a living link back to where we began. The gorilla's genes have survived from that mysterious moment when man had barely separated himself from the rest of the animal kingdom, and though the gorilla has been modified by time as we have, these genes perhaps retain protohuman characteristics. I find the idea of a gorilla curiously thrilling; like a rock from the moon or a seed from an Egyptian tomb.

I telephoned Stanford and was connected with Penny at the trailer. Her voice was friendly, but our talk was a bit disjointed; every few sentences she broke off to say the sort of thing mothers say to a distracting child. "Koko! No. Please put that down!" I heard Penny laughing and sounds of a scuffle. "Please, Koko. You can't talk on the telephone. Penny is talking!" For a moment breathy sounds came through the receiver, then Penny's voice returned. "I'm sorry," she said. "Koko is a bit competitive when I talk on the phone." She invited me to visit them whenever I wanted.

In August 1975, I flew to California, rented a car, and drove to the campus. Following Penny's instructions, I parked beside a chain-link fence that closed off the yard behind the museum. I opened a gate and saw a trailer parked in an open space of dry earth and withered grass, a setting far removed from the leafy jungles that are Koko's natural birthright. As I walked toward the trailer I was excited. I'd seen zoo gorillas, of course, but those I happened to see were always sitting in huge, psychotic apathy in their prison cells. I expected meeting Koko to be quite different; perhaps a little scary. I'm not entirely trusting of my primate cousins. The only monkey I ever met socially took my forearm in his hands, inspected it, selected a choice spot, and bit it. He seemed gratified when I yelped.

I mounted wooden steps at the side of the trailer, opened a sliding door, and found myself looking into a wire enclosure filled with a welter of objects such as might be found on any nursery floor—preschool toys, a ball, a doll, a rumpled blanket, a rubber tub, and an inflated inner tube. A tall, slim girl dressed in blue jeans and a short smock was bending over and being hugged by two hairy, black arms. Penny straightened up and I saw that she is pretty and looks, coincidentally, quite like Jane Goodall. Penny's nose has an upward tilt; her chin is pointed; her eyes almond-shaped and dark brown. She greeted me with a charming smile, and introduced me to Koko.

Koko, naturally, looked like a gorilla; a small very lively gorilla. She was then almost five years old, a little over three feet tall, and weighed a hundred pounds. Koko focused on me instantly and with effortless motion came to the wire partition, where she sat on her haunches, grasping the mesh and inspecting me closely. I knelt down so that my face was on her level. We looked each other over. Koko is covered with straight dark hair except for her face, which has shiny black skin. Her hands and feet also are mostly bare, but the skin is grayish rather than shiny. Her head seems large, but she has small, neat, human-like ears, not the comic-strip ears of the chimpanzee. Her nose looks like a human nose that has been ironed flat. Gorillas lack the nasal bones that make human noses project. She has a heavy ridge of bone over her eyes and the top of her head has a helmet-like crest. I have read that though the gorilla brain is shaped like the human brain there is an extra layer of bone on top of the skull to anchor immensely strong jaw muscles. These strong jaws and big canine teeth are designed not for any savage purpose, but to chew tough woody plants. In the wild, gorillas are vegetarians, unlike chimpanzees, who sometimes eat meat.

The most fascinating thing about Koko, I found, is her eyes. Humans unconsciously communicate with their eyes and constantly judge, usually subconsciously, what other people's eyes reveal. Koko's eyes are light brown. They show less white than a human eye, but, for reasons I cannot analyze, gave me a confusing sensation of looking into the eyes of someone almost, but not quite, like me. All simian eyes, of course, have more candlepower than even an intelligent dog's and are quite different from the one-way glass one finds in the eyes of a feline, who looks out but doesn't allow us to look in. Koko's eyes gazed directly into mine and left no doubt that if I am *Homo sapiens* she is *Ape sapiens*.

I pressed my hand against the wire mesh, offering it to Koko to smell. She sniffed it and poked a thick black forefinger through the wire to touch it. Penny stood close by, softly admonishing, "Be nice, Koko. Be nice." Koko ran her finger over my hand very gently. Her hands are human, though much larger in proportion to her size. Where my fingernails are pink, hers are gray.

Again we sat looking into each other's eyes. Koko put her face close to mine, pursed her lips, and gently blew. As with all vegetarian animals, her breath smelled fresh. "That's a greeting," Penny said. "She likes it if you blow back." I returned the greeting. After we had exchanged a series of gentle blows Koko picked up a stone and gave it to me. I said, "Thank you, Koko." She watched intently while I held the stone, wondering what to do with it. Unsure of etiquette, I handed it back. She took it, put it down, and handed me a rubber dog bone. I tried to look grateful. Then Penny and I began to talk. Penny explained their housekeeping arrangements. Koko's room is partitioned from the kitchen by wire mesh. She has kitchen privileges, but can be closed into her room when it is necessary. The kitchen has all the usual equipment as well as Penny's desk and telephone and serves as her headquarters.

Koko put up with our boring conversation for a few minutes, then she rose and bounded around her room, ricocheting off various objects; the wall, her rubber tire, a small, raised springboard, and a metal toy chest. Each time she passed the toy chest she gave it a resounding slap and added to the noise by slamming her rump against the opposite wall. Penny explained that Koko dislikes being left out of any conversation and hence was showing off.

Koko bounded into the kitchen and came over to its wire-mesh door, close to where I sat in the aisle, making notes. "Sometimes walks on two feet," I wrote. "Sometimes two feet and knuckles of one hand, sometimes all fours . . . effortlessly . . . athletically . . . seems on springs." While I wrote Koko squatted down, crossed her arms on her breast, and watched my pencil move. After a while she picked up a toy car and tried to push it through the wire. Penny laughed and said, "Koko, I know what you are up to." To me she explained, "She's trying to lure you close so she can get your pencil." Sure enough, a long, black arm had squeezed fluidly through the crack in the doorjamb. I evaded her groping fingers.

Penny intervened. "Koko, would you like a sandwich?" Koko turned and Penny made rapid hand signals. Koko responded with a sign that Penny translated as "yes." Penny went to the kitchen counter. Koko followed and bounded on top of it, squatting down to watch while Penny spread peanut butter on a slice of bread. Koko seemed to take in every quick motion of Penny's hands. Penny cut the sandwich in two and held up half. Koko made a sign that Penny translated as "please give me sandwich." Penny gave it to her. Koko took it in her hand, put it between her teeth, and leaped off the counter. She walked over to a tall kitchen stool. Standing upright, she dragged it into a corner, climbed on top, and sat down while she ate the sandwich. I asked Penny if Koko always retreats to eat. Penny said, "No. It's because you're here. She's afraid you might ask her to share it."

When Koko had finished her sandwich she got down from the stool and stood before Penny, looking up and signing "more" by putting her fingertips together. At that moment she resembled a hairy human child except that she was not quite erect. Also her legs are short compared to her wide chest. Gorilla leg bones and muscles exhibit one of the few anatomical differences between our two species. Humans have a long fibula which helps prevent the ankle from turning. The short-legged gorilla walks, not flat-footed as we do, but on the outside of the foot, sole turned inward. Standing, Koko seemed somehow pathetic. When she dropped to all fours she was transformed from a misshapen human to a well-designed animal. I cannot walk on all fours without awkwardly bending my knees and elevating my behind. Koko's arms are longer than her legs and on all fours her shoulders are higher than her rump; her motions easy and graceful.

Penny and Koko began a dialogue in sign language. Koko signed "more." Penny signed "more what?" Koko signed "more eat sandwich nut." Penny explained that such conversations constitute Koko's lessons. She gave Koko the remaining half of the sandwich. Koko took it and sat down beside me. She surveyed me between bites, handling the sandwich as a human would, though I thought her way of stuffing rather large pieces into her mouth unrefined. It occurred to me that I was judging her by human standards and that her sudden transformations from human to animal and back again were bewildering.

While Koko ate, Penny filled three plastic cups, two green and one red, with fruit juice, explaining that their purpose was to teach Koko to sign "same" and "different." Koko accepted a green cup, emptied it promptly, and signed "same." Penny gave her the second cup. Holding it carefully in one hand, Koko walked "on all threes" into her room and sat down on the springboard. Her sitting posture was so human that as she sipped from her cup she looked like a rather odd guest at a picnic.

Koko drank slowly, shifting her attention like a polite listener as Penny and I talked. Suddenly Penny noticed that juice was trickling from the cup in Koko's hand and snatched it from her. "Koko, did you bite it?" she asked reproachfully, talking and signing at the same time. Koko looked away like a sulky child. Penny scolded her, her hands moving rapidly as she said severely, "Mess! Dirty! Bad! Teeth bad!" Koko endured the storm in silence. Penny picked up a sponge and handed it to her. "All right, young lady," she said. "You may clean it up!"

Koko jumped up and, bending from the waist with enviable ease, vigorously sponged the wet spot on the carpet. "She loves to clean," Penny said. Koko dropped the sponge, picked up the empty cup, and bounded over to the wire to give it to me. Penny said, "She is generous with dregs, rinds, and stuff like that. She'll give you the banana peel any time, and once in a while she will share something really good." I took the cup and thanked Koko. Koko blew at me and then stuck out her long pointed tongue. Penny explained that she wanted to know what I taste like. I licked my finger and offered it. Koko touched it with the tip of her tongue. Curiosity satisfied, she searched the carpet and picked up a tiny blue straw about the size of a toothbrush bristle and offered it to me. I was interested that she not only noticed an object so small, but also thought it of value. It is commonly believed that one reason apes walk on their knuckles with their fingers folded inside is to protect the tactile sensitivity of their fingertips.

Penny and I began to talk and Koko retired to her room to play, becoming increasingly noisy and acrobatic as she swung on her swing and rolled on the floor. She is so flexible she can grasp her elbows with her toes or put her toes in her mouth like a newborn human. Among Koko's playthings was a large, black rubber tub. Koko overturned it and managed to squeeze most of herself under it, though her feet stuck out on one side and her dark face was visible as she peered from beneath the rim.

Penny picked up the cue and bustled around saying, "Where is Koko? Where can she possibly be?" She lifted the edge of the tub. Koko's hands emerged, signing rapidly. Penny, full of laughter, exclaimed, "Oh, Koko, you funny little kid!" To me she explained that Koko had signed "Go away. I am hiding." Suddenly Koko sprang from under the tub and jumped into Penny's arms. Penny got down on the floor and they rolled around in a wild melee, wrestling and tickling. Penny laughed with genuine enjoyment while Koko gave soft grunts of delight. When her mouth opened wide in a huge, silent laugh, I glimpsed her pink gums and large white teeth. Penny saw them too. Between giggles she admonished, "Watch teeth, Koko! Watch teeth!" As Koko became more excited Penny slowed down the pace of their play. She disengaged herself, pushing Koko away reproachfully, and scrambled to her feet. Panting and flushed, she bent over while she scolded. "Koko! Did you scratch? Did you scratch Penny?" She pointed to her cheek, then to Koko's fingernails, signing as she talked. "Nails, Koko! Nails!"

Koko sat huddled and crestfallen. She soberly regarded her nails, then held a forefinger to her mouth. Penny shook her head. "She has just told a lie," Penny said. "She knows darn well she scratched me, but she said it was her teeth. A play bite wouldn't hurt another gorilla; that may be why she thinks that's better." Koko made another sign. "She says she is sorry," Penny told me.

Koko was downcast for only a moment. She embraced Penny's legs and made signs asking to be tickled. Penny relented quickly. She smiled and tickled while Koko grunted with pleasure. Koko grasped Penny's slim legs and I realized that Koko's wrists are thicker than those of a grown man. She pulled off Penny's slingback shoes, and while Penny hopped around giggling, Koko tickled her bare feet. "She's crazy about tickling feet," Penny gasped, "and she really digs it when you laugh." Penny tickled Koko's

large flat feet in return. Koko's joy was tremendous. A moment later Penny and Koko were rolling around on the floor; a whirl of flying yellow hair, hairy black arms, and Penny's long, blue-jean-covered legs. Gradually Penny slowed Koko down until they lay still, resting with their arms around each other.

Their peace was shattered when a girl in a lab coat arrived bringing a cardboard box containing several mice that Penny had asked for with the thought that watching mice might provide Koko entertainment and give her an awareness of living things other than humans. Penny shut the door of Koko's room while she talked to the visitor in the kitchen. Koko leaped to her feet and bounced wildly from corner to corner, creating a thunderous din. "That's enough," Penny exclaimed with stern authority. "Your audience is leaving!" She opened the kitchen door and led her visitor down the steps to the yard. As Penny started to leave, Koko sat down abruptly. When Penny actually disappeared from view Koko emitted a shriek. It was a terrified appeal. Penny bade the girl goodbye and quickly returned. Koko sat quietly, looking chastened. Penny went to her and they hugged.

Penny had a glass tank full of shavings ready for the mice and invited Koko to watch as she transferred them from the box. Koko appeared fascinated. "Mousies! Koko. Mousies! Little animals. Two white. One black." Koko touched one gently with the tip of her finger. Penny put the mouse tank on the floor just outside the wire. Koko sat down to watch them with rapt attention. It occurred to me that a mouse is certainly a marvel if you have never seen one before.

After my first meeting with Koko I did some reading on gorillas. They are the largest primates; males average about five feet six inches and females about five feet, but for many years travelers' tales portrayed them as being monstrous in size. They are in fact heavier than most men and far stronger. A mature male weighs over three hundred pounds; a female over two hundred. Zoo gorillas tend to obesity and several have grown to over five hundred pounds. However, a newborn gorilla weighs less than five pounds and is as helpless as a newborn human. At birth there is little difference between the brain size of human and gorilla, but as growth proceeds the human child pulls ahead. Structurally human and gorilla brains are very similar.

I remember reading once that some jocular scientists had formed a committee to inform animals of their taxonomic position. If they began with apes, they could give them the news that apes, monkeys, and men are all members of the primate order, but man has accorded himself a superfamily—Hominoidea —containing only one living species—man. Old World monkeys and apes are in another superfamily, Cercopithecoidea. Gorillas, chimps, and orangutans are classed together in the family Pongidae. Chimpanzees and gorillas have been distinct from each other for many millions of years and the ancestral human line split off from our common ancestor long before that. Yet despite millennia of separation without any mingling of genes the major physical differences between apes and men relate to size and rate of growth. Since man and ape look very different and under natural conditions do very different things, there is an implication that their genetic difference is also large.

However, recent studies comparing the genes of man and chimpanzee show that the differences are no greater than in what are called "sibling species," two species morphologically similar but reproductively isolated. Why then, if man and ape are so close genetically, do they have such different traits? One theory holds that certain key genes influence the regulatory system and set the timing of development by turning other genes on and off. Perhaps it is a difference in this key gene that makes us human by retarding our rate of development. Adult humans mature more slowly than apes and, as adults, retain more juvenile proportions and mental characteristics. Protracted youth provides a longer opportunity to learn. Another question that is often asked concerning men and apes is the possibility of a fruitful mating between the two species. I found that Dr. Stephen Jay Gould of Harvard had tackled this subject. "The very low genetic distance between humans and chimps," Gould wrote, "might tempt us to try the most potentially interesting and ethically unacceptable scientific experiment I can imagine—to hybridize our two species and simply to ask the offspring what it is like to be, at least in part, a chimpanzee. I am delighted to report that this almost certainly cannot be done." He then explained that though genetic differences are small they include at least ten instances in which the genetic material is in a different position in the reproductive cells of ape and man. For two species to hybridize, their chromosomes must lie side by side so that each pairs with its opposite number. In ape and man the difference in position would probably make this gene-by-gene pairing impossible.

There has also been much speculation on why apes can't learn to speak vocally. They can make a variety of sounds, but only baboons seem able to produce "humanoid grunts" that resemble the resonance of human speech. In 1947 Cathy Hayes, whose husband was a psychologist at the Yerkes Primate Laboratories in Florida, acquired a newborn chimp named Viki. Mrs. Hayes began giving Viki speech lessons when she was five months old. At ten months Viki finally "spoke." "It was an ugly sound, hoarse and strained," Mrs. Hayes wrote. "It was like whispering 'ah' as loudly as possible and with great effort. When Viki said it her face contorted while her eyes assumed the tense preoccupied stare of a stutterer. Then from her lips burst this rasping, tortured 'aaaahhhh.'" Viki's vocabulary never got beyond "mama," "papa," and "cup." As a result of Viki's failure, many scientists deduced that chimpanzees lack something essential in the organization of the brain. Recently, however, Phillip Lieberman, of the Yerkes Primate Center, advanced a different explanation. He pointed out that the vocal tract of a gorilla is more nearly like that of a human baby than that of a human adult and a human infant can no more imitate human speech than a gorilla can. The tongue of both gorillas and human babies almost fills the mouth cavity, while in adult humans it is relatively smaller and can move to alter the size of the vocal tract. Apes have long, flat tongues that can't execute the changes needed for speech. In addition, the human pharynx is a flexible tube, expanding and contracting to produce different sounds. The vocal tract of the ape is more like a trumpet; it can expand at the end, but does not vary in cross section as ours does when we speak. Penny has made no effort to teach Koko to speak vocally, but for a time Koko seemed to try silently to shape her mouth in imitation of Penny. After a while she gave it up, but still likes to answer the telephone. She picks up the receiver and utters a soft, breathy "whoooo" sound.

The history of man's relations with gorillas reflects no great credit on human intelligence. Twenty years ago, the gorilla was invariably and falsely described as a fierce, terrifying, and murderous beast. In 1959 George Schaller went to Africa, watched gorillas for a number of months, and reported that they are the gentlest of all primates. They live in groups of up to thirty, led by the oldest male. Younger males have lesser rank, but all adult males dominate females and the young.

Unlike humans and wolves, gorillas do not fight over rank. Precedence is amicably acknowledged. Conflict is almost nonexistent, both within the group and between separate groups that happen to meet. In fact, the daily life of the gorilla would strike most humans as deadly dull. They spend most of their day in peaceful foraging for tasty plants. Between meals the elders lounge in the sun while the young play; wrestling, chasing, and swinging on branches. To make life duller still, it seems that the Serpent barely got its foot in the door of the gorilla's Eden; sex doesn't interest them as much as it does other primates. They copulate casually and infrequently. Jealousy does not ruffle their tranquil relationships. When females are in heat they invite attention and sex play is quite similar to that of humans though gorillas do not kiss. The erect penis of the largest primate is only two inches long.

I wanted to know more about Penny's scientific work with Koko, and since Koko's competition made it difficult to talk at the trailer, I arranged to meet Penny at her house. Early one morning we sat in the backyard and talked for an hour or so.

The title of Penny's preliminary report is "The Acquisition of Sign Language and Behavioral Development in a Lowland Gorilla." Koko's progress, Penny wrote, "suggests that certain aspects of man's linguistic abilities are not solely human, as Noam Chomsky et al. assume, but are based on capacities that humans share with apes."

One of the characteristics linguists deem essential to distinguish true language from mere communication is the use of grammar. This obviously entails a more complex thought process than does a single, invariable signal.

I asked Penny if she thought Koko understood word order. Penny said that Koko knew the difference between "Koko tickle Penny" and "Penny tickle Koko" and similar simple phrases. Penny has kept daily records of Koko's activities together with videotape samples to show the development of her gesture vocabulary. Every day Koko becomes more "talkative." When she was three and a half, she used seventeen different signs in a day. A year later she was using ninety-four. Her vocabulary covered almost the full range of concepts expressed by human children in the early stages of talking. Koko asks questions as deaf people do by "gesture intonation," keeping her hand in the sign position and looking into the eyes of the person addressed. Penny gave an example: One day when Barbara Hiller (Penny's good friend and helper, who also knows how to sign) was with Koko a woodpecker began to tap outside. Barbara signed "Koko, listen, bird." Koko signed "Bird?" She turned her head to Barbara, cocked it, opened her eyes wide, and almost raised her eyebrows. Barbara signed "Yes, bird tapping outside. Listen." Barbara tapped on the counter and pointed outside as the woodpecker tapped again. This time Koko signed "Listen. Bird," with a positive intonation.

The concept of time is an especially slippery one, but Koko can use some time words such as "time me toilet go." When Penny promises something "later" or "in a little while," Koko seems willing to wait. Motivation is important to Koko's learning. Her early vocabulary was heavy with the names of pleasant things. She learned "swing," "berry," "soap," and "pinch" within minutes, but the names of two things she dislikes, "egg" and "hand lotion," took months. Possibly Koko hopes that if she refuses to recognize them they will go away. Like Lucy, a chimpanzee schoolmate of Washoe, who invented terms for novel objects—"drink fruit" for watermelon and "cry food" for radish—Koko invents startlingly descriptive combinations. She called a stale roll a "cookie rock" and a mask an "eye hat." Human children do the same. Koko generalizes, using a single term for a number of things that are in some way similar. She learned "straw" to mean a drinking straw, but now applies it to other long, thin objects—plastic tubing, cigarettes, a radio antenna. She has progressed from "open the door" to "open the box" and so on.

Like small human children, Koko talks to herself while playing alone. Going to bed, she may sign "this red" as she arranges a red cloth; "note bird," pointing at a toy; and then "sleep," as she lies down in her nest. She also "reads to herself," signing the names of things she recognizes in her picture books, such as "bird," "man," "baby."

Penny records many of Koko's conversations and as a sample offered this one in which Koko was talking with Barbara Hiller:

Koko: You chase me.

Barbara: My name is Barbara.

Koko: Barbara chase me. (Barbara does so.)

Koko: You tickle me.

Barbara: Where?

Koko: Tickle arm.

Barbara tickles and then Koko leads her to the kitchen, signing "you me there" and pointing to the refrigerator.

Barbara: What want?

Koko: Eat drink.

Barbara: Eat or drink? Which?

Koko: Glass drink.

Barbara (getting juice): That?

Koko: That.

I asked Penny what she thought about Koko's awareness of herself. Viki, Mrs. Hayes's chimp, was able to sort pictures of animals and people into appropriate categories, but always put a picture of herself in the "people" pile. Koko seems to know she is a gorilla. When Penny gave her a tiny toy gorilla Koko gestured "Me! Koko!" Even such intelligent animals as dogs and monkeys do not recognize their own image in a mirror, but children can do so at two. Koko showed self-recognition at three and a half. Penny put a spot of paint on Koko's face and Koko, seeing it in a mirror, wiped it away.

I wondered what other clues Penny had found to Koko's inner thoughts and feelings. Penny said that at first when Koko used the word "sorry" it had seemed merely a tool to obtain forgiveness. Human children use it in the same way. Now, Penny thought, it had become meaningful. "If I am upset she tries to make me feel better. Koko is very responsive to my moods. She

knows when I'm sick or sad. I don't have to tell her. She reads
my body posture and then she hugs and kisses me. She becomes
very sad and worried. I had a broken toe that hurt awfully. I
bumped it and cried. Koko hugged me and licked away the tears.
When I'm sick she senses it and is gentle. When I get mad, she
gets mad. I handle her by treating her like a human kid. If I
treated her like an animal, I'd get nowhere. She is so sensitive; as
sensitive as any child that age and *more* perceptive. She notices
very small, subtle things. Her vision and hearing are terrific;
much better than mine."

Penny described the problem of discipline. In the wild, youngsters who annoy their elders are admonished with a hearty
whack. Gorillas are tough enough to absorb a blow that would
knock a man down. Penny, however, has decided not to run the
risk of teaching Koko dangerous behavior; she uses only scolding
and nonphysical punishments. She believes that Koko can exert
considerable self-control, but there is no way to know if this will
continue into maturity. So far Koko has never behaved in a way
that Penny calls "chimpy"; she has never had a tantrum as
chimps frequently do. Her most troublesome and unruly behavior is in response to strange people. "At two she was very anxious
and fearful with new people," Penny said, "but she was a 'beautiful three.' I could leave her with anyone. Now she is a problem
again; all that rough stuff that you saw only happens when new
people are around. When we're alone together we have a peaceful, lovely time."

At the time I visited Penny the director of the San Francisco
Zoo wanted to reclaim Koko as a zoo animal and had predicted
that if Penny kept her into maturity someday Koko would "get
mad and slam her against the wall." I asked Penny about this potential danger and she said she felt confident she would always
be safe with Koko provided she had the proper physical surroundings—secure and free of disturbance. She pointed out that
adult chimpanzees are successfully handled at several primate facilities and that chimps are, in her opinion, more dangerous than
gorillas because they are more volatile emotionally. Penny has

formed a Gorilla Foundation and has purchased Koko from the zoo. Thinking of the tremendous demands that life with Koko makes on Penny, I wondered how long she wanted to continue it. "I want to stay with her forever," Penny said simply. "I love Koko, but I am not thinking just emotionally. My life work is the study of primates. Koko and I are just at the beginning. The potential is terrific. I believe ape communication studies can change, not just our view of apes, but perhaps of all other animals and ourselves as well."

On another morning I climbed the steps of the trailer for a final visit to Penny and Koko. I came upon a peaceful scene. They were sitting on the floor looking at a book of Cinderella. The moment I entered it was disrupted. Koko leaped up and came to the wire to greet me. I had brought her a nasturtium. She smelled it and then ate it. She turned and, picking up the book, held the cover picture of Cinderella plastered to her chest. The symbolism of the story fitted my mixed-up feelings about Koko. Is language her glass slipper? I had a sudden image of Koko's large, hairy foot shoved into a high-heeled shoe. Koko dropped the book and picked up a rubber duck. She kissed it and then presented it to me to be kissed. I pecked at it. Koko put the duck in her mouth and crossed her arms on her breast. Penny said Koko was making the sign for "love." "Koko love what?" Penny asked. "Love baby," Koko signed. "That not a baby, that a duck," Penny replied. Koko dropped the duck and picked up a large, naked doll, missing one leg, and held it in a loving posture. Penny told me she had a new toy for Koko. She reached in her pocket and gave her a police whistle. Koko took it eagerly and managed to produce a few toots; then lost the knack and blew fruitlessly. She sat down abruptly and pounded the whistle on the floor, making a sound like "uh, uh, uh" that Penny said meant annoyance. Petulantly she threw the whistle through the wire mesh, then instantly tried to retrieve it. It lay on the floor just beyond reach of her fingers. "Help," Koko signed to Penny. Penny handed her a fork and Koko succeeded in raking in the whistle.

Again Koko sat regarding it; then, using the fork, tried to pry out the ball, visible through the aperture at the front of the whistle. Failing in this, she picked up a plastic drinking straw, put the tip into the hole, and tried to suck out the elusive ball. Penny remarked that Koko has an urge to take things apart; in the wild this might be useful in opening nuts. She will work on a problem for thirty minutes or more. "What is interesting," Penny said, "is that she shows so many capabilities that are not apparent in the wild. Apes seem to have potential abilities stored within them that they don't use."

Koko's work on the whistle was interrupted by the arrival of a laundryman with the bundle of forty-two clean towels that Koko uses each week. At night Koko makes a nest as she would in the wild, except that hers is made of towels rather than leaves. When the towels had been stuffed in a closet Penny announced that it was time for a walk around the yard. "Do you want to go out, Koko?" she signed. Koko signed "on, on necklace," pointing to her neck. Penny put on her collar and leash. Then she decided Koko should sit on the toilet first. There was a small potty chair in a corner of her room. Koko has learned to use it, though wild gorillas are rather casual about these matters. She squatted on the potty quite willingly and then impatiently signed "time to get off." Penny said, "All right, but if you do it outside we're coming right back. Let's go see cows."

I had an idea that Koko was more interested in meeting me without the intervening wire. She hustled to the door and while Penny was undoing the latch her arm groped for me through the crack in the doorjamb. I felt a flutter of uncertainty about what would happen when we were face to face. Penny opened the door and Koko bounded forward, then stopped just in front of me. She half stood, half squatted, while we surveyed each other. Then she raised her arms to me. I bent down. She clasped her arms around my neck and with mixed emotions I felt her pull me to her with irresistible force. She sniffed my face carefully. "Be nice, Koko," Penny said. "Give her a hug." Koko hugged and released me and she and Penny went down the steps into the yard. I followed. Koko turned to me, grabbed my wrist in her left hand, and walked on three legs as she pulled me along, making a strange little murmuring sound. Penny called it "purring" and said it denoted pleasure.

Linked together, we wandered around the yard, as weird a threesome as ever graced the pages of a fairy-story book. Penny might be the golden-haired lassie, Koko the bewitched sister. My role was ambiguous. Koko tugged us toward an enclosure that held a group of calves. She jumped easily to the top rail of the fence and dropped over it. The calves bunched up and stared with uncomprehending surprise. Koko politely gestured "come here." Strangely, the calves moved toward her. When they were close Koko rushed at them to the limit of her leash and the calves scattered. Penny tugged and Koko returned. Koko could easily break the leash, but Penny has taught her that if she fails to obey a tug the outing is immediately ended.

Koko's attention returned to me. She sat on the fence and embraced me. She signed "tickle" and I tickled while she wriggled with pleasure. She tried to climb onto my shoulders. She felt like a ton of bricks. To my relief Penny extended her arms and Koko climbed onto Penny, who is used to carrying her weight. Koko dismounted and, taking my hand again, led us to a big outdoor cage full of rhesus monkeys. She banged on the wire and the monkeys obligingly shrieked and leaped about. Koko looked delighted. I can't explain how I was able to read her expressions since her features are relatively immobile—but I had distinct impressions of changes in her feelings.

We moved on and now Koko flung one arm around my shoulders. Penny said this was a friendly gorilla gesture. Since I was two and a half feet taller than Koko, I had to bend over, but I wanted to be friendly too, so, stooping, I accompanied her to an outdoor water faucet with a hose attached. Koko turned the handle and we took turns drinking from the hose. While I drank Koko put her face close to mine, watching each swallow go down. Penny said Koko is fascinated by watching people eat and drink. I, in turn, looked deep into Koko's brown eyes, set among black wrinkles, and felt what might be called very strange vibes. It seemed as though I could see intelligence in pure form, unadulterated by the ambiguities and inhibitions that veil human eyes.

We went on strolling about the yard in the sunshine. Koko searched the ground for novelties; picking up and examining an empty matchbook, a plastic spoon, and so on. Penny followed patiently, the leash slack, and I was reminded of similar hours spent in the park when my son was very young and I followed him about, watching his interest shift from gum wrappers to puddles to piles of leaves. Koko plucked leaves from a dusty shrub, tasted them, and spat them out. She turned to me and made a grab for my skirt. Penny caught her hand and reproved her. Koko quickly signed a phrase. Penny shook her head ruefully. "Oh, Koko," she said, "I know you better than that!" She explained that Koko had said she merely wanted to smell the flowers printed on my skirt, but that in truth she enjoys ripping up fabric and knows it is bad.

We wandered back to the trailer, Koko still holding my hand in her strong grip. At the steps I squatted down to say goodbye on her level. Koko took the opportunity to look down my bosom. She thrust her hand down, pulled my blouse toward her, and peered inside with interest. She chuckled enigmatically, then raised her face and brought it very close to mine, and I heard her purring softly. Her long arms went around my shoulders and she hugged me, gently but firmly pulling me toward her. To evade her kiss I put my head down and buried my face in the soft hair on her chest. In the darkness of her embrace I smelled a long-forgotten smell. Koko smelled like a teddy bear. At last she released me. Penny said, "Let's go, Koko." Koko stood up and thumped her chest with her fists. Penny said, "She's saying goodbye her way. That's a gorilla greeting, but it also means goodbye."

6
THE WHOOPING CRANE

My acquaintance with the whooping crane began with a small item in the New York *Times* in the autumn of 1963. It said that forty-two cranes had migrated from Canada, where they nested, and had reached their wintering grounds on the Gulf coast of Texas. It added that the Fish and Wildlife Service had been trying to protect the cranes for many years, but that the birds were, nevertheless, in danger of extinction. I cut out the item, and the more I thought about it, the more intriguing it became. The precise figure—forty-two cranes—puzzled me. The birds with which I was familiar—songbirds or even larger birds such as crows and hawks and migrating geese—seemed to come and go as interchangeably as windblown leaves without giving any clue to their individual identity or total numbers. I might note a lot of blue jays around the farm one year and the next wonder if perhaps there were fewer swallows, but I had no idea how anyone could determine just how many swallows or blue jays existed. My second question was equally naïve. I wondered how it was possible that if the Fish and Wildlife Service really wanted to protect cranes from extinction it had not succeeded.

Two years later I had found at least partial answers to these questions and lost some of my innocence. I had learned how whooping cranes are counted and that restoring a species to health may be infinitely complex; a modern problem on which studies have only recently begun. At the time I wrote about the cranes—1966—the protection of endangered species was just emerging from the Dark Ages, and the survival of the whooping cranes hung by the slenderest of threads.

What is the bird on which so much effort and anxiety have centered? Is it all worthwhile? In a world teeming with problems the survival of one particular species may strike many people as of minor importance. As I worked on the story of the cranes I had my first lesson in the interrelatedness of life and answered the question, at least for myself—the cranes are precious beyond price and we must not let them go.

My first inquiries about whooping cranes made it clear that the answer was not to be found in any one place, but must be sought in a number of areas and from an unexpectedly varied cast of characters. In one way or another an astonishing number of people have become concerned, in some cases embroiled, in the fate of the cranes. Nor was it possible to understand the birds' present situation without looking into their past. What I attempted, then, was to reconstruct the chronicle of the cranes year by year since they became officially wards of our government.

The only wild whooping cranes on earth spend their winters stalking regally about the sand flats and shallow waters of the Aransas Wildlife Refuge, which occupies a small peninsula on the Gulf coast of Texas, seventy-five miles north of Corpus Christi. Each autumn whooping cranes arrive there, not in a flock but singly or in family groups, during October and November, and settle down on the marshes along the shore. Even from a distance their tall, gleaming white forms are easily seen against the pale yellows of salt grass and sand.

During the quiet months of winter the birds, with the young of the past summer still at their parents' sides, gather strength for the effort ahead; a flight of more than twenty-five hundred miles to northern breeding grounds, and the production of a new generation. Then, in April, family by family, or sometimes several families together, the whooping cranes begin their extraordinary and hazardous flight to their nesting grounds.

For years the cranes' destination was one of the most tantalizing of ornithological mysteries. In the words of one baffled observer, "It was as though they flew north each spring and vanished from the face of the earth." In 1955 their secret nesting place was discovered in a far northern corner of Canada's Northwest Territories, within five hundred miles of the Arctic Circle. Summer there is short and capriciously variable. The birds must nest and rear their young on a tight schedule. Any that are delayed even a few weeks will perish in the sudden cold of au-

tumn. In late September the cranes and their newly fledged
young begin the return trip to Texas. In the autumn the long
flight over Canada and the central United States is even more
perilous than in spring, for in the hunting season lakes and
marshes, the natural resting places of cranes, are ringed with
guns. Rarely in the past thirty years have all the whooping
cranes made the round trip without apparent loss—and even then
young birds whose existence had not yet been recorded may
have been shot between Canada and Texas.

In addition to this group of wild birds there were, in the fall of
1965, seven captive whooping cranes. One of them, a young male
named Canus (derived from "Canada" and "U.S."), was injured
on the wilderness nesting ground in the summer of 1964, rescued
by helicopter, and put in the custody of the United States government. The six other captive whooping cranes were housed at
the Audubon Park Zoo in New Orleans.

The Audubon Park Zoo and the National Audubon Society are
both named after the great naturalist, and both are involved in
the history of whooping cranes, but they are in no other way
connected. The Society was founded in 1905 for the purpose of
saving endangered wildlife, and is supported by the contributions of its members. The zoo, whose funds come from the city
of New Orleans, is managed by civic officials as part of the city's
Park Department. Its primary purpose is to provide recreation
for New Orleans' citizens. Tropical verdancy, an air of shabby
ease, old buildings of beige brick—all make it a pleasant place for
a Sunday stroll; but its lack of trained staff or special facilities
make it an unlikely site for a crucial experiment in aviculture.
Nevertheless, it was here that fate chose to deposit a whooping
crane named Josephine who deserves to be known in the annals
as the "Dowager Queen of Cranes."

For sixteen years, until her sudden, tragic death in September
1965, Josephine, at that time the only breeding female crane in
captivity, laid eggs that were almost literally worth their weight
in gold. With the help of her mate, a splendid old bird named
Crip, Josephine laid fifty-two eggs at the Audubon Park Zoo.

Twelve of these eggs hatched live young whooping cranes, of which four lived to maturity. In addition to Crip and these surviving young there was a female named Rosie, who, for nine years, had idled away her time in sterile captivity at the San Antonio Zoo, which possessed no male whooping crane with which to mate her. In the spring of 1964 Rosie was moved to join the others at Audubon Park in the hope that she might take the torch from the aging Josephine.

During the years that Josephine and Crip labored to preserve their species, the scene at New Orleans was dominated by a man named George Douglass, who was superintendent of the zoo from 1941 until his death in November 1964. Douglass' monopoly of the world's supply of captive whooping cranes, coupled with the meager production of young, was a source of embitterment to a variety of people. Although united in little else, Douglass' critics were unanimous in feeling that his most outstanding zoological skill was his ability to hang on to a whooping crane once he got his hands on it. The situation at New Orleans, combined with the ever imperiled condition of the wild whooping cranes, brought into head-on collision two groups of people, both passionate about whooping cranes and passionately opposed to each other on the question of how to preserve them.

One group was composed of people who believed that the species could be saved from extinction only by breeding whooping cranes in captivity. They argued that offspring from this flock might later be turned loose, or, if this proved unfeasible, there would at least be representatives of the species safely tucked away in zoos and aviaries. The proponents of this plan included men of a variety of backgrounds, ranging from backyard duck breeders to distinguished museum directors, loosely organized under the banner of aviculture—the science of breeding birds in captivity. The initial step would be, of course, to capture a number of wild whooping cranes or take their eggs for artificial incubation.

Opponents of this plan, chiefly the National Audubon Society and its friends, felt that the helping hand of aviculture, if allowed to meddle with the cranes in the fashion proposed, would quite likely finish off the wild flock then and there. The Society's biologists pointed out that the capture of large wild birds inevitably involves a high percentage of accidental death or injury. The loss to the cranes of those captured, plus those injured or dispersed, could be a deathblow, reducing the flock below any chance of regeneration. Was it worth such a risk, they asked, in order to attempt breeding experiments whose success could by no means be guaranteed?

A corollary point of disagreement was the tricky biological question of whether there could be any hope of releasing zoo-bred whooping cranes, either to rejoin the wild group or to establish a new wild population. Anyone thinking of the English sparrow and the starling might assume that this would be a simple matter of opening the door of the cage and wishing the whooper Godspeed. Unfortunately, previous experiments with other large, slow-maturing birds have indicated that there are many problems involved in returning captives to the wild. In the case of the cranes, these might or might not be soluble. Thus the argument between those in favor of capturing cranes and those against it approached the philosophical question of the difference in value between wild birds and birds in perpetual captivity.

As the National Audubon Society saw its mission, it was to protect creatures in their natural state, not to provide breeding stock for zoos. In their view a caged and pinioned whooping crane is simply another form of fancy poultry, an ornamental shell representing its once proud but vanquished race. Thus, if the wild birds perish, the whooping crane will, in any real sense, have become extinct. To this the aviculturists retorted simply that the species would be better off in zoos than in oblivion.

Of the people concerned in the whooping crane's plight, the National Audubon Society was the earliest on the scene, the most dedicated, and the most idealistic. It was able to point out that the only serious research on the natural history of the whooping cranes was the result of its interest and sponsorship.

This study was the work of Robert Porter Allen, who was

research director of the National Audubon Society. His mono-graph *The Whooping Crane*, published by the National Audubon Society in 1952, is considered a classic of wildlife research. Until then no accurate information on the natural history of the whooping crane existed. The habits of the species, its diet, nest-ing, relationship to its habitat, and dozens of other factors bear-ing on its survival, were all unknown.

Allen dedicated himself heart and soul to finding the answers to such questions. He combed libraries for historical records of whooping cranes. He struggled through the mud of the Texas salt flats to stalk the wintering birds. In summer he flew several hundred thousand miles searching for the mysterious nesting places. In the course of this work Allen became a passionate champion of the whooping cranes. He not only knew more about them than anyone had before him; he also cared more about them than anyone else ever had. It is typical of the bad luck that besets the whooping cranes that they lost such a friend. Allen died suddenly in June 1963.

Ultimately, decisions affecting the wild whooping cranes are made neither by their avicultural friends nor by the National Audubon Society, but by officials of the United States and Cana-dian wildlife services. The U. S. Fish and Wildlife Service has more than cranes to worry about. It is perpetually short of the funds to carry out its plans, and equally short of the prestige needed to wage its battles. It has little appeal for voters and hence for congressmen. On the contrary, its mandate to conserve natural habitat for wildlife constantly runs afoul of local eco-nomic interests. There are also well-financed and highly organized sportsmen's organizations that see the Service's primary duty as the provision of game animals. Cattlemen and farmers urge it to concentrate on controlling pests. Conservationists implore it to hold the line. Officials of the Service are accustomed to compro-mise as a way of life. It was therefore no novelty for them when the problem of the whooping crane—and how to preserve it— grew thornier as the birds' fate aroused ever wider interest. It was clear that if the whooping crane became extinct as the result of something the Service did—or left undone—there would be not only tremendous regret among conservationists but also recrimination from those whose advice had gone unheeded.

When I saw my first whooping crane, it was accompanied appropriately enough by a large placard that bore, in red capital letters, the word EXTINCTION. The bird was stuffed, and it stood, looking tall and surprised, one foot lifted and its extraordinary neck in a proud arch, in a glass case in the Natural History Section of the Smithsonian Institution in Washington. This was Exhibit Number 27, dedicated to a few of the birds that are going or recently gone.

"Extinction," the placard continued, "is the dying out of a species. While this has happened to countless thousands of kinds of animals and plants throughout the ages, here we are concerned only with those birds that have disappeared within the memory of man, as well as some others that are now so reduced in numbers as to be in danger of doing so. Directly, by hunting, or indirectly, by virtue of the changes he has wrought on the earth's surface, man is today the chief factor in extermination."

Beside the whooping crane in the case were other birds whose rigid attitudes seemed extraordinarily eloquent of personality. The brown and buff Labrador duck (this one a female; last known specimen collected December 12, 1878) had a rounded, turned-up bill, half open, that made its expression oddly beseeching. The condor, perched on a branch, a huge, dark bird, majestically unattractive, looked as though it would go down to oblivion grandly, scornfully, disdaining any appeal.

At the bottom of the case, appearing to step busily through the artificial leaves and grass, were two little heath hens, their heads inclined toward each other as though nodding in sociable chat. Their smartly barred feathers of russet brown covered plump figures that made me think of Victorian ladies in a fashion book, tripping innocently along to some gay event. The death of the last heath hen was announced on April 21, 1933.

I stared in some disbelief at the great auk, or garefowl, a tall, flightless bird not unlike a penguin, but with an improbable nose-like beak. It might have said, "I am not beautiful, but I am me!" Later I read an account of how the last great auk met its death on a tiny island off the coast of Iceland on the morning of June 3, 1844. For hundreds of years these birds, which once lived in multitudes on the coasts and islands of the North Atlantic, had been slaughtered in their rookeries by sailors from passing ships. By 1840 the North American rookeries were empty. Suddenly museum directors awoke to the fact that there were few skins or eggs in their collections. They offered large sums to fishermen to raid the remote, rocky islets on which a few survivors still nested and raised young. After several raids a few dead birds and eggs were brought back, and then the fishermen reported they could find no more garefowl. The museums, still unsatisfied, raised the price even higher. At last a man named Vilhjalmur Hakonarsson agreed to make one more search on the tiny island of Eldey where some birds might have escaped previous raids. The scene on the island was later described by an ornithologist, Seimington Grieve:

"As the men clambered up they saw two garefowl sitting among numberless other rock-birds and at once they gave chase. The garefowl showed not the slightest disposition to repel the invaders, but immediately ran along under the high cliff, their heads erect, their little wings somewhat extended. They uttered no cry of alarm, and moved, with their short steps, about as quickly as a man could walk. Jon Brandsson, with outstretched arms, drove one into a corner, where he soon had it fast. Sigurd Islefsson and Ketil Kentilsson pursued the second, and the former seized it close to the edge of the rock, here risen to a precipice some fathoms high, the water lying directly below. Ketil then returned to the sloping shelf whence the birds had started, and saw an egg lying on the lava slab, which he knew to be a garefowl's. Whether there was not another egg is uncertain. All this took place in much less time than it takes to tell it."

A second later the men had wrung the necks of the two birds

and flung their bodies into the boat. Ketil threw the egg away because it showed a tiny crack. At that moment the great auk became extinct.

I turned away from the great auk in the case at the museum to look at a display of Carolina parakeets, small, cheerful-looking green birds with yellow heads and curved beaks. There were sixteen of them placed in a lifelike tableau on branches against a painted snow scene. The clever arrangement gave a feeling of arrested motion, as though a movie projector had been stopped on a still picture. At any moment, I felt, the film might start again and the birds break out of their frozen postures and resume hopping and fluttering and talking among the branches.

In 1881, an ornithologist wrote of the parakeets: "Their enemies are legion; bird catchers trap them by the hundreds for the northern markets, sportsmen shoot them for food, planters kill them because they eat their fruit, and tourists slaughter them simply because they present a favorable mark." The last reported Carolina parakeet was seen in 1904 by Dr. Frank Chapman in a remote swamp in Florida.

In the next case nine beautiful passenger pigeons were placed as though roosting on an oak branch, their necks curved toward each other in graceful bows. A painted backdrop suggested that in the distance were flocks so large they darkened the sky.

The story of the pigeons has been told often, but I find their extermination involves such astonishing figures that they are hard to grasp. From the 1850's until the end, slaughtering pigeons for market was an industry that involved thousands of people, hundreds of thousands of dollars, and billions of birds.

Killing reached such efficiency that it took only a short time to destroy the flocks utterly. The pigeons vanished very quickly between 1870 and 1880. By 1890 there were only a few captive birds in zoos. Suddenly, to everyone's surprise, it became apparent that there was only one. It lived for quite a few years in the Cincinnati Zoological Gardens. This very last bird happens to be in the same case in the Smithsonian as the whooping crane and the others that I looked at that day. It is accompanied by a note: "Martha, the last of her species, died at 1 P.M. September 1, 1914, aged 29."

I came away thinking that the extinction of a species, no matter how alien to us the creature may be, is an awesome thing. In its presence we experience a sort of shiver, perhaps an instinctive (should I say premonitory?) awareness that this is a death quite different from the death of an individual; that it has a different finality. This extinction of something that will never, in all eternity, be duplicated, is an occurrence that seems to break a strand of time itself.

Theodore Roosevelt wrote: "The destruction of the wild pigeon and the Carolina Paroquet has meant a loss as severe as if the Catskills or the Palisades were taken away. When I hear of the destruction of a species I feel just as if all the works of some great writer had perished; as if we had lost all, instead of only part, of Polybius or Livy." I think of these words when I hear people ask why there is so much fuss about wildlife, such as whooping cranes—or whenever I wonder myself why it seems worthwhile to document the crucial and possibly final years on earth of a small band of white birds.

2

Although the whooping crane is the tallest North American bird, it is not mere size but something that can best be described as total personality that makes it so striking and impressive a creature. An adult male whooper weighs perhaps twenty to twenty-five pounds, and stands a little over four feet tall. Its height is in the long, delicate legs and agile neck, longer and more sinuous than that of a swan, to which the spear-shaped bill is in elegant proportion. Its tapered white body is poised on its black legs in an almost upright fashion, so that the bird's silhouette is something like that of a man in a swallowtail coat. At rest the bird appears pure white except for a ruby crown and cheek patches that are, in fact, red skin bare of feathers, and a mask of glistening black featherlets that ends in points on its cheeks, suggesting a Victorian mustache of the fiercer sort. When the crane's wings are spread to their astonishing breadth of seven and a half feet, it can be seen that the wing tips are satiny black. The innermost flight feathers, the tertials, are white, and longer than the primaries. Allen describes them as "exquisite and plume-like." Curving backward, they trail over the edges of the folded wings, hiding the black tips; or, if the bird desires, it can raise these plumes over its back in display. Except when the whooping crane is feeding, it holds its narrow, patrician head high. The color of its eyes is a cold, frosty yellow. The bird has an alert, far-sighted gaze that seems to scan distant horizons with a fierce, wild recognition of some primeval challenge invisible to human beings. At least, that is the sort of notion that the whooping crane is able to inspire.

The female whooping crane is outwardly identical with the male (which adds a baffling factor to the problem of crane "management," as the professionals term human attempts to interfere in the private affairs of wild creatures), except that she is a trifle smaller and her demeanor gentler (Allen called it "more domestic"), while her mate's is heavily masculine. The difference, however, is obvious only when the birds are a mated pair.

In flight, whooping cranes are fully as regal as they are on the ground. After watching the cranes in Texas, at the Aransas Refuge, Allen wrote:

"The sight of a Whooping Crane in the air is an experience packed with beauty and drama. We see the broad sweep of the great wings in their stiff, almost ponderous motion, the flash of sunlight on the satin white plumage. As we drive down the narrow trail that borders the low salt flats a trio of the big fellows may appear, quite suddenly, in the waist-high oak brush, where they have been feeding on acorns. Their heads come up and the shrill, bugle-like notes send a shiver along your spine. They are up at once, leaning forward, running a few steps and then lifting their heavy bodies in straight-away, horizontal flight. Neck and head are extended forward, like a spear or lance, and slightly down. The long black legs stretch out behind. The wing stroke is like that of the other cranes, and of the limpkins as well. The complete arc of the stroke is narrow and there is a powerful *flick* on the upbeat. Normal flight produces about two beats to the second and there is ease and competence in the way these giants skim low over the salt grass towards the shore of the bay.

"In the grim aspect of the features, in the whole trim of the birds as they move, silently now, there is a dignity and a sense of unconquered wildness, of an obstinate will to survive. We watch them with admiration and with hope. In spite of its glowing reality, it is like a brief and unexpected look at the World as it was in the beginning."

Earlier writers have described a spectacle that nowadays no more than a handful of people are in a position to witness—an aerial ballet of whooping cranes high in the sky, an exercise the birds may indulge in just before and during migration. In a book entitled *Our Feathered Game,* published in 1911, the author, Dwight W. Huntington, tells of watching a flock of migrating whooping cranes rise from a marsh: "When quite overhead in the azure sky, their white feathers gleaming in the sunlight, they proceeded to go through many graceful evolutions, flying about in a circle, forming sides and crossing over and back and dancing in midair to their own loud music."

Yet whooping cranes are great walkers as well as flyers. In the winter months at Aransas they walk more than they fly. But "walk" is not a properly important word to describe the gait of a whooping crane. The bird moves with a peculiar, stately step, marked by a tiny pause just before the lifting of each foot. It brings to mind solemn human ceremonies, clerical processions and the aisle of Westminster Abbey.

The mighty voice that gives the crane its name is produced from a trachea five feet long coiled like a French horn behind the breastbone. The sound has been variously described as a whoop, a bugle call, or a trumpet sound. The whooping crane can modulate its voice through a fairly extensive vocabulary of sound. Both sexes trumpet when they are disturbed, angry, or wish to threaten an intruder. Under the right conditions the whoop can be heard for a mile or more. Probably the cranes sometimes whoop just for the joy of it. Or did. So few people have heard them lately that old sources are the best witness. In 1883 *Forest and Stream* published this account:

"In fine, calm weather he [the whooping crane] delights to mount up, in great, undulating spirals, to the height of a mile or so, and take a quiet float, while he whoops at neighbors in the adjoining counties.

"After airing himself to his heart's content, he descends, sometimes spirally as he rose, at other times with great plunges and wild, reckless dives, until within about 50 feet of the earth when he hangs himself upon the air, with his long, spindling legs down, gently settles and alights."

Whooping cranes mate for life. In the wild, family ties are very strong; so much so that if one member is shot the others remain close to the wounded or dead bird, and thus they, too, are exposed to danger. Parent cranes share the month-long job of incubating the eggs—only two are laid in a setting—and later share the care and defense of the young. A newly hatched whooping crane is no more than half the size of a full-grown robin. It is covered with soft, reddish down. It spends its first days within the warmth of its parents' feathers, but then can run about, following the older cranes as they search for food. By the time the young whooping cranes start the southern flight from Canada to the Aransas Refuge in the autumn, they are nearly five months old. The plumage of immature birds is not white, but a calico mixture of grayish whites and brownish reds. At a distance they look almost pink. Unknowing hunters can easily mistake them for some other sort of bird, particularly when the whooping cranes are feeding with their grayish cousins, the sandhill cranes; and so the coloration of the immature birds adds yet another hazard to the fall migration.

The scientific name of the whooping crane is *Grus americana*.

Cranes, members of the order Gruiformes, which includes other cranelike birds—rails, coots, gallinules, sun grebes, sun bitterns—are quite high on the evolutionary scale by which birds are classified. They rank above the herons (with which laymen often confuse them), above swans, geese, ducks, hawks, grouse, and quail, and just below the plovers and their relatives. It is in Asia that crane species are most abundant. Of the twenty-three species and subspecies of cranes now living, eight are native to Asia. They are the birds whose gracefully curving forms appear so often in Oriental art. South America is the only continent that has no cranes. North America has two species, the whooping crane and the sandhill crane, *Grus canadensis*. Sandhills are divided into four races, forms that do not differ enough to be termed distinct species, but are still distinguishable. All four are smaller than whooping cranes, and their plumage is predominantly gray. Unlike whoopers, sandhills are gregarious birds, and much less demanding of special habitat. As a result fairly large numbers of sandhills survive quite nicely in conditions that their inflexible cousins cannot tolerate.

Grus americana probably evolved from marsh-dwelling ancestors during the Pleistocene period, some 500,000 years ago, a time when the vast prairies, inland seas, and wet savannas of our continent presented a quite different landscape from that of today. After the withdrawal of the last glacier, during the long period when grass was the predominant vegetation, the cranes increased to their maximum numbers. Fossil bones show that in this, their Golden Age, whooping cranes ranged from coast to coast and from the Arctic to central Mexico. In time, however, forests emerged to encroach on the grasslands, the water table subsided, and a relentless shrinking of crane habitat began. It was probably then that the sandhill crane adapted itself to a less watery world while the whooping crane, victim of what has been called "crystallized psychology," and unable to change its habits, stayed within ever narrowing confines. Imprisoned by this need for a land like that which gave it birth, a land of shallow waters and vast seas of grassy, marsh vegetation, the whooping crane retreated in numbers as well as range. Robert Allen believed that even before there was significant human interference the whooping crane population had shrunk to no more than fifteen hundred birds.

These birds were never a single flock, and claimed no single area as their home. Rather they could be found wherever there was the proper combination of water and vegetation. On the East Coast whooping cranes wintered on the Atlantic shore from the Carolinas to New Jersey. But by far the greatest wintering ground for cranes was in southwestern Louisiana, where, until settlers arrived, there were two million acres of tall-grass prairie ideal for whoopers.

Also resident in southwestern Louisiana was a peculiar group of whooping cranes that for some reason did not migrate, but nested in the same area in which it wintered. Allen speculated that these birds might be the descendants of a group that formed this nonmigratory habit during a prehistoric period when glaciation forced all the cranes to nest far to the south of their later breeding grounds, and had, for some reason, clung to it ever after.

A remnant of this tribe survived until recent times, hidden in a sort of watery version of Conan Doyle's Lost World. This was a marsh of forty thousand acres of yellow grass, or "paille fine," as the Cajuns call it, near White Lake, Louisiana. There were a goodly number in the colony until about 1900, when hunting had so reduced it that the remaining birds, which had retreated to inaccessible portions of the marsh, were forgotten by the outside world. Then in 1929, the United States Army Engineers, in the course of their ceaseless improvements, extended the Intracoastal Waterway from the Vermilion River to Grand Lake. As they drove through the marsh, they incidentally "rediscovered" the lost colony of cranes.

Although Louisiana was the heartland of the migratory cranes' winter territory, the species was by no means confined to it.

Other whooping cranes, in lesser numbers than the Louisiana population of migrant whoopers, spent their winters patrolling the sea-rim marshes of the Gulf of Mexico, from New Orleans to the Rio Grande delta. In the interior grasslands of Texas and northern Mexico there were also scattered sites where lakes and marshes once provided good whooping crane habitat. Probably the whooping cranes of different localities did not mix, and met only accidentally when migration paths converged. For generation after generation individual whooping cranes remained bound by racial memory to the territories of their ancestors both in winter and in summer.

The original breeding grounds of the cranes ranged from the prairies of the central United States on up through Canada to the point beyond which severe weather made it impossible to rear young.

Allen wrote that "its preferred niche, especially when nesting, is a flat, or slightly rolling, open area interspersed with bulrush, cattail and sedge marshes and swales, covered with standing water and having the biotic characteristics found in the willow communities of the aspen parkland. There must be a great abundance of small animal life, including basic invertebrate forms. The entire area must be several hundred (or even several thousand) acres in size and completely isolated from human disturbance of any sort."

It is hard for us to realize now that less than a hundred years ago the lush prairies that then stretched from central Illinois westward across northern Iowa, western Minnesota, and eastern North Dakota fitted this description. Best of all whooper nesting habitat, and the heart of their nesting area, was the prairie of northern Iowa. An ornithologist, J. W. Preston, wrote a description of the marshes at the headwaters of the Iowa River that gives a picture of this general habitat:

"Years ago, when northwestern Iowa was a vast prairie, out onto which few settlers had ventured and the monotony was seldom broken save by some wood-fringed lake or a herder's shanty

. . . my way lay along the Iowa River, from the headwaters of which stream, westward, was a great, flat prairie, interspersed with marshes and small lakes, about which swarmed countless numbers of shore birds."

Preston, in search of eggs, reached a marsh where whooping cranes were nesting: His notes bear witness to the comparative rarity of the birds even then, in the 1880's:

"Pond and shallow water, overgrown with rushes, stretched for miles with occasional tracts of tussocks. Among these I wandered about, getting sight of a pair of Geese here, a frightened Rail there. Occasionally a flock of Sand-peeps whistled by me. Hours passed away, and when I was turning campward I caught sight of the snowy forms of a pair of White Cranes flying slowly toward me."

The nest grounds of the whooping cranes were connected with their winter homes by more or less fixed pathways of migration. Birds from the Louisiana area flew north to their nest sites in Illinois, Iowa, Minnesota, and eastern North Dakota. Texas migrants converged at the Platte River in Nebraska, and then, after following the river for a time, spread out to nesting grounds in the northern United States and Canada.

Even in migration whooping cranes never formed flocks in the sense that more social birds do. Early records describe migrant groups as numbering ten to twenty birds; on rare occasions as many as thirty or forty were sighted at one time. The Platte River was (and remains) a major resting place on the migration route where the birds might come to earth and stay for several days. Allen found old-timers who recalled seeing the great white forms of whoopers dotting the sandbars in the river at nightfall. There were still a few buffalo on the plains, and in the morning the whooping cranes moved to the riverbanks to hunt for insects and frogs in the buffalo wallows or to stalk grasshoppers through the open grassy stretches.

When the cranes were ready to resume their journey, usually in the afternoon, they would gather together, then rise and circle higher and higher until, as one old man said to Allen, "they found the right air current." The old man remembered how the great birds could be heard calling to one another as they disappeared into the depths of the sky.

3

For a good many thousands of years whooping cranes ranged a continent as yet untroubled by the advent of human beings. In that time layers of ice stretched out and receded; mountains moved, and new shores rose out of the seas. Finally the first human beings entered the hemisphere from Asia, and spread to its farthest extremity. But *Grus americana,* as Allen wrote, "unchanged, moved through these shifting scenes with the same nobility, the same dignity we know today. After unknown generations of existence, the drama—the tragic drama—of its meeting with 'civilized' man—was about to unfold."

Nobody knows which of the several accounts by early explorers of North America that speak of "cranes" deserves the honor of being considered the first written record of that meeting. For instance, Captain Luke Fox, who visited Hudson Bay in 1631, wrote that there was brought on board his ship "two goodly Swannes, and a young Tall Fowle alive; it was long-headed, long-neckt, and a body almost unanswerable. I could not discerne whether it was an Estridge or no, for it was but pen-feathered. Within 3 or 4 dayes, the legges by mischance were broken and it dyed."

This could have been a sandhill crane or, just as easily, a whooping crane. Other accounts are similarly ambiguous until we come to that of Mark Catesby, an English naturalist, who visited South Carolina in 1722. During his travels along the coast, an Indian presented him with a skin that Catesby realized belonged to a hitherto undescribed species of bird. He recorded it in his *Natural History* as *Grus americana alba*. Twenty-two years later the whooping crane was mentioned again, this time by a French explorer in Canada who, in 1744, wrote with an accuracy uncharacteristic of whooping crane annals: "We have [in Canada] cranes of two colors; some are all white, the others pale grey, all make excellent soup." Then, in 1748, a certain Mr. Isham brought a dried whooping crane skin from Hudson Bay to London and gave it to George Edwards, author of *A Natural History of Birds the Most of Which Have Not Hitherto Been Figured or Described,* who described it therein. In 1770 these sketchy references to *Grus americana* were amplified by the explorer Samuel Hearne, again with an accuracy that was to become increasingly rare: "This bird visits Hudson's Bay in the Spring, though not in great numbers. They are generally seen only in pairs, and that not very often. . . . It is esteemed good eating. The wing-bones of this bird are so long and large, that I have known them made into flutes."

Thereafter, for many years, even though the continent was increasingly explored, the written record of whooping cranes remained meager and frequently misleading. Audubon painted a whooping crane at New Orleans in 1821, but his notes show that he confused it with the sandhill. So, most probably, did an English botanist named Thomas Nuttall, who, while "leisurely descending on the bosom of the Mississippi" in 1811, saw what he took to be a vast migration of whooping cranes passing overhead "in such legions" that their "deafening clangor" continued throughout the whole night. Nuttall further described roosting flocks of whooping cranes emitting "clamorous cries . . . braying tones . . . jingling and trumpeting hurrahs." Allen, obviously affronted by such an insulting description of *Grus americana*, wrote that in the first instance Nuttall probably witnessed a sandhill migration and in the second must have "stumbled upon a hidden corral full of jackasses," since whooping cranes could not conceivably utter such sounds. Nuttall's errors, however, were not so clear to the ornithologists immediately succeeding him. His remarks about "migratory hosts" were preferred to less flamboyant testimony on the scarceness of whooping cranes, and have continued to be quoted, to support a widespread myth that whooping cranes were once as numerous as buffalo.

The period around 1850 was a turning point in the history of the whooping crane. Until then the sparse settlement of the land west of the Mississippi posed no serious threat to crane habitat. Suddenly, changes that had been in the making for fifty years seemed almost to explode. Economic and political events had sent a great tide of settlers westward. Railroad surveys opened up virgin land. Canada was rapidly explored. The Northwest Territories from the Great Lakes to Tennessee had become part of the Union in 1819, and thereafter were steadily settled and civilized. The Southwest, Louisiana, Texas, the Oregon Territory, all were opened up during the extraordinary first fifty years of the century.

In 1858, it occurred to Dr. Spencer Fullerton Baird, a leading ornithologist of the day, that the whooping crane had been scientifically neglected. He wrote: "The *Grus americanus*, though common in Texas and Florida, is yet one of the rarest birds in collections. There are none in any of the public museums of the United States, as far as I have been able to ascertain."

Baird's errors (*Grus americana* was common nowhere, and nonexistent in Florida) reflect the scientific ignorance of which Baird himself complained. It was indeed true that the whooping crane, because it was comparatively so rare, had been barely described. In 1858, its life history, its numbers, even its true range were still unknown. Ironically, it was not until thirty years later, when the crane population was melting like snow, that ornithologists began recording accurate information about the species.

Dr. Baird obtained a whooping crane skin, which he presented to the United States National Museum, where it still resides as catalogue item No. 10384. As though mobilized by Dr. Baird's remarks, collectors became eager for whooping crane skins and eggs. These trophies became increasingly valuable. In 1887, whooping crane skins went for $2.50 each, or at the wholesale rate of $2.00 if purchased in lots of one dozen or more. Only three years later, skins were sold at $8.00 to $18.00, depending on their condition. At first, eggs could be had for as little as $.50 each. By 1890, they had risen to $2.00 each.

It is probable that 90 percent of the whooping crane population disappeared in the thirty years between 1870 and 1900. No single human activity was to blame for the loss. Almost every change that occurred was inimical to the species: agriculture, drainage, cattle, settlement, hunting, even egg collecting—all were interwoven in their destruction.

The first to go, and numerically the biggest loss, were the whooping cranes that wintered on the Louisiana prairies and nested in the north-central states, for these were attacked on both winter and summer territory. Settlers came into northwestern Louisiana in the early 1800's. Undoubtedly they shot whooping cranes wherever they found them. Grus gumbo must have been a tempting dish. But it was the introduction of rice as a major crop in the 1880's that suddenly changed the face of the southern prairie. Within a few years millions of acres of grassland were turned to rice fields.

The last record of migratory whooping cranes in what was once the heart of their winter kingdom is of an incident on the prairie above Sweet Lake in 1918, when a farmer named Alcie Daigle shot twelve whooping cranes that were feeding on rice fallen from his threshing machine.

While rice farmers were taking over the whooping cranes' Louisiana wintering grounds, other settlers were moving into their summer territory in Iowa, Minnesota, North Dakota, and Illinois. The wild, wide spaces became wheat fields, homesteads, and cattle ranches. Streams were diverted and marshes drained. By 1880, whooping cranes no longer nested in Illinois. Nesting birds had disappeared from North Dakota by 1884, and the last Minnesota eggs were collected in 1889. On May 26, 1894, an ornithologist named Rudolph M. Anderson searched a marsh near Eagle Lake, Hancock County, Iowa, where crane eggs had been collected in the past. He sighted a pair of whooping cranes that "rose with slow, heavy flaps of their great wings," and moved to the far side of the marsh. There they stalked along with "long strides, as fast as a man could walk." They bugled protestingly, but did not defend their nest. This was the last wild pair found nesting in the United States.

In Canada the known nesting places of the cranes lasted a little longer. Then, on May 28, 1922, at a place unromantically known as Muddy Lake, Saskatchewan, a game warden named Fred Bradshaw came upon a pair of nesting whooping cranes. He later told how the birds attempted to lead him away, one bird circling within a hundred yards of him while he photographed the nest.

Then Bradshaw heard a "strange, piping whistle," which he discovered to be the cry of an infant whooping crane, just broken from the shell. He seized it easily and deftly wrung its neck, in order, as Allen wrote, "to efficiently collect this uttermost nib of surviving offspring and give it immortality in the form of a tag with a number on it." The chick is No. 30393 in the Royal Museum in Toronto. This was the last live whooping crane nestling that anyone would see, in the wild, for over thirty years. Until the discovery of the one remaining wilderness breeding ground of the whooping cranes, in 1955, it seemed that it might be the last ever to be seen. Meanwhile, in 1946, in the first phase of the long search for the hidden nests of the cranes, one of the searchers flew over Muddy Lake in an airplane. He found the lake as dry as dust.

Today, of course, almost all the United States and Canadian nesting sites accessible to man have been changed beyond recognition. Some that were marshes are now dry land. Others have become summer resorts, farms, towns, or the environs of towns; dumps, wrecked-car lots, gravel pits, and such. In just a few spots, which have not been attractive to development, there are still water, food, and isolation. These places still shelter nesting ducks, but no whooping cranes nest there.

In Texas the destruction of the habitat of the whooping crane was neither so sudden nor so simple as in Louisiana, but proceeded as inexorably. The Rio Grande area, once wet enough for cranes, gradually dried up as a result of drainage, farming, and grazing. Overgrazing changed the character of the vegetation and lowered the water table so that once verdant areas of southern Texas became near desert. Along the coastal strip north from the Mexican border to New Orleans, almost every acre of land has been altered by human use. Marshes have been filled and shallows dredged. At the mouth of the Brazos River whooper territory is now the scene of oil refining, sulfur extraction, and kindred industrial uses. It is as congenial to whooping cranes as the center of Houston, only sixty miles away. The sea-rim marshes of coastal Louisiana have been less dramatically altered, but even so whooping cranes did not survive there. In the 1920's there was a sudden boom in muskrat fur. The price rose to a dollar a pelt. Thousands of trappers came to the marshes between New Orleans and Port Arthur, hastening the end of the small groups of cranes that still wintered there.

Loss of territory was the major reason for the disappearance of the cranes, but it was never the only hazard to them. Another major factor was, and remains, hunting. A whooping crane is an easy target. Its double curse of size and beauty seems especially to arouse the killing instinct in gunners.·

Early sporting journals contain enthusiastic descriptions of shooting the "big white fellows." The greatest number were shot during migration, and the heaviest loss was in Nebraska, where the whoopers followed a route that was highly accessible to hunters. The greatest number were killed in the 1890's. After that, the kill record declines as the whooping crane population declines. Since 1916 and the ratification of the Migratory Bird Treaty between the United States and Great Britain, and hence Canada, it has been illegal to shoot whooping cranes, yet they are still being shot. In the ten years from 1939 to 1948, thirty-nine adult whooping cranes were lost. Allen estimated that less than half died of "natural causes"; the rest were shot on migration. There is no way to know how many juvenile whooping cranes died on their maiden trip from their birthplace to Texas.

Egg collecting is no longer a problem for obvious reasons, but there was a time when even this pretty Victorian pastime took a toll. There was a particular vogue for it in the 1880's and 1890's. Ostensibly the object was scientific, but the majority of "eggers" failed to keep records. Of the 121 whooping crane eggs that Allen was able to find in museums and private collections, hardly any were accompanied by such simple data as time, place, and circumstance of collection, so that the eggs are valueless to the scientist. This dearth Allen ascribed to the "childishly competitive" aspects of egg collecting.

Eggers robbed nests and at the same time blandly deplored the growing scarcity of material. The only legacy of value bequeathed us by the eggers are quaint descriptions of nest sites and the behavior of the nesting birds. Some of these were written with true Victorian sensibility of the pathos of the situation. In 1876, a man named George B. Sennett, an inveterate collector, set out to gather whooping crane eggs at Elbow Lake, Minnesota. He found a nest built on top of a muskrat house in a marsh. After frightening off the birds he hid himself nearby:

"Fully half an hour went by [Sennett later wrote] . . . when one noble fellow flew over the slough and lit on the opposite shore. Cautiously he began to survey the situation and shortly his mate came swooping down to his side. . . . Some fifteen minutes of strutting back and forth when she boldly walked out in the water, some eight or ten inches deep, directly toward me, mounted the rat house and sat down on her two eggs.

"I could see her wink her eyes, watching me and her mate constantly. Her eyes gleamed like fire. How anxious and how handsome, was ever a sight so grand! The male stood on the ridge watching her closely for a few minutes, when, feeling all was safe, he calmly commenced to plume himself in grand style and shortly walked off away from me, the proudest of birds. I slowly arose, turned, and gave her one barrel as she was rising from the nest and the next before she had gone six feet and dropped her in the water."

J. W. Preston, the ornithologist and writer who described the Iowa marshes where the last nest in the United States was found, also did his share of egg collecting. He described how, from a hiding place, he saw a female whooping crane alight and walk into the tall grass that concealed her nest. Preston followed:

"To my delight she was sitting on her heavily marked drab eggs, which lay in a neat cavity in the top of a well-built heap of tough, fine marsh grass one and a half feet high on firm sod. The eggs were the first I'd seen and were a rare prize to me. When I approached the nest, the bird, which had walked some distance away, came running back . . . trotting awkwardly around, wings and tail spread drooping, with head and shoulders brought to a level with the water; then it began picking up bunches of moss and sticks which it threw down in a defiant way; then, with pitiable mien, it spread itself upon the water and begged me to leave its treasure, which, in a heartless manner, I did not do."

Fortunately another pastime, more fruitful than egg collecting, was also born in the 1880's, and gave ornithology a new dimension. Bird-watching was virtually invented by Wells B. Cooke, an ornithologist with the Division of Economic Ornithology of the United States Department of Agriculture. Working from his desk in Washington, Cooke organized a vast correspondence soliciting reports on birds from amateurs all over the nation and in Canada. In effect, Cooke mobilized an army of observers; a motley group whose ranks included hunters, housewives, teachers, eggers, farmers, and small boys. The result was a hitherto impossible coverage reaching into the far corners of the country. Cooke's bulletin on migratory birds, published in 1888, was a landmark in whooping crane history, in that it provided the first reasonably accurate picture of their winter distribution. And just in time: a few years later the birds had disappeared from 90 percent of this range without trace.

Even so, reliable information on the numbers of whoopers was not easily come by. Somehow, perhaps dating back to Nuttall's accounts, there was a fixed belief that whooping cranes had once been abundant, and that "somewhere" they were abundant still. The myth took a long time to die. While some ornithologists were warning that *Grus americana* was alarmingly scarce or possibly already extinct, others maintained that the species was in no danger. This confusion among people who should have known better was typical of the whooping cranes' bad luck, and helped postpone the rescue operation until almost too late.

In 1912, a year when, according to Robert Allen's reconstruction of their history, there were actually eighty to a hundred whooping cranes alive, the bell was tolled by an authority named Edward Howe Forbush, who wrote a history of the game birds of New England. "The whooping crane is doomed to extinction," he declared. "It has disappeared from its former habitat in the east and is now found only in uninhabited places." Dr. William T. Hornday, of the New York Zoological Park, who had a captive whooping crane for which he had been unable to secure a mate, was ready to concur. "This splendid bird will almost certainly be the next North American species to be totally exterminated," he wrote in 1913. He added that a standing offer of $1,000, made by an English gentleman, for a live pair of whooping cranes had gone unanswered for five years.

At about the same time, a certain Professor Myron H. Swenk, of Lincoln, Nebraska, took a hand in whooping crane history. An admirer and champion of the birds, his long and patient labors to rally interest in them were neatly canceled by his blunders in appraising their situation. Swenk made, and published, spring and autumn tallies of the number of migrating whooping cranes observed in Nebraska. His mistaken reports of large numbers clouded the truth during the critical decades from 1912 to 1934.

Despite Swenk's optimistic reports, others erred on the darker

side. In 1923 *The Saturday Evening Post* published an article by
Hal G. Evarts, a popular nature writer, which announced that
the whooping crane had already "travelled the long trail to oblivion." Evarts had been given the skin of what he thought was the
"last straggler," and presented it to the museum in Yellowstone
Park. His account of the trail to extinction included a description
of how the whooping cranes were shot year after year as they migrated over a salt marsh near Hutchinson, Kansas. An enterpris-
ing resident of the area captured two crippled survivors of the
sport and, reportedly, sold them for $1,900 to a dealer in New
York who intended to ship them to Australia. Before they could
be sent off, the birds died in the Bronx Zoo.

Two years after Evarts wrote their epitaph Dr. Swenk reported
a spring flight of sixty-five whooping cranes across the Platte
River. This "firsthand" report entered the ornithological literature and tended to lull alarm over the birds' status. It apparently
helped to reassure Dr. T. Gilbert Pearson, president of the National Association of Audubon Societies, for in 1932 he told a
convention of conservationists that current information from Nebraska showed the cranes to be "somewhat more numerous" than
indicated by the gloomy figures previously reported.

In truth, as far as it can be reconstructed, after 1918 there
were only three groups of migratory whooping cranes in existence: The King Ranch in Texas was the wintering ground of perhaps sixteen birds; at the site of the present Aransas Refuge on
the Blackjack Peninsula there were approximately twenty-five
whooping cranes; and on the sea-rim marshes of the Louisiana
coast six or eight birds held out during the 1920's. Allen calculated that the grand total for 1918 was forty-seven birds. This
figure had probably been somewhat reduced by 1925 when Dr.
Swenk made his report of sixty-five migrating whooping cranes.

During this critical period of decline in the fortunes of the
cranes, Dr. Swenk continued to be the only person seriously interested in their fate, but unfortunately he remained convinced
that the birds were holding their own—or better. In 1933, he

wrote that while he didn't want to minimize the danger of their situation he felt that the number of whooping cranes migrating through Nebraska had in fact increased since 1916. Dr. Swenk had come to believe that somewhere there was a great flock of whooping cranes and that the scattered individuals seen in spring and fall were simply wanderers from this flock. He clung to this belief even though, year after year, the "great flock" failed to appear. The truth is that in later years Dr. Swenk was seldom in the field himself. He confused an increase in the number of bird-watchers with an increase in the number of whooping cranes. As Swenk's years of devoted missionary work to educate Nebraskans about whooping cranes enlisted a growing army of farmers, hunters, and housewives scanning the skies in the spring and fall, his graph of "whooping cranes" sighted steadily rose. Years later, Robert Allen tracked down similar amateur reports of whooping cranes and found them to be in reality an assortment of pelicans, gulls, sandhills, and snow geese. Undoubtedly Swenk's well-meaning friends made the same mistakes.

Dr. Swenk's miscalculation was almost fatal to the cranes. "On the strength of this rosy picture," Allen wrote, "direct action on their behalf was seriously delayed." Poor Swenk, whose error was born of concern, would have been one of those most grieved had he realized the true situation.

Dr. Swenk's figures were not challenged because no one was in a position to refute them. As late as 1941, the American Ornithologists' Union reported: "Estimates made in 1938 place the whooping crane population at less than three hundred." That estimate was at least technically correct. Allen reconstructed the actual population of 1938 as consisting of eleven birds in the nonmigratory flock at White Lake, Louisiana, and eighteen migratory whooping cranes on the Blackjack Peninsula, Texas.

There were no others. The last of the King Ranch birds had vanished the year before. The last migrants of the Louisiana coastal marshes had perished. There were twenty-nine whooping cranes left on earth. Swenk's great flock was a phantom, and the species itself very nearly one.

At this critical moment, in December 1937, the United States Biological Survey, forerunner of the Fish and Wildlife Service, made its first move, riding up like a cavalry regiment in a romance of the Old West, just in time to untie the heroine from the railroad tracks.

4

One of the few occasions when an encounter between a man and a whooping crane has been fortunate for the crane occurred in 1936. Early that winter a biologist named Neil Hotchkiss, on a scouting mission for the Bureau of Biological Survey, visited the Blackjack Peninsula and saw four whooping cranes, as well as a fine assortment of water birds. Hotchkiss recorded the cranes in his notes on wildlife observed in the area, and reported to Washington that the peninsula merited further investigation as a possible waterfowl refuge.

A few months later, in the small town of Brady, Nebraska, some thousand miles distant from Texas, one other event important in whooping crane history took place. It was described thus by the Lincoln County *Tribune:*

BRADY, NEBRASKA, June 10 (Special to the *Tribune*)—A large white Heron was sighted by the Henry George girls while riding their bicycles Friday and returning to the house with the news, Mr. George took the car and drove the Heron for a mile into a 5-foot wire netting fence where it was caught. It had been shot and one wing and its eye were injured. It easily looked over the fence. It was turned over to the Gothenburg Sanctuary where it was let loose.

The sanctuary was a large pen where the whooping crane lived, one-eyed and unreconciled, refusing to make peace either with its keepers, members of the Gothenburg Gun Club, or with the assorted poultry sharing its quarters, for the next twelve years.

Hotchkiss' visit to Texas had not been accidental. During the 1930's nature and economics, dustbowl and depression suddenly combined in favor of conservation. The depletion of all our natural resources, including wildlife, had become dramatically apparent. At this moment, too, federal funds were flowing. Thanks to the herculean efforts of J. N. ("Ding") Darling, the Iowa cartoonist who had become the crusading chief of the Bureau of Biological Survey, Congress for the first time consented to spend sizable amounts on wildlife. The result was a brief Golden Age of acquisition when hundreds of thousands of acres were bought for sanctuaries. The refuge program of the Biological Survey, transfused with money, leaped into life. Biologists were dispatched on survey missions to select the most useful sites from among the scores of possibilities. Thus it happened that Hotchkiss made the difficult trip over the narrow dirt road that led to the last redoubt of the whooping crane.

A short time later Hotchkiss returned with two colleagues: J. Clark Salyer II, chief of the Refuge Branch, and George B. Saunders, a Bureau ornithologist. Again whooping cranes were noted. Then Saunders, who had studied the whooping cranes' cousins in Africa as well as in North America, spent several weeks looking over a wide stretch of coast. He saw whooping cranes nowhere but in the Blackjack vicinity, a circumstance that interested him deeply. As a result he recommended the purchase of the Blackjack Peninsula and of the two protective islands of Matagorda and St. Joseph, just off its shores, where he had also seen whoopers.

Adjacent to the land for sale on the Blackjack Peninsula was another tract—the Hallinan Ranch—which, Saunders noted, was an ideal habitat for Attwater's prairie chicken, and so he recommended that also. The answer from Washington was that the Bureau couldn't buy that much territory in one place; if he couldn't have it all, which portion was the most important? Saunders, thinking of the whooping cranes, as well as the waterfowl, replied, "Blackjack." Thus the refuge does not include the islands of Matagorda and St. Joseph, which could have been protective barriers to the privacy of the peninsula. The Bureau's decision to eliminate the islands and the Hallinan Ranch was sadder and more consequential than anyone could possibly have known. Not long thereafter the prairie chickens gave up their habitat to large-scale farming. Today the species is high on the danger list.

Nevertheless, it was a crucial moment in whooping crane history when the Bureau decided to purchase the Blackjack Peninsula. There is no reason to doubt that the whooping cranes would otherwise have vanished years ago. The Bureau bought 47,261 acres, roughly 74 square miles, for $463,500. On December 31, 1937, President Roosevelt signed an executive order that transformed it into the Aransas Migratory Waterfowl Refuge, a title later transmuted into its present one—the Aransas National Wildlife Refuge.

The entire Gulf coast of Texas is a strategic area for water birds. Its crescent coastline, extending some 360 miles between Louisiana and Mexico, is protected for much of its length by a chain of long, thin, sandy islands that follow the shore like a breakwater. Between the islands and the mainland are shallow lagoons where oyster reefs and marine meadows of seaweed provide splendid feeding grounds for waterfowl.

The Aransas Refuge region has an especially rich variety to offer wildlife. It is part of a peculiar area where it seems land and water have not finally made up their minds to part. Much of the land is as level as the sea itself, and there is a wide, intermediate zone where bays, lagoons, sloughs, and ponds make lacework of the shore. Wide expanses of marsh just barely rise above the water. Like islands in these seas of salt grass are mud flats that are sometimes claimed by the land, sometimes by the water, depending on wind and tide. The tides here are peculiar, too. They do not rise and fall on a predictable, moon-determined schedule, but are influenced by the strong, persistent winds characteristic of these shores, especially in spring and fall. The level of the water may rise, covering the low land, and stay at the flood for days or even weeks. Then, with wind from another direction, the water is blown offshore, out of the ponds and sloughs, and will remain at ebb until the wind changes.

The Blackjack Peninsula, or what has now become the Aransas Refuge, is a thumb of land pointing southwest. It runs almost parallel to the mainland shore, something like the thumb of a man's hand in relation to the other fingers. To the west a sliver of water, St. Charles Bay, separates the peninsula from the mainland. On the east the peninsula is flanked by a long lagoon beyond which the sandbar islands of St. Joseph and Matagorda face the open Gulf.

This eastern shore is fringed by a salt marsh, twelve miles long and a mile or two in width, that Robert Allen called "one of the most fascinating water environments that I have ever wet my feet in." The marsh, and its network of ponds, inlets, and mud flats, is the home of small sea animals, particularly the blue crab, on which whooping cranes depend for food. This marsh, together with some similar stretches on the shores of Matagorda and St. Joseph, is the true kingdom of the cranes. Here they stake out their territories and spend most of their winter days. Behind the marsh the peninsula rises into low, rolling sandy soil, densely covered with live oak and sweet-bay brush. Groves, or "mottes," of blackjack oak provide acorns and shelter from storms for a variety of creatures. The interior is host to dozens of species of birds and mammals, but the whooping cranes as a rule visit it only when storm or drought drives them from the marsh, or to feed on acorns when they are in season.

The Blackjack Peninsula was first settled in the early 1800's. Homesteaders cleared the high ground for small farms. In time a post office, a fish factory, and a general store graced the settlement. However, its remoteness made farming marginal. After 1900, the homesteaders began to drift inland. The fish factory closed. In 1923, a San Antonio millionaire named Leroy Denman bought the entire peninsula. He used it to graze cattle and as a shooting preserve. It was thanks to Denman's protection and the isolation of the peninsula that the cranes survived there, but one other aspect of Denman's ownership was less fortunate for them. When he sold to the government he retained mineral rights which provide that there may be oil exploration and drilling anywhere on the refuge. The arrangement included a royalty to the government that will eventually refund the entire purchase price of the land. This bargain was a good one, perhaps, for the taxpayers, but it rendered the sanctuary less than inviolable at its very inception.

In 1938, Aransas Refuge began to function with the installation of a resident manager, James O. Stevenson. His first important contribution to the cranes was an attempt to count them. Nowadays Fish and Wildlife men count the cranes from a low-flying airplane or from roads that overlook the salt flats, but in Stevenson's day the plane was not available and the roads had not been built. By tramping over the flats, Stevenson found fourteen cranes in the autumn of 1938. Four of them were rusty-colored young. Stevenson felt that, because of the difficulty of scanning the entire shoreline, he probably missed a few cranes and that there may have been as many as eighteen whooping cranes in the area.

Meanwhile, in Louisiana, John Lynch, a Fish and Wildlife Service staff biologist who had been keeping track of the small resident population of whooping cranes in the marsh at White Lake, found that they had increased to thirteen.

These two reports, adding up to no more than thirty-one whooping cranes, suddenly made clear the impossibility of the Nebraska reports of large flocks. The bad news, no longer conjecture, began to seep through ornithological circles.

The first winter on the refuge was comparatively tranquil. The weather was clear and mild. Hunters shot 7,806 ducks and 136 geese in the waters around the refuge, but fortunately shot no whooping cranes. A CCC camp was built on the refuge, and the boys began to work on roads, paved with oyster shells, and on a headquarters building.

Stevenson, fascinated with the cranes, made an effort to study their behavior, noting particularly the tendency of each pair to choose a certain territory and to remain within its limits, driving off any other whoopers that sought to intrude. Then, in the weeks between mid-April and mid-May, Stevenson found fewer cranes each time he counted them, and presumed that the missing individuals had flown north. No one could do more than hope they would return.

Stevenson's summer, though isolated, could hardly have been lonely. The bureau had given a permit to the San Antonio Loan and Trust Company, representing Denman, allowing it to graze four thousand head of cattle for a fee of thirty cents per head per month. This meant that cowboys handling the cattle came and went. In addition the first explorations for oil had shown a promising area at the inland edge of the refuge, and Continental Oil, which had leased the rights from San Antonio Loan and Trust, was making preparations to drill. These workers plus the CCC boys formed a large and busy human population.

In October the first crane reappeared—then a family—followed by others, until by mid-November Stevenson counted what proved to be that year's maximum of twenty-two cranes. Six were young. One pair had brought twins.

The mild, dry winter weather of 1939–40 gradually became drought. The cranes visited an artesian well to drink twice a day. Stevenson built a blind nearby from which he watched the cranes. In this neutral territory the crane families called a truce and did not dispute each other's right to the water. Geese, widgeons, and pintails lined up at the side and humbly waited their turn to drink when the lordly cranes had finished. One large crane disciplined any geese that got out of line.

In 1938, a strip of water around the refuge had been declared legally closed to hunting by presidential proclamation, but the ban was not immediately enforced. When, in the winter of

1939–40, Stevenson closed these waters, it was a sorrow and annoyance to the St. Charles Bay Club, a hunting club on the shore of St. Charles Bay, whose manager was found in "closed" waters attempting to drive ducks out of the safety zone and in front of the gunners' blinds. Of the club's fifty-one blinds, thirty-three were just offshore from the refuge. Eventually the sportsmen became reconciled to the idea that the refuge actually enhanced their shooting, but at the time, Stevenson reported, they were "provoked, to say the least."

In January, Stevenson recorded the odd behavior of a family of three whooping cranes that suddenly took to frequenting inland farmlands to the southeast of the refuge. There they were perfectly visible from the highway, but paid little attention to the automobiles passing a few hundred yards from them. Stevenson was greatly relieved when, at length, they returned safely home.

The truce between man and whooping crane at Aransas was doomed to be shattered by the Army Engineers who appeared on the scene in the spring of 1940. The engineers had been inexorably working their way down the coast, dredging a channel along the shore in order to extend the Gulf Intracoastal Waterway south to Corpus Christi. Upon reaching the refuge they did not turn aside. As they surveyed the area they found that a route along the edge of the cranes' precious salt marshes would offer more protection to boats and be cheaper to maintain than the otherwise equally feasible offshore route winding through the chain of bays that bound the refuge. As the engineers pressed on through the refuge, they drained and thus destroyed acres of whooping crane territory on the salt flats. The spoil from their ditchdigging smothered another wide area, rendering it useless as far as cranes were concerned. The loss of territory, although unfortunate, was minor compared to the main misfortune that had now befallen the cranes. Their sanctuary was now pierced by a broad highway of water, open to all comers. As Robert Allen wrote bitterly, "The ditch, nine feet deep and one hundred wide, over a three-hundred-foot right-of-way bisected the very edge of salt flats where whooping cranes had found safety for perhaps two million years. This once isolated tip is no longer secure, or isolated."

Even if the Fish and Wildlife Service had fully foreseen the sad results—the danger from guns, from disturbance and pollution that were the inevitable results of having the waterway on the doorstep of the refuge—there was very little they could have done about it. This was by no means the first, and far from the last, time that the plans of the engineers have collided with the interests of wildlife. Almost invariably the engineers roll on, no matter what the protests. As one official of the Service, a veteran of a thousand lost battles, has sadly remarked: "To say that the Engineers are unmoved by our wishes is putting it mildly." And so, as the engineers swept through Aransas, the Service could only watch sadly and philosophically, and hope for the best. It is quite likely, too, that at that time very few people thought the whooping cranes would be around long enough for conditions at Aransas to make much difference.

While the engineers were digging, the Continental Oil Company had begun drilling. On January 27, 1940, its first well blew in and caught fire. Stevenson, who was having trouble enough policing the roughnecks working the rig, now had to cope with streams of sightseers come to view the blaze. Fortunately, the well was on the inland side of the refuge, at a place called Little Devil Bayou, far from the cranes' usual haunts and in an area of low value to wildlife. The well was eventually capped, and Con Oil went to work on a second.

During April and May the twenty-two whooping cranes flew off to the peace and quiet of Canada, leaving Stevenson to a hot, busy summer.

Humble Oil began drilling in the bay just outside the water boundary of the refuge. A dredge started digging a channel in the oyster reefs. Finally news was received that the Army Air

Corps proposed to use part of Matagorda Island as a bombing and machine-gun target range.

In Louisiana another misfortune was waiting in the wings. In August 1940, a cloudburst and windstorm hit White Lake. The thirteen resident whooping cranes that John Lynch had counted the year before were flushed out of their seclusion and blown inland. From this visit to the haunts of man only six returned to the marsh. Of the seven that were lost, it is presumed that six were shot and eaten and that the seventh, though wounded by a gunshot, survived.

Any population, animal or human, has a numerical threshold below which it cannot produce enough young to counterbalance normal attrition. Apparently the six survivors at White Lake were below that threshold. By 1942 they had dwindled to five; in 1943 there were four; the next year three. For the next two years a lonely pair hung on, but did not nest, and then, in 1947, there was only a single bird.

A year after the disastrous storm at White Lake, a fateful sequel took place. On November 25, 1941, a whooping crane with a crippled wing was brought to the Audubon Park Zoo in New Orleans. This was undoubtedly the only survivor of the seven lost White Lake cranes. The bird had been captured by a farmer in Evangeline Parish in the fall of 1940. He gave it to a Mr. La Haye of Eunice, Louisiana, who nursed it to health. La Haye assumed that his crippled pet was of no particular distinction, but a year later a Federal Game Management agent, Houston C. Gascon, happened to see the bird, and identified it as a whooping crane. The bird was brought to the zoo by Gascon and State Wildlife and Fisheries Officer John McCloskey.

The bird was received by George Douglass, who had recently become director of the Park Department and hence of the zoo. Its arrival at Audubon Park was noted on a card in a filing cabinet in the zoo's office. The card read, "Josephine . . . whooping crane . . . 4 feet tall . . . wing spread approximately seven feet

. . . adult . . . pure white . . . found in a rice field in Eunice, La., 1941 . . . donated by L. O. La Haye of Eunice, La." Handwritten in pencil across the bottom of the card were the words "because so rare priceless."

For once the concept "priceless" was almost literally true. Possession of this bird would eventually give control of the entire captive breeding population of whooping cranes to the Audubon Park Zoo. However, it is safe to assume that at the time this thought occurred to no one, including Douglass. He put the bird in a small cage, placed her on 'exhibit, and there she remained, causing little remark of any kind, for the next ten years.

At Aransas on October 22, 1940, Stevenson saw the first crane returned from the north, and by December he had counted twenty-six birds. There were five young. In all, the increase these first three summers seemed extremely promising.

In the spring, however, an apparently healthy group of three, a pair with their yearling, failed to migrate. They spent the summer on the refuge, but did not nest. From time to time since then, others have done the same. No one knows why.

One day in May 1941, when all the cranes except these three had left, a string of barges tending a wildcat well, recently drilled in the bay a short distance from the east end of the refuge, suddenly discharged a quantity of oil into the water. As it happened Stevenson was standing with a visitor looking over the marshes. The visitor was Robert Allen, who had recently come to Texas on an assignment from the National Audubon Society to study the roseate spoonbills that are found on the outer islands. The two men saw with dismay that a wide slick was slowly traveling inland toward the entrance to the canal. If the oil entered the waterway, it would wash into the ponds and mud flats, bringing an abrupt black death to the plant and animal life of the shore. There was nothing Allen and Stevenson could do, so they just watched. Then, the wind changed and the deadly stuff moved off in another direction. If the wind had not shifted when it did, the cranes would have returned to a lifeless shore, which would, quite likely, have ended their story right there.

Stevenson and Allen drove to Houston and called on the president of the oil company concerned. He listened sympathetically as they described what had almost happened. Then he said that such things occur despite the best of precautions. He turned up the palms of his hands. "Let us trust, gentlemen," he said, "that this does not happen again."

In the autumn of 1941 the whooping cranes returned, but though Stevenson searched repeatedly he was unable to locate more than fifteen birds. Of these, three had summered on the refuge; two were young of the year. Thus, of the twenty-three migrants of the previous spring, only ten had returned. "We can only wonder about the rest," Stevenson wrote as he recorded the loss of the thirteen birds in his regular report to Washington of events at Aransas. However, it is likely that not many people gave the matter much thought. At this moment Pearl Harbor tended to eclipse whooping crane affairs no matter how unfortunate they might be.

The war began to be felt at Aransas when Army and Navy planes started to fly low over the refuge. Local hunting guides grumbled that revenues fell because these flights broke up the concentrations of ducks and geese. Stevenson called on military commanders at nearby bases and informed them that low-flying airplanes might drive the whooping cranes from the refuge. They promised cooperation, and in fact fewer planes flew low. The CCC camp closed, and the boys went off to war. Stevenson caught a hunter on the refuge, and charges were brought against him.

That year (1942), by enormous good fortune, the fifteen surviving cranes made their summer journey without the loss of a single adult bird, and brought back four young ones.

In July 1943, when the nineteen cranes had left for the summer, the Army Air Force began to use its practice range on Matagorda Island. The range is a strip twenty-two miles long and three miles wide, situated ten miles southeast of the refuge headquarters, but at one point only five miles from crane territory on False Live Oak Point. The site for the range had been chosen, according to the Air Force, "because it would affect comparatively few people." In the years since then the Air Force used it for bombing practice, at both low and high altitudes, sometimes with live ammunition and sometimes only for dry runs in which an imaginary impact point was calculated by radar.

As in the case of the Army Engineers, the wishes of the Fish and Wildlife Service made no perceptible dent on the Air Force. However, whereas the engineers dig and move on, the Air Force settles down to stay. In this situation the Fish and Wildlife Service had no choice but to establish neighborly relations in an attempt to minimize the damage. This they proceeded to do at Aransas. Communications between the two services were cordial. The only trouble was that the Air Force bombing range was there at all.

Despite the air activity on Matagorda, the cranes continued to use the marsh at the easterly portion of the island. This half of the island is privately owned. It is the property of a prominent Texas rancher named Toddie Lee Wynne. From time to time bombing miscalculations resulted in the disappearance of one or two of Mr. Wynne's herd, but as far as is known no whooping cranes were pulverized. Close calls—and there must have been some—are not on record.

5

In 1943, Stevenson wrote an article about the whooping cranes that was published in *Audubon Magazine*. Even as late as this, no one knew with certainty that the cranes at Aransas were the only migratory whooping cranes in existence. Stevenson harbored the hope that others—perhaps the birds reported as migrating through Nebraska—would still turn up, and spoke of the species as being reduced to a "sorry remnant of perhaps two hundred birds."

What was perfectly clear, however, was that new dangers had appeared at Aransas at almost the same moment that the establishment of the refuge had promised safety to the whoopers. Stevenson listed these obvious threats: bombing and machine-gun ranges established by the Army Air Force on the barrier islands; target-shooting boatmen riding through the refuge on the Intracoastal Waterway; exploration for oil on the refuge; the drilling of oil wells in the waters of the bay. "Are the birds to be driven from their last stronghold?" he asked.

Shortly thereafter, in the autumn of 1943, sixteen of the nineteen cranes that had migrated came back to Aransas, bringing with them five young, for a net gain to the flock of two birds. The twenty-one whoopers were greeted by a new manager at the refuge. Stevenson had been transferred in accordance with a Fish and Wildlife policy of moving its men from post to post at regular intervals. The new manager was Earl W. Craven. "The whoopers are still struggling for existence," Craven reported to Washington, "and there is still hope for them as long as they continue to produce young." Craven also reported that Continental Oil Company was still drilling and now had four producing wells. The skies over the refuge were still busy with airplane traffic. Craven noted that most of the wildlife on the refuge was becoming adjusted to airplanes, although the geese remained a bit nervous about them.

The twenty-one whooping cranes migrated normally in the spring of 1944 and vanished toward the north in their customary manner. On October 20, 1944, Craven saw the first autumn arrivals. A family of three alighted on the territory opposite Rattlesnake Point. By November, Craven had counted a total of eighteen whooping cranes, of which three were young. Thereafter, all during the winter, the birds behaved restlessly and moved in and out of the refuge, making it impossible to be sure of the true number. Robert Allen later guessed that four birds were overlooked or possibly had wintered off the refuge, so that the flock actually numbered twenty-two in the winter of 1944–45.

In an effort to locate the cranes, Craven was now making his surveys from a plane leased from a local airport. In the spring he told Washington that the whooping cranes had apparently scattered up and down the coast. They had been reported both north and south of the refuge, and often only half the flock could be found at any one time. Craven guessed that low water levels on the salt marshes had made food conditions unfavorable and caused the birds to look elsewhere for feeding grounds. In the spring of 1945 the entire flock departed for the north. It was lucky that no whoopers remained behind, for in August the refuge was in the path of a particularly savage hurricane that would surely have swept them away.

During the five years following the establishment of the Aransas Refuge, the indisputable and bleak figures on whooping cranes resulting from each winter's census in Texas were at last attracting the attention of the ornithological world. Reports published by the American Ornithologists' Union and the Wilson Club pronounced the whoopers' situation more precarious than ever and, in 1944, called for action to save the remnant of the species.

Shortly thereafter the National Audubon Society took up the problem of the cranes with the United States Fish and Wildlife Service—the new agency in the Department of the Interior that had taken over wildlife management from the Biological Survey. The director of the Service was Dr. Ira N. Gabrielson. Both he and Dr. Clarence Cottam, its chief of research, were well aware that despite protection at Aransas the whoopers were holding on to life by the slenderest of threads; but, lacking funds for such obscure and exotic projects as the salvation of whooping cranes, the Service was unable to take any special measures on their behalf. In this situation the National Audubon Society was the only agency in the country willing and able to lend a hand.

The National Audubon Society was formed in 1905 to meet a specific and urgent threat. The combined onslaught of sportsmen and commercial exploiters had finished off the pigeons and the parakeets; plume hunters were reducing the great egret colonies from tens of thousands of birds to a handful; and so on through a sorry list. In the case of the pigeon and the parakeet, the Society came on the scene too late. It saved the egret, dramatically, by forcing the passage of laws that banned further slaughter. A generation later, however, it was apparent that human expansion posed a new and more subtle danger as it altered environment and shattered the delicate balance of plant and animal life. It is of little use to ban hunting when an entire habitat may be wiped out, as has happened in the case of the ivory-billed woodpecker, which depended on a certain kind of forest and could adapt to no other. By the 1930's the Society had realized that henceforward in order to help a threatened species it would be necessary to understand how its life cycle was related to its environment and to the new conditions confronting it.

In 1945, the president of the National Audubon Society was a tall, serious-minded Bostonian named John Hopkinson Baker. He was the son of George Pierce Baker, director of the famous drama workshop at Harvard and, later, Yale. He had been an amateur naturalist since boyhood, a World War I pilot, and a successful businessman before he took on, at the age of fifty, the leadership of the Society. One of the first questions to cross his desk was that of the whooping cranes, and it was his decision that the Society should intervene.

As John Baker surveyed the situation of the cranes, it was obvious that there was an almost complete lack of information on which to base a program of help. Not only did no one know, surely, how many whooping cranes there were; but there were no reliable data on the most elementary factors in their life cycle. Their food, nesting habits, the rearing of their young, their behavior on the long flight to their mysterious nesting grounds, all presented unanswered questions. During the thirties the Society had come to the aid of the ivory-billed woodpecker, the California condor, and the roseate spoonbill by underwriting exhaustive biological studies. It now decided to do the same for the whooping cranes. John Baker conferred with Gabrielson and Cottam of the Fish and Wildlife Service. An alliance called the Cooperative Whooping Crane Project was formed. Its announced purpose was to determine "what steps may reasonably be taken toward further protection and restoration of the species." Beyond this the terms of the partnership were unwritten, an omission that the Society may later have viewed with regret.

The first step in the project was, of course, to find a biologist willing to take on what promised to be a long, strenuous, and financially thankless task. The job would involve not only a study of the whooping cranes at Aransas but also a search for the hidden nests whose location was considered one of the most crucial questions in the puzzle of how to preserve the species. At that moment, in early 1945, the Society's research director, Robert Porter Allen, who had studied the spoonbills and was obviously the man for the whooping crane job, was in the Army. Most of the other men who might have qualified were unavailable for the same reason. The gap was filled, momentarily, when a Canadian devotee of the whooping crane, Fred Bard, curator of the Provincial Museum in Regina, Saskatchewan, offered to search for the whoopers' nests. In the summer of 1945 Bard spent two months in fruitless airplane flights over central Saskatchewan, without seeing so much as the tail feather of a whooping crane.

That autumn the Whooping Crane Project was taken on by an ornithologist, Dr. Olin Sewall Pettingill, Jr., who spent several winter months studying the birds at Aransas. In the summer of 1946, Mr. Terris Moore, president of the New England Museum of Natural History, offered the use of a plane and his own services as pilot. Pettingill and Moore flew over several thousand miles of what seemed promising territory in Alberta and Saskatchewan in an unavailing search for whooping crane nests. In the autumn Pettingill had to drop the project in favor of a teaching job, but by then, luckily, Robert Allen was on his way home.

Bob Allen, then forty-one years old, was a stocky, dark-haired man with a strong-featured, smiling look of humor and friendliness that belied both the sophistication of his mind and the fierceness of his dedication to his cause: the protection of threatened species. His character combined a capacity for strong feeling with a rare sensitivity and gentleness. What made these qualities so effective was an extraordinarily patient doggedness—once committed, it seemed impossible for him to give up until the cause was won. At the time Allen took on the whooping crane project, no one could foresee what the job would entail. When he had finished his monograph, he had spent three years and three months of intensive study, twenty-seven of them in fieldwork. He traveled more than twenty thousand miles by plane and six thousand by jeep, searching the Canadian wilderness for the secret nesting sites. He spent many freezing nights in tents; some of them in northwestern Saskatchewan, where late-spring sleet storms suddenly iced the canvas, and others on the flats of Aransas, where chill, hard "northers" can blow exhaustingly night and day. He often ate badly and overworked for long stretches of time. These are conditions that can appear romantic from a comfortable distance, but are more likely to be depressing when experienced at first hand. In Allen's case his sense of the romance of the whooping cranes proved unquenchable, no matter what the conditions of his work.

Allen wrote a great deal about the birds: a number of articles, a popular book, and the monograph with its supplement on the nesting grounds. In all these, even in his most objective scientific reports, he conveyed the sense that he had fallen in love with the cranes and become committed to their cause. He presented the case for the survival of the cranes not simply as the continuance or extinction of one species among many now in danger, but as the cause of all simple, beautiful, and defenseless living things vanishing before the relentless force of human expansion. Since Allen was a romantic, somewhat of a mystic, and a man of violent belief and fierce determination, he refused to concede that the outcome of the conflict is inevitable.

Robert Allen was born in South Williamsport, Pennsylvania, on April 24, 1905. His early surroundings were a combination of the literate and the rural. His mother was a schoolteacher and his father a lawyer. Their home was in mountain country where deer, bear, bobcat, and other game survived in abundance. Allen's own account of his boyhood makes it clear that he was called to his work with wildlife as surely as some receive the summons to the Church. In Allen's case the first mystic whisper came when, at the age of ten, he read Ernest Thompson Seton's *Two Little Savages*. For a while thereafter Allen spent as much time as possible in the role of an Indian stealing through ancestral hunting grounds. Seton has endowed the wild with magic for many young boys; for Allen this magic remained constant to the end of his life.

By the time he reached high school, Allen had joined a junior Audubon Club and shifted from deerslayer to bird-watcher. Thenceforward ornithology was the only thing he really cared about. Upon graduation he reluctantly left the woods to enter Lafayette College in Easton, Pennsylvania. He spent two years there; in his opinion, quite uselessly. Allen described himself at this period: "In my outmoded Norfolk jacket I was a trifle rural among my new friends, although I knew that I could outrun the whole lot of them on a mountain trail, outpaddle them in a canoe, and make jackasses of them in a river-bottom swamp. I did learn a few things about the world that lay beyond Bald Eagle Mountain, but I remained an undisciplined nonconformist, incapable of learning many of the graces and determined to find a way of life wherein the kind of shoes you wore and the sort of knot in your tie were of no importance."

As a practical matter Allen found that his skill in ornithology seemed unlikely to finance any way of life whatever. For a time he avoided the question of a career by taking a job on a freighter bound for Singapore. In three years he sailed twice around the world. His adventures included a shipwreck in the Sulu Sea. He came home forty-eight cents richer.

Ashore in New York, Allen went to a party at which he met a girl named Evelyn Sedgwick, who had just graduated from the Juilliard School of Music, and fell in love with her. Love produced a sudden urge for solvency, and Allen set out to look for work. He called on Dr. Chapman, of the American Museum of Natural History, with whom he had once corresponded on the subject of birds. Chapman sent him to see Dr. T. Gilbert Pearson, then president of the National Audubon Society, who gave Allen a trial job sorting books in the basement. Allen was jubilant. He had found a milieu in which the knot in his tie was not important; he was dealing with books and birds, and he was able to marry Miss Sedgwick.

In 1930, when Allen came to the National Audubon Society, it was modestly housed over a funeral parlor on Broadway. During the next ten years the Society not only expanded but, in accordance with new needs, began a program of research and field studies. Allen was promoted from book sorter to full-time ornithologist. He emerged from the basement to make a study of gulls on the Maine coast. A friend commented that sending Allen into the field was like "ordering a duck back to water." The Society had also begun to set up a department of sanctuaries. In 1934, after growing a mustache in order to look old enough to satisfy the board of directors, Allen became sanctuary director. Five years later, in 1939, the plight of the roseate spoonbill, a large, gaudily beautiful, shore-dwelling bird native to Florida and Texas, became urgent. Allen was assigned to a full-scale study. With his family, which by then included a son and daughter, he moved to Tavernier, a little town on Key Largo at the tip of Florida. The Allens set up housekeeping in a trailer close to the home of the spoonbills on Bottlepoint Key. A year later he was able to make recommendations that undoubtedly saved that colony of birds. His spoonbill monograph, published in 1942, is considered a classic life history. By the time it had appeared in print, Allen was in the Army, on sea duty, serving as a mate on an Army minelayer.

When, on his return, John Baker told Allen that the whooping cranes were now his problem, he already had an inkling of what the project would entail. Six years before, the study of spoonbills had taken him to the Texas coast, where he saw his first whooping crane. "I wondered idly," he later wrote, "what poor, un-suspecting soul would some day be assigned the rugged task of making a full-scale study of them."

Meanwhile, at Aransas, the whoopers had been doing slightly better than holding their own. In the winter of 1945–46 official refuge figures showed only seventeen cranes, but Dr. Pettingill, who twice searched the coast by plane, concluded that the total population was twenty-five, with nine of the cranes spending most of their time on the island of Matagorda. There were, however, only three young whoopers, including a pair of twins.

In the spring of 1946 four of the flock stayed behind to summer on the refuge. Two were the young twins who, for some unexplained reason, failed to follow their parents north. The others were two single birds, both of them crippled and unable to fly, who joined forces during the summer. Luckily the summer weather was calm and the four came through without incident. When, in the autumn of 1946, the rest of the flock returned, they had again brought with them only three youngsters. Robert Allen reached Aransas in November to begin work on the Whooping Crane Project, and found that the world's population of migratory whooping cranes was twenty-five.

6

When Allen came to the Aransas Refuge in November 1946, it was approached as it is now, by a state road that cuts through vast flat, tilled fields. In winter the furrows look like black corduroy stretched out to the horizon. Far-off houses and a few windmills stand up like ships at sea. In this openness the sky seems higher and wider than elsewhere. Often the sky is busy with fast-moving clouds that darken and lighten the landscape in quick succession. There may be sudden showers followed by dramatically golden sunbursts. Gradually, approaching the shore of San Antonio Bay, the land becomes more wooded, with clumps of oak and mesquite breaking the geometric pattern of the fields. Just before the gates of the refuge there is a pebbly shore, white with shells—at the moment inhabited only by a collection of rusted tin shacks called Pete's Camp—and beyond it the shallow waters of the bay whose horizon is dotted by offshore oil rigs and the lumpy craft that tend them.

The road leads through modest gates to the refuge, and to a different landscape. Here there has been little cutting for over thirty years. There are handsome groves of oaks and everywhere lush tangles of shrub and vine. Things are more manicured now than they were when Allen arrived. There are a neat, cement-block headquarters building and pleasant little houses for the staff. At almost any time there are apt to be white-tailed deer—two or three or perhaps more—browsing in the clearing around the buildings. When visitors arrive, the deer stare as though incredulous at the intrusion, and after a moment's thought leap suddenly into the thickets with a rocking motion, as though their legs were pogo sticks.

Although Aransas is tidier now than it was when Allen worked there, its essential appearance is unchanged. The shell-paved roads wind past shrub and thicket and grove. Armadillos creep nearsightedly through the wiry grass. It is possible to glimpse wary, tough little javelinas—small, native peccary—and big wild pigs that are descended from European boars released there years ago by Leroy Denman. From time to time there is a boar roundup followed by roast pork on the menus of deserving local institutions and a barbecue for the staff. There are thirty or forty species of mammals on the refuge—and almost three hundred species of birds have been sighted there. But all this goes on in the wooded uplands, and is for the most part remote from the world of the whooping cranes out on the marsh.

In November, the Allens arrived and set up housekeeping in the town of Austwell, eight miles from the gates of Aransas. Austwell was an extremely modest settlement (population 287) housed in a collection of gray frame buildings. The social head-

quarters in Allen's day was in Cap Daniel's combination beer
parlor, gas station, and garage. Here Allen sounded local opinion
and found that the town's leading citizens were either indifferent
to whooping cranes or resentful because birds that had been declared legally inedible were supported in idleness on taxpayers'
money. Allen regarded it as an important victory when, two
years later, the proprietor, a great collector of junk and me-
mentos, not only asked for a photograph of a whooping crane
but, in order to make room for it, unhesitatingly wrenched from
the wall a large lithograph of Judge Roy Bean holding court west
of the Pecos. In Texas this is almost a sacred scene. Such a grat-
ifying change in local attitude was due to a great deal of patient
missionary work on the part of both the Allens. Mrs. Allen, a
woman with a talent for making friends in whatever social milieu
she found herself, did not scorn to put her Juilliard training to
work. She played the organ in Austwell's tiny church, and little
by little helped to convince even the most skeptical of her neighbors that ornithologists are not necessarily lunatic feather collectors.

On a dismally gray, cold day in November, Allen began his
study of the cranes. He and the new refuge manager, Bud Keefer,
who had recently replaced Craven, tramped along the higher
ground overlooking the flats until they caught sight of two white
forms, distinct against the golden-tan sand. Allen made his first
field notes on the cranes: "Two adult wh. cranes on wet mud flat
in Redfish Slough. Fed a little and rested, preening. ½ to ¾ mi.
distant from our position on dike." Later he added: "I remember
that those first two birds seemed very far away—not only in a
physical sense. Their arrogant bearing, the trim of their sails, as
it were, would intimidate the most brash investigator. I reached
our cabin that first night feeling very humble and not too happy."

Getting close to the whooping canes in a physical sense was a
very real problem. The birds proved to be extremely wary of
anyone moving on foot. Later, Allen found that they are less easily disturbed by the approach of an automobile and that a boat

on the Intracoastal Waterway can come within fifty yards as long as it keeps moving at a steady pace. But Allen had no boat and there was no automobile road from which he could scan the marsh. For his first surveys he and Keefer used a tractor to draw an old farm wagon—Keefer at the controls and Allen standing in the wagon, trying to hang on to his field glasses and the wagon at the same time—following a rough trail along the twelve miles of shorefront.

In these first winter months crane-watching remained frustrating, chilly work. For a time it seemed as though a half a mile were as close as Allen would get to them. Then one day he suddenly surprised a pair not fifty yards away. "They were already moving," he later wrote, "sounding their bugle-clear trumpet blast of warning and running with amazingly lengthy strides before getting airborne. The red skin on top of their heads stood out clearly, and so did the grim, almost fierce cast of their features . . . like great, satin-white bombers, with their immense wings flicking upward in short arcs and their heavy bodies fighting for altitude, still calling, they glided over the tops of the scrub, slowly gaining elevation. . . . I had forgotten how cold I was . . . my hand was shaking when I started to write my notes."

At one point in his efforts to get close to the cranes, Allen, who had noticed that the birds were indifferent to cattle wandering on their territory, went so far as to construct a portable blind in the shape of a bull. His contraption, consisting of a red canvas hide stretched over a wire frame, turned out so convincing that he named it "Bovus absurdus." This realism was almost Allen's undoing. He had placed Bovus on the marsh and hidden himself inside, waiting for cranes to appear, when, to his horror, he saw a real bull—huge and baleful—advancing to challenge the supposed interloper. For a few dreadful moments the real bull glared at Bovus, and its quaking occupant, with puzzled hostility. Then, apparently deeming Bovus unworthy of combat, the bull wandered off. Allen scrambled out of his disguise determined to find other means of observing cranes.

As Allen became more familiar with the marshes, he found vantage points from which he could creep within fifty yards of feeding cranes without flushing the birds. Gradually each family took on an identity in his mind. He named them according to the territory they occupied—the Slough Pair, Middle Pond Family, Dike Pair, and so on. Gradually, too, he became acquainted with the invisible boundaries separating the domains of each pair, and began to discover some of the essential rules of whooping crane behavior.

In addition to watching the cranes as they went about their daily rounds, Allen spent long hours painstakingly putting together notes about the habitat on which they depended. He studied the action of wind and tide on the food supply in the ponds, and how this in turn caused the cranes to move here or there. He counted two hundred marine worms per cubic foot of Aransas mud, and watched the comings and goings of the blue crab, a vital link in the food chain that feeds the cranes.

When Robert Allen took over the Whooping Crane Project from Dr. Pettingill, he noted with interest that Pettingill had discovered two whooping cranes in captivity: Josephine, the White Lake survivor who had been at the New Orleans Zoo since 1941, and the one-eyed whooping crane, now named Pete, who had been kept by the Gothenburg Gun Club in Nebraska since 1936. Although no one knew the sex of these birds, Pettingill had suggested that bringing them together might be worth a try. Allen was intrigued by the idea, and decided to take time off from the work at Aransas to visit New Orleans and look at Josephine. He recorded his impressions in these notes:

"Audubon Park, New Orleans, December 4, 1946. I found the second known whooping crane in captivity in an ordinary exhibition pen, between similar pens containing a lone sarus crane on one side and a group of peafowl on the other. The sign on the wire of the cage, black letters painted on a white board: 'whooping crane—North America.' Most people visiting this section of the zoo were more attracted by the Nile Hippos. Whether this bird is a male or a female is impossible to decide. It is evidently in good or even excellent health, alert and with a good appetite. According to the employees of the zoo it will eat almost anything offered to it; peanuts, popcorn, potato chips, bits of bread and uneaten portions of hamburger, frankfurters. . . . We tried salted peanuts and the crane came close to the wire, catching them in the air as they were thrown through the netting. As it approached and while waiting for additional offerings it gave a low clucking note. Every now and then, as a number of salted peanuts were eaten, the whooper walked with dignity to its concrete water trough and drank, raising its head to swallow. The tameness of the bird is remarkable in view of its shyness in nature. It seems perfectly adapted to its life behind wire, and seems on good terms with its environment, with the crowds of staring people, the noisy children, the traffic along the adjoining road, the shrill blast of the nearby train whistle and even the endless barking of a seal in an adjacent aquarium.

"This captive whooper is an appealing individual, and even though its confinement has taken from it some of its majesty, its very tameness lends it a charm that is undeniable. And yet much of the majesty remains, even in the act of catching peanuts in midair."

As it happened, the zoo director, George Douglass, was not in his office that day, and he and Allen did not meet.

During the winter Allen made one other excursion from Aransas. He had still not given up hope that there might be other whooping cranes besides those at the refuge. In a plane chartered by the Fish and Wildlife Service he flew low along the entire coast from Louisiana to Mexico, but saw no whoopers. At the same time the Fish and Wildlife Service sent Dr. Saunders, the ornithologist who had originally surveyed Aransas, to search the former haunts of the whooping cranes in Mexico, again to no avail. Now the ornithological world at last regretfully concluded that the twenty-five cranes wintering at Aransas and the Louisiana remnant at White Lake—by then reduced to two—were the only whooping cranes left at large in the world.

In March 1947, Allen temporarily put aside his biological studies at Aransas to take up another phase of the work, a study of the whoopers' migration and a search for the nesting grounds. From an analysis of old reports Allen felt sure that the migrating cranes followed a more or less fixed pathway north, and he guessed that at one point they would cross the Big Bend of the Platte River in Nebraska. He left Aransas ahead of the cranes —who would not start their flight until April—hoping to intercept them in what would be one of the most unlikely rendezvous ever attempted. If he succeeded in meeting whooping cranes in Nebraska, he would know how long they had taken on this first leg of the migration, and thus calculate when they would reach the mysterious nesting grounds.

Allen chose North Platte, Nebraska, as his headquarters. The local paper obligingly printed his request that anyone sighting a whooping crane telephone him at the Hotel Pawnee. During the next month he got tips daily from housewives, truckdrivers, farmers, and other bird-watchers. Collectively they reported 144 whooping cranes. Allen checked each report, and identified the birds as ring-billed gulls, white pelicans, lesser sandhills, or snow geese.

In the first week of April the cranes at Aransas began to move about restlessly, and even to join up in groups as though some attraction were breaking down the social barriers of winter. The refuge manager counted the cranes daily and wired Allen each time he found a family or group missing from its usual haunts, presumably having started on the long flight north. Two crippled cranes remained on the refuge for the summer. Allen had mapped out a two-hundred-mile stretch of the Platte River where the whooping cranes were most likely to appear, and he tried to patrol at least part of the area each day. During the two weeks that whooping cranes were in flight, he flew 800 miles, drove 3,172 miles along the river, and walked more miles of river bottom than he could keep track of.

Finally, on April 14, he got news of a trio of whooping cranes, identified by a reliable informant, near Overton, Kansas. Since the only trio in flight had left Aransas on April 9, Allen now knew that the cranes had flown 920 miles in four days and a few hours.

Allen redoubled his efforts to be everywhere along the whooper front at once, but for five days there were only false alarms. Then, at last, he made his improbable rendezvous. "My five birds landed in Earl Mathers' corn stubble field, three miles east of North Platte at 7:35 A.M. April 19," Allen wrote to Baker. "Thanks to the radio publicity, he recognized them, dropped his farm chores, and sped one mile to a telephone. Meanwhile his wife saw the whoopers move out, flying off southwest. Shortly after 8 A.M. I was at the Mathers farm. No whoopers, but a hundred and twenty-four white pelicans were on the nearby Diversion Dam. After fruitlessly trudging the adjacent river bottom with Mathers, I drove to the airport and chartered a plane. In ten minutes I located the whoopers bunched together on a sandbar in the South Platte River." As the plane swept low over the birds, Allen saw a tinge of russet in the plumage of one of them and thus recognized it as the youngster of the North Family that had left Aransas in company with their winter neighbors, the Slough Pair. Allen felt as though he were greeting old friends.

The next day the whoopers had moved on. Allen got a few more reports of cranes sighted on their way to the Canadian border. After that, their trail vanished. Ahead of them lay the most dangerous part of their journey, over the wheatlands and prairies of Saskatchewan, once the heart of their territory. Here the farmers are particularly hostile to any birds that invade their grain fields, and here, Allen suspected, the whoopers, particularly the unmated yearlings, may be tempted to linger, lured by what he called their "biotic niche."

As the cranes vanished toward the north, Allen prepared to

pick up the search for the nesting grounds where Dr. Pettingill had left off the summer before. Mrs. Allen and their two children joined him and, equipped with camping gear, they set forth in a station wagon and trailer, headed for the Canadian bush.

Although to hunt for twenty-odd birds, even big white ones, in millions of acres of wilderness presented a fantastically difficult assignment, Allen was convinced that finding the nests was of crucial importance in order to answer a number of biological questions. He was vitally interested in knowing what percentage of the flock was attempting to breed and how many young were being lost because of weather, predators, or other factors on the breeding ground. A count of fledglings at the nesting ground compared with the number of young reaching Aransas would show what proportion were lost on the fall migration. Finally, of course, it seemed important that conservationists find the nesting grounds before some commercial project stumbled over and destroyed them.

As Allen set out on his search, the trail of the migrating whoopers was dim indeed. Plotted on a map, all the available clues—and there were not many—seemed to describe a straight line from Aransas to Regina, Saskatchewan, but then the birds fanned out toward the northwest, and vanished. Allen decided to drive north of Regina to the end of the road and then search by air.

He found that each summer the Canadian Fish and Wildlife Service sent a small plane to make an aerial census of waterfowl nesting in the Northwest Territories. The Service's biologist, Robert Smith, was eager to help in the search for whooping crane nests, and the Service agreed that he should take Allen along in the plane.

In early May, Allen and his family drove to Flotten Lake, Saskatchewan, at the edge of the bush, and made camp. Allen found it a disappointingly busy wilderness. Indians, loggers, and mink ranchers had taken over all the marshes and lakes that might have sheltered nesting whooping cranes.

On June 6 Smith picked up Allen, and the two men spent weeks flying at low altitude and scanning the wilderness beneath for any sign of a white bird. Their flight path, covering almost six thousand miles, took them across northern Alberta, then north to the Lake Claire area, and finally to Great Slave Lake in the District of Mackenzie. Here, on June 25, finding nothing but endless barrens ahead, unlikely for cranes, they turned back in defeat and headed south and east toward their base at Fort Smith. Their route home took them over the northern corner of a wilderness preserve named Wood Buffalo Park. Beneath the plane was a wild region of muskeg, sparsely covered with tamarack and pitted with pothole ponds and lakes. Here Allen's psychic sense should have given him a nudge, but, as the plane suddenly ran into heavy rain that blotted out his view of the ground, Allen noted only, "1:40 P.M. Rain squall. Rough going. Poor visibility all the way in . . . This ends our search. We have no further possibilities on our list!"

Years later, when the nests had been found, Allen realized that as he wrote those words he was directly over the whooping cranes' nesting place, at that moment veiled by the sheets of rain.

If Allen's search had produced no whoopers' nests it had at least stirred a wide public interest in the quest. Most news accounts were friendly, but one Canadian magazine wrote of "a bird's nest hunt that has cost $75,000 without an egg yet to show for it." The truth was, of course, that the search had been done on a shoestring. Allen's flights with Smith were combined with the Service's regular surveys, and cost the taxpayers nothing extra, but the story launched a rumor of extravagance that haunted the Whooping Crane Project for years.

More helpfully, *Life* magazine ran a story on the cranes that stirred sympathy for their plight, but also added its mite of confusion. It spoke of a plan to trail the cranes to their nesting grounds. Some readers assumed that Allen, aboard a plane, would cruise along beside the birds at forty-five miles an hour, wing to wing and perhaps roosting on an adjoining sandbar at night. Helpful readers suggested that the birds be banded with "radar bands" to make such tracking easier. Somehow this caused the Air Force to issue a straight-faced report on "minimum reflective surface for radar waves" and the technical inadvisability of following metal-banded birds with radar-equipped aircraft.

7

On his return to Texas after the summer search of 1947, Allen again took up his study of the habitat at Aransas while he waited, in considerable suspense, for the migrant cranes to come back from Canada. He was happy to see that the two crippled whooping cranes that had remained on the refuge had come safely through the summer. He named them the Summer Pair.

In early October an east wind that blew day after day filled the pond system of the refuge to overflowing with salt water, so that a bounteous harvest of blue crabs and small marine creatures awaited the whooping cranes. On October 21 the first migrant whooping crane, a single, was seen on the refuge. Five days later it was joined by a pair and a trio of adults. The first pair to bring back a youngster arrived November 2. Allen was able to watch them as they rested and fed near Mustang Lake. They seemed very quiet, and visibly tired by their tremendous journey.

Day by day more travelers returned. Allen checked off each arrival with mounting satisfaction. A second young bird arrived, then a third. Families with young are often the last to arrive because they must fly more slowly to accommodate the youngster. Finally all twenty-three birds that had migrated in the spring were back, safe and sound, and there were six young birds with them. Counting the Summer Pair, there was now the fine total of thirty-one whooping cranes; the highest in the nine years that records had been kept at Aransas and the third time on the record that there had been no losses during the summer.

Allen now took up the problem of how to spy on the private lives of the whoopers. Considering the failure of Bovus absurdus, he abandoned the idea of a portable blind, and decided to try to attract them by scattering corn in strategic locations.

The cranes were briefly enthusiastic about these handouts. Then, to Allen's dismay, all but one family tired of corn, and would stalk off to their ponds to fish, leaving Allen alone in his blind. The exceptional family, however, saved the day for Allen. They were the Middle Pond Family, a fine pair with a young bird. Their appetite for corn remained constant. Allen worked out a method of baiting an area near the blind in the early dawn while the family still slept in their night roost across the pond, then creeping into his hiding place to await their arrival.

Once the birds were near, he dared not even sneeze lest he give the whole show away—and sometimes he sat in his cramped hiding place watching for ten hours at a stretch. In these hours of busy, quiet vigil Allen filled notebook after notebook with the tiny details that make up the winter life of the whooping crane. Rarely has a creature been so painstakingly documented.

When whooping cranes are *en famille* it is easy, Allen found, to tell the sexes apart. The male is not only larger than the female; he is also the acknowledged head of the family. It is he who decides where to feed, when to rest, when to move on. His mate and young may wander from his side, but they always return to him, not he to them. He is not influenced by their whims. His chief occupation is to guard and defend his family, and this is a role he takes with extreme seriousness. "His head is always snapping up to attention, his cold, yellow eyes scanning the complete arc of the horizon," Allen wrote. Even his step, the way he holds his head seem to express the solemnity of his responsibility.

The attitudes of the female, on the other hand, seemed to Allen to convey a gentler, more domestic character. Although she will support her mate in defensive actions, she seems to leave decisions in these matters up to him, as though she acts upon his orders. Her main activity is the care and feeding of her young. In the early winter months she keeps the youngster always at her side, and painstakingly teaches it the primary business of life—getting food.

In the autumn as the cranes arrive—in pairs, families, or singly—there is a short period in which the birds shift about on the marsh. The wanderings of the single birds, particularly, give a sense of confusion to the territorial scene. Then, in a series of brief, but intense, ceremonial encounters the strongest pairs establish their land titles. Thereafter, except for slight misunderstandings and skirmishes at the borders, there is usually a quiet and peaceful routine throughout the winter. The social relations of the whooping cranes on the wintering ground are as cool and orderly as in the most decorous suburban community.

The occupants of a territory, Allen found, do not usually leave that territory from the time they claim it until just prior to the spring migration. Toward the end of March, as migration nears, the rigid segregation breaks down, but until then each pair or family lives strictly alone. Cranes spending the winter in a territory at the east end of the salt flats never see those in territories at the west end. The birds move inland only under special conditions: when a severe "norther" drives them to find shelter in the oak groves, or "mottes," that dot the higher land behind the marshes; when they are attracted by some special delicacy, such as a new hatch of frogs in a freshwater pond; or in a drought year when the brackish water of their feeding ponds becomes too saline and they must search for fresher drinking water elsewhere.

Allen charted fourteen territories strung like adjoining house lots along the shore of the refuge. He felt that the limits of each may have been established many whooping crane generations in the past and that each pair returns to the same territory year after year—or attempts to—for it is always possible that a stronger pair will evict a weaker. Conceivably, territories are handed down in whooping crane families. If so, it is likely that primogeniture would apply.

Each territory on Allen's map covers a little more than four hundred acres, and includes all the necessities of whooping crane winter life. For the most part each is true salt flat, with waterfront for feeding, brackish ponds for drinking and sleeping, and an inland border of oak brush in which to shelter when the wind is high. Not all the territories are equally desirable. The best of all at Aransas, judging by the fact that birds that stay behind in the summer always choose it and that in winter its owners defend it with outstanding zeal, is the Middle Pond territory. Like most of the others, it has about a mile of beachfront, but its superiority, Allen felt, derived from its varied and well-balanced complex of ponds and estuaries, which remain stocked with food after others have failed.

Geese and whooping cranes are among the few birds in which the family does not break up at the end of the breeding season. In each case they migrate together to the winter quarters, spend the entire winter as a family, and do not separate until sometime during the spring journey north, or perhaps even later. Social status, among whooping cranes, depends upon the marital and parental situation. At the top of the social order are a pair with a young bird. It appears that the presence of the youngster stimulates a quicker temper and a fiercer attachment to home. Thus parents will defend their territory with greater determination than a childless couple, and usually triumph in a dispute. A mated pair, though childless, in turn makes stronger territorial claims than do either the lonely "singles"—who may be widowed or adolescent birds—or "companions," birds whose relationship is purely platonic. Singles or companions surrender their territory to the first challenger. They then wander, living hand to mouth as it were, chivied by the lords of whatever territories they chance to invade.

Whooping cranes are monogamous, and the attachment within a family is strong. A widowed parent continues to care for a young one. Both widows and widowers will accept new mates. However, it is suspected, on the basis of evidence that is not confined to the bird world, that the male whooping crane will make marital readjustments more readily than will the female.

Allen did not know at what age whooping cranes become mature and mate, nor when they become too old to produce fertile eggs. The oldest whooping crane on record lived to be more than forty—how much more is again unknown. This was a female purchased in 1892 by a certain Lord Lilford, who kept many species of cranes at Lilford Hall in England. For many years this bird, which lacked a mate, laid infertile eggs. When it ceased to lay eggs of its own, it brooded the eggs, also infertile, of a Manchurian crane with which it was penned. This whooper died on August 19, 1930, presumably of old age. At the time Allen wrote his monograph, the staying powers of Josephine and Crip had not yet been demonstrated, and he could find no evidence on which to base a guess concerning the whooper's life-span. In the wild, of course, there are few species whose members regularly reach old .age. Most whooping cranes in recent times have died violently. Since 1938, more than a hundred yearling whooping cranes have been recorded at Aransas. Had "natural causes" been their only enemy, and these all survived to breed, the flock would now be many hundreds strong.

Documenting the behavior of the subadult whooping cranes is a difficult matter. By the time it is a year old the young whooper has lost the outward signs of immaturity and from a distance cannot be distinguished from an adult. Thus, at Aransas, Allen could not determine which of the singles were subadults and which unmated for some other reason. From an analysis of records of birds sighted during the summer, he concluded that although unmated birds migrate they do not go the full distance to the breeding grounds but become what he called "summer wanderers."

Single whooping cranes, moving about in response to varying food and water conditions, have been reported in the prairie provinces over an extremely wide area. They have turned up in central Saskatchewan and in sections of western Alberta. Often they appear close to settlements in the neighborhood of crane nesting locations abandoned many years ago. Sometimes these nonbreeders travel together, in pairs, or even small groups, but quite obviously do not nest. Allen estimated that as much as 50 percent of the flock, during the years that he observed it, were in the nonbreeding category. How many of them were young, where they went in summer, and when they mated were things that he would have given a great deal to know.

The first whooping crane Allen came to know personally, as it were, was the male of the Summer Pair, a large and lordly individual that Allen named Crip because of his damaged left wing. Although Crip was unable to fly, he was strong and alert. Once Allen and Olaf Wallmo decided to corner Crip, and learned at first hand how fast a whooping crane can walk. The two men advanced on Crip from opposite sides of the marsh. "Crip calmly hiked up his bad wing," Allen later wrote, "and, head high, started off with those steady twenty-three-inch strides that a crane uses when he wants to run down a skittering blue crab or outwalk a couple of boy scouts, which is what we felt like. Olaf and I, floundering across mudholes, were hopelessly outdistanced in ten minutes." Crip had joined forces with another flightless bird that, like him, had probably been shot on the way south, and they had spent the summer of 1947 together on the salt flats of the choice Middle Pond territory, only to be ignominiously evicted by the stronger pair with young that Allen knew as the Middle Pond Family.

Eventually Crip and his mate settled on unclaimed territory near the canal in the vicinity of what is known as Rattlesnake Point Road. Allen put out corn for them here, as he had for the Middle Pond Family. They took to it and quickly learned to come for it daily. They seldom wandered far from the baited area except to fish along the canal near the lower end of the road.

Although the Middle Pond male had triumphed over Crip, he still had the Dike Pair to the east to keep in line. On December 19, for instance, Allen made these notes: "At 2:07 (as the Middle Ponders were preening and resting on a sandbar), the pair occupying the Dike territory to the east called. It was the usual challenging call, repeated several times. The Middle Pond male responded at once. Drawing himself to what seemed an amazing height, bill pointing straight up, he threw an answering challenge into the air. On the second call the female joined him, the young bird, although suddenly alert, made no sound. Abruptly all three took off, the male arching his neck and beginning his take-off a fraction of a second ahead of the other two. They flew about fifty yards to the east, which brought them to the buffer strip between the two territories. Then, with another series of calls, they ran forward, launched themselves in a low, skimming flight and headed straight for the offending Dike Pair. This carried them well inside the Dike Pair's territory. They seemed to feel that this was enough to satisfy their honor, for they landed again, nearly two hundred yards short of where the two Dike birds were standing, their heads high and whole manner one of extreme alertness. This ended the affair . . . both groups soon resumed their endless feeding, the Family gradually working back into their own bailiwick. This was a typical demonstration of the zeal and overpowering confidence of pairs with young, compared to a pair without young."

Allen had the opportunity to watch an unusual territorial problem when, in December 1948, a lone adult accompanied by one youngster made a belated arrival. From the parent bird's manner Allen guessed it to be a female. Apparently she had lost her mate along the migration route. From her late arrival it seemed likely that the male had been badly wounded, but lingered long enough to keep his family at his side for some weeks. When the two arrived, all the choice refuge territories were already occupied.

"This 'Extra Family' . . . ," Allen wrote, "insisted on trying to squeeze in between the Middle Pond Family and the Dike Pair, a boundary that was already jealously guarded. Again and again the two newcomers were chased, chiefly by the completely intolerant male of the Middle Family. Sometimes, during these chases, he would bear down on the lone female on the wing, force her into the air, and then harry her mercilessly, flying close on her tail for a mile or more. The fatherless youngster would fly also, but the chase always passed it by and an hour or more was often required for the homeless female to join her offspring again.

"Eventually the Extra Family spent much of its time in wet swales in the oak brush, beyond the limits of regular territories, where they were seldom bothered by other Whoopers. From these observations we decided that the presence of the male of a pair is essential to normal establishment of a territory and, further, that the insistence of the Extra Family on a site between the Dike and Middle Pond might indicate that the female had family connections with one of those areas. Perhaps the irate male of the Middle Family was her own father!"

However, not all meetings between crane families are hostile. Once, for example, Allen watched two adjoining families perform a strange ceremony for which he could not account:

"From the shelter of a live-oak thicket overlooking the flats I saw six Whooping Cranes close together in a bed of salt flat grass. . . . The first look showed them to be . . . two pairs and their rusty-plumaged young-of-the-year. They were some twenty-five yards apart, but as we watched the two males . . . separated themselves from their families and strutted slowly towards each other. Their strides were exaggerated and stiff, the wings dragging slightly, . . . their whole manner seemingly formal and almost self-conscious. . . . They came on until only a yard separated them, then stopped and looked about them. One dropped his head in a feeding movement and the other did likewise. But whatever emotion it was that spurred them on was strong medicine. They came within less than two feet of each other and repeated the feeding movement. Then both retreated a couple of feet. Suddenly they were close together again, and simultaneously their heads came up, bills pointing skyward, wings drooped, plumes raised over tail and back. Across the gray, misty flats we heard the thrilling trumpet call of the Whooping Crane. . . . After the first blast, during which the two males had their heads almost together, the females joined in, their posture the same as that of the males. The two young birds, standing idly on the outskirts of this performance, seemed to have no interest in the proceedings. . . . The males repeated their performance without the females' cooperation, then drew away from each other in a curious circling walk, heads down as if feeding. After a little, the males came together again, bowing this time, in short, stiff little nods. . . . They stood, finally, with their crimson crowns almost touching, bowing so low that their bills went back under the breast feathers and very nearly between the legs. . . .

"This remarkable show lasted over a period of 50 minutes, after which the two families calmly separated, each withdrawing into its own territory. The location of the demonstration had been the exact boundary between the two territorial claims."

8

When the Middle Pond Family arrived at Aransas their youngster was approximately five months old. It had learned to fly perhaps only six weeks before and yet had been able to follow its parents across more than two thousand miles of alien territory. On the ground it still looked small and awkward. Its wings, pinkish buff and cinnamon splotched with dull white, appeared too big for the rest of its rusty-plumaged body. Its head bristled with reddish feathers, giving a gawky, callow appearance that reminded Allen of an overly tall twelve-year-old boy whose hair needs brushing. But on the wing it would suddenly seem as large and capable as the adults. It had no trouble keeping up with them as they skimmed across the salt flats, and it landed with what Allen called "at least a simulation of dignity, to explore, with expert and solicitous guidance, the many wonders of their new habitation."

During the winter Allen was able to watch the young bird's maturation. In the first weeks it trailed closely after its parents. The female and young bird particularly were always side by side. The youngster's main interest was food, and at first it was fed almost entirely by the parents. (If there is only one youngster, the female takes on most of the feeding, Allen found, although the male will also offer it morsels from time to time. If there are twins, it later became evident, both parents care for both youngsters, but each is inclined to have a favorite to which most attention is devoted.)

At first the adult cranes feed the young by actually placing morsels, which they have broken into suitably small pieces, in the youngster's beak. Later the adult merely catches the prey, breaks it up, and places it before the youngster. By January the young crane has learned to search for its own food, with supplementary handouts still welcome, and by February it is feeding itself almost entirely. By this time, too, it is beginning to look like an adult, with the reddish plumage dropping away and being replaced by gleaming white.

Until the prenuptial dances of the parents become intense, in March or April, family life is orderly and calm. By that time the young crane has gained considerable confidence and taken experimental trips off on its own. Nevertheless, it quite evidently comes as a shock when, almost without warning, its parents' attitude changes and the painful process of weaning begins.

As Allen saw it: "One day, the young hopeful who has been so carefully guarded and nurtured for so many weeks, suddenly becomes a source of annoyance. Its own mother turns on the bewildered creature and drives it from her presence. The male, in his turn, chases it too, sometimes flying after the poor youngster for a mile or so before leaving it to its own, uncertain devices."

However, the tie between parents and young has not yet been totally severed. When it is time to migrate, the parents recall the young one to their side, and the three, a family once more, migrate together. Somewhere in the north a final parting occurs, but just when or where no one knows.

The dance of the whooping crane is a justly celebrated performance that has long fascinated human beings because of its

eerie resemblance to some human rites of spring. It is not peculiar to whoopers alone. Sandhills and other cranes perform a very
similar ballet. Allen believed that the dance has an emotional
basis and becomes more frequent and intense as the birds' sexual
cycle progresses through its various stages to full breeding condition. It may then serve to strengthen and cement the bond between the pair. There are other times, however, when the cranes
dance simply as a physical and emotional outlet, a means of
releasing tension. Later, when Allen was able to watch nesting
birds, he saw a bird, relieved from duty, arise after a long,
wearying spell on the nest, walk a short distance, and then
silently whirl and leap in a solitary dance.

Allen saw the first signs of a new breeding cycle at Aransas in
late December or early January. At first only one bird of a pair
would begin a dance, leaping into the air, flapping its wings and
bowing, but then quickly settle down again. As the season
progressed its mate joined in. Allen described a brief but complete dance thus: "The 26th [of January] was warm and clear, in
contrast to the wet and chilly weather of January 10. The same
pair that we had watched in a partial dance on the earlier date
were observed moving slowly along the far bank of Middle Pond.
Suddenly one bird (the male?) began bowing his head and flapping his wings. At the same time he leaped stiffly into the air, an
amazing bounce on stiffened legs that carried him nearly three
feet off the ground. In the air he threw his head back so that the
bill pointed skyward, neck arched over his back. Throughout this
leap the great wings were constantly flapping, their long black
flight feathers in striking contrast to the dazzling white of the
rest of the plumage. The second bird (the female?) was facing
the first when he reached the ground after completing the initial
bounce. She ran forward a few steps, pumping her head up and
down and flapping her wings. Then both birds leaped into the
air, wings flapping, necks doubled up over their backs, legs
thrust downward stiffly. Again they leaped, bouncing as if on
pogo sticks. On the ground they ran towards each other, bowing

and spreading their huge wings. Then another leap! The climax was almost frantic, both birds leaping two and three times in succession. Quickly it was all over, after about four minutes, and an extended period of preening followed."

As the day of migration draws near, the birds' emotions become increasingly hair-trigger. Any small excitement can provoke a dance, as when Allen saw a male crane leap to threaten a group of intruding ducks, and suddenly transmute these leaps into the pirouettes of a dance.

On April 3, 1948, just a few days prior to migration, Allen watched his now familiar Middle Pond Family in a typical display. "On this particular day the female was more interested in dancing than the male. While he fed, she and the now well-grown youngster were bathing, the offspring imitating the movements of the female. They were standing in water about 15 inches deep. The female would crouch hesitantly, like a bather cautiously feeling the water with an exploratory toe.

"Then she would dip all the way under, except for her head and neck, splashing up and down, shaking her partly open wings, wiggling her tail and throwing her head about so that her crown stroked the feathers of her back. The immature Whooper imitated all this awkwardly. Then both birds stood and shook themselves vigorously, flapped their wings, wiggled their tails, ran their bills through their dripping primaries and began jumping up and down. The male kept on with his feeding. Then the female began leaping and flapping in a wide circle, running as she leaped. The immature crane watched and started to follow suit. The female turned and, with head lowered as in an attack, chased the youngster. She chased it repeatedly. Though obviously bewildered, the youngster continued following her and attempting to leap and circle as she did, wings flapping. After a little, the male, looking up from his searching, walked towards the female, leaped and beat his wings a few times. But no complete dance resulted. The routine of the long winter months was nearly broken. There was an air of excitement, of impending change. The cranes seemed almost as if poised, ready, waiting for the sound of a starting gun."

Unfortunately, not all the events that Allen observed on the marsh were as orderly as the private lives of the cranes. In the course of the two winters that he spent at Aransas, Allen became increasingly distressed as more and more threats pressed in upon the refuge.

Oil, under the water or on land, was a sword always poised over the refuge. In early 1948, Allen learned that the Western Natural Gas Company of Houston, on a sublease from Continental Oil, was preparing to drill on the sand flats in prime whooping crane territory. This, it seemed, might be the beginning of the final disaster. Allen telephoned John Baker in New York. A conference was arranged with the company's officers at which Allen and Baker explained the probable consequences to the cranes. To its great credit the company saw the point. While they did not abandon the plan entirely, the officers agreed to drill in summer when the cranes would be absent, and to take other precautions designed to protect the cranes' winter habitat.

Meanwhile, it became increasingly obvious to Allen that poachers could come and go on the refuge almost as they pleased. In March 1948, someone—who was never caught—came onto the refuge and shot the flightless female of the Summer Pair. Allen found the bird lying wounded on the salt marsh. As Allen approached she managed to get up and struggle into the brush, but he had seen that her breast was stained with blood. The next day Allen and Refuge Manager Keefer found her again. They caught her and carried her to refuge headquarters, hoping that a veterinary might save her, but the bird died within a few hours. In addition to the old wound crippling her wing, there was a recent bullet wound through the trachea.

Allen reported her death in a long memorandum to Washington. Then, in a "Progress Report" he made a vehement plea for better protection for the whooping cranes. "Direct protection," he wrote, "is a first essential. There is no point providing a habitat if no wild life remains to live in it. In the case of the whooping crane every loss is a calamity and every calamity is a long step toward the extinction that we are making it our business to prevent."

Allen reviewed the way in which the whooping cranes' security had first been breached by the waterway: "The cranes are disturbed every day by lines of great barges that bear down on these ancestral shores, pushed by throbbing, purposeful tug boats; or by fleets of fast-moving shrimp boats, sending up a swirl and wash of churned water that engulfs the *alterniflora* on the banks and scatters the schools of small fry in whirling eddies of sudden and unfamiliar motion."

Allen told how he had often watched whooping cranes, feeding quietly on the shore of the refuge, forced to fly as oil barges or shrimp boats bore down on them. He cited a specific episode in which a pair of feeding whoopers were so repeatedly disturbed by boats that they gave up feeding and flew to a different strip of shore, only to be harried by a light airplane: "It continued to dive and circle the poor birds until they rose and flew toward the outside edge of their territory." In doing so the whoopers passed directly over a fleet of fishing boats in the canal where there might easily have been a gunner unable to tell a crane from a pelican.

There was ample evidence that there were gunners aboard the boats that passed within easy range of the feeding cranes. Once Allen saw a boy on a passing shrimp boat fire at ducks and feeding whooping cranes. The whoopers, sounding their loud alarm notes, took wing, and escaped. On another occasion, as Allen was watching the East Family of cranes he saw a barge approach. On deck was a man with a shotgun in his hands, firing at ducks along the canal. Luckily, the whooping cranes were just out of range and did not fly, but they could as easily have been at the edge of the canal. At the end of the 1947 shooting season, Allen found a duck blind on the refuge within the territory of a family of whooping cranes. The litter of empty shells around it showed that it had seen considerable use without being noticed by refuge personnel. "I want to make it clear," Allen wrote, "that I have no intention of censuring Refuge personnel or the Service . . . on the other hand if some of these facts are known . . . it should be possible to overcome many of the inevitable barriers." He then listed measures that might give the cranes the extra protection they needed. The most urgent problem, Allen felt, was a full-time patrol of the waterway. At that time the refuge possessed no boat, nor even a place to bring one ashore through the shallows. Allen proposed that a channel be dredged and the refuge equipped with a small, fast boat so that a refuge patrolman could overtake and disarm poachers.

Allen's memorandum also discussed ways in which the cranes could be lured from dangerous proximity to the waterway by supplementary feeding. He suggested that grain crops be planted for them and brushy plots burned over regularly to make acorns and insects accessible. He stressed the increasingly serious menace of oil pollution of the refuge waters and the need for stronger legal power to prevent it. Finally, he took up the matter of "improvement" of the refuge for the benefit of ducks and geese, pointing out that any tampering with the water systems of the refuge that would allow fresh water to flood the marshes and lessen their salinity would be a blow to the food supply of the cranes.

Washington officials of the Fish and Wildlife Service make the decisions ultimately carried out in the field, but as in all bureaucratic systems, orders travel a route that is often long and complex. The Service's refuges are not administered directly from Washington but through a system of five regional headquarters, each responsible for all the refuges within its area. The Aransas Refuge is the responsibility of the regional director in Albuquerque, New Mexico. Washington therefore replied to Allen's memorandum by saying that his recommendations would be given close attention. The problem of patrol would be taken up with the regional director with the request that Aransas personnel redouble their efforts.

What Washington didn't answer, of course, was the question

implicit in all of Allen's warnings and recommendations: How far out of its way would the Service go in its efforts to preserve the whooping cranes? How much of its limited funds should it spend on them, if it meant neglect of other urgent needs? With the Aransas Refuge serving to protect most of its animal inhabitants quite adequately, how much more should be done for such difficult, finicky guests as the cranes—guests who might at any moment take it into their heads to depart?

9

Shortly after his initial visit in 1946 to the New Orleans Zoo to see Josephine, the captive whooping crane, Allen began negotiations to bring her together with Pete, the one-eyed whooper that had been the guest of the Gothenburg Gun Club in Nebraska since 1936. He wrote to the custodian of each bird, carefully explaining the critical situation of the species and the great benefit to the cause of the cranes if the meeting of the two birds should prove fruitful. Both George Douglass, superintendent of the New Orleans Zoo, and the spokesman for the Gun Club replied that they would be glad to cooperate by lending their birds.

The next step was to find a suitable place in which to attempt to breed them. Allen toyed with, and discarded, the idea of turning the flightless birds loose at Aransas and letting nature take its course. A second possibility, that of caging them at Aransas in a large enclosure, would involve persuading the Fish and Wildlife Service to spend a considerable sum to build a fence. There was a third possibility—to have the birds kept at a zoo where, presumably, there would be the advantage of expert care. Among the possibilities were Chicago's Lincoln Park Zoo, which had a large flying cage, or the St. Louis Zoo, which had had considerable success in breeding rare birds. Fred Stark, director of the small but excellent San Antonio Zoo, was also notable for his interest in aviculture. Finally, of course, there was the Audubon Park Zoo, which had the advantage that Josephine was already accustomed to life there.

During the summer of 1947 Allen and John Baker of the Audubon Society discussed the pros and cons by mail. Washington was cool to the idea of building a large pen at Aransas. The northern zoos had the disadvantage of cold climate. Allen had been far from impressed by the upkeep of the New Orleans Zoo. On the other hand, John Baker felt that it would be tactless to ask George Douglass to send his crane to San Antonio, also a southern zoo. In November 1947, John Baker visited New Orleans and met Douglass for the first time. He found him a cordial host, and eager to cooperate in the breeding experiment. "You'll like him," he wrote Allen at one point, and in another letter admonished him, "For Pete's sake, don't tell him his zoo isn't good enough!"

From Aransas, Allen wrote Baker that he now agreed that because of the difficulty of getting a proper enclosure at Aransas the best plan would be to send Pete to join Josephine at New Orleans.

It was a solution that Allen accepted without much enthusiasm. In a letter to Baker he apologized for "being difficult." He conceded that "despite a rather varied diet and exposure to crowds, noise and carbon monoxide," Josephine seemed to be in fine condition, but he insisted that a better cage, with running water, seclusion, more natural food, and enough headroom for dancing, would be essential to the success of the venture. Shortly thereafter Baker wrote Allen that Pete would arrive at New Orleans about December 15. Douglass had agreed to build two new, isolated pens. If things failed to work out well at New Orleans, Douglass would send both birds to Aransas.

The tricky business of organizing the transfer of Pete was handled by George P. Vierheller of the St. Louis Zoo. Pete arrived at the Audubon Park Zoo in late December 1947. His meeting with Josephine has not been recorded; but in early February, Baker wrote Allen relaying word from Douglass that the captives had been put together and were getting along well, although they showed no great interest in each other.

On March 15, 1948, Allen left Aransas to see for himself what was going on at New Orleans. What he saw there and how he felt about it is recorded in a memorandum dated March 29, and addressed to the Fish and Wildlife Service in Washington:

"On March 17th [1948] . . . I visited George Douglass at Audubon Park, New Orleans, and observed the two captive whooping cranes in their special enclosure on the grounds of the Audubon Park Zoo. I would be a dissembling coward if I did not admit that I was shocked and distressed by what I saw. The two birds are merely existing, shut up in a ridiculously small pen scarcely large enough for a pair of tame ducks. The pen is located in the 'backyard' of the zoo, close to rubbish and without anything even remotely resembling isolation from noise and casual, disinterested disturbances. The floor of the pen is covered more or less by short grass, now well trampled. There is no natural water, but the original pans of water have been replaced by metal washtubs filled with dirty water. The bottom of the wire does not meet the ground all around, and we saw rat tracks running through the mud around the tubs, indicating that rats come and go at will.

"There is no shade except the wood shack at one end. Mr. Douglass said that both birds go inside this shack on occasion. There is a bed of straw on the floor.

"The head room and ground space are both entirely inadequate for whooping cranes that have been placed together for the purpose of pairing off and, presumably, breeding. Even worse, their diet is almost certainly a guarantee that they will never breed again! Each bird is being fed the following daily amounts:

"1 and ½ lbs. scratch grain, 1 and ½ lbs. fish (cut in small pieces), 1 and ½ lbs. bread.

"Some time ago I wrote Mr. Douglass suggesting *live* crayfish and blue crabs. The blue crab, in particular, is unusually rich in nutritious values, including a high protein content and a wealth of vitamins A, B, and C. He recently offered a half dozen crayfish to the birds but they 'were too excited' to pay any attention to them. He wanted to know if soft-shelled crabs were 'anything like' blue crabs! While I was present he called a nearby café and ordered soft-shelled crabs from their deep-freeze with the idea of 'testing' my claim that the birds would take blue crabs and improve their general tone and condition on such a diet. Wow!! I tried to explain what poor food value is contained in ordinary store bread under these circumstances. I also attempted to describe the outward signs that demonstrate good physical condition in the species and especially the increasing gonadal development. The soft part color changes that I have noted in my wild birds are very definite, and I assured Mr. Douglass that until their *environment* and *diet* were greatly changed he would see no soft part color changes in these captive birds and could expect no breeding. I have a feeling that all this was mere mumbo-jumbo as far as he was concerned.

"Douglass seems to mean well, but he should not have charge of those precious birds! They both look bad, have poor color, general lack of tone. The Nebraska bird is highly nervous, almost hysterical (its original enclosure in Gothenburg was large, without a roof and was traversed by channels of the Platte River from which he secured live fish, frogs, etc.). I fear for the survival of both birds, particularly the Nebraska bird.

"To expect them—*if* male and female—to pair and breed and deposit a set of fertile eggs under the conditions described, is nothing short of idiotic. I must be absolutely honest and outspoken on this subject because it is too important to misrepresent or waste time being polite about or soft pedaling in any way in this type of private communication. Those birds must be moved and moved soon. Their present condition is a disgraceful thing! The species has suffered much but those two birds represent the lowest rung. I could have wept when I saw them, if I hadn't been so numb with anger and shame.

"I have an immediate suggestion. Directly southeast of the Aransas headquarters buildings and adjacent to Webb Point is an extensive salt flat marsh. Wind tides keep its ponds supplied with crabs, fish and other marine life from the open bay. In back of, and to the west of the salt flat area are heavy growths of *typha* and other fresh water aquatics, creating a splendid nesting environment. The location is sufficiently extensive to be isolated and yet near enough headquarters to be easily watched. It is far removed from the Intracoastal Canal.

"All that is needed to make this area a safe and adequate location for the two captive birds is some additional fencing. I have discussed the suitability of the habitat with Lynch, Keefer and others and the fencing problem with Keefer and other refuge personnel. All are enthusiastic about the location and willing to cooperate fully in working out plans for creating a practical enclosure.

"I have invited Douglass to come over here and he may do so soon. He will, I think, be eager to get rid of the two birds. He realizes, I believe, that they are more of a responsibility than he can handle with the facilities and experience at his command. When I show him the cat-tail marsh and adjacent salt flat ponds and outline our plans for an extensive enclosure I feel that he will cooperate whole-heartedly. He may wish to retain 'title' to his crane, so be it. We can keep it here more or less indefinitely and eventually, if no breeding occurs after several seasons and he wants it returned, it will not be difficult to catch."

Allen's report got prompt action in Washington. Within a few days the chief of the Division of Wildlife Research, to whom Allen had addressed himself, wrote that he would urge that the birds be moved to Aransas in accordance with Allen's recommendations. Shortly thereafter the Service ordered a wire fence nine feet high, enclosing the tract of a hundred and fifty acres that Allen had described. The fence would cost two thousand dollars. Until it was completed, however, Josephine and Pete would have to remain at New Orleans.

Douglass agreed readily enough to send the pair of cranes to Aransas. John Baker, who had taken on the task of keeping pleasant relations between all parties, wrote to thank him for permitting "the indefinite loan of your bird." "Certainly it should be understood," he wrote, "that if the experiment be a definite failure, your bird would be returned to you; moreover, that should your bird unfortunately die, or be injured while at Aransas, there would, of course, be no claim made by your Park Commission."

With relief Allen returned to the work of completing his notes on the biology of the cranes' habitat. A primary object of Allen's two years of study was to discover exactly what whooping cranes eat, a subject at that time completely undocumented. As Allen attacked the problem, he found himself in the frustrating position of watching the birds feed and yet being unable to see what was actually going down their throats. The first step was a painstaking study of the flora and fauna of the marsh. Then, from watching the cranes and studying the ground they had covered, he was able to deduce a great deal. A certain diagram of whooping crane tracks accompanied by scattered claws and shells showed where the birds had dug blue crabs out of their burrows. Elsewhere the birds had walked in a straight line, probing to right and left to pluck tiny marine worms from the soft mud. Eventually Allen was able to make a list of the main items on the whooper's menu. He felt that the blue crab was of such importance to the cranes' survival that the bureau should make a special study of its life cycle and make sure its numbers do not diminish. Next in importance are mud shrimp, annelid worms, and a miscellany of small marine creatures. Small fish appear on the list, but the cranes do not depend on them as they do on the crustaceans. When the whoopers feed in fresh water they are partial to crayfish, frogs, and aquatic insects. On land they will pursue grasshoppers, or almost any small "chance prey," including reptiles and birds. Vegetable food, in Allen's opinion, is not normally a major part of the cranes' diet, but they accept it on occasion.

As Allen watched the cranes in their final weeks before departure for the north, late in the spring of 1948, he happened to witness the next episode in the life story of Crip, the survivor of the Summer Pair. Crip had of course been single since the shooting of his mate in March. In April, as members of the flock began leaving, it seemed that Crip would be doomed to summer alone. Then, on April 17, a clear, bright spring day, Allen chanced to be walking down Rattlesnake Road when he heard a whooping crane call. "A single bird was in flight, headed north," Allen wrote. "On the far bank was Crip calling to it. The single bird answered, circled, and came to earth. She descended within ten feet of Crip. He walked off with dignity and she followed." Crip's call must have been a persuasive one, for his new lady stayed by his side all through the long, hot summer.

During the winter Allen had been making plans for a second trip to the north in search of whooping crane nests. A number of tips had come in. A Royal Canadian Air Force pilot wrote that he had seen cranes of "tremendous size" just south of the point where the Mackenzie River flows into the Arctic Ocean, a spot almost a thousand miles north and west of the areas that had previously been searched. A second suggestion mentioned Lac la Martre, north of Great Slave Lake; a third recommended the western shore of Hudson Bay.

These ideas fitted into a manageable pattern. The complete failure of previous searches in more southerly areas led Allen to think of territory farther north. There is a natural flyway for ducks, geese, and swans that channels northward along the Athabaska, Slave, and Mackenzie river routes. It seemed possible the cranes followed it as well.

As it happened, the wildlife services of both the United States and Canada were interested in getting estimates of waterfowl populations along the Arctic coasts. Again Allen arranged to join Robert Smith, the pilot-biologist with whom he had flown the previous summer. The two men could combine their missions so as to count waterfowl and at the same time look for whooping cranes in the far north.

In May, Allen drove from Texas to Regina, Saskatchewan, where he met Smith. On June 3 the two men started off in the little Widgeon belonging to the United States government. Again they flew to Fort Smith, unaware that they were, comparatively speaking, within a stone's throw of the hidden target, and flew on, almost a thousand miles farther north, to make what Allen called "a painstaking, low-altitude hunt—lake by lake, muskeg by muskeg."

In a month of flying, Allen and Smith covered more than fourteen thousand miles, going as far north as Point Barrow, Alaska, and the shores of the Arctic Ocean. In all that vast country they found not a single clue that might unlock the secret. The miserable climax of these futile miles was a forced landing in an Arctic lake. For sixteen hours, until the wind dropped, the two men stood in icy water, holding the wings of the light plane to prevent it from being battered to pieces on the rocky shore.

When the trip ended, Allen felt utterly baffled and discouraged. He wrote: "Once more we failed to locate the nesting grounds. Our only consolation is the realization that wherever this unknown place may be it is evidently hidden not only from us, but from anyone who might disturb the birds or do them harm. One thing seems certain: the place we are looking for is in virtual truth a lost land. It is probable that no human being, white or aboriginal, lives there, at least not in spring or summer. This would account for the unknown character of this enchanted spot, a never-never land that has resisted discovery by a naturalist since earliest times."

After this second summer of failure, Allen gave up the idea of further organized searches, since he now had no idea of where to look. There was always the hope, though, that someone else might accidentally come across new clues. Both the Canadian and United States Fish and Wildlife Service men in the north had been made thoroughly aware of the great whooping-crane-in-the-haystack hunt, and would be alert for any sign of the birds as they made their rounds.

Because Allen's field research at Aransas was now complete, on his return from Canada he went, not to Texas, but to his home in Florida, to write the monograph whose findings and recom-

mendations, he earnestly hoped, would help the Fish and Wildlife Service to help the whooping cranes survive. Checking up
on the summer's events at the refuge, he learned that it had been
a hot, dry summer. Crip and his new mate had ranged widely in
search of acceptable habitat, but had nevertheless come through
the summer in good condition.

In November 1948, the flock of twenty-eight that had migrated
in the spring returned. They had brought back three youngsters,
but three adults had fallen by the wayside, neatly canceling the
gain. With Crip and his mate there was now a flock of thirty
whooping cranes. This was a far healthier figure than the low
twenties of only a few years before, but it was one less than the
count of the autumn of the previous year. As Allen sat down to
work, it was with the sense that the whoopers were still operating on the thinnest of margins but that given any sort of chance
they could and would survive.

10

The enclosure at Aransas that was to receive the two captive
whooping cranes was ready in October 1948. The fence surrounded 150 acres that combined brackish marsh typical of
whooping crane winter territory with a freshwater cattail marsh
similar to the whooping cranes' natural nesting habitat. It was
the nearest thing possible to freedom. Meanwhile, Allen and
Baker had managed to have Josephine and Pete transferred from
New Orleans to the San Antonio Zoo. Fred Stark, its director, one
of the most skillful aviculturists in the country, had successfully
bred several species of rare cranes. He pinioned the captives'
crippled wings in order to reduce the chances of their injuring
themselves in an attempt to fly, and fed them a rich diet calculated to put them in breeding condition. Finally the birds were
trucked to Aransas, and released. Much to Allen's gratification,
they settled down almost immediately. They took up the busi-

ness of leading normal whooping crane lives—stalking blue crabs, fishing for shrimps, and searching the grass for frogs and insects —as though their freedom had never been interrupted. Josephine was already relatively tame, but Pete had always maintained an aloof manner during his twelve years of captivity. Now, however, he made friends with Mrs. Keefer, the wife of the refuge manager. Pete and Josephine came up to the fence every day for a ration of corn soaked in wheat-germ oil, and also, apparently, for the pleasure of Mrs. Keefer's company.

"As long as she stays there they stand, preen and snooze," Keefer wrote to Allen. "When she leaves they move off. They know her voice and when she talks to them, answer with a sort of guttural, rolling sound like they were trying to 'purr.' They will eat from her hand, but only from hers; not mine."

In December, Josephine and Pete performed a prenuptial dance. This hopeful news was relayed to Allen in Florida, to John Baker in New York, and to Fish and Wildlife officials in Washington and Canada. Rarely has the announcement of a betrothal been better received.

The dancing of the captives became more intense during March and April. Then, on April 27, at the hour when both birds usually came to the fence for their ration of corn, only one bird appeared. Keefer wondered if possibly the missing bird was on a nest. The next day again only one bird appeared. On the third day Keefer was able to see Pete crouching in the cattails while Josephine came up for corn. On April 30 Keefer went into the enclosure and sneaked toward the clump of cattails that sheltered Pete. As Keefer approached, Pete whooped a warning and rose to drive back the intruder. Keefer was pecked on the arm and hand before he retreated. He had seen the nest. It contained a single egg.

Four days later Keefer again approached the nest to photograph it. Both parents "raised an awful fuss, whooping and scolding." Josephine pecked at his right thumb, drawing blood, then grabbed his sleeve and tried to pull him away. She finally pecked him, hard, on top of the head. Keefer got his picture, but was glad to retreat. During the commotion Pete stood on the nest, hovering excitedly. There were now two eggs.

Allen, who was in Florida at the time, hurried to Texas and arrived on May 12. He posted himself in an observation tower overlooking the nesting area. There he spent each day, from dawn to dusk, keeping a minute-to-minute record of the activities of the nesting cranes.

The nest was a flat mound constructed chiefly of salt-flat grass, with some strands of cattail leaves and sea oxeye. Almost six feet across, but no more than ten inches high, it was well hidden in a dense growth of cattail, and surrounded by water that was at first almost a foot deep, but later went down to a few inches. The parents took turns incubating. At first there were usually six nest reliefs during the day. As the weather grew warmer, the birds exchanged duties more often. The male spent more time on the eggs during the day than did the female, averaging two hours at a spell to her one and a half hours. Overall, Pete did more than 70 percent of daytime incubation. Although it was impossible to see what happened at night, Allen assumed that Josephine was mostly on the eggs while her mate stood guard.

In his monograph Allen made this report: "When the incubating bird stood on the nest it was in plain view, from this vantage point, but when it settled on the eggs it was extremely difficult to see and was often out of sight completely. However, with the aid of a 19.5 spottingscope its movements generally could be followed without much loss of detail.

"The male was sometimes extremely restless and particular about his position on the eggs. On May 12th, after relieving the female at 8:12 A.M., he did not stir until 9:04 A.M. Then he stood and rearranged the position of his feet and of the eggs four times in the next 45 minutes. At 9:55 A.M., with the female standing close by, he walked off the nest, possibly to drink, and was back again within a few seconds. Although he stayed on the nest, except for momentary excursions of a few seconds each, until 12:55

P.M., the male rose and fussed with the eggs and the nest five more times. Once he added more nesting material. Some of the excursions were evidently for water.

"Also on May 12th, at dusk (7:10 P.M.), the male was on the eggs and the female, standing near the nest, raised her wings and jabbed with her bill at something in the cattails. The male remained motionless. Four minutes later the female sounded an alarm note and ran, wings partly opened, towards something in back of the nest. The incubating male never moved. Then we saw a large doe . . . retreating rapidly with the enraged female in pursuit. The male, low on the nest, sat like a statue.

"On occasion the incubating bird seemed to grow extremely weary. On May 14th, after the usual noontime relief, during which the two birds might exchange places on the eggs twice, or even three times, within a half hour, the male resumed his incubation at 1:30 P.M. . . . and when the female did not come near the nest by 4:20 P.M., the male simply stood up and with bill open, as if very hot and tired, walked off. The female, who was perhaps 20 yards off, immediately started directly towards the nest, covering the eggs two minutes later, after arranging them to suit her. . . .

"In both leaving and approaching the nest, the free bird nearly always followed a devious route through the cattails, disappearing for a space and then emerging 40 or 50 yards to one side. Once in the open this caution diminished and . . . the bird might dance briefly, but silently, or relax enough to bathe in a pool of fresh water. . . .

"The bird that was relieved at the nest often showed real pleasure at its release. Once Josephine stepped off the mound and Pete took over, . . . Josephine stood for a moment and then went running and skipping off toward the open marsh, her wings flapping gaily. Another time she walked as far as the nearest salt pond and, standing on the bank, did a wonderful little dance— apparently through sheer exuberance—twirling and leaping around and around, dipping her body low, wings extended, and then leaping sideways.

"In addition to feeding, the free bird spent a lot of time coping with real or imaginary dangers. One day when Pete was probing around on the higher ground, where painted buntings were singing beautifully from the mesquite brush, he came on a large rattlesnake, half coiled on a patch of bare ground. Pete walked up to him and started dancing up and down, wings flapping. Around and around the snake he went, the reptile's head turning slowly to watch him. After a few minutes Pete broke the impasse by suddenly walking off. On another occasion, however, he attacked a large cotton mouth moccasin, beat it to death by stabbing furiously at its head, and then swallowed it entire. . . .

"Most guard duty however consisted of chasing off other birds, especially American egrets, snowy egrets, Ward's herons, Louisiana herons, and roseate spoonbills. The Ward's heron and American egret were a particular anathema to him. At times the male would chase egrets the entire length of the salt pond, or nearly a mile. He seemed more cautious in attacking Ward's herons, but never failed to evict them, no matter how far from the nest the chase carried him.

"On May 21st, the male was relieved at 2:52 P.M. and walked immediately to the salt pond, where he chased a group of American egrets. When they simply flew to the far side of the pond he charged after them again. At this juncture a Ward's heron flew across the pond and came down on the west shore. The male turned from the egrets and gave his full attention to the Ward's. He actually *whooped* at it several times, strutting very stiffly and with an air of great dignity. Then he lowered his spear-like head and neck and charged, running with huge strides and flapping his wings rapidly, fairly skipping across the surface of the water. The heron, glaring at the male in what seemed a very disconcerted manner, stood his ground until the juggernaut was almost upon him. Then he rose and flew. The male, with only one complete wing, usually ended his charge at this point, slowing and shortening his stride, using his wings as a brake, arching his neck until it looked like that of a swan, and coming to a rather abrupt but wholly dignified stop. Two hapless egrets were standing nearby, uncertain whether to stay or fly, and the male settled the issue for them by walking towards them, his head high, his manner aggressive. The Ward's heron, discouraged, flew out of the enclosure. After another moment, the male charged the two egrets, and they quickly followed the Ward's. When every last intruder had been sent packing and the entire pond and salt flat were his, the male strutted back towards the nest, his solemn grandeur a joy to behold. . . .

"The female, a younger bird and in finer plumage, always looked clean and neat. The old male, from so much chasing through mud and water, was usually dirty and ruffled-looking. Sometimes, after a series of exhausting chases, he walked back towards the nest dripping wet and black underneath from the splashing mud. He was a game old warrior and did the best he could."

The exact period of incubation of whooping crane eggs was unknown, but there is usually a correlation between the volume of an egg and the time it takes to hatch. On this basis Allen guessed that Josephine's eggs should hatch on about the thirty-third day. But on the twenty-fourth day the routine of incubation was suddenly broken. Allen, watching in the tower, saw both birds acting strangely. They got on and off the nest in a restless fashion and poked anxiously at the eggs. Abruptly they left the nest, walked toward the open meadow together, and danced. Allen descended the tower and crept toward the nest. Josephine and Pete made no effort to stop him. He found the two eggs smashed—evidently by the parents. The remains were merely empty shells; the infertile contents dried up and futile.

Pete lived only another two months. At dawn on July 22 Josephine trumpeted in distress. The refuge manager, Julian Howard, who had taken Keefer's place, found her standing alone, whooping wildly. Pete lay dead, on his back, in shallow water. Postmortem showed no new injury. His death was ascribed to natural causes.

Since Josephine had shown herself willing and able to nest in captivity, it seemed urgent to find her another mate. Crip was the obvious candidate. He and his new mate had not nested, so Crip's potential was being wasted. Therefore, shortly after Pete's death Allen sent a memo to John Baker: "I strongly urge that our experiment be continued and that the first move should be to place Crip in the enclosure. Of course the odds are considerable that nothing will come of such a move, but it seems to me that at this stage of the game we can't very well afford to overlook any chances whatever. Even with a successful breeding next Spring the thread between survival and extinction remains very thin."

Washington agreed that Crip should be captured, but it was also decided to postpone the capture until cool weather. In early October a four-man posse chased Crip and his companion through the brush. Although the second bird was able to fly, it stayed at Crip's side until the men had almost closed in on them. Then it flew. Crip, struggling valiantly, was caught in a fishnet and released in Josephine's enclosure. Apparently Crip did not mourn his wild companion. To the satisfaction of all concerned, he and Josephine were compatible. Crip became tame quite quickly and soon joined Josephine at the fence at four each afternoon for dinner.

There was also satisfaction in the whooping crane circle, which now engaged in a regular exchange of information between Aransas, Washington, New York, and Florida, when the entire complement of cranes made a safe return from Canada with four young birds. The flock in the autumn of 1949 was thirty-four, the highest number in Aransas records. Allen was especially elated that the cranes had made the round trip without a fatality. He felt that perhaps the publicity of previous years might at last be influencing the hunters who would otherwise have shot at the migrant whoopers.

The winter on the refuge was relatively serene. Fortunately, the oil well that had been drilled on the marsh during the summer was dry, and no new drilling on crane habitat was impending. Although there were now ten producing wells, they were safely distant from the marsh.

During the ·winter, as it became certain that the capture of Crip had been a success, the whooping crane circle began to give serious thought to the idea of salvaging yet another bird as a potential breeder. This bird was the sole survivor of the White Lake colony to which Josephine had once belonged. Ever since the storm that had blown her and her companions out of the marsh five years earlier, John Lynch of the Fish and Wildlife Service had been keeping tabs on the small remnant that had returned. One by one this handful of birds dwindled. For the past two years Lynch had been able to find only a solitary bird. Everyone agreed that it should be captured, but how to do it was a perplexing problem. The bird ranged so widely that to lure it into a snare or trap seemed impractical. At length Allen and Lynch worked out a scheme to capture it by helicopter; their idea was to hover over the bird in such a way that the downdraft of the propellers would pin it to the ground. John Baker approved the project and so did Dr. Clarence Cottam, now the assistant director of the Fish and Wildlife Service, but Cottam warned Lynch: "Be careful! Biologists are expendable; whooping cranes are not."

On Saturday, March 11, 1950, a capture party assembled. Allen had arranged for the services of a helicopter and pilot. Lynch had the use of an ancient Stinson L-5. In addition to Lynch and Allen and the two pilots, the group included Nick Schexnayder, superintendent of Audubon's Rainey Wildlife Sanctuary south of Lafayette, Louisiana. The posse flushed the lone whooping crane from the marsh without too much difficulty, and then a wild air rodeo began. The Stinson managed to stay on the bird's tail as it twisted and turned, dived and soared. The crane's airspeed was clocked at forty-five miles an hour. Eventually the bird landed on the marsh and took cover in a clump of sawgrass. Allen and Schexnayder, in the helicopter, came to earth beside it. Both leaped out and grabbed the bird. In a moment they had a sack over its wings and its legs tied together. The captive seemed in good shape, considering what it had been through.

The men had planned to fly the bird to Aransas immediately, but bad weather suddenly made this impossible, so they decided to drive instead. The whooping crane, quickly named Mac in honor of the helicopter pilot, shared the back seat of Allen's sedan with Schexnayder. Lynch and Allen took turns driving through the night. For a while, as Allen drove, his companions fell asleep and began to snore. The crane evidently remained awake, for Allen heard it answer each snore with a low, guttural talking noise.

In the morning at Aransas they lifted the crane out of the car and prepared to turn it loose. To their dismay they found that the captive was in bad shape—too weak, in fact, to stand. It also occurred to the captors that this crane, unlike the Aransas whoopers, was accustomed to a freshwater environment and, in its weakened condition, might die of thirst on the brackish marsh. After considerable worried consultation, it was decided to pen the bird beside a small freshwater pond. While the refuge manager and his men hastily put up a fence, enclosing an acre or so, the others worked over the sick crane. The bird drank water and accepted small frogs that the men caught in the cattails. After its legs had been massaged to restore the circulation, the crane was able to stand, and it then allowed itself to be walked up and down the road. When the bird seemed to have picked up enough strength to look after itself, the flight feathers of one wing were clipped and it was turned loose in the enclosure. Then, hoping for the best, Allen and Lynch left the crane in the care of Howard, and returned to their homes.

On Monday, the second day of his captivity, Mac still would not feed himself, but walked ceaselessly along the fence of his pen, trying to get out. At length Howard decided the bird might do better if turned loose. He force-fed him and then took him to a freshwater area and released him. From here Mac walked a half a mile into the domain of a pair of wild whoopers, who attacked him. Mac, because of his clipped wing, was unable to escape. On Tuesday, Howard found the bird on the marsh, wet, dazed, and with blood from gashes on his head staining his feathers. Howard carried the wounded crane to his house, where he put him in the kitchen, and sent for Fred Stark. Stark treated the wounds, which turned out not to be serious. Again the main problem was the bird's refusal to eat, and after force-feeding him again, Howard decided that it would be best to turn Mac loose. This time he released him at a freshwater lake far from any other cranes. Here Mac seemed to get along well enough. Howard saw him from time to time during the spring and summer. Then, on September 1, Howard found Mac's corpse by the lake. The cause of death, whether injuries, disease, or improper environment, was not determined, but autopsy showed the bird to have been a female.

The death of Mac left Josephine the sole representative of the Louisiana strain of whooping cranes. No one knows if the Louisiana whoopers' ability to nest without migration was a trait determined by genetic makeup, but it is considered quite likely that it was. If so, this trait could have been invaluable in saving the species. If it were possible to breed whooping cranes of sedentary habit, it would be far more likely that captive-bred birds could be acclimated to the wild to start new flocks of whooping cranes. Sedentary cranes could be protected with infinitely greater ease than birds that must fly the length of the continent twice each year. Thus the loss of the next-to-last Louisiana bird was more than the loss of one individual—it was the loss of precious genes and irreplaceable opportunity.

Robert Allen felt, bitterly, that here was an object lesson in the perils of ignorance in handling wild whooping cranes. From this time forward he opposed all proposals to capture any of the wild flock. He had many reasons for his conviction that it should not be attempted, but among the strongest was his fear that further experiments in capturing cranes could turn out as fatally as they had in the case of Mac. And, as he had said before, "Every loss is a long step toward the extinction we are making it our business to prevent."

11

In April 1950, as the wild cranes were leaving the salt marshes of Aransas, Josephine and Crip built a nest. They built it far out on the open flats, amid short grass and in plain view, about a thousand feet from the tower. Newspaper stories announcing that the birds were nesting suddenly caught the public imagination. A flood of letters, wires, and telephone calls asking for news began to arrive at Aransas. Tourists from thirty-six states and from Canada and New Zealand visited the refuge, hoping for a glimpse of the celebrated birds. Julian Howard, the manager, found that his duties as host were taking a great deal of time. He also found it necessary to close the road to the marsh to all but refuge cars to prevent disturbance of the birds. Still the nesting cranes were occasionally bothered by trespassers who approached the nest site from the waterway.

As interest in the nesting of the whooping cranes continued to mount, shedding a warm radiance of publicity over everyone associated with them, George Douglass, in the shadows of the New Orleans Zoo, began to grow restive. He expressed his discontent to John Baker, who had persuaded him to continue his "loan" of Josephine for another year after the death of Pete.

Again Baker begged him to allow the experiment to continue. On April 30 the *Times-Picayune* ran a story under the headline WHOOPING CRANE LAYS EGG—PARK WANTS RARE BIRD BACK. The story said in part: "Douglass said he hadn't been notified about the egg laying, but that the event was expected. He is anxious to get Josephine . . . home. He plans to swap her, on a loan basis, to a northern zoo for a panda: 'The folks there have never seen a whooping crane and our people haven't seen a panda. I expect our crane back after the egg is hatched so we can make the swap.'"

Meanwhile, at Aransas, Josephine and Crip continued the

same diligent routine that Allen had recorded the year before. Allen, who was now at home in Florida finishing his monograph on the cranes, kept in close touch with Aransas, and came there on May 23 when the hatching was expected shortly. And indeed, on the very next day the birds' behavior changed as though a momentous event were at hand. Both birds seemed extremely tense. Josephine took on the brooding at ten in the morning and from then on scarcely moved. Allen and Refuge Manager Howard, posted in the tower throughout the day and watching every wink of Josephine's eye through a spyglass, guessed that she could hear the chick trying to break out of the shell. But darkness fell and still nothing had emerged. They left reluctantly, hardly slept that night, and climbed the tower again before dawn the next day.

With the first light of day they saw that both birds were standing by the nest, intent on whatever was hidden within its center. The two men waited all day, in almost unbearable impatience, and still no chick appeared, yet from the intentness of the parents Allen was convinced that there was a live infant crane within the grassy walls of the nest.

Later Allen wrote: "The following day, May 26, at a few minutes past six thirty in the morning I saw him. He was so tiny I could scarcely believe my eyes, but there he was, a rusty-colored downy little thing, moving about on the nest on his wobbly legs."

The news that for the first time in history a whooping crane had been hatched in captivity was on the air and on the front pages of newspapers here and abroad. For that moment at least, literally millions of people were poised over the bassinet of the baby crane and no doubt wishing it happiness and long life. Dr. Cottam, who flew to Texas from Washington, still recalls that it was a deeply thrilling moment when he got off the plane at Corpus Christi and picked up a newspaper with a full eight-column headline: WHOOPING CRANE IS BORN! Farther down in the paper he noticed a small item announcing the birth of a royal child to a European queen. He laughed with satisfaction and then sent both clippings to his wife with a note saying, "At last things are in proper proportion."

On his third day the chick, named Rusty, left the nest. Allen wrote: "I saw Rusty run across his father's big feet, running with the tottering friskiness of all small precocial birds. Then he came trotting back again, between the towering columns of Crip's long legs, and stopping, he looked up. No doubt he was uttering the 'strange, piping whistle' that Bradshaw heard when he saw the young whooper on the last Saskatchewan nest. Then Crip bent over with a soft and graceful tenderness, and finding the tiny mouth with the tip of his great bill, fed him. In all my experience with birds, this was the most wonderful, and the most moving scene I ever witnessed."

That afternoon the parent cranes began to wander in search of food, the chick running at their feet. Since the chick was no more than six inches high, Allen and Howard, who had still hardly left the tower, lost sight of it in the foot-high grass. With some anxiety they noticed several raccoons running along the flats. Howard sent one of his men out with a rifle, but by then the raccoons had disappeared.

The next morning, the chick's fourth day, Allen mounted the tower at dawn. There was a cold, biting rain. The parent birds were by the nest, and one of them seemed to be brooding the chick. Then suddenly the brooding bird arose and both birds walked away from the nest. They walked rapidly and without looking down. Allen, filled with horrible foreboding, called Howard on the field telephone in the tower. When he arrived the two men entered the enclosure. Josephine and Crip, who before had been so vigilant, were indifferent to their entry. Allen and Howard searched the muddy grass for hours, but found no trace of the chick. The empty nest was soggy in the rain. A few shards of eggshell lay nearby. Everywhere in the mud were the tracks of raccoons, making the chick's fate quite clear.

Rusty's loss was not the only misfortune to befall the cranes that year. The wild cranes, too, were having a hard time. All during the winter strong, dry winds had blown over the flats day after day. Little rain fell. Lakes and ponds on the refuge became mere stagnant puddles or vanished entirely. Along the shore the vegetation was thin, and inland the grass was as yellow as straw. With food hard to get, the wild cranes dispersed over a wide area. They migrated early. When they returned in the autumn of 1950, it was to unbroken drought.

The first bird appeared on October 5. For some time thereafter Howard was able to find only twenty birds. Then, searching by plane, he located twenty-eight. There were five young, of which two were twins. Still hoping to find more cranes, perhaps scattered by the abnormal weather, game agents were asked to search along the coast from the Sabine River to the Rio Grande, but they found nothing. The count of birds on the refuge remained uncertain because of the way they moved about, but after a great deal of figuring Howard decided to put down the official figure of twenty-six adults and four young. It appeared that seven cranes had perished in summer and that sometime in early January one of the twins had disappeared from the refuge. Its carcass was not found. Possibly it graced the dining table of some passing tugboat.

Howard's report for the last months of 1950 makes this seem the likeliest explanation, since he notes that "more than once" he saw shooting from boats but that they were too far away for him to identify their numbers and that without a boat of his own, pursuit was impossible. He also turned back several fishermen who came ashore on the refuge, and reprimanded two boys caught driving around the refuge with a gun and a dead goose— shot elsewhere, he believed—in their car.

As the drought continued in the winter of 1950–51, it became the longest dry spell on record. Besides lack of rain there were abnormally low tides. Tidal pools were drained and cracked. It was possible to drive a jeep in areas that usually were too soft even for walking. To provide drinking water for the waterfowl, turkey, and deer, Howard used a dragline to excavate potholes in the dry lake beds. The cranes found the small puddles that remained on their territories too salty, and came inland to drink. One family came daily to a pothole dug in one of the lakes. They made an odd picture as they climbed out of the hole. Because of the low tides Josephine and Crip were able to leave their enclosure at will by walking around a fence that had once extended into deep water. Usually they did not wander far, and returned daily. Sometimes, when they lingered too long, Howard would go for them, rattling corn in a bucket, and they would quickly accompany him home to their enclosure.

The year 1950 was black not only for cranes but also for friends of cranes. In October 1950, Robert Allen left the annual meeting of the American Ornithologists' Union, in Minneapolis, literally writhing with pain in his back. For months before this he had suffered a malaise that had been diagnosed as the result of a slipped disk. A doctor had put an uncomfortable cast on his neck which Allen had removed the first time he wanted to turn his head to count whooping cranes from an airplane. But this new pain could not be ignored. He got home to Florida and was given the grim diagnosis that he suffered from a form of progressive arthritis. He was told that the prognosis was unremitting pain, while his back stiffened, until he became immobile. After some months of contemplating such a future he was rescued by the then brand-new drug cortisone. Its effects were so beneficial that in a month he was able to get up and shortly was tramping through southern swamps searching for ivory-billed woodpeckers. In May 1951, six months after the acute attack, he was able to make a strenuous trip to the Bahamas to study the nesting grounds of flamingos—a species whose troubles were next on the National Audubon Society's—and Allen's—agenda.

To prepare for a second season's nesting by Josephine and Crip, Allen designed a new pen, carefully planned to keep out predators. The original 150-acre tract was reduced to a rectangle a quarter of a mile long and a hundred yards wide, which included salt flats, shell ridges, and a portion of cattail marsh. An inner rearing pen, a hundred yards square, was built in the center with the thought that the parents and young could be herded into it when the young had hatched. As a further precaution the raccoons in the vicinity were done away with. On the advice of Fred Stark, of the San Antonio Zoo, Josephine and Crip were fed an enriched diet of yellow corn, chicken laying pellets, shrimp, ground horsemeat, hard-boiled eggs, and wheat-germ oil.

April passed, but though the captives danced they did not nest. Then, on May 12, 1951, Howard discovered a nest containing one egg on a small peninsula that extended into a tidal slough. The happy news was relayed to Washington, New York, and Florida.

Two days later a strong, steady east wind brought in the tide, and water crept to the edges of the nest. As the water rose the birds abandoned their incubating and both worked, in an anxious fashion, building up the nest. With growing dismay Howard saw that they were fighting a losing battle against the rising water. Nevertheless, he was reluctant to interfere. Finally, at nine-thirty that night, when it was obvious that only drastic action could save the egg, he waded out to the nest.

An overcast dimmed the moonlight, but he could see the white shapes of the cranes. He found the nest almost submerged. The egg was a quarter of an inch above the water, and cold droplets were splashing upon it. He withdrew and with his helpers brought armloads of dry hay and salt grass. They managed to lift the egg and nest together, so that the egg was untouched by their hands, and put a platform of hay under the nest. By now the nest site was an island with only the tops of the salt grass above the water. The wind was still blowing with gusts of thirty and forty miles an hour. Josephine and Crip, who did not attack, but bugled furiously, were dim white forms against the black water. The work of building up the nest took the men ten minutes. Then Howard climbed the tower and waited. At last, two hours later, one of the birds returned to the nest and began to brood. Relieved, Howard went to bed.

The next morning he could see that the reinforced nest had indeed weathered the storm, but instead of incubating the egg

both birds were standing by the nest, probing at it in a peculiar fashion. Howard waded out and found that though the nest was sound and dry, the egg had disappeared. After a brief search, he found it smashed and floating amid the reeds. It seemed likely that the cranes had tried to rearrange the nest, causing the egg to roll out of its shallow resting place, and broken it as they attempted to push it back in place.

Although birds often nest a second time after such a loss, Josephine and Crip did not.

While these events were taking their course, twenty-nine wild cranes had migrated from the drought-stricken flats, leaving one bird behind. In September 1951, Howard found its carcass, a month dead, on the refuge. Its major bones were unbroken, so it may have been that old age or illness prevented its migration and eventually killed it. The first migrants did not return until November, a little later than usual. One of the first to come in was obviously crippled. On November 12 a state employee found it on the ground near a windmill, unable to fly or stand, and brought it to headquarters. One leg had been shattered by gunshot. It had been hobbling on the injured leg until it grew too weak. Howard fed it corn and water and took it to San Antonio for care by Fred Stark, but it died shortly. A month later Howard found a whooping crane's corpse. This bird had lost a foot and had a break in the leg bone. It, too, had probably starved to death.

Compounding these losses was the fact that the summer toll had been terrible. Eight birds had been lost. This more than canceled the addition of five young that the survivors managed to bring back. The flock was back to a mere twenty-five. The death of eleven birds—one third of the flock—in a single year had wiped out all the gains of the past ten years.

It was at this point, when the fortunes of both wild and captive cranes were at a low ebb, that George Douglass grew tired of waiting in the wings and stepped to center stage to play a decisive role in the future of the species. He demanded the return of "his" bird, Josephine.

Fate could not have selected a character more incongruous as custodian of what was now undoubtedly the single most valuable feathered creature in the world. Douglass was a politician by profession and a zoo keeper by accident. He had been born in New Orleans in 1905. His father was an engineer who worked for the city and became a member of the Water Board. As a youth Douglass studied both accounting and law at Loyola University, but left without a degree to join his father in the Department of Waterworks. He worked in the personnel and accounting departments for five or six years, eventually becoming supervisor of several departments. In 1941 the director of Audubon Park died. A replacement was sought, and Douglass applied for the job. The Board of Commissioners of Audubon Park—twenty-four local civic leaders who are appointed by the mayor—did not feel that Douglass' inexperience in zoological matters was any hindrance to his appointment, since running the zoo was considered mainly an administrative job, and in any case merely one segment of Park Department affairs.

Douglass' qualifications included membership in the business and political fraternity of the city. He was personable, friendly, a natty dresser, and popular at businessmen's luncheons. As director of the zoo, then, Douglass' single drawback was that he knew very little about animals. Even this wouldn't have mattered much in the course of world affairs had not fate made Josephine —the only captive female whooping crane on earth—his charge.

Until the moment Josephine began to lay her golden eggs no one had given any thought to the question of her ownership. Was she a gift or a loan to the zoo? Since wild migratory birds are under federal protection, had anyone the right to give her to anyone else? After ten years the circumstances of her arrival at the zoo were undocumented and confused. There was no written record beyond the file card in the zoo's office. The state and federal game wardens who brought the bird to the zoo had not bothered to inform anyone else of the incident, so, until Robert Allen conceived the idea of breeding Josephine and Pete, Washington officials of the Fish and Wildlife Service not only didn't care who had custody of Josephine; they hadn't known she existed.

There is no truer truism than that possession is nine tenths of the law. During the negotiations that preceded bringing Crip and Josephine together, not only common sense but common courtesy prompted all concerned to request the "permission" of Douglass—and the Audubon Park Board—for the "loan" of "the Park's" bird. John Baker had given assurance that if the experiment were a "failure," Josephine would be returned. What, exactly, constituted failure had, of course, not been defined.

In any case, late in 1951, Douglass came to his own decision that the breeding experiment was a failure and that it was his duty to demand that she once again ornament the New Orleans Zoo. He expressed this line of thought to the local newspapers, with the result that his and Josephine's name appeared in large type. The Texas newspapers were quick to take up the issue, arguing against her removal from Aransas. From this evolved a states'-rights editorial battle that amused everyone except the few people—like Robert Allen—who viewed Josephine, not as a tourist attraction, but as the final, fragile possessor of genes that no power on earth could duplicate.

On December 13, 1951, Douglass made a sudden move that apparently caught the United States Fish and Wildlife Service off balance. He got into the zoo's panel truck, drove to Aransas, strode into the office of manager Julian Howard, and told him, "I've come to get my bird." Howard asked him to wait while he telephoned Washington. That day Dr. Cottam was acting director in the absence of Director Albert M. Day, and received the call. As Dr. Cottam now recalls the events of that day, he was both taken by surprise and appalled. He had been interested in the cranes since the early days of Aransas. Now that captive breeding had come within an ace of success, he was deeply anxious to have the effort continue. Furthermore, he did not feel that Douglass' accidental possession of Josephine had made the bird his private property, or that of the Audubon Zoo.

In legal matters the United States Fish and Wildlife Service is counseled by the Office of the Solicitor of the Department of the Interior. Douglass' claim on Josephine was clearly a matter for legal decision. Cottam told Julian Howard to keep Douglass waiting, and on no account to surrender Josephine, while he consulted the department's lawyers. He has described what happened next as "just another one of those unfortunate things that dogs the cranes." According to Dr. Cottam, the lawyer into whose hands the question happened to fall was a man who saw no importance in a problem involving a single bird. He shortly delivered the opinion that Josephine should be returned to Douglass.

Dr. Cottam was, in his own words, "fit to be tied." He determined to take the question up another rung of the ladder, to the head of the Legal Department. A second call from Howard at Aransas saying that Douglass was now threatening to take Josephine by force did not help Dr. Cottam keep cool. To the misfortune of the cranes, the lawyer who had ruled in Douglass' favor had already reached his superior and recited the story. Dr. Cottam is still convinced that had the issue been differently presented at this time the outcome would have been different. As it was, the chief solicitor backed the opinion of his subordinate, and ruled that the Service must relinquish Josephine. Dr. Cottam had no further recourse. He telephoned Aransas and told Howard to surrender her. Then, on the slim hope that Josephine and Crip would breed at New Orleans, Cottam offered to allow Douglass to take Crip as well, provided Douglass would sign a release acknowledging the government's ownership of Crip. "They were a mated pair and I felt it would be criminal to separate them," Cottam has since said. "But I was so damn mad and rattled that I didn't think to put in a clause covering ownership of their offspring. Don't think I don't kick myself for that."

Victoriously, Douglass bore off his two prizes. At the zoo he put them on exhibit in a cage ten feet square.

Once the transfer of Josephine and Crip had become a *fait accompli* the losers elected to bow to defeat gracefully. A news release was issued from Aransas blandly stating: "After a visit since the fall of 1948, Josephine . . . is leaving Aransas for her home state. She has been on loan from the Audubon Park Commission to the Fish and Wildlife Service in their efforts to perpetuate the species. . . . The U.S. Fish and Wildlife Service has agreed to loan Crip for one breeding season or until another mate for him is secured. . . ."

John Baker, too, felt that nothing would be gained by further public airing of the affair. The next issue of *Audubon Magazine* ran a story that reviewed how the Audubon Park Zoo had "generously loaned" Josephine to the Fish and Wildlife Service and the National Audubon Society for three nesting seasons. It went on: "When the Audubon Park Commission recently indicated that, in view of the circumstances, it would like to be given the opportunity to demonstrate whether it could succeed . . . in raising young whooping cranes at a zoo, for later liberation in the wild, it was felt by the Fish and Wildlife Service and your Society that the request was a reasonable one, even though we both believe it would be preferable to continue the breeding experiment under as natural conditions as possible, and that the chances of young cranes surviving in the wild, after being raised in a zoo, are slight. It was felt . . . the captive adults should stay together and so decision was made to offer to loan the male to the Commission for ten months . . . as well as return the female. This decision was . . . disheartening to the Refuge Manager, who had done so much to give the captives all possible aid and who had become very much attached to them. . . . While the incident caused considerable publicity in Texas and Louisiana papers, with expressions of rival claims as to jurisdiction, and involvement of the issue of states' rights, all was in good humor!"

This was the first, but by no means the last, time that the circumstances of Josephine's residence at New Orleans were politely withheld from public discussion.

12

In early 1952, Robert Allen's monograph *The Whooping Crane* was published by the National Audubon Society. It was a massive piece of work, analyzing in painstaking detail all the information, both historical and current, that he had been able to gather about whooping cranes and their environment. Since the entire purpose of the study was to provide the Fish and Wildlife Service with practical information to be used in providing help for the cranes, the most important sections of the monograph were those labeled "Survival: Protection and Conservation."

Leading Allen's list of recommendations were those concerned with the food supply at Aransas, the reasons for the periodic failure of marine life along its shores, and steps that could be taken to prevent dearth of food and water from driving the cranes into alien territory. He noted that an alert manager at Aransas could foretell winter food scarcity, and act accordingly. Certain bayous might be equipped with tide gates so that marine food animals could be stocked. Inland ponds could be dug and stocked with killifish, frogs, and crayfish. "We feed game birds in winter," he wrote, "why not whooping cranes?"

The report discussed means of protecting the cranes from shooting and disturbance at Aransas. It named those areas of the bay, the waterway, and adjacent islands that should be more adequately protected. "Constant patrol by a deeply interested and able warden would do immeasurable good," Allen wrote. He suggested that the boundaries of the area closed to shooting should be enlarged so that it would no longer be legal to shoot ducks from blinds within two hundred yards of the cranes' territory and that an effort should be made to persuade the state of Texas to close Mustang Lake to fishermen. Ideally, the lake should be added to the refuge, as should every other available inch of whooper habitat, for as things stood, if the population of cranes increased, the shortage of habitat would become critical.

Allen took up the threat of oil pollution, pointing out that if a quantity of oil were accidentally spilled from rigs working in the bay it could be fatal to the whooping cranes. Meanwhile, the disturbing effects of drilling on the refuge could be kept at a minimum only by continued cooperation from the oil companies concerned.

Harrassment by low-flying aircraft that might drive the whoopers from the refuge was a similar problem. As a practical matter, the refuge manager dealt with it by informally asking the local commanding officers to caution their pilots; but, Allen suggested, it would be better if an official ceiling could be established, as well as a definite arrangement with the armed services to safeguard whooping crane territories on Matagorda and St. Joseph islands.

Allen also felt that more could be done for the cranes to guard them on their migration route: "The Platte River has long been a major stopping place for the whooper migrants, yet no safe resting place has been provided for them. A Federal refuge for waterfowl and whooping cranes should be established along no less than fifty miles of the Platte River in Nebraska." In addition he urged the importance of continual effort to reach hunters along the cranes' route by all possible means of publicity.

Although Allen's monograph was primarily a scientific document, he was never entirely successful in preventing his passionate feelings about the cranes from cropping up among his dispassionately presented facts; as when he wrote:

"When you sit crouched in a blind and watch an adult Whooper stride close by you, his head high and proud, his bearing arrogant and imposing, you feel the presence of a strength and of a stubborn will to survive that is one of the vital intangibles of this entire situation. Certainly it cannot be overlooked. We have a strong conviction that the Whooping Crane will keep his part of the bargain and will fight for survival every inch of the way. What are we going to do to help? Here, in this report, is the challenge, here is the job that must be done."

To underscore Allen's warnings on dangers to the cranes, Howard's reports to Washington reflected increasingly hectic activity at Aransas. During 1951, oil wells 19 and 20 had been drilled. Increased production prompted Continental Oil and its sublessee, Western Natural Gas, to plan a new barge-loading dock requiring a pipeline and road laid directly across whooping crane territory. They were finally persuaded to choose another route—at some financial sacrifice. For this forbearance the National Audubon Society presented them with a Citation of Merit.

A total of 3,422 visitors registered at headquarters during 1951, and it was manager Howard's belief that most of them came in the hope of glimpsing, from the tower, the distant white forms of whooping cranes. Not counted as "visitors" were the fifty or more people who came to the refuge daily to tend the cattle and to work on the oil company's fast-developing installations on the interior of the refuge. The road traffic to the oil sites became very heavy: "a continuous stream day and night," Howard wrote.

In the autumn of 1951 the refuge was plagued by a rash of

hunting violations. One of them involved a man from Rosenberg, Texas, who, as Howard put it, "takes the furlined bathtub for the blunder of the year." After registering at headquarters the man drove half a mile south and blazed away at some ducks in a roadside pond, believing, he said, that this was a public hunting area. The bathtub winner was stopped before he hit any ducks, and later fined $100 in a state court.

In early December, Howard caught a man shooting from a boat on the waterway, and the next day nabbed two more shooting on the refuge itself. In the course of an air survey to count whooping cranes, Howard discovered a man and his wife who had been squatting for a month at a pleasant spot within whooping crane territory known as Cape Carlos. They were allowed three days to pack and leave.

In the early months of 1952 there was some rain, but because the thirsty sands soaked it up like a blotter, the drought was not entirely ended. Owing to a shortage of food on the marshes, the cranes "continued to feed within easy slingshot range of the canal." This, Howard noted, "constitutes a hazard to the wintering population."

On March 20, 1952, around midnight, Howard was awakened by gunfire. He leaped from bed in his pajamas and arrested three men who had shot a doe directly in front of headquarters.

That spring Howard was unsure of the number of whooping cranes on the refuge. He reported that at least twenty-five migrants had returned from Canada, with twenty-three surviving the winter, but it was possible that two more had gone uncounted. Several single cranes that moved restlessly about caused the confusion. Whether twenty-five or twenty-three, the last of the migrant cranes left Aransas at the end of April. Howard saw the final pair flying in a circle and calling to each other, then drifting up and away until they vanished in the sky.

During the summer there was constant drilling in San Antonio and St. Charles bays. Howard reported: "It is apparent we are entering a period of rapid and intensified exploration for gas and oil. Despite cooperative efforts to reduce damage and disturbance to water fowl areas, it is visualized as an uphill struggle between the dollar and the duck."

In the autumn of 1952 there were rains in the northern part of the state, but the showers missed Aransas and, as waterfowl and whooping cranes returned, the shortage of drinking water was critical. Only nineteen adult and two young whooping cranes reached the refuge. Of the six (or eight) adults that had been lost over the summer, the fate of one became known. On October 31, children near Olathe, Kansas, found a wounded whooping crane in a cornfield and brought it to school. A game warden drove all night in an attempt to get it to the San Antonio Zoo, but it died on the way.

A few days later game agents in Regina, Saskatchewan, telegraphed to Washington: "Have a live, injured whooping crane. Immature. Wing tip off. Knee badly damaged. Will try to force-feed." Washington dispatched a plane to get the bird, but it, too, died en route.

Audubon Magazine commented, "Each year it becomes more apparent that illegal hunting is the major factor in reducing the numbers of the whooping cranes."

In the spring of 1952, when Josephine and Crip should have been nesting, Dr. Cottam visited them at Audubon Park. He found them on exhibit in their ten-foot coop. Mustering all his self-control, Dr. Cottam explained gently to Douglass that whooping cranes require both solitude and large premises in order to nest. Dr. Cottam's effort was rewarded: some time later, when John Baker also visited the two captives, he found that their enclosure had indeed been enlarged and moved behind the elephant house, where it was out of the way of heavy traffic. Having decided to keep smiling in public, Baker made no published comment on any shortcomings he may have noticed, but wrote in *Audubon Magazine* that he had found the birds "in fine condition," in a special enclosure three hundred feet square.

Josephine and Crip evidently felt differently about things, for they did not nest, either that spring or the next.

During 1953, John Baker, distressed at the plight of Josephine and Crip, and the waste of their valuable potential, cast about for a means to rescue the birds. At length he hatched a plan to persuade Douglass to "lend" the birds to the National Audubon Society's Rainey Sanctuary, a large and secluded tract in southwestern Louisiana.

Baker entered into tactful correspondence with Douglass, pointing out that to all who truly cared about the preservation of the species the furtherance of a successful nesting by Josephine and Crip overrode all other considerations and that quite possibly the semi-wild habitat at the Rainey Sanctuary would be more conducive to success than the necessarily unnatural conditions of the zoo. Douglass replied smoothly that of course his greatest concern was for the safety of the two precious birds. Therefore, a decision of such importance as their transfer to Rainey Sanctuary must rest, not with him, but with the New Orleans Park Board.

On January 4, 1954, Baker again wrote Douglass a cordial note expressing surprise that he had heard nothing further about the plan to move the captive whooping cranes to the Rainey Sanctuary in time for a possible nesting that spring. Douglass answered that the question of transferring the whooping cranes to the sanctuary had been discussed at the Park Board meeting in December and laid over until the next meeting on January 27. He wished Baker a very happy New Year.

Just prior to this January 27 meeting of the twenty-four New Orleans civic gentlemen who now, curiously, were being called upon to make a decision that might settle for all time the fate of *Grus americana*, John Baker again wrote to Douglass: "Dear George . . . I had hoped you would have visited the Rainey Sanctuary to determine to your satisfaction that the transfer would be practical."

On January 28, the day after the meeting, Douglass replied to "Dear John" that several members of the board were acquainted with the location of the sanctuary and that none of them thought well of the idea. He went on to say that the Rainey Sanctuary lacked blue crabs, knowledgeably quoting Robert Allen on "blue crabs as a principal item of whooping crane diet." He closed by mentioning a fear of predators, which could hardly have been an unintentional reminder of the death of Rusty. John Baker remained unruffled on paper. "Dear George," he wrote, "I am rather surprised that several members of your board do not think well . . ." He politely pointed out that the Rainey Sanctuary was in an area that once supported many wild whoopers and that the National Society planned to build a vermin-proof enclosure a hundred acres in extent that would be patrolled by a full-time warden. Here, for the moment, the correspondence rested.

The zoological world is bigger than the average sewing circle; nevertheless, news gets around it fast. By this time a good many ornithologists, related scientists, and bird lovers had become interested in whooping cranes, and were by no means generally satisfied to have Josephine and Crip remain at the New Orleans Zoo. One of those who felt most deeply dissatisfied was Dr. S. Dillon Ripley, who at that time was Curator of Vertebrate Zoology of the Peabody Museum at Yale, and is now Secretary of the Smithsonian Institution in Washington. The situation of the whoopers had caught Dr. Ripley's eye for two reasons. He is a vigorous member of several international organizations for the preservation of endangered species, and his hobby, to which he is ardently devoted, is breeding waterfowl in captivity. When, by the end of June 1954, it was clear that the captive whoopers at New Orleans had let another season go by without breeding, Dr. Ripley decided to see what he could do about it. He wrote a long letter to a number of men who were, in various ways, influential in wildlife conservation, describing the sorry situation of the species *Grus americana*, both captive and free, and urging that some way be found to provide Josephine and Crip with skilled avicultural care.

Rearing captive cranes, Dr. Ripley wrote, might turn out to be the basic factor in saving the species. "There is now in existence a known, proven, breeding pair of captive cranes . . . these cranes will breed again, given proper surpervision and care. The nub of this entire problem lies in the proper supervision and care. . . . Technicians of this sort are unfortunately rare in the United States. . . . There are not more than two or three men in the USA who could be entrusted with such precious charges, or such a weighty assignment. However, in the meantime I for one consider it a criminally irresponsible thing to *waste* the present proven breeding pair, to eke out their meager and barren lives in the Audubon Zoo in New Orleans. The chance of their breeding further is simply being thrown away, and the Audubon Zoo should be encouraged to realize this and to cooperate to the full to save the species. . . ."

This letter proved to be something like a large rock thrown into a small pond; the ensuing waves hit the shore in all directions, and were to surge back and forth for the next ten years.

One of the first ripples evidently reached George Douglass at New Orleans, who thereafter became noticeably touchy on the subject of captive whooping cranes. Some months later he found means to take a countermeasure when the zoo was visited by French-born Jean Delacour, an ornithologist of renown, who became an American citizen and who was then curator of the Los Angeles County Museum.

After a tour of the zoo and a pleasant dinner, Douglass elicited from Delacour a testimonial to the quality of the zoo's care of the cranes. Under the date November 17, 1954, Delacour wrote, in part: "In the company of Dr. George Lowery of the University of Louisiana, Baton Rouge, I went to the New Orleans Zoo to see a pair of captive whooping cranes in that establishment. I found the accommodation was very good. It is large and secluded enough, and well protected against any possible predators. The food given the birds, consisting of laying pellets, corn, crabs and shrimp, seems to be excellent. . . . I see no reason why they should not breed in this pen. . . . I would recommend therefore, that the birds be left at the New Orleans Zoo under the present conditions and it is very likely that now that they have settled down completely in their new pen, they will start breeding." For the next ten years Douglass kept a supply of mimeographed copies of this curious document in a desk drawer at the zoo, ready to hand out to visitors.

Meanwhile John Baker had not yet relinquished his hope of getting the captive cranes moved to the Rainey Sanctuary. When Douglass sent him a copy of Delacour's report, Baker replied with thanks, and again mentioned the Rainey Sanctuary project. Douglass did not reply. On May 26, 1955, Baker wrote again. "Dear George . . . Not having heard from you about any nesting of the captive whoopers this spring I rather assume they again failed to lay . . . time is marching on and I hope you will feel as I do that some new efforts should be made to obtain young from the captive birds. . . . You have had the birds for three years: the Aransas Refuge had them for three years before that, and I think you know I feel there would be a better attitude on the part of some of our ornithological friends if an arrangement could be worked out whereby someone . . . known to have had successful experience . . . were given an opportunity to show what . . . he could obtain at a new location."

Douglass' reply a week later was a shock. He wrote to "Dear John" that on Sunday, May 29, he had found an egg in a nest of straw in the whooping crane yard. The egg was discovered at 7 A.M. and at 10:30 it was found to be broken. He had hopes that another would be laid. In regard to Baker's letter, he did not feel any new effort should be made to obtain young from the captive birds. He felt he was doing well enough as it was. He further remarked that Baker's statement that there "would be a better attitude, etc." was out of order.

Thus, at the very moment when, after so much disappointment there again seemed to be hope of breeding captive cranes, and when, therefore, skilled handling would be most crucial, Douglass had slammed the door on Baker and, it seemed, on any project to move the captives. John Baker's feelings at this juncture may well be imagined. However, he sent back a soft answer. His letter disclaimed responsibility for any hostile remarks about Douglass, and closed with the whisper: "You seem to be having somewhat the same kind of heartbreaking difficulties that were experienced at Aransas."

Douglass did not notify Baker of the particular heartbreaking difficulty he experienced when Josephine laid a second egg. Douglass, delighted, allowed reporters and photographers to view the historic scene. In the course of the hustle and bustle of newcomers around the nesting pen, someone took it into his head to tease the whooping cranes by poking a stick through the wire. Crip became so furious in defense of the nest that he accidentally stepped on the egg and smashed it. Josephine laid no more eggs that year.

13

After Allen's two unsuccessful searches for the cranes' nesting grounds, ending in 1948, there were no further organized efforts, although each summer Fish and Wildlife biologists making their regular rounds to count waterfowl kept on the lookout for whoopers. For three summers no new clues showed up; then, suddenly, Robert Smith, the biologist with whom Allen had flown, sighted two whooping cranes in a remote area north of Great Slave Lake. On July 15, 1952, he wrote to Allen: "Two of the elusive great white birds found north of Great Slave Lake— just north of Deep Bay. The first one was found July 11 and the next day we went back and saw it again. . . . We then found another one about 30 miles away. The way they act there might be nests nearby. . . . It is not possible to land anywhere near the birds and it would be quite a project to get to them on foot. . . . You and I flew over the same area twice, once in '47 and again in '48, and from my experience the other day they could have been there then. It took us 20 minutes to locate the first one a second time and we knew almost exactly where he was."

This was tantalizing news but difficult to follow up. Baker and Allen decided to postpone a search on the ground until there had been further reconnoitering by air. In August, Smith flew over the region again, but this time found nothing, so further search was put off for another year.

In early June 1953, Smith again surveyed the area, and drew a blank. Then, on June 21, a Canadian helicopter pilot reported encountering a huge white bird in the air close to the spot at which Smith had seen the two whoopers the previous summer. Finally, in October, W. Winston Mair, then chief of the Canadian Wildlife Service, telegraphed Washington: "Eight whoopers reliably reported southbound along Slave River October 6."

Thus, as the summer of 1953 ended, although no whooping crane nests had been seen, there was reason to hope that soon, perhaps in one more season, the mystery of the nesting grounds would be unlocked at last.

While this was exciting and hopeful news, there was nothing cheering in the situation as it had developed at Aransas during the past year and a half. In the autumn of 1952 there were only twenty-one wild whoopers. The following summer, thanks perhaps to a massive publicity campaign in which the Audubon Society, the State Fish and Game departments, and the Canadian and United States wildlife services all cooperated, the flock made the round trip without losing a single adult bird. Nesting, however, was less successful, or possibly the young perished en route south. In any case, only three young were added, and so the flock numbered twenty-four in the autumn of 1953—a precarious figure, to say the least.

There had been few improvements at Aransas to brighten the picture. Nature had helped somewhat, for the drought broke in 1953, but otherwise matters were much as before. The refuge now possessed a boat, but there was no regular patrol of the waterway or the marshes to guard against poachers, and no supplementary feeding, so that whenever their food supplies deteriorated some of the whooping cranes moved off the refuge.

In April 1954, when the twenty-four cranes left Texas, the Society and the two wildlife services agreed to launch a ground expedition to search for the nests as soon as there were any new reports of cranes sighted in Canada. May and June passed without news, and then the Canadian Wildlife Service dispatched from Ottawa what Allen called "an electrifying message." Dated July 2, 1954, it read: "Dear Mr. Baker, We have just received a telegram from W. A. Fuller, our mammalogist at Fort Smith, Northwest Territories, stating that four or possibly six whooping cranes were seen from a helicopter in Wood Buffalo Park, NWT, on June 30th. The group included a pair with one young. . . . We expect more details next week."

The details came in a letter from William Fuller. The discovery, he wrote, had been due to the sheerest accident. On June 30 a fire had broken out in a remote section of Wood Buffalo Park, which because of its forbidding terrain is one of the least-known regions of Canada. A helicopter belonging to the Canadian Forest Service was dispatched from Fort Smith, at the northeast corner of the park.

Aboard the helicopter were the pilot, Don Landells, and G. M. Wilson, Superintendent of Forestry. On the return trip from the fire they flew low over a swampy region near the Sass River. Both men chanced to look down, and there, standing tall, and gleaming white against the dark terrain, were two birds that Wilson was certain were whooping cranes. Most marvelous of all, he could clearly see beside them a long-legged, rusty little bird, about the size of a large rooster—obviously a whooping crane fledgling. He radioed the discovery to Fort Smith.

That same evening the helicopter set out again, this time with William Fuller aboard. As they circled the area that Landells had marked on his map, Fuller spotted two whooping cranes. There was no doubt of the identification—he could see the vivid red crowning their heads. The only question was whether this was a second pair or the original pair with the young bird now out of sight. Finally, as a sort of dividend, they saw yet another whooper, a single, near the Nyarling River, some miles to the northwest.

Fuller had wanted to land near the cranes, but the terrain was too formidable. It was, he reported, an area dotted with small, shallow, muddy lakes separated by narrow zones of spiky black spruce. Ground travel appeared to be nearly impossible. Fuller guessed that the only access would be the twisting course of the Sass River.

John Baker telephoned the news to Allen, who was in Florida. That evening Allen wrote to him, "Our telephone conversation this afternoon . . . has been, for me, like the clanging of a bell to an old fire horse!" However, he added regretfully, he felt it was too late to undertake an expedition that season.

The Canadian authorities agreed, but promised to keep tabs on the area by helicopter and protect the nests by banning unauthorized aircraft from that section of the park. As an added precaution the exact location of the nests was kept as nearly secret as possible. On this point Baker felt strongly. "Our experience leads us to recommend extreme caution," he wrote. "There are individuals who will go to almost any length to get a specimen of a species . . . threatened with extinction."

In this instance Baker need not have worried. The spot the whooping cranes had chosen was almost literally impenetrable in summer, and this, of course, was why the nests had eluded observation for so long.

Wood Buffalo National Park covers 17,300 square miles—more than Massachusetts, Connecticut, Rhode Island, and Delaware combined. Once considered economically valueless, it had been set aside in 1922 as a preserve for the last of Canada's herds of wild bison. The cranes' nesting ground in the northeast corner of the park, although only a hundred miles west of Fort Smith as the crane flies, might as well have been in the center of the Land of Oz, since it was cut off by natural barriers so formidable that it had been virtually unexplored. Airplanes usually avoided flying over it because it offered no landing places in case of emergency; its lakes were too shallow for pontoon planes and the muskeg too soft for conventional aircraft. Its rivers were so choked by fallen timber as to be practically unnavigable. Thus it is likely that very few men, white or Indian, had ever set foot within the cranes' enclave.

In the autumn of 1954, the return of the cranes to Aransas was awaited with more than usual eagerness. In September, Howard began daily trips to the marsh. At 10:00 A.M. on October 17, his assistant, Everett Beaty, saw three adults fly into Mustang Lake. Their weary behavior made him think that he had seen an actual arrival for the first time. Two more pairs appeared that afternoon. Gradually the population built up until there were twenty-one adults on the refuge. But the little bird that had been seen in Canada never got through. For the first time since records had been kept, all the young of that summer somehow perished. Three adults had also been lost. Howard reported to Washington: "With a drop of three, and no young, the situation becomes ever more critical."

The fact that no young had arrived at Aransas made Allen feel that it was more than ever vital to explore the breeding ground. He hoped to determine whether the nests, or the young whooping cranes, were being destroyed there, perhaps by storms or by predators, or whether the losses were, as he suspected, the result of shooting on the flyway. In November, Allen went to Ottawa to see Winston Mair, chief of the Canadian Wildlife Service, and planned an expedition for the summer of 1955. He arranged that Fuller, at Fort Smith, would begin air surveys in early May; as soon as nesting cranes were sighted a ground party would try to reach the spot.

In April the whooping cranes began moving north from Aransas. On April 12 Julian Howard happened to be watching a pair at the moment they departed. As he wrote later: "A pair was located near the bay . . . we stopped to watch them. The weather was overcast with low clouds and a strong southeast wind. . . . After eight or ten minutes the pair extended their necks . . . two or three quick steps and they were airborne. With the high wind they quickly gained altitude and circled the first time at approximately 150 feet. As they continued circling they gained altitude and drifted with the wind. . . . In three or four minutes they were lost against the low gray clouds."

Eighteen days later, on April 30, a pair of whooping cranes, possibly this same pair, had covered the twenty-five hundred miles from Texas to Wood Buffalo Park. William Fuller wired to Mair that from the air he had sighted two birds on the Upper Sass River within a mile of the spot at which cranes had been seen the year before. In a memorandum he added: "The Sass River is navigable at the present stage of water (it is now open and flowing fast), although there may be some difficulty with beaver dams. . . . My recommendations would be for the ground party to commence operations as early as possible."

Meanwhile, Robert Allen, who had not expected such an early summons from the north, was in the Bahamas studying flamingos when John Baker radioed him to return immediately. He reached Fort Smith on May 20. Two days before, on another air survey, Fuller had seen a grand total of seven cranes, one of them near a nest in which he was even able to see an egg. The birds were all within an area of approximately five hundred square miles—a pocket handkerchief from the air, but an immensity on the ground. A few days after Allen arrived, he, too, flew over the nesting area: "There beneath us was the sight I had been hoping to see for almost ten years—a wild whooping crane on its nest! The incubating bird continued to sit as we flew by, circling at 1,000 feet. Its size and outline, even its posture, were unmistakable. I could see that it was turning to watch us as we passed, its head up and its yellow eye doubtless glaring at us with hostility and a total lack of fear."

The search party assembled by Allen consisted of himself, Ray Stewart, Fuller's assistant in place of Fuller, who was unable to go; and Bob Stewart of the United States Fish and Wildlife Service. From aerial photographs Allen had concluded that the best way to reach the Sass—the swift and narrow stream that twists through the heart of the nest area—was to travel some forty miles downstream on the Slave River to a spot known as the Grand Detour, and thence make a long portage overland to the Little Buffalo River. A few miles' travel upstream on the Little Buffalo would lead them into the Sass, which would, after many twists and turns, take them into whooping crane country.

On May 23 the three explorers set forth on the Slave. With them were ten Indians who were to carry their five hundred pounds of equipment over the Grand Detour portage. The air was bright and cold. Ice on the riverbank glittered in the sun. At Grand Detour the overland trek began. Allen was relieved to find that his ailing back stood the strain of the heavy going. They traveled through damp spruce woods and then across marshy prairie to the shore of a slough connecting with the Little Buffalo River. There the Indians put down their loads and left them. The searchers were on their own. After a second day of hard going— on foot and by canoe—and another long, cold twilight night in camp, they reached the Sass River. Spirits high, they launched their canoe. Rounding the first bend, they found the river blocked by a mighty logjam. After a half hour of hacking they cut through it only to find a bigger jam just ahead. One of the men made his way through the brush along the riverbank and reported that beyond the second jam was a third, beyond that a fourth, and so on, undoubtedly ad infinitum. The Sass River was hopelessly unnavigable, and the whoopers' nests as tantalizingly unreachable as ever. Four days later, after a difficult return trip, the party was once again at Fort Smith. It was as depressing a moment as Allen had faced in all his endeavors for the whooping cranes.

Defeated on the ground, Allen now arranged to charter a commercial helicopter. On June 4 the party was in the air heading for a spot near the Sass where a distinctive limestone escarpment marked the vicinity of the cranes' nests. In due time the helicopter landed them in the wilderness, and departed. The men made camp and then began to hunt for the landmarks, shown on their aerial maps, that would lead them to the cranes. After four futile days of tramping in all directions, they realized the bitter truth: the helicopter had put them down near the wrong escarpment. For almost two weeks the party remained marooned in the wilderness while Forest Service officials at Fort Smith—whom they could reach by radio—tried to find a helicopter to rescue them. At length Fort Smith radioed that no helicopter could be procured, and recommended that they try to get out under their own steam. Their escape took five days of infinitely painful travel. One entire day was spent on the Sass River, hacking through forty logjams and three beaver dams in order to cover an airline distance of a mile and a half.

They reached Fort Smith exhausted and defeated. Since it appeared impossible to charter a second helicopter, their expedition seemed at an end. Robert Stewart, the United States Fish· and Wildlife man, left by plane immediately. Allen planned to stay on for a few days to tie up loose ends.

On the following day, Allen dropped into district headquarters to see Ward Stevens, Superintendent of Game, and found a message that a helicopter would be available two days hence. Weary as they were, Allen and Ray Stewart went back to work, repacking their battered equipment and compiling a grub list.

For this third attempt Stevens offered to transport the expedition in the Service's riverboat to a rendezvous with the helicopter on the Slave River. A landing strip was created by lashing a large wooden platform to the bow of the boat. The party set off on the river in the rosy dusk of midnight and reached the rendezvous point by morning. At noon the helicopter appeared and settled neatly on the platform.

Later, Allen wrote John Baker as follows: "It was about 1:15 P.M. on June 23rd when we made our second try by helicopter. . . . We flew west until we saw the Little Buffalo and then, after a few anxious minutes, located the twists and turns of our Nemesis, the Sass. Soon we could make out the strange dark patches, three in number, that we had selected as our landmark. Studying them and their relative size and positions carefully we were certain, from their appearance on the aerial photographs, that this was the spot. . . . Holmgren [the pilot], without a moment's hesitation, landed exactly where we indicated. As soon as we were unloaded he took off for the second run, which would deliver the remainder of our gear.

"I wrote in my notes: 'It has taken us 31 days and a lot of grief, but let it be known that at 2 P.M., on this 23rd day of June, we are on the ground with the whooping cranes!'"

From the air Allen had seen a pretty green-and-brown pattern of ponds, lakes, and snaky streams, interwoven with patches of forest and brush. From the ground the terrain was more forbidding. They had landed close to the Sass, at the edge of an open area—a brûlé—burned over perhaps fifteen or twenty years before. Here and there the dark skeletons of spruce and tamarack stood naked and bereaved-looking. To the east the marshy banks of the river had stopped the fire, and beyond it were thickets of mixed brush and stunted trees that, Allen knew from their air survey, surrounded a bewildering network of shallow ponds. Amid those ponds and bogs and brush-covered ridges was the inner sanctum sheltering the nests of the whooping cranes. As so often happens in moments of final achievement, Allen and Stewart were unable to feel the high elation they had so long looked forward to—they were too weary and too oppressed by the grim inhospitality of the landscape. They made camp by the river—accompanied everywhere by the customary cloud of mosquitoes—and settled down, wanting nothing more but sleep.

The next morning they set out to explore. Allen later wrote to John Baker: "The walking was difficult across the mushy surface of the burn, and once we had dropped into the pothole area to the west, it was even worse. Unexpectedly, the land between the ponds and tiny lakes is thickly grown with dwarf birch, willows, tamaracks and scraggly black spruce. Once in the middle of such a thicket one's vision is strictly limited. Often we were unable to see fifty feet in any direction."

To avoid becoming hopelessly lost, they decided to find a particular lake that could be identified in the aerial photos and serve as a reference point:

"As we moved ahead, in the direction of a glitter that must turn out to be water, we were startled to see an unmistakable flash of white just beyond. A second later it had assumed a strikingly familiar outline and we were staring straight at an adult whooping crane! Then, in another moment, we saw a second bird. . . . Both birds were very alert and they were moving in opposite directions, one to the left and one to the right. The bird to the right quickly disappeared behind the thickets, but the other whooper kept in view, although walking away from us with long strides. As we came out on the open shore of a little pond he rose from the brush on the other side, calling a series of alarm notes. Immediately he was attacked by a short-billed gull, which must have had downy young hidden along the edge of the pond. Wheeling in a short circle, and still calling, the whooper was soon out of sight. . . ."

Allen and Stewart spent ten more days at the nesting ground exploring the surrounding country, collecting plants and samples of the animal life of the ponds, and listing the birds and mammals that share the summer home of *Grus americana*. Allen's notes on the sights and sounds paint a vivid picture: "High ground, rises like islands above the surrounding confusion of ponds . . . Fires have swept over them . . . The only live trees that remain are clustered about wet depressions or along the course of the river. . . . The Sass is deep and swift and the water appears quite dark . . . Upstream, in a meager growth of poplars, there was a deserted beaver dam and the series of little water falls made a pleasant and somewhat drowsy music. Other songs were contributed by the birds in the river thickets—chiefly song sparrows, Lincoln's sparrows and redwings—while snipe winnowed in the twilight that passes for night in that latitude, and bitterns boomed from marshy ponds. . . . Now and then we heard the guttural notes of sandhill cranes and on a few occasions, the clear trumpet calls of whooping cranes. . . .

"Other birds were seen on the open burn—sparrow hawks, rusty blackbirds, juncos, chipping sparrows and flickers. A pair of lesser yellowlegs had built a nest on the moss-covered ground not far from our tent. . . . Once a bald eagle flew over and twice we saw ravens soaring, gliding and stooping in the wind.

". . . The weather was hot and dry, the thermometer reading 92° Fahr. at 6 P.M. on the 23rd, and frequently starting the day in the low 80's. . . . Elsewhere there was heavy rain and violent electric storms. . . . We were thankful that the storms had passed us by, for our campsite and surroundings were as dry as tinder."

The bottoms of the ponds were too soft and spongy to risk crossing, but it was possible to walk along their rims: "We discovered small numbers of fish in some of the larger ponds . . . which we had not expected." Frogs were numerous. "No snakes were noted. Mollusks were very abundant and nine species were collected from the crane ponds. These creatures, and the frogs, must be important items in the whooping crane's diet."

Allen found that the mammals include the red fox, moose, black bear, and wood bison but that probably none is plentiful there.

Despite their constant watchfulness during these ten days, Allen and Stewart saw no more whooping cranes, though they heard their calls and found their seven-inch footprints, mingled with the smaller prints of the young, on the shores of the ponds. The birds seemed deliberately to stay out of sight. Allen wrote: "It was maddening to know that at least one pair of whooping cranes, with young in tow, was within a half mile of us most of the time, yet we were unable to watch them. Our visions were filled with them, a hundred yards away perhaps, calmly picking up snails, the young one quite possibly darting after a white admiral butterfly! Earthbound and weary, we could not tell. But we were on the spot. We had gazed at its features and felt of it with our bare hands. It is real and it is reasonably understandable. But most important of all, it is no longer unknown."

On July 2 a radio message told them that their helicopter would pick them up that afternoon. Allen and Stewart broke camp and lighted a smoky fire to guide their pilot. He arrived late that afternoon. This time the return to their old home base— the Hotel Mackenzie at Fort Smith—was triumphant. For Allen, the finest fruit of the expedition was the assurance that the whooping cranes could hardly have chosen a better place to rear their young in isolation and safety. He was satisfied that food and water were adequate and predators scarce. Fire, which had seemed a possible threat, would be stopped by the wet ground surrounding the nest sites. Allen wrote to Baker: "It is in truth a lost and unknown place, and the nesting whoopers should continue to prosper here . . . as they have evidently done for so many years. Only man can reach them here and do them harm, and, if not permitted to fly low over these ponds or land beside them by helicopter, even man need not be feared."

As the finale of his visit to crane country, Allen made a flight from Fort Smith over the territory he and Stewart had explored on the ground. To their delight they spotted two pairs of whooping cranes, each with twin young. The existence of two sets of twins made Allen wonder how often twin young reach flying age but die on the migration route. Only five times in the previous sixteen years had twins arrived at Aransas, and there had never been two sets in the same year.

After Allen had left for Florida, William Fuller continued to survey the crane nests. On one flight he saw eleven adults and six young. He last saw cranes in the area on October 12, much later than Allen or anyone else had imagined they would remain.

Only twice in whooping crane records had as many as six young birds reached Aransas from the nesting grounds. Thus Fuller's discovery of such a crop was fine news. In fact, this, plus Allen's findings on the safety of the nesting grounds, would have made the outlook for *Grus americana* seem unusually bright were it not that all through the summer the United States Air Force had been relentlessly grinding ahead with a plan that, if carried out, promised a sudden end to the whooping cranes' sanctuary at Aransas and thus, inevitably, to the cranes as well.

14

The first news of the Air Force's threat to Aransas came in the early summer of 1955. At approximately the same moment that Robert Allen and his companions were struggling through the Canadian wilderness, the Air Force announced its intention to use the bombing range on Matagorda Island for practice in photoflash bombing. Photoflash bombs are spectacular devices used at night to illuminate large target areas. Their effect on wildlife has been demonstrated. Every creature that can walk, fly, or crawl leaves the vicinity with all possible speed. The use of the bombs at the edge of the Aransas Refuge would have emptied it of wildlife with dramatic suddenness.

In order to begin Project Photoflash, however, the Air Force found that it would be necessary to extend the danger area on both sides of the range. This was highly fortunate, for, instead of simply going ahead and dropping the bombs, the Air Force had to announce its plan and request that additional waters both on the Gulf and in San Antonio Bay be closed to traffic. As is required in such cases, a local public hearing was held by the United States Corps of Engineers.

Here again luck was on the side of wildlife, for this proved to be one of the rare occasions when the interests of commerce and cranes were united. Neither the local oil interests, real estate interests, nor fishing interests were at all pleased with the Air Force proposal. Their opposition resulted in a second hearing. By this time virtually all national conservation organizations, including of course the National Audubon Society, had mobilized their opposition. The United States Fish and Wildlife Service called the attention of the Air Force to the presence of the whooping cranes, and also entered its protest. The outcome of this combined opposition was that the Air Force, in due time, decided to go ahead with its plan.

During the summer the controversy simmered on. Most of the activity was now behind the scenes: letters, telephone calls, pleading, exhortations, and various forms of wirepulling by conservationists, all of which apparently left the Air Force unmoved. The Fish and Wildlife Service had emptied its arsenal quite early in the game. Dr. Cottam, who had retired from the Service the year before but was still deeply interested in the whooping cranes, recalls that he upbraided his former colleagues for not carrying the struggle further. If the project went through, he told them, they might as well cut the whooping cranes' throats and get it over with.

When rescue for the cranes came it arrived, as usual, at the eleventh hour. Without doubt Robert Allen's hard work in Canada that summer had a great deal to do with saving the cranes. Had he given up and failed to find the nests there would have been very little whooping crane news in the papers. As it was, his discovery brought the birds greater publicity than ever before. The New York *Herald Tribune* had sent John O'Reilly, an old friend both of Allen and of whooping cranes, to Canada to cover Allen's expedition. O'Reilly's vivid stories brought the whooping cranes worldwide attention. Canadians, particularly, became proudly aware that they were custodians of something rare and beautiful. Thus they were unpleasantly startled to learn, so soon after a dramatic triumph in conservation, that the precious birds were about to be blasted out of their southern sanctuary. Somehow, the Canadian newspapers felt, this didn't make sense; particularly when the blasting was a mere by-product of military convenience. Such headlines as THREAT TO WHOOPERS ALARMS OTTAWA—U.S. BOMB RANGE PROTESTED appeared in Canadian papers. Canadian politicians, in turn, proved to be more sensitive to the protests of their citizens than had those in Washington. On October 20 the Canadian Embassy in Washington sent a formal note to the United States State Department: "The Canadian Ambassador presents his compliments to the Secretary of State of the United States of America and has the honor to draw his attention to a proposed photoflash bombing range. . . . It is hoped that the existence of the whooping crane will not be imperiled at a time when the prospects for the increase of the species have at last become bright."

John Foster Dulles, to whom this note was addressed, may have other distinctions in histories of the times, but it is nonetheless to his credit that, on November 1, this reply was delivered to the Canadian ambassador: "The Secretary of State presents his compliments to His Excellency the Ambassador of Canada and has the honor to acknowledge the receipt of his note No. 657 of October 20, 1955, drawing attention to reports of a proposed Air Force photoflash bombing range. The Department of State informed the Department of Defense of the Canadian concern, and has now received a reply stating that the Department of the Air Force is withdrawing its proposal for extension of the Matagorda Island Air Force Range, which is the matter referred to in the Ambassador's note."

At the moment that their survival was being decided at the highest diplomatic level, the whooping cranes were in flight between Canada and Aransas, running the gauntlet of gunfire that Allen was now convinced was the major cause of attrition. Once again the National Audubon Society made an effort to spread the word of the cranes' special status to hunters along the migration route. A leaflet describing the cranes and their plight was widely distributed. Local editors took up the cause, printing the leaflet's closing words: "We Appeal to the Sportsmanship and Humanity of Every Person, from Saskatchewan to Texas, to Withhold His Fire, and to Give Any Large White Bird God-speed, Instead of a Charge of Shot."

This autumn, of course, there was particular suspense as to whether the six young, seen in Canada, including the two sets of twins, would come through safely. On October 18, Julian Howard found that the first pair of cranes had arrived at Aransas. They had one youngster with them. In the next two weeks several singles and childless pairs drifted in. Then, on November 3, Howard saw the first set of twins, as well as three pairs of adults with one young each. The next day, to the delight of the whooping crane circle, the second pair of twins was seen with its parents on Matagorda Island. By December 1955, the grand total was eight young, the largest number of young to come through safely since crane records began, and twenty adults, representing a loss of only one adult bird. To the anxious bystanders it almost seemed as though the cranes themselves had, in some eerie way, responded at the right moment. Their unprecedented crop of young, and their good luck on the skyway, had once again staved off disaster.

Eventually the fate of the lost bird became known when the Service got word that a whooping crane had been shot at a lake near Sioux Falls, South Dakota. One of a party of hunters shooting from a blind brought it down with a kill of snow geese. According to newspaper stories, the hunter was arrested by game wardens.

As the cranes settled down at their winter quarters, Howard noted that the summer's events inspired more letters, telephone calls, and visits to Aransas than ever before. Hardly a day went by without someone phoning the refuge to report a stray flock of whooping cranes, which most often proved to be sunbathing pelicans. Most of the public feeling about the cranes was friendly to them, but there was a sprinkling of humorists and, what was more sinister, there were a few people who were furiously hostile. In the first category, one would suppose, was the lady who mailed an envelope of white chicken feathers to Aransas with a note advising the Service that it could cease its search for the missing whooping crane. A Louisiana man sent a carton of pelican bones labeled "fossil whooping crane." On the hostile side was a letter, printed in a Corpus Christi newspaper, from a man who signed himself "Disgruntled," complaining about the attention lavished on a handful of birds. From here and there samples of hate mail reached Allen, and some of them made his blood run cold. A farmer in Saskatchewan proposed to put a stop to the fuss by killing the few remaining birds and thus saving both farmers and taxpayers further trouble.

Although Howard had counted twenty-eight whooping cranes on December 22, 1955, he was thereafter never able to locate more than twenty-seven. In his report on refuge events in the first quarter of 1956, he noted that two barren pairs had shown signs of being loosely united, and he guessed that one of these had lost a member. Because no corpse was found, the cause of the bird's disappearance was never known.

In April, as the cranes were leaving the refuge, Howard saw an oil slick drifting to shore from an offshore rig. He found that the contractor had washed down his equipment with diesel oil. Howard called in Texas game wardens, and the violator was ordered to install proper drip pans under his machinery.

On May 3, Howard found that all but three whooping cranes had left the refuge. A lone immature crane lingered on Matagorda Island, where a family had wintered, and there was still a pair on the refuge. Shortly thereafter the tardy pair took wing, but got no further than Lampasas County, Texas, where one of the birds collided with a high wire and crippled one wing. Its mate voluntarily came to earth with it, and the two cranes took refuge by a farm pond on a ranch owned by a Mr. Ed Kirby. For some weeks Kirby noticed the two huge white birds feeding at the edge of the pond, which was shrinking in the summer heat. At length the pond dried up entirely. After a day or two without water, the uninjured whooping crane deserted its mate and flew away. The cripple, driven by thirst, approached a water tank near the ranch house. Mr. Kirby chanced to see it, took his lariat, neatly slung the rope around the crane's neck, and dragged it into the house. Mrs. Kirby gave the captive food and water while Mr. Kirby telephoned the San Antonio Zoo and told Fred Stark that he had a big white bird tied up in his kitchen. Stark quickly dispatched a truck that brought back to the zoo the captive whooping crane now known as Rosie. Stark guessed by the size and conduct of the bird that it was a female and, because of the character of the markings on its head, thought it to be a yearling.

Although the circumstances that brought Rosie to Stark's zoo were similar to those that had brought Josephine to New Orleans, Stark made no effort to claim her as his property. After a conference with Fish and Wildlife officials in Washington, it was arranged that Rosie would remain at the zoo on loan from the Service. She was assigned a large cage with running water and began what proved to be a nine-year wait for her nuptial day.

In the summer of 1956, Julian Howard was transferred, and in the autumn a new manager, Claude F. Lard, took his place at Aransas. It had been another hot, dry summer, and by autumn the water situation was very bad along the whole Texas coast. During November, conditions of food and water were growing ever worse and, as usual in this situation, the newly arrived cranes moved about so much that it was difficult to count them. It was at last clear that only two young had come through from Canada. Just as sad, there were only twenty-two adults. Of the twenty-eight of the year before, one was in the San Antonio Zoo; one was the bird that had disappeared from the refuge without trace; and four had been lost in the migration of 1956. Thus, in only one year, the seesaw of the cranes' luck had again tilted from high to low.

Nor was Aransas exactly an ideal refuge that winter. Lard reported to Washington in December 1956: "All ponds and small lakes on the Refuge were dry until latter part of December . . . the only fresh water was the overflow of windmills. Every place we had a little fresh water we had an enormous concentration of ducks and geese, and the fresh water soon became a dirty looking green from overuse and we were afraid we would get an outbreak of disease at any time."

Lard also reported that the lure of the cranes brought an all-time high of 9,309 visitors to the refuge. Those registered were only a fraction of the so-called "visitor load," the tally of visits rather than individuals, which was estimated to be about 15,000.

There were also unregistered visitors who were potentially a menace to the cranes, but the Service had to rely on state officers, who seldom took court action against them. Lard recorded three cases of trespass on crane territory, and added, "The entrance of visitors and fishermen into unauthorized areas is very common despite the fact that all roads are marked off limit."

Lard's notes echo the warnings that Allen had expressed in his memoranda to Washington eight years earlier, warnings that had been almost entirely ignored. By this time, of course, Allen's official work on the cranes had ended. Little by little he had been made aware that his continued comments on what he considered the Service's neglect of the cranes at Aransas were less than welcome; nevertheless, he continued to visit the refuge and express his views. In the summer of 1956 he wrote to John Baker: "I was shocked at what I saw there last March. Much can be done . . . and would greatly benefit the whooping cranes. They need all the breaks we can arrange for them."

15

Meanwhile, at New Orleans, Josephine and Crip had come through the year in a chicken-wire enclosure, a hundred feet square, behind the elephant house. Josephine was now more than sixteen years old; how much more, no one knew. Some observers thought she must surely have come to the end of her reproductive span. Dr. Cottam, for one, was doubtful of her ability to carry on. However, on April 28, 1956, Josephine laid an egg on the bare earth in the same spot that she had made her ill-fated effort the year before. On May 2 she laid another egg, and then she and Crip began the month-long ritual of incubation. As the magic day drew near, the newspapers became increasingly interested. Again George Douglass found himself host to reporters and photographers. The slate roof of the elephant house overlooking the crane yard became a lookout post and press room from which the visitors watched the nest, forty feet below, and waited for the drama of hatching to take place.

At about the same time Robert Allen had come down with a second illness, as yet undiagnosed, and was in bed in Florida. John O'Reilly, who spent a week perched on the roof reporting on the cranes, sent him an account of events. In the first place, he wrote Allen, it is obvious that whooping cranes will eventually get used even to the strangest surroundings. All the odd sights and sounds of the zoo had become routine to the birds, and did not alarm them, but anything that did not fall into the raucous pattern was a disturbance. When O'Reilly's hat blew off and sailed to the ground, Crip rushed to the fence, ready to attack, and Josephine rose nervously on the nest.

The two parents shared the incubation as they had at Aransas. Crip was a cooperative partner, and came over promptly when Josephine gave her low call. At each relief the bird taking over rolled the eggs carefully with its beak. From time to time they pulled dried grass up around the eggs, and although there had been no nest when the eggs were laid, by the time hatching was near there was a mat of dried grass beneath them.

On what turned out to be the final day of incubation both birds were very tense. Josephine would not allow Crip to sit on the nest, but he stood over her as though on guard. At about 10:15 on the morning of May 29, the rooftop spectators saw Josephine get up and turn the eggs. A hole was visible in one of them. Four hours later, when she rose again, they saw a wing sticking out of the egg and, half an hour later, at 2:36, she got up, and a chick emerged from the broken shell. It was tiny, brown, and wet. Josephine called Crip, who had moved off to feed. He came to the nest. Both birds put their beaks together, pointing downward, then slowly stretched their necks skyward and gave a long, bugling call. The chick quickly dried out and became fluffy. It spent most of its first two days buried in Josephine's feathers while she incubated the second egg.

The chick's progress was astonishing. In two days it seemed to double in size and then was strong enough to leave the nest and flounder around in the grass. During this period Josephine's allegiance seemed to be divided between feeding the chick and incubating the remaining egg. Crip was greatly concerned over the chick. He kept close to it as it ran about, and he was constantly treading the grass, with toes extended, to flush out grasshoppers and other insects. When he caught a morsel he would mash it with his beak and then hold it at the tip of his beak in front of the chick's beak. The chick grabbed at the food readily, and, if it was a large piece, gobbled and gulped like a robin swallowing a worm.

The second egg hatched four days after the first, and another tiny crane emerged. From time to time both parents left the second chick in the nest while they wandered about the pen, feeding the first. Occasionally Josephine would return to the nest as though to check up on the younger chick. At night both little birds crawled into Josephine's feathers.

The second chick lived only two days. It vanished overnight, presumably the prey of an owl that could have swooped into the roofless cage, or perhaps carried off by one of the big rats that reporters had seen scuttling about the zoo. After the loss of the chick, Douglass had a wire top installed on the pen.

Poor Douglass, now in the embarrassing position of having failed in the care of the precious birds for a second time, while all the world watched, as it were, through the eyes of the reporters and cameramen assembled on the slate rooftop, was considerably upset. One of the reporters later wrote Allen his observations of the scene: "The more I think about it the more astonishing the whole thing becomes. In the first place it was ironic that a New Orleans politician should be the one under whose supervision the hatching took place. Douglass is a well-meaning guy, but his thirty-one years as a city employee have not prepared him for anything so vital as having nesting whooping cranes under his care. However, he is aware of his shortcomings in animal husbandry. He has no veterinarian at the zoo. If an animal gets sick he gets in touch with Stark or George Vierheller, or somebody who specializes in the branch to which the sick animal belongs, and asks them what to do about it. In an emergency he calls in a professional vet. I don't think he fully realized the significance of a successful crane nesting until the eggs were in the nest and national interest began to manifest itself. Then it was too late to improve the chicken wire pen in which Crip and Josephine were housed. As events progressed Douglass became more and more concerned. He would squat on the roof during the daytime and return to the zoo at night, sleeping but little and at the same time trying to keep up with his other duties as director of the park and swimming pool."

The result of all this strain was that the unfortunate zoo keeper came down with a stomach-ulcer attack, and was hospitalized.

The surviving whooping crane chick grew rapidly. Within a few weeks it was a long-legged, ungainly youngster with tremendous feet and fluffy plumage colored cinnamon and buff. Its eyes were brown, rather than the acid yellow of its parents' eyes. It seemed to be always hungry, and the adults foraged for it, digging up the dirt of the pen in a search for earthworms. When the keeper filled their food pan the parent birds picked out shrimp and crab, which they broke up and presented to the chick with the tips of their beaks. Sometimes Crip or Josephine would throw a morsel on the ground and prod it until the chick noticed it and picked it up. Both birds were constantly vigilant, and fierce to intruders. When an unfortunate gray squirrel got into the pen, Josephine attacked it. The little beast barely escaped alive.

As the month of June wore on, there was increasing sultry heat. The chick seemed to tire easily and often dropped to its haunches to rest in the shade of a camphor tree, which was the only shelter from the blazing sun. In the first week in July one of the keepers noticed the chick sitting and gasping for air. By the second week it was doing this frequently. On the morning of July 13 the keeper saw the chick lying prostrate in the yard. He entered the cage, fending off the attacks of the parents with a chair, and picked up the little bird. It was quite dead. Autopsy showed it had died of aspergillosis, a fungus of the lung that afflicts domestic poultry. It had lived forty-five days, was thirty-three inches tall, and weighed four and three-quarter pounds.

Dismay over the little chick's demise was not limited to the immediate family, as it were. The circle of those interested in whooping cranes had been widening rapidly. Other zoo keepers, aviculturists, and an assortment of scientists and conservationists, both American and Canadian, had become intrigued with the problem of *Grus americana*. To some of these people the failures at New Orleans seemed to indicate that success in breeding whooping cranes in captivity was tantalizingly close, but could, in fact, be achieved only with more skillful handling than seemed possible under George Douglass' direction. A variety of proposals were made: that the Service take Crip and Josephine by court proceedings and, since the Service possessed no avicultural facilities of its own, put them in the custody of someone qualified to try to raise captive whooping cranes; that adults be captured from the wild flock at Aransas to start a breeding experiment in another zoo and perhaps provide a mate for Rosie, whose sex was still undetermined; that young whooping cranes be captured at Aransas and distributed to zoos, or to private aviculturists, who might have the technical skill to raise them and breed a new generation; that eggs be taken from the whooping crane nests in Canada and artificially incubated.

Since the Fish and Wildlife Service showed no disposition to make a legal issue of Josephine's custody, those interested in captive breeding of whooping cranes were led more and more to think of taking birds from the wild. In this way the fate of the wild birds was becoming entwined with the fortunes of the captives at New Orleans.

The question had of course been simmering for some years. By 1953, the idea of capturing whooping cranes had been urged often enough so that Allen had felt it worthwhile to express his strong feelings against it. In *Audubon Magazine* he wrote: "A few well-intentioned people have suggested that the wild cranes ought to be trapped, their great wings pinioned and the entire flock grounded on the Aransas Refuge in Texas. . . . We can fully understand the feelings that have inspired this plan but we would deplore its execution . . . it would be a fool-hardy and dangerous experiment; even if two or three birds were successfully caught, the loss and injury and the scattering of others would be a most deplorable price to pay for highly dubious results."

Allen's opposition had not, however, altered Dr. Ripley's conviction that only aviculture could save the whooping crane, and Ripley had in turn convinced a number of people whose opinion carried weight in conservation circles. Nor had Allen been able to persuade his old friend John Lynch (who in addition to his work as a Fish and Wildlife Service biologist was an aviculturist and privately raised waterfowl) that talk of capturing whooping cranes was doing more harm than good. Lynch had been studying the population figures of the Aransas flock, and concluded that without artificial aid the wild whooping cranes were unquestionably doomed. Meanwhile, in Canada, Fred Bard, of the Provincial Museum in Regina, who had maintained his interest in the whooping cranes ever since his efforts ten years before to find their nests, was likewise positive that the cranes were fluttering their last and that the remnants of the flock must be captured before it was too late to preserve them even in zoos. Like Ripley in the United States, Bard worked in Canada to line up support for this point of view.

In June 1956, those in favor of captive breeding of cranes brought the issue to the fore at a Canadian meeting of wildlife managers—the Twentieth Federal-Provincial Wildlife Conference. United States representatives had been invited, but neither Allen nor Baker was able to go. Allen, still ill at his home in Florida, prepared a rebuttal to the arguments that he knew Lynch would present.

Allen's paper, read aloud in his absence, opened up the touchy question of whether an avicultural program could honestly hold out any hope of ever returning zoo-reared birds to the wild, or would in fact be merely a means to preserve specimens of the whooping crane in perpetual captivity. This, Allen was convinced, would be the inevitable outcome.

"The time has not yet come," Allen wrote, "for taking such drastic and perhaps dangerous action as suggested in these plans. . . . It is not our wish to see this noble species preserved behind wire, a faded, flightless, unhappy imitation of his wild, free-flying brethren. We are dedicated to the job of preserving the whooping crane in a wild state. We do not feel . . . that we have failed in this. If the day comes when we have reason to feel otherwise, then that will be time enough, perhaps, for someone to consider such improbable techniques as capturing all young-of-the-year by running them to earth with helicopters (as has been seriously proposed!), sorting them out in rearing pens, pushing them to lay several sets of eggs, which would then be incubated artificially, and produce whooping cranes—or what would presumably pass for whooping cranes—like so many mallard ducks or barnyard chickens! No! The whooping crane faces enough dangers without turning it over to such an uncertain program as that."

However, of the two points of view Lynch's turned out to be the more persuasive. The conferees, most of them Canadian Fish and Game officers, voted to endorse Lynch's resolution that "a program of capture, artificial breeding and subsequent release to the wild" be undertaken for the whooping crane. Allen's proxy vote, cast by the representative who had read his paper aloud, was the only dissent.

An odd footnote was appended to the proceedings when someone mentioned that among those in the audience was Mr. Fred Bradshaw, the man who had found the last whooping crane nest in Saskatchewan in 1922 and, as Allen had written, immortalized its tiny occupant with a numbered tag.

Following this meeting the National Audubon Society girded

itself for what it saw as a battle to defend the whooping cranes from their friends. Since wild whooping cranes could be captured only by the wildlife services of the United States and Canada, or through their authorization, the opposed camps, pro- and anti-capture, went to work to try to convert officials of these services to their point of view. John Baker immediately wrote to the chief of the Canadian Wildlife Service, who replied that though he agreed in theory with Lynch, he had strong reservations on the practical application of the plan, particularly when it came to "any molestation of the birds on their summer range." Perhaps the Canadians felt that if a debacle were to result, it would be preferable to have it take place elsewhere.

To John L. Farley, director of the Fish and Wildlife Service, Baker wrote that "our Society is absolutely opposed to [Lynch's proposal], which we believe is based on an erroneous assumption [that the cranes are doomed in the wild]. We believe that if cranes are wanted by zoos and aviaries, the source should be the production of young by the present captives."

On this point, if no other, the National Society and Dr. Ripley were in agreement. Dr. Ripley had been convinced all along that if the Service were sufficiently determined, a legal way could be found to transfer the two captives from New Orleans to more skillful hands and that healthy young whoopers would undoubtedly result from better care. Furthermore, he felt that the two precious birds, Josephine and Crip, were in truth natural resources belonging to the people of the United States and Canada, and should be so declared, even if it took an Act of Congress to do it. Privately, Dr. Ripley expressed the view that the Fish and Wildlife Service was paralyzed by bureaucratic terror of stirring up a ruckus over ownership of the cranes; that it was principally the fear that Douglass, if attacked, would appeal to his congressmen for help that prevented more vigorous action.

Following the Canadian meeting, Ripley continued his efforts to line up supporters who would in turn urge the Fish and Wildlife Service to capture whooping cranes.

In July, Ripley wrote to Fish and Wildlife director Farley, expressing pleasure that Rosie had been put in the custody of Fred Stark at San Antonio, but added that "failing a parthenogenetic birth," the Service should consider trapping a mate for this new addition to the captive ranks. He also tackled the issue of whether it might ever be possible to return captive-bred whooping cranes to the wild: "There is no pertinence to the discussion as far as I can see, as to whether in future captive-reared birds will or will not survive in the wild state. The situation has gone beyond that, and in discussing such peripheral and conjectural matters we lose sight of the basic question of whether we want future generations to see the species alive at all or merely stuffed in museums. In the future, *all* live whooping cranes may have to be in parks or preserves of one sort or another just as the Buffalo occur today."

It was, of course, exactly this facet of Ripley's view of the cranes' future that sent cold chills up Robert Allen's spine and prevented any rapprochement between the National Audubon Society and Dr. Ripley on behalf of the species.

In September the American Ornithologists' Union came partway into Ripley's corner with a resolution, at its seventy-fourth meeting, stating that "whereas the whooping crane, one of the most remarkable and spectacular birds of North America, is in imminent danger of extinction," the Department of the Interior and the Congress of the United States should provide funds for a full investigation "of all methods whereby this bird may be saved."

With pressure mounting "to do something" about the cranes, the Fish and Wildlife Service found itself uncomfortably wedged between the opposing forces. It met the dilemma by calling a meeting. Invitations were sent to all national ornithological and conservation organizations, and to the directors of several zoos and museums. At 9:30 A.M. on October 29, 1956, what Allen described as "some forty highly interested gentlemen" filed into a conference room in Washington to confer on the plight of the whooping crane. The forty included all shades of opinion in the whooping crane capture controversy, ranging from Allen and Baker on the one hand to Ripley, Lynch, and Bard on the other. Like medical specialists at the bedside of an ailing patient, the conferees found themselves not only offering totally different remedies, but unable to agree on the condition of the patient. It was one of the ironies of the situation that both sides—pro- and anti-captivity—had backed themselves into corners on the outlook for *Grus americana*. The National Audubon Society, which had for so long been calling for help for the wild whoopers, now found itself declaring that their condition in the wild was sufficiently robust as to make the drastic step of capture unwarranted; while the captivity bloc was equally vehement in its contention that the species had more than one foot already in the grave.

When, seven hours later, the forty interested gentlemen filed out again, the only thing that had been decided was that the director of the Fish and Wildlife Service would choose a committee to study the problems of the whooping crane and to offer advice to the Service. Its members, chosen from among those present at the meeting, represented both sides of the captivity fence.

From the point of view of the National Audubon Society the creation of the committee, known as the Whooping Crane Advisory Group, was indeed a blow, since it elevated to the status of "advisors" people who had heretofore been merely spectators. There were no interment ceremonies, but, as it turned out, the birth of the Advisory Group marked the death of the Cooperative Whooping Crane Project, so idealistically conceived eleven years earlier.

Deepening Robert Allen's gloom as he left Washington was his conviction that the real purpose of some of the captivity proponents was to capture *all* young whooping cranes as they reached Texas in order to build up a large captive supply. Even such a firm believer in aviculture for cranes as John Lynch had been rather taken aback by the drastic elaboration of his original ideas. If, by any chance, the Fish and Wildlife Service yielded to the proposals of the aviculturists, the struggle of the wild cranes would indeed be at an end.

16

Early in 1957 the Fish and Wildlife Service was subdivided. A number of its departments were grouped within a new pigeon-hole and given the unhandy title of Bureau of Sport Fisheries and Wildlife. The director of the new bureau was Daniel H. Janzen, a veteran Service administrator who had been a regional director in the Midwest. Janzen deputized his assistant, Dr. Frederick C. Lincoln, to take responsibility for whooping crane affairs and to represent the Bureau on the Whooping Crane Advisory Group.

Meanwhile Dr. Ripley had continued to ponder the stalemate at New Orleans, and concluded that as an interim solution it might be possible to move the mountain to Mohammed: if the birds couldn't be sent to a qualified aviculturist, then the next-best thing would be to send an aviculturist to them. He and Fairfield Osborn, president of the New York Zoological Society, enlisted a retired bird keeper, George Scott, to supervise a nesting season at New Orleans. The Bureau agreed to pay Scott's salary. All that remained then was to persuade George Douglass to accept outside guidance. Thus the subsequent chapter in the whooping crane saga might have been entitled "The Wooing of George."

In February 1957, Ripley and Lincoln flew to New Orleans to pay Douglass a visit, and found him a cordial and receptive host. The three men sat down for a chat in the crane pen, while Josephine and Crip circled them suspiciously. Douglass accepted the offer of Scott's help. He listened attentively as Ripley made tactful suggestions on ways to improve the food, housing, and sanitary care of the whooping cranes. Ripley and Lincoln left New Orleans well satisfied. Lincoln issued a cheering report to the Whooping Crane Advisory Group: "Mr. Douglass was most cooperative and eagerly accepted every suggestion. . . . Mr. Douglass makes no pretense of being an aviculturist. . . . The two birds are in excellent condition and Crip is already putting on occasional dances to which Josephine remains rather coy. Both Dr. Ripley and I were very much pleased with the conditions we found and with the attitude and interest of Mr. Douglass."

Dr. Lincoln's memorandum then moved on to the tricky matter of who really owned Josephine and Crip—a question that was being raised with uncomfortable persistence by some members of the Advisory Group. To answer it, Dr. Lincoln now resorted to a bit of word mincing perhaps designed to mean all things to all people and avoid the unpleasantness of a showdown with Douglass. The whooping crane, he said, is a migratory bird and cannot be possessed either in Canada or in the United States except upon definite authority in the form of a permit from either of the two services concerned. "Such being the case," he went on, "a statement of ownership either of the adult birds or of any progeny is more or less academic and can be determined when the occasion arises."

Josephine laid two eggs at the end of April, and on May 11 George Scott arrived to supervise the hatching. The nest in which the eggs lay was merely a small flattened pad of hay that Josephine had made by lying down and drawing the hay to her with her beak. It was placed precisely where it had been the year before, in an open, unprotected area of the enclosure. The fierce heat of the semitropical sun made the task of incubation a difficult ordeal. During the noonday hours the incubating bird sat with half-closed eyes, panting visibly. The eggs were rarely left uncovered for any length of time. The birds exchanged shifts without any particular ceremony. Ordinarily when one bird seemed to feel its turn was over it rose and the other willingly took its place. Scott noticed, and was amused by, an incident that was exceptional. On an especially hot, steamy day Josephine incubated, gasping in the direct noonday sun, while Crip stood nearby, preening comfortably in the shade of a tall bush. Finally Josephine arose and looked about. Somehow Crip managed to avoid noticing the cue to take over. He turned his back and stalked away. Josephine finally hurried over to the water pail, took a long drink, and walked resignedly back to the eggs.

At 9:25 A.M. on May 18, Scott saw that one egg had been pipped as the chick within cut a narrow chink in its shell. The day was extremely hot, but Josephine sat all morning. At noon she allowed Crip to relieve her for two minutes. At 2:30 P.M. Josephine rose and turned the eggs. Crip made awkward attempts to settle on the nest but Josephine drove him off and resumed her place.

The hole was now much larger, and Scott had seen the chick moving inside the egg, but it wasn't until nearly midnight that the chick finally freed itself. The hatching had taken almost fourteen hours to complete. The next morning at dawn Crip came over and coaxed the chick from the nest while Josephine continued to incubate the remaining egg. The chick ventured only a few feet from the nest, and after twenty minutes found its way under Josephine's wing. On May 21, twenty-four hours after it had first pipped its shell, the second chick made its way out. It was dry and fluffy within an hour, and shortly made a daring excursion of six feet from the nest. It seemed more vigorous than the first chick even though its hatching had involved a longer struggle.

The chicks took their first food when they were approximately a day old. At this stage the behavior of the birds was recorded by William Conway, Curator of Birds at the Bronx Zoo, who had come to New Orleans especially to see the infant cranes. "The entire feeding process," he wrote, "is one that shows a delicacy of relationship and a degree of parental attentiveness that some ornithologists might be loath to credit to a bird." He noted how carefully the parent worked the food in its bill and then, gently and precisely, offered the small particle, perhaps a piece of shrimp or a dragonfly, putting it directly in front of the chick's bill without quite touching it.

If the chick failed to take it, the adult might cock its head and softly drop the food in front of the chick. The chicks at first pecked clumsily at the offerings, and then, with increasing strength, became more accurate. Unlike young songbirds, the whooping crane chick doesn't beg with fluttering wings and open beak, but the parents are so attentive that it is offered food almost constantly.

Conway was fascinated by the interplay that accompanied Josephine's brooding of the chicks. The process of bedding down for the night involved many preparations and false starts: "At 5:50 P.M. the male began a strange ritualized tramping procedure in an area of high grass [perhaps to flatten the grass as a precaution against predators, Conway guessed]. Josephine joined in as the chicks wandered nearby. She drew grass and bedding toward the center of the area. At 5:58 she lay down and drew more bedding grass about herself. The youngest chick pushed at the long tertials extending back near her 'elbow' and gained entrance under her wing. Shortly a minor uproar took place high up in the feathers of the mother's back. A small, fuzzy head appeared and looked about. At 6:10 the chick tumbled out of its feather bed and Josephine arose." A half hour later Josephine again lay down, and both chicks crept beneath her. Suddenly the second chick popped out from the feathers of her neck and walked off to get a drink of water. When it had drunk, Crip offered it a bite to eat, and the chick, thus distracted, began to follow Crip, looking up as though it hoped to be brooded, and eventually uttering a soft, cricket-like, twittering distress call.

Josephine, who had in the meantime been trying to call the chick to her side with a low, murmuring sound, now arose and went to fetch the errant one. Then, finally, the family settled down for the night. Throughout the hours of darkness Crip stood silently some three or four feet away, awake and alert for possible danger. In fact, for the first five days of the chicks' lives he was never seen to lie down.

Despite their parents' assiduous care, the young whooping cranes were still at the mercy of chance. One day, for instance, there was a sudden, drenching rain. Josephine immediately lay down to shelter the chicks. The smaller found its way under her wing, "pushing toward a warmth that might mean life or death at this delicate point in its existence," Conway wrote, but the larger chick seemed unable to find an entrance, perhaps because of Josephine's injured wing. While it struggled Josephine showed great anxiety, jerking her head and calling, but seemed unable to assist the youngster. The chick was thoroughly soaked by the rain and finally took shelter under a large leaf on a nearby bush. Fortunately, it was not fatally chilled.

The chicks grew rapidly. At the end of a week they were seven inches tall, and with increasing strength showed increasing rivalry. Rising to their full fluffy stature, they would spar, each trying to grasp the other's bill and twist it. Occasionally Crip and Josephine became quite excited by these small battles. They would put their heads down close to watch, and then, throwing their heads high, sound a loud, rattling call.

Scott stayed on until August to care for the young birds. By then they had become strong enough so that their survival seemed assured, and he felt it safe to leave them in the care of regular keepers. The young whooping cranes had been named George and Georgette in honor of Scott and Douglass. Their survival not only made avicultural history but also gave people on both sides of the captivity controversy a new factor to think about.

In September 1957, Dr. Lincoln issued a new memorandum to the Whooping Crane Advisory Group reflecting further thought, and possibly behind-the-scenes maneuvering, on the ownership of the captive cranes. "Final disposition of the two birds raised this year is of course a decision that must be made by the Director of this Bureau," the memo stated bravely. "The young birds probably can remain with their parents until next spring." As for Josephine and Crip, Lincoln wrote, it was his opinion that they had best remain at New Orleans. Josephine, he pointed out, was an old lady, over seventeen or eighteen years of age, who might not be productive much longer. The transfer from Aransas to New Orleans had been followed by four barren years, and another transfer might result in an interruption of her egg laying. There were grounds for this thought: Aviculturists have noted that captive cranes of other species sometimes stop laying for a time after a change of scene. On the other hand, immediately after moving from New Orleans to the relative freedom of Aransas, Josephine had nested for the first time.

Meanwhile, Douglass appeared to be enjoying his new situation as the world's only whooping crane breeder. At a meeting of the National Audubon Society at which he spoke on the "Reproduction and Rehabilitation of the Whooping Crane," he handed around feathers to the audience. "I have here something which I doubt anyone has seen and I'm going to ask our future Congressman down there if he'll step up and pass these around, because these are whooping crane feathers and these here are the feathers that are changing color from brown to white." Douglass also had photographs of George and Georgette. "This will show you a parent bird, and two young birds . . . and you will see them in the process of changing color. Oh, I would say in about another two months at the rate they're going they will be a total white!" Mr. Douglass may not have been a whooping crane expert to begin with, but he was fast on the road to becoming one.

In the discussion period that followed, someone asked Douglass what would be done with George and Georgette when they matured.

"That's a serious question," Douglass replied. "There's been so much discussion about what we are going to do about them and the easiest way out is to say, well, we'll have to see what develops. . . . Now what would happen to the birds if we had a successful nesting year and we had, say, two more? That is in the future, but I want to say this; that the Audubon Park Commission and your speaker are not trying to have in Audubon Park an exclusive flock of whooping cranes."

Douglass also acknowledged: "It is quite possible that the birds could hatch elsewhere in this country and do as well. I don't think they could do better because of the condition of the birds, the plumage and their health, but I do believe we should not keep all our eggs in one basket. . . ."

Ten days after his platform appearance before the National Audubon Society members, Douglass took part in another public ceremony in a way that made the whooping crane circle shudder. On November 22, 1957, the United States Post Office issued a whooping crane commemorative stamp. In New Orleans the day was marked by an elaborate program of ceremonies. Dr. Lincoln later ruefully informed the Advisory Group that the program had included the personal appearance of the whooping cranes from the Audubon Park Zoo. The cranes had shared the television cameras with two senators and several congressmen. "An incident that is to be regretted," Lincoln wrote, "as it brought much criticism not only on this Bureau but also on the Audubon Park officials. Fortunately the birds suffered no harm, but it is only in thinking of what might have happened that there was cause for alarm."

This episode later resulted in a formal recommendation by the Twenty-third North American Wildlife Conference that the captive whooping cranes make no more TV appearances, and be removed from their pens only with the approval of the director of the Bureau of Sport Fisheries and Wildlife.

Meanwhile, the Bureau's director, Daniel Janzen, had appeared on the same program at which Douglass handed around crane feathers, with a rueful story of his own to recount. This concerned an episode at Aransas wherein Janzen, new to the job of dealing with whooping cranes, had learned at first hand of the possibilities for disaster that somehow so often attend all efforts, no matter how well intended, to handle *Grus americana*.

The story began with a report from Aransas in the spring of

1957 that three whooping cranes had not joined the others in migrating, and seemed to intend to spend the summer together on the refuge. The three were a mated pair and a young single that had wintered alone on the King Ranch and had also failed to migrate the summer before. Hearing of this, Dr. Ripley urged Janzen to have the single captured during the summer while it was molting and flightless, with the hope that it might turn out to be a mate for Rosie, confined in sterile solitude at the San Antonio Zoo.

Dr. Cottam, who was now director of the Welder Wildlife Foundation at Sinton, Texas, a two-hour drive from Aransas, agreed with Ripley, and added the explicit recommendation that the tricky business of capture should not be left to the judgment of the refuge staff, but should be supervised by himself and Fred Stark. Under no circumstances, he warned, should the bird be captured in the heat of the day.

Janzen later told the Audubon Society members how, knowing himself to be green at the job, and knowing, too, the danger that the bird might be killed or injured in an attempt to capture it, he put off the decision as long as possible. Finally, in June, the refuge manager notified Janzen that because the three summering whoopers were in full molt, and unable to fly, it would be easy to drive them into a net. Janzen then gave his approval to the capture, but included the instruction that Cottam and Stark be on hand. Unfortunately, this last proviso was not fulfilled. On the morning of July 1 the refuge manager found the single bird separated from the pair, and decided to take the opportunity to capture it without bothering the other two birds, even though this decision allowed no time for Cottam or Stark to get to Aransas.

"Then," Janzen told the Audubon Society members, "I got a call from the refuge manager and he was in tears. And I don't blame him. What happened was this. . . . They put a net across one narrow spot, and they started to work these birds toward this narrow spot. . . . When they started to drive [them] . . . the bird cut off into some heavy brush, and [the men] moved up and captured the bird. The bird showed no sign of injury of any kind, and they took it to headquarters. The bird apparently was all right. Stark came out. He looked at the bird. He said, 'Well, it's breathing rather rapidly.' And about that time the bird collapsed. It apparently went back on its feet later on, and it was all right, and all of a sudden it collapsed again and it was dead within two hours."

The embarrassed Janzen went on to say that autopsy had shown that the bird had an enlarged spleen and was thin, but uninjured. Often, he said, in the capturing of wild animals a certain percentage keel over for no apparent reason. In this case the cause may have been shock, fright, or exhaustion.

Dr. Cottam, who was indignant that the refuge manager had acted alone and sent for Stark only after the damage had been done, thought the unfortunate bird had died of heat exhaustion. John Baker did not let the episode pass unremarked. In view of this "complete fiasco," he wrote to Winston Mair, chief of the Canadian Wildlife Service, he hoped there would be less talk about capturing wild whooping cranes.

Apparently the lesson was not lost on Janzen, for he told the National Audubon Society that he now felt the danger in capturing wild cranes was such that it would be better to wait and hope that an accidentally crippled bird would be saved to provide a mate for Rosie. "I am right now in the mood that we have two flocks of whooping cranes—those in captivity and those on the outside—and I am not disposed to capture any more wild birds. I say again 'disposed' because I feel that no decision ever made is ever final. You might find that later you may change your mind. . . ."

Meanwhile, the migrants who spent the summer of 1957 in Canada had a fairly successful season. The first pair returned on October 21. By November 14 the number of whooping cranes on the refuge had built up to twenty-six, of which four were young. One summer casualty was seen, crippled, on October 29 on

Grand Lake, two miles north of Ketchum, Oklahoma. Unfortunately, the Bureau didn't hear of it until months later, and by then it had disappeared. On November 17 another single was sighted in Manitoba, and the sighting verified by a staff member of Ducks Unlimited, but this bird never appeared at Aransas.

17

As the winter of 1957–58 wore on, the problem of the captives at the New Orleans Zoo remained a vexing one for the Bureau. Members of the Whooping Crane Advisory Group continued to press the Bureau to find some way to take the birds away from Douglass. The Bureau continued to temporize—as though it hoped to catch more whooping cranes with honey than with vinegar. In February 1958, Dr. Lincoln visited New Orleans for another pleasant talk with Douglass. He presented him with a permit from the Bureau authorizing him to keep Crip, Josephine, and their progeny. Bravely, but somewhat unrealistically appended to the permit was the condition that the Bureau "reserved the right to take them into custody at any time.

Lincoln also discussed with Douglass the position of George and Georgette, whose sire, Crip, was indubitably government property. It was the consensus of opinion, Lincoln said, that the young whoopers should be moved to another zoo so that all the world's captive whooping cranes wouldn't be in one basket. The very excellent San Antonio Zoo was the first choice.

Politely, Douglass replied that his "curator of birds" was making a study of the plumage development of the young, so the transfer would not be convenient at that particular moment. Douglass' curator of birds had been recently hired and would not stay long, but he served his purpose, for there the matter rested.

In truth, it was far from safe to have the birds so concentrated, regardless of the care they received. A hurricane, an avian epizootic, or even a bucket of spoiled shrimp mixed with their rations, could wipe them out at one blow despite the most careful guardianship.

A freak accident was always possible. An anecdote current in the whooping crane circle described the visit of a northern zoo director to inspect the captives. Josephine was on the nest. There was knee-high grass in the pen, and the visitor remarked to Douglass that the grass might shelter rats or other predators. Douglass ordered a workman to cut the grass, and then led his colleague off to look at something else.

Shortly the two men heard a fierce bugling and hurried back to the crane pen. Crip, in the full majesty of his protective fury, had hemmed the workman in a corner. Crip was lunging and thrusting at the man, who was swinging the blade of his scythe within inches of Crip's long, priceless neck, and crying, "Bird, you come closer and I'm gonna cut off your head!"

Lincoln had hoped that Scott would return to New Orleans to supervise the 1958 breeding season, but Scott was unable to come, and no other qualified man could be found. The regular care of Josephine and Crip was now in the hands of a new keeper, a kindly little man named Leo Buras, whose greatest avicultural qualification was his boyhood experience in raiding the nests of egrets and raising the nestlings. Leo and Josephine had something in common, in that many years before his arrival at the zoo a hurricane had blown Leo out of his birthplace, at the tip of the Delta, just as a storm had blown Josephine out of hers at White Lake. Leo wandered north to New Orleans, where he found work in a bakery making cookies. He baked cookies for thirty-seven years until the bakery closed in 1957. He then applied at the zoo and soon found himself cleaning birdcages. Then Leo, the small, gray-haired cookie baker, was gradually transmuted into a whooping crane keeper, a job he had performed with great conscientiousness and the anxious manner of a man who lives in fear that the cookies may burn.

In the spring of 1958, Josephine laid four eggs. Three were infertile, but one was successfully hatched. Under the care of Leo

Buras the third whooping crane to be born in captivity survived the perils of infancy. Leo christened the young bird Peewee. The world supply of captive whoopers now numbered five at New Orleans and, of course, solitary Rosie at San Antonio.

During the summer of 1958 the wild whooping cranes, as though to refute the charge that they couldn't possibly survive on their own, had nested with remarkable success. In the autumn the flock, which had numbered twenty-six in the spring, came back thirty-two strong. Four families with twin young and one single youngster made a total of nine young whoopers, the largest number in the twenty years that records had been kept. Actually, ten young had been produced. A young bird and an adult were sighted at the Mingo National Wildlife Refuge near Puxico, Missouri, after the others had reached Aransas, but they were never seen again. Two other adults also vanished. Thus the net gain to the flock was six. The increase seemed to Allen and Baker a splendid affirmation of what the whooping cranes could do on their own—given just a little luck, and protection from man.

It was indeed fortunate that the wild cranes had been able to help themselves, for no one else had been able to accomplish much in their behalf. One particularly sad failure was the defeat of a proposal to enlarge the refuge area at Aransas and rename it the Whooping Crane National Wildlife Sanctuary, thus giving the cranes top billing over ducks and geese.

Ever since Allen had discovered what he considered the immutable territorial requirements of the cranes, he had been troubled by the paradox at Aransas: If the cranes increased as everyone hoped they would, there would not be enough refuge land to accommodate them. The problem was, of course, compounded by the cranes' insistence on a certain type of habitat. Thus the possibilities for extra crane territory were narrowed to a very few: these were portions of Matagorda, St. Joseph, and Mustang islands and of the King Ranch. These lands were already being utilized by millionaire ranchers; men who were in the main sympathetic to whooping cranes, but whose sympathy was not sufficient to cause them to wish the refuge enlarged at their expense. In spite of this ready-made impasse, Congressman John Young of Corpus Christi and Senator Ralph Yarborough were persuaded to introduce the necessary bills in Congress. In December 1957, H.R. 9353 was discussed at a public hearing in Corpus Christi. Opposition was expressed by a spokesman for the Sportsmen's Clubs of Texas, of which one of the millionaires in question, and owner of crane territory on Matagorda, happened to be president.

The spokesman, Cecil Reid, argued that while no one was more ardently in favor of aiding whooping cranes—or in fact all wildlife—than the sportsmen of Texas, they saw no need to enlarge the refuge, because the ranchers owning the lands adjacent to it were also keen conservationlists who protected the cranes quite adequately. This argument changed Congressman Young's mind, and he has since then held the same view as the Sportsmen's Clubs of Texas. The bills died.

On a smaller scale, but on the same note, was John Baker's experience in trying to persuade the owner of St. Joseph Island to set aside a bit of whooping crane territory there and post it against hunting. This project failed, thanks to the protests of a local man who rented out hunting boats and found the site a convenient one for duck blinds.

After being laid up for almost a year with his second bout of illness—which had finally been diagnosed as a rare metabolic disorder that could be controlled—Allen was able to go back to work late in 1957. In the autumn of 1958 and in early 1959 he returned to Aransas to check up on the cranes. It was distressingly apparent that despite his two years of work, and his carefully documented recommendations, the situation there was quite unchanged. Allen reported to John Baker: "I was impressed by the fact that the whooping cranes are pretty much left to shift for themselves. They receive no special attention. The only Refuge patrolman spends 90 percent of his time trapping wolves, coons, possums, and skunks! Meanwhile, entire crews, with their families, housing provided, live on Aransas to look after the oil interests, the cattle interests, and the administrative affairs of the area, but not one solitary soul is there to tend to the welfare of the wintering whoopers. Actually this is nothing new, nothing we haven't faced before, but the point is there does not seem to be any official awareness of the problem and no effort to do anything about it."

Allen was also much concerned about a new menace to the cranes that had loomed up in the north. The Canadian National Railway had announced plans to build a branch line to reach zinc and lead deposits near Great Slave Lake. Two routes were possible. The shorter, and cheaper, would go through Wood Buffalo Park, and pass within eight or ten miles of the edge of the nesting grounds. If it were put through, Allen foresaw that the railroad would be likely to change the course and flow of rivers; start fires along the right-of-way that might sweep on to the nesting grounds; and bring in telegraph lines, which are always a hazard to large birds. Finally, and worst, it would provide ready access by people.

Once again the Canadian Audubon Society, and its friends, leaped to the defense of the cranes, and once again the issue of their safety was on the front pages of Canadian newspapers. This time, though, it would be more than two years before the final decision was made.

Meanwhile, the news from New Orleans had been especially tantalizing. On Valentine's Day, 1959, Josephine surprised everyone by laying an egg well ahead of schedule. Three days later she laid a second. She then proceeded to break one of the eggs and, picking up the broken pieces, carried them to the water trough and placed them in it. She broke her second egg and put it, too, in the water trough. Three days later, George Scott, who had agreed to supervise once more, arrived. Josephine laid a second clutch of eggs, which Scott took from her and put in an incubator. She then laid a fifth egg, which Scott left in the nest.

By April 15 the incubated eggs had passed the normal hatching period by almost a week. Scott opened one of them and found a partially formed chick dead inside it. By then the fifth egg, on which Josephine was setting, was within three or four days of maturity. Scott took it from the nest and put it with the egg that still remained in the incubator. Four days later, when it was obvious that nothing would emerge, Scott opened both eggs and found both rotten. Two weeks passed, and then Josephine laid a sixth and a seventh egg. Scott left them in the nest. Josephine and Crip incubated these for almost a month. Then, on June 3, Crip arose from the nest, revealing a broken egg. He picked up the shell in his beak and put it in the water trough. Scott was unable to tell if it had been fertile. On June 13, when the last egg was long overdue, Scott opened it and found a fully formed dead chick that for an unknown reason had been unable to escape from the shell.

This time there was no ready explanation for the disaster. For once Mr. Douglass could not be blamed, since Scott had been in attendance. It could only be hoped that Josephine's poor performance was simply an example of the uncertainty of raising whooping cranes, and not an omen for the future.

While the news from New Orleans was saddening to the entire whooping crane circle, it made life particularly difficult for the Bureau of Sport Fisheries and Wildlife. Dr. Lincoln had hoped that if Josephine and Crip raised enough young to produce other mated pairs, Douglass would share some of the young with the other zoos and aviculturists who were pressing the Bureau with increasing insistence. Not long before this, a number of aviculturists had joined together in an organization called the International Wild Waterfowl Association. Its president was Jean Delacour, the French-American scientist who had once given Douglass a testimonial. Dr. Ripley was vice-president. Soon after its creation the International Wild Waterfowl Association formed a standing committee to study the whooping crane problem. This committee, which later decided to call itself the Whooping Crane Conservation Association, dedicated itself to making two basic points: (1) wild whoopers must be captured to create a breeding stock; (2) the Bureau must somehow wrest some of the already captive whoopers from Douglass' grip and, since the Bureau possessed no facilities for raising cranes, spread them around among other zoos.

There was, of course, nothing the Bureau would have liked better than to be able to settle the matter by removing the cranes from New Orleans—provided it could be done neatly and without fear of political reprisals. In April 1959, Bureau director Janzen asked the Solicitor of the Department of the Interior to look once again at the legal possibilities. In July the answer came back. The Solicitor stated that the United States had no title to the birds and—even sadder—no claim on the young cranes, George, Georgette, and Peewee.

During the winter months of 1958–59 the wild whoopers, twenty-three adults and nine young, spent a quiet season without any loss, and began their departure on schedule in April. This year the Bureau had assigned a biologist, E. L. Boeker, to appraise the cranes' situation. Boeker made a particular effort to discover just where the unmated yearlings wandered during the summer, for it seemed quite clear they did not come to the nesting grounds. There had been a growing suspicion that somewhere these young birds encountered unknown hazards and that an unduly small percentage of them survived to become breeders. In May and early June, Boeker searched likely portions of Saskatchewan by plane. Of the nine young whooping cranes that had left Aransas, he was able to sight only one bird. The summer whereabouts of the young remained as much of a mystery as the location of the nests had once been.

That spring the breakup of ice in the Sass River area was three weeks later than usual, and the weather that followed was unsettled. The Canadian Wildlife Service, which each summer made regular aerial inspections of the nest areas throughout the breeding season, was able to locate unusually few pairs and, what was worse, only one fledgling.

In October, as the cranes started their flight south, a series of early and severe storms struck the northern states and apparently forced the birds to change their route, for very few were sighted on the traditional path. True to the gloomy prediction from the Canadians, only two young reached Aransas. Fortunately, only one adult had been lost, so the flock was now thirty-three.

Meanwhile, Allen and Baker were still discussing, by mail, their dissatisfaction with what they considered the laissez-faire policy at Aransas—a policy the Bureau would justify whenever it was criticized on this score by pointing out that whooping crane mortality at Aransas was relatively small compared to summer losses.

In the autumn of 1959 Allen wrote Baker another memorandum: "All the old difficulties are still present and still unsolved. Trespass violations and buzzing by low-flying aircraft are completely out of hand. There seems to be no official consciousness of these problems and no long range plan for dealing with them. As the human population increases in that area they can only get worse."

In sixty days at Aransas, Allen had frequently seen trespassing fishermen drive the whooping cranes into the air. Twice he saw private planes buzz the birds as they fed. Air Force jets flew low over the refuge, but the cranes didn't seem to mind them. Regular practice bombing and target runs were taking place on Matagorda Island just east of Panther Point.

"The cranes occupied all available territories and are being pressed on every hand by the increasing human population," Allen wrote. He urged Baker to try once more to persuade the owners of Matagorda and St. Joseph, and the state of Texas, which controls Ayres and Roddy Island, Mullet Bay and Mustang Lake, to set these areas aside for the use of the cranes. The owner of St. Joseph was amenable, but his tenant was not. Allen's hope was partly realized, however, in 1960, when the National Audubon Society was able to lease 4,003 acres of Matagorda from Toddie Lee Wynne for the use of the cranes. The next year they subleased a further 1,717 acres from Mr. Wynne, thus giving the cranes the use of all the suitable marshes outside Air Force territory. As a further safeguard the Society placed the leased land in the care of a full-time warden equipped with a motorboat. Thus, for as long as the present owners control the land, and continue the lease, the cranes that use the island are protected, provided another war does not bring live bombing back to the bombing range.

Ironically, the human pressure at Aransas was being hastened by the whooping cranes themselves. Over the years publicity had made them an important tourist attraction. Dr. Cottam estimated that tourists visiting the cranes brought the state of Texas a million dollars a year. An excursion boat, the *Mary Lou,* out of the bayside town of Rockport, made a profitable business bringing sightseers to the cranes at five dollars a head. Traveling the waterway through the refuge, the *Mary Lou* often brought the visitors within a stone's throw of the feeding whoopers. Later, as business increased, the *Mary Lou* was joined by an even larger craft, named the *Whooping Crane.*

Fortunately, a boat moving at a steady speed doesn't bother the cranes—nor is it likely that bird-watchers would molest them —so this facet of the cranes' popularity was not a source of worry. Much more important was the increasing settlement of the whole area. Rockport was growing rapidly as a center for hunting, fishing, boating, and even bird-watching. The value of shorefront property was rising, and more and more the gay little flags of developers marked the places where bulldozers would roll into the brushland bordering the highway between Rockport and Aransas. Thus, when Allen visited Aransas in 1959 he found the picture vastly different from the wild, lonely emptiness of ten years earlier—and since then it has changed even more.

It was obvious to Allen that the chances of getting more space for the cranes would diminish with each passing year. In 1960, he wrote: "Each pair and family requires approximately four hundred acres. This fact I have checked and rechecked. If the flock increased to a hundred birds where are they to winter? I know that area and every acre surrounding it, and the only possible room for expansion is on Matagorda Island and possibly on St. Joseph, but the habitat there is limited. To tell the truth there is not much room to spare right now, and if we had as many as fifty birds to deal with they'd be hard put to it to find undisturbed, honest-to-God whooping crane habitat. It is a problem that has worried Baker and me for some time. It is something we've been trying to interest the Bureau of Fish and Wildlife in taking seriously."

A short time later Allen wrote in *Audubon Magazine:* "Do we really want to save the whooping crane? For the first time there is grave doubt by some people whether, for all our pious words to the contrary, we can continue to provide sanctuary for large, wilderness-seeking species like the whooping crane."

In this, for the first time, Allen seemed to be on the verge of admitting that defeat might be inevitable, no matter how he, or anyone else, labored to save *Grus americana.*

In June 1960, Robert Allen retired from the National Audubon Society, for which he had worked for thirty years. His retirement at fifty-five was something he had long promised himself in order to work on his own writing and research projects unhampered by routine assignments. Once or twice more in the next three years Allen would make yet another effort on behalf of the cranes, but in truth his retirement marked the end of what he could do for them.

Allen continued to feel, passionately, that it was the wild flock of birds, not captive whooping cranes, on which attention should be centered; that it was the problem of helping the small flock increase its numbers beyond the danger point that presented the true challenge. In his monograph he had written: "As the human population curve goes up, the Whooping Crane curve goes down.

This is a bird that cannot compromise or adjust its way of life to ours. Could not by its very nature; could not even if we had allowed it the opportunity, which we did not. For the Whooping Crane there is no freedom but that of unbounded wilderness, no life except its own. Without meekness, without a sign of humility, it has refused to accept our idea of what the World should be like. If we succeed in preserving the wild remnant that still survives it will be no credit to us; the glory will rest on this bird whose stubborn vigor has kept it alive in the face of increasing and seemingly hopeless odds."

After his retirement Allen lived in Tavernier, and in 1961 finished writing *Birds of the Caribbean.* He was making new studies of flamingos and spoonbills—his two greatest loves next to whooping cranes—when in May 1962 he had a severe heart attack. He recovered from it and impatiently went back to work. He had a second heart attack, and died on June 28, 1963.

Robert Allen's work for the whooping crane had been the most profound involvement of his professional career. He had laid all he had, emotionally, physically, and intellectually, on the line in his effort to save the wild birds. They had come to symbolize some of his deepest moral beliefs regarding conservation. He was convinced that with the proper effort they *could* be saved—and yet—at the time he died—there was little in the fortunes of the whooping cranes to give him very great hope.

18

It would be difficult to choose any particular moment as a turning point in whooping crane affairs, but it does seem that in 1960 a good many changes that had been in the making for some time took effect. Of these, by far the most important was the Bureau's realization that it couldn't remain forever wedged between the upper and nether millstones of the aviculturists and the National Audubon Society, while the whoopers quietly faded away, but must indeed do something—if not necessarily what either suggested. Late in 1960 the Bureau did what everyone now agrees was the right thing to do—it launched avicultural studies of its own. This program did not, of course, spring into being full-blown; it was a measure that had been persistently urged—in various forms—by almost everyone: the National Audubon Society, Dr. Ripley and his friends, and men within the Bureau itself, for five years or more. In a sense the National Audubon Society and the aviculturists had worked together better than they knew; as opposing forces they had pushed the Bureau in yet a third direction that combined elements of the course desired by each.

As far back as 1956, Dr. Ripley's gadfly tactics had forced the Bureau to do some homework in preparation for its Whooping Crane Conference, and this included an effort to make an up-to-date biological assessment of the whooping cranes' situation. John Lynch had prepared an analysis of the cranes' vital statistics that was in turn given for review to another Bureau biologist, a quiet, dark-haired young man named Ray C. Erickson. Dr. Erickson took his assignment with a seriousness and a thoroughness that hadn't been matched since Allen's studies. Erickson disagreed with Lynch's conclusions—since he thought it would be unwise to capture wild whooping cranes at that time, or allow any aviculturists to capture them—but suggested that the Bureau should prepare itself for the eventuality by experiments with the whooping cranes' abundant cousins, the sandhills. Working with them, it might be able to devise techniques of capture, rearing, and even reintroduction to the wild that would show the way if the time ever came to capture whooping cranes. This suggestion for pilot studies with sandhills was put forward by Erickson in a memo to Janzen. Then, for almost five years, a short period as time is measured within government agencies, nothing tangible resulted.

As Erickson continued off and on to work at his whooping crane assignment, studying whatever data came his way, he noticed a peculiar feature of whooping crane statistics. On several occasions the population suffered a major loss of birds, yet the following year brought back as many young as ever. This led him to think that the losses had occurred not among mated pairs—the elders of the flock—but among the subadults, the wanderers of summer. It was this idea that prompted Boeker's efforts to trace them in the summer of 1959.

Erickson made still another interesting discovery. The major losses to the flock had occurred during years when the ground water level was high in the prairie provinces of Canada, filling the potholes that dot the land. Conversely, it seemed that during the dry years more adults—presumably yearlings—survived. Making a guess to account for this, Erickson put forward the idea that when the prairie potholes dried up, the yearling cranes flew elsewhere, possibly northward into the wet brush country, and for some reason prospered; while in wet years they stayed on the prairies and fell prey to farmers defending their wheat, to four-footed predators, or some unguessed danger. Supporting this surmise was the fact that cranes have been seen in the pothole country southeast of Regina only during wetter years. In Canada wet years usually run in cycles of two or three or more, during which ground water builds up. This, coupled with the amount of winter snowfall, makes it possible to predict, with reasonable success, whether prairie potholes will be full or empty in any coming summer.

Coupling the two ideas of high mortality of yearlings in wet summers—and the predictability of wet summers—Erickson came up with the proposal that four to six immature whooping cranes be captured at Aransas when a wet summer was in prospect. In this way it would be possible to acquire the breeding stock for which the aviculturists clamored and at the same time salvage birds that would otherwise quite likely be lost in their maiden season. He again urged that the groundwork be laid by experiments with sandhills.

In this work of Erickson's, the Bureau saw hope of finding a way out of its dilemma. Biological studies accompanied by success in breeding sandhills might convince the Audubon Society of the rationality of capturing whooping cranes and, at the same time, hold off the criticisms of the aviculturists. And last, but not least, it seemed possible that through experience with sandhills the whooping crane might indeed be saved.

In 1960 the Bureau announced that it was going to begin its own propagation of whooping cranes. Thus, for the first time in quite a long while the Bureau was about to do something in relation to the whoopers with which few could find fault.

In the spring of 1960 Josephine and Crip had performed their nuptial dances within their cramped and arid quarters at the Audubon Park Zoo. Josephine began her annual effort to raise young. Her first three eggs were infertile. In mid-April she laid two more. On May 17 the first egg hatched a fine little chick. The second hatched on May 18. The next day the second chick was found dead in the grass. Douglass took the survivor from the parents and put it in a brooder, where it was fed by hand. It seemed to do well until, without warning, it collapsed and, as Douglass described it, "died without a struggle." Again aspergillosis was to blame.

At this time George and Georgette were approaching their third birthday. No one knows, exactly, when whooping cranes are old enough to mate, but since sandhills pair at three there was reason to think that the young birds were approaching maturity. Douglass began to view them hopefully for signs of difference in sex, but the young cranes, penned together since infancy, now showed quite the reverse of prenuptial behavior. From time to time one or the other would become excited and run back and forth against the side of the pen until its wings were raw. The birds calmed down as soon as they were separated. The two-year-old chick named Peewee, in a pen divided from the others by chicken wire, showed nothing but alarm in the company of its siblings.

Meanwhile, the wild whooping cranes had been continuing their uphill struggle with that strange, last-ditch tenacity that Robert Allen had termed a "vital intangible of the situation."

The drought at Aransas had broken in the summer of 1959 and been replaced by a protracted wet spell that was as bad for the cranes as the drought had been. Thanks to the dikes and channels that had been built on the refuge, floods of fresh water washed over the marshes, upsetting the precarious balance of salinity and destroying the marine life that usually provided the cranes with food. The thirty-three wintering cranes spent more time on the canal as the winter progressed, and then a number of them moved to Matagorda and St. Joseph. When the spring migration took place, a pair elected to stay behind and summer on Matagorda. In the summer of 1960, the nesting birds had above-average luck and that autumn brought back six young to the still-flooded refuge. The summer's loss was three and so there was a new record of thirty-six whooping cranes on the refuge.

Unfortunately, conditions on the refuge prevented any complacency. The cranes wandered far and wide in search of food, sometimes within the limits of the Matagorda bombing range. As in the previous year, heavy rains caused trouble in the marsh.

"The whooping cranes gave us nothing but fits," the manager wrote in his report on the 1960–61 winter. "We attribute the cranes' strange actions to the fresh water intrusion. Fresh water was impounded behind the east shore road and released comparatively slowly through control structures and washouts to spread over the coastal marsh, polluting the tide pools and lakes which are normally whooper food lockers." In an effort to keep the cranes on the refuge, the manager dropped paper bags full of wheat on the marshes, thus at last putting into effect one of Allen's suggestions. "Whoopers took readily to this supplemental feeding," the manager reported, "and more than once were observed rushing to the air-dropped wheat."

Before the eventful year 1960 ended, there had also been important changes in the personnel of the whooping crane circle. John Baker followed Robert Allen into retirement, and became president emeritus. His place was taken by Carl Buchheister, a graduate of Johns Hopkins, and former teacher, who had served the Society in various ways for years.

The circle also lost Dr. Lincoln, who died in September. The crane portfolio was handed on to the Bureau's assistant director, Lansing Parker, a tall, genial administrator who had been in the Service since 1945. Parker picked up where Lincoln had left off in the ticklish job of maintaining polite communication with Douglass, with the aviculturists, represented by the Whooping Crane Conservation Association, and with the Bureau's old friend and critic, the National Audubon Society.

In the spring of 1961, Parker had pleasant news to report. Josephine laid four eggs, and though three were infertile the fourth hatched a healthy young whooping crane that gave every promise of surviving. The fourth whooper born in captivity was named Pepper.

In the spring of 1961, the wild cranes left their flooded home at Aransas early and departed for Canada, where, though they could hardly have been aware of it, luck had turned to their side. Protests over the proposal to put a railroad line near the nesting ground had reached the highest political levels. Prime Minister John Diefenbaker, in a speech from the throne, had asked Parliament to appropriate funds to survey the western route that would detour Wood Buffalo Park. At considerable cost, this route was adopted. The summer was fortunate in other ways also. Only two birds were lost, and five young returned in the autumn of 1961. Again there was a new record: thirty-nine cranes. Meanwhile, in September, Hurricane Carla had swept the refuge, erasing many of the works of man and recharging the salt flats with seawater and crabs.

As winter wore on, the members of the flock wandered about, even though there was plentiful food on the refuge. Perhaps their high number caused their restlessness. In December the foreman of the ranch on Matagorda found a dead whooping crane on the island, a discovery he decided to keep to himself. When, months later, the news got out and the refuge manager learned of it, the foreman explained his silence by saying he'd "sooner be caught with an illegal whiskey still than have anything to do with a dead whooping crane."

In the spring of 1962, the flock of thirty-eight migrated normally, but were met by cold, wet weather in Canada. The Canadian Wildlife Service surveyed the nesting grounds and found that high water had drowned out most of the small grass islands on which the cranes are in the habit of building their nests. It predicted a poor nesting season. This was borne out in November when the flock returned. For only the second time in twenty-five years they came down from the north without a single young bird. To make matters worse, six adults had been lost and the flock was back to thirty-two birds.

The aviculturists seized upon this disaster to prod the Bureau on the subject of capturing cranes. John A. Griswold, Curator of Birds at the Philadelphia Zoo, was reported by the Philadelphia *Inquirer* on December 30, 1962, to have said that the "tiny population of whooping cranes is inevitably yet needlessly doomed to extinction in its natural environment.

"There is no doubt about it," the paper quoted him, "the small population is bound to die if man doesn't breed them in captivity. The Fish and Wildlife people are well aware of it, but they're sort of namby-pamby because if something went wrong they'd get it in the neck. . . . Birds raised in captivity won't ever be able to return to the natural state, but at least people will be able to see what they look like."

The words "inevitably yet needlessly doomed to extinction in its natural environment" were more nearly exact than perhaps even Mr. Griswold was aware. At the time he spoke, the whooping cranes were suddenly beset by added danger at Aransas. That autumn they had become innocent bystanders at the Cuban crisis. With the coming of the war threat, the Air Force began to drop powerful live bombs on their range on Matagorda. The refuge manager, Huyson Johnson, reported the fact to Washington. "Whatever they are using really rattled the windows for twenty miles around," he wrote in his report of December 31, 1962. "While they did not bomb every day, this activity put a lid on our census flights into the restricted area without a mess of red tape. No whoopers were using Matagorda . . . however a potential danger did (and does) exist."

At the same time food conditions on the marsh were poor. In his next report Johnson told how the birds, "unhappy over conditions on their habitat, moved restlessly about. Live bombing of Matagorda added chaos to the confusion."

At length Johnson concluded that three whooping cranes were missing, then four. He visited the Air Force officer in local command and was provided with a helicopter to search the refuge and the bomb range, but no white corpses were found. The Bureau then assigned Erwin Boeker, the biologist who, with Erickson, had been studying the crane problem, to make a further search for the missing whoopers. Boeker reported:

"On December 4, 1962, when bombing commenced, ten whoopers were utilizing Matagorda . . . the number remained constant through February in spite of the bombing. Thus, there is no direct evidence available to indicate that the bombing program adversely affected whooper behavior, or that it was instrumental in causing the disappearance of four of the birds.

"Intensive aerial search over the bombing range failed to disclose any carcasses. On the other hand, the bombing did create a hazardous condition and, along with other human activities, may have contributed to the general unrest of the wintering population. Rather than point at any one disturbing factor on or near the whooping crane wintering grounds as being the responsible factor for creating discontent, it appears we should take a long, hard look at the entire situation.

"At almost any hour of the day or night the area is a beehive of human activity ranging from oyster dredges to SAC bombers. A constant stream of boat and barge traffic moves through the Intercoastal Canal and oil exploration and drilling continue to increase in waters near the Refuge. The question is, how much disturbance can the whooping crane tolerate without creating obscure psychological effects which eventually will cause the entire population to scatter and disappear? Perhaps this point has been reached.

"Another factor that should be considered in connection with the disappearance of four whoopers is a possible shortage of food. Last fall the whoopers made more use of the Refuge interior than usual. This suggests that marine organisms were not abundant even before a series of northers lowered water levels drastically. Supplemental food in the form of wheat and hegari was dropped during this period.

"The fate of the four missing whoopers will probably never be known unless they moved to some undisclosed area last winter and will return to the known wintering grounds this fall. As previously stated, there is no evidence that they were lost due to the bombing program on Matagorda. Yet this activity as well as others on the wintering grounds must be curtailed if the whoopers are to receive sanctuary and maximum safety."

At the time of which Boeker wrote, bombing was certainly not the only danger at Aransas. In February, Shell Oil, drilling just offshore, began to discharge sludge directly into the bay. It continued to do so for ten days before complaints stopped the pollution. Poachers were common on the marshes, where there was no regular patrol. On the waterway the sign warning approaching boatmen that they were entering a protected area had been blown away by the hurricane two years before and had not been replaced because the necessary funds had not been authorized by the Bureau's regional office.

In May the last of the twenty-eight cranes that had somehow survived the perils of the refuge flew north. On May 22 the manager wrote: "No cranes on the Refuge . . . this closes the book on the whooping crane season of '62–'63 with an indicated loss of six birds during the summer of 1962, no young reared and a loss of four on the wintering grounds."

Summer was kinder to them than the almost disastrous winter. The flock lost only two of its number, and triumphantly added seven young for a total of thirty-three birds in the autumn of 1963. As an indication of their symbolic, if not their real, status in American life they were welcomed home by Secretary of the Interior Stewart Udall, who issued a statement announcing the arrival of the whooping cranes at Aransas that November. The secretary said, "The good news on the flock's growth is heartening evidence that thoughtful men can help undo the ravages of thoughtlessness." Perhaps he should have added a line giving equal credit to the tenacity of whooping cranes.

19

A sine qua non of breeding birds in captivity is an ability to distinguish between the sexes. As time wore on and the young birds at the Audubon Park Zoo still refused to declare themselves, the puzzle of their gender became more and more exasperating to all concerned. Whenever the young cranes were penned together, or even adjacent, as a prelude to possible mating, they showed nothing but hostility. It was impossible to tell whether their behavior stemmed from their unnatural circumstances, their immaturity, or the inherently difficult disposition of whooping cranes. There was also the unlikely but dismaying possibility that they were all of the same sex. Of course, the whooping crane circle not only hoped that a mated pair could be found among the four young but also that one of them would turn out to be of the opposite sex from San Antonio Rosie, whatever that might be. However, whenever anyone suggested to Douglass that he send one of his young birds to San Antonio on a trial basis, he invariably replied that, being ignorant of their sex, he couldn't know which one to send but that Rosie would be welcome at the New Orleans Zoo anytime the Bureau chose to send her to him.

Finally, in 1961, when George and Georgette were four years old, the Bureau could stand the frustration—and the prodding of the Whooping Crane Conservation Association—no longer, and assigned a biologist to study the problem of sex determination in whooping cranes.

The biologist chosen, a tall, dark-haired woman with a soft Georgia voice named Mrs. Roxie Laybourne, discovered that a colleague at Johns Hopkins was facing a similar problem with penguins. In both birds the distinguishing features are hidden within the cloaca of the bird and, at that time, could be identified only by autopsy. Mrs. Laybourne and her friend designed an instrument, which they called a cloacascope, that enabled them to take an enlightening look without damaging a live bird.

In 1960 the Bureau had opened a shooting season on sandhill cranes in Texas and New Mexico—a move that greatly dismayed the National Audubon Society, but incidentally provided Mrs. Laybourne with a supply of subjects on which to practice. She visited the refuges where shooting was taking place, and as hunters brought dead cranes to a Bureau checking station Mrs. Laybourne examined them and then verified her guess by autopsy. She then moved on to working with live sandhills at the Washington Zoo. When handling live subjects she taped their legs, tarsus to tibia (as though hand to shoulder in a human), taped the bill closed, and enveloped the bird's wings in a crane jacket of her own design, made of Canton flannel and closed down the front with a zipper.

By November 1962, she was satisfied that her method was reliable and did no physical or psychological harm to the birds. The sandhill cranes, she found, recovered their aplomb quite rapidly after the experience.

In the spring of 1962 Mrs. Laybourne packed her crane jacket and cloacascope and journeyed south, hoping to determine the sex of the young whooping cranes at New Orleans and of Rosie at San Antonio. At Audubon Park she found that Douglass was not at the office. He had, however, left word that he would be unable to see her and that she was on no account to lay hands on his cranes. Mrs. Laybourne went on to San Antonio. She examined Rosie and found her to be a female.

The reason Douglass later gave for not allowing Mrs. Laybourne to examine the young cranes was his fear that she might damage them in some way. He had also, of course, kept intact his reasons against sending any young to San Antonio, but at the same time condemned himself to continued suspense. In this dilemma he turned for advice to a man who worked for the Purina Chow Company and from whom he purchased the Game Bird Crumbles and Purina Checkerettes that were part of the cranes' diet.

The Purina Company maintains a laboratory at St. Louis where it does avicultural research. The company offered Douglass the aid of its experts, and Douglass' friend told him that if he could get sandhills to practice on, as Mrs. Laybourne had, he might be able to duplicate her method of sexing whoopers. Sandhills cannot be captured except by permit, so Douglass asked the Bureau to provide him with some sandhills. Understandably, the request was refused.

That spring of 1962, Josephine began to lay in early March. Of her first clutch one egg was infertile, but the other hatched on April 8. By April 12 Douglass had realized that the chick had a defect of its right leg. He decided to entrust it to the Purina Company. The chick was flown to the laboratory in St. Louis and a veterinary there operated to correct a slipped tendon. The original operation was a success, but the stitch tore out. The bird was given anesthetic for a second time, and died on the operating table. It was ten days old. In May, Josephine laid a second clutch. Both eggs were taken from the nest and sent to the

Purina laboratory for incubation. Neither hatched, but it was found that both had been fertile. There was, of course, no way to tell if the trip to St. Louis and the method of incubation had caused the death of the embryos, or if it would have occurred in any case.

Finally, at the end of May, Josephine made a third attempt to raise young whoopers, and for a time it seemed as though she might succeed. On June 25 a young crane was hatched, but lived only a week. It was found dead in the yard of causes that were not determined or recorded. The day before its death Crip broke the remaining egg in the nest. It contained a dead chick.

As word of the spring debacle at New Orleans reached the whooping crane circle there was mounting chagrin. Dr. Ripley, for one, decided to make a new attempt to free Josephine and Crip. Going over the Bureau's head, he wrote a strong letter to the Assistant Secretary of the Interior, Frank Briggs. He told Briggs that the situation of the five captive whooping cranes at New Orleans was a travesty. Scientists all over the world were distressed by the critical situation of *Grus americana*, Ripley wrote, and it was both distressing and embarrassing that the United States government was, in truth, doing very little to prevent the extinction of the species.

To this the Assistant Secretary politely reiterated the Solicitor's opinion that Josephine and her offspring belonged to the New Orleans Zoo; an attempt to take the birds from Douglass would forestall any chance of the Bureau's getting young birds from him voluntarily. He had, he said, been informed that Mr. Douglass would give up a young bird when he had a mated pair in addition to Crip and Josephine. Dr. Ripley was neither satisfied nor convinced. Like some other indignant bystanders, he felt that the Solicitor's opinion was legal mumbo jumbo with which the Bureau had allowed itself to become burdened. Since Ripley was a man not easily quenched, he wrote Assistant Secretary Briggs a second letter, again urging legal steps to take

Josephine and Crip from Douglass, describing him as a man who, "for one reason or another, seems to have taken extraordinary pains to jeopardize the future of the species in captivity."

Possibly Dr. Ripley's letter spurred the Bureau to greater efforts, for in the following spring it was happy to inform Dr. Ripley and other members of the Whooping Crane Advisory Group that it had at last made progress at New Orleans. Douglass had agreed to surrender Josephine's first set of eggs to the Bureau, and the Bureau had selected William Huey, an aviculturist employed by the New Mexico Department of Fish and Game, to stand by, ready to hatch them.

The spring laying season was awaited with more than usual anticipation. On March 12, 1963, Josephine laid an egg. She pecked a hole in it the same day. In succeeding weeks she laid a second and a third, and as promptly destroyed them. Finally, in April, she laid an egg that was snatched from beneath her before she could break it, and delivered to Mr. Huey in Sante Fe, New Mexico. While this prize was being incubated there, Josephine laid four more eggs; but of these, two were infertile and two were broken before they could be taken from the nest.

The new spirit of cooperation between Douglass and the Bureau was destined to be brief. The very week that Douglass relinquished an egg to Mr. Huey, *Life* magazine published a full-page photograph of Douglass dolefully staring at the broken shards of Josephine's first three eggs. The accompanying text stated that out of thirty-four eggs laid by Josephine, thirteen had hatched but only four chicks had survived. To Douglass the story seemed to imply criticism of his management, and he became highly incensed. He telephoned the Bureau and accused it of being instrumental in bringing about this unfavorable publicity. All deals were off, Douglass angrily declared, and the Bureau could expect no more whooping crane eggs from him.

To make this rupture unhappier still, the egg Huey incubated in Sante Fe turned out to be infertile.

Word of the Bureau's latest reverse soon reached the Whooping Crane Conservation Association. Its president was now a man named Jack Kiracoff, a hobbyist who had been breeding birds, particularly waterfowl, for many years. Kiracoff mulled over the problem of how relations between Douglass and the Bureau might be restored. Kiracoff's proposed solution produced one of the stranger episodes in whooping crane history. He suggested that the International Wild Waterfowl Association, originally the parent of the Whooping Crane Conservation Association, present Douglass with an award for his "outstanding contributions to aviculture." In view of the fact that a recent meeting of the IWWA had roundly condemned Douglass as a hindrance to the propagation of the whooping crane, some of Kiracoff's confreres were a bit doubtful of the wisdom of the stratagem, but it was decided to give it a try.

Douglass was invited to come to the IWWA's annual convention in October 1963 to receive the award. He accepted with pleasure. Then, on the day the presentation was to take place, there was a hitch of a bizarre nature. Members of the association were assembled in the hall when word came that Douglass had been robbed. He had lost not only his money but his clothes, and was thus unable to leave his room.

A hastily formed subcommittee sped to the motel to take the imprisoned zoo keeper's measurements. On the way, someone remarked that this was the first time George Douglass had ever been restrained by modesty, but otherwise old enmities were generously put aside. The delegation quickly bought and delivered to Douglass a suitable ensemble.

This strange episode helped to lessen whatever strain might otherwise have existed between Douglass and his hosts. The award was given in a glow of mutual cordiality. Kiracoff felt that his scheme had indeed served its purpose when, shortly afterward, Douglass renewed his offer to give some of Josephine's eggs to the Bureau in the coming year.

To prepare for further efforts to raise young whoopers from Josephine's eggs, the Bureau hired a full-time aviculturist, a young man named C. Eugene Knoder. Because the Bureau still possessed no suitable laboratory of its own, it was decided that the eggs would be incubated at the Bureau's Lafayette, Louisiana, Research Station, where John Lynch would make available his private avicultural facilities. On March 28 and March 31, 1964, Josephine performed her annual miracle. Knoder was standing by, ready to take the eggs. They were moved in heated, padded boxes to Lafayette, where John Lynch had been conditioning silky bantam hens, weighing only a pound each, to brood half-pound whooping crane eggs; a trick performed by artfully substituting bigger and bigger eggs for the bantam's own clutch.

The hens, whom Lynch had named Patience and Petulance, did their duty, but once again lack of experience in dealing with whooping cranes brought failure. The first chick was premature because the aviculturists had not realized that the egg should be cooled for periods during incubation. The chick died when it was thirty hours old. The second egg hatched a chick that appeared viable, although it had a defective leg muscle. When it was six days old, Lynch and Knoder decided to move it to the Monte Vista Research Station in Colorado. It died there of a hemorrhage of the ischiadic vein at the age of eighteen days.

Josephine, meanwhile, continued to lay. She broke all records by laying a total of ten eggs. She broke one of them by pecking a hole in it. The others were taken from her and put in the zoo's incubator, but all of them were infertile.

By now there was more than ever reason to fear that Josephine or Crip, or perhaps both of them, were too old to produce viable young, and it was more than ever important that Rosie—now, at last, known to be a female—have an opportunity to do her share. It also occurred to the Bureau that Rosie might perform a further service. If she were exposed to the young birds at New Orleans, any that were hostile to her might be presumed to be female, and any that were friendly might be male.

Therefore in April 1964 the Bureau decided to accept Douglass' offer and move Rosie to New Orleans. Before sending her, the Bureau took the precaution of obtaining a firm legal agreement that any offspring from her would be the property of the federal government.

At Aransas the winter months of 1963–64 were more peaceful for the wild whooping cranes than they had been the year before. The wild acorn crop was good, and the birds were also fed with grain. The Air Force ceased using live bombs. The only untoward event was the discovery, in March, of the scattered remains of a whooping crane on Bludworth Island, just off the refuge. The corpse, found only a hundred yards from the canal, was of an immature bird, one of the twins of a family that had only a single parent. The loss reduced the flock to thirty-two, all of whom migrated normally in the spring.

In early summer the Canadian Wildlife Service predicted an unusually good season. From the air its biologist, Nicholas S. Novakowski, saw four breeding pairs of cranes. By June, one pair had hatched a single young bird and two pairs had twins.

For the rest of the summer Novakowski made only occasional flights, for fear of disturbing the nestlings, but in September he flew low in a helicopter for a thorough look. As he passed over the spot where he had seen a pair of twins, Novakowski saw only one young bird, and it seemed to be in trouble; its right wing dangled and it tripped over the primary feathers every few steps. Novakowski asked the pilot to bring the helicopter down low for a closer look, but the adults dashed at the plane with flapping wings, and the pilot was barely able to veer and rise quickly enough to avoid them. Novakowski flew back to Fort Smith with all possible speed and wired his discovery to the two wildlife services. Within a few hours he had been instructed to capture the injured bird.

The next day, with an assistant, Novakowski returned to the nesting area. The youngster was spotted next to a dry lake where, fortunately, the helicopter was able to land. The men chased the young bird through the brush until it tripped and fell.

Then they caught it easily. It was surprisingly unresistant as it was wrapped in sacking and put in a cage tied to the outside of the helicopter. At Fort Smith the bird was put aboard a commercial flight to Edmonton, where it was immediately taken to a local veterinary clinic. An X ray showed that the injured wing was partially dislocated and that a two-inch sliver of charred wood had pierced the bird's breast muscle. Probably the youngster had flown against a burnt tree and impaled itself on a branch while learning to fly. To the surprise of its captors, the young bird seemed quite unafraid as it was handled, and readily accepted a meal of minced egg, mealworms, hamburger, and fresh smelts.

That afternoon Eugene Knoder, the avicultural expert the Bureau had hired to handle Josephine's eggs, arrived by plane to take the little crane, nestled in a cardboard box, to Monte Vista. The trip was interrupted by a stop at Cutbank, Montana. Here Knoder took the crane out of the carton for exercise. A crowd gathered, but the bird walked up and down the cement apron quite unconcerned, eating and drinking as though it were already used to people. Knoder came to wonder if perhaps at this stage of their lives young whoopers assume people are other birds and learn to fear humans only when their parents teach them to, during migration and on the wintering ground.

For the first two weeks at Monte Vista, the young whooper, now named Lady Bird, did well, and then, without warning, became very ill. One morning it was barely able to stand. As the day passed it refused to eat or drink, and seemed near death. Knoder sent for all the medical help he could gather. Four veterinarians arrived and administered a barrage of medicines. The bird responded, and within a day made a remarkable recovery, only to get in trouble again.

The young crane was penned indoors at night. In the morning it customarily celebrated its release by flapping its wings and running about. One morning, during these capers, it caught one toe in the bandage on its wing, and fell, breaking the already injured wing in two places. Again veterinarians went to work and repaired the damage, and again the whooper recovered. It was soon strong enough for a session with Mrs. Laybourne, who pronounced it a male. The name Lyndon Bird was rejected by officials mindful of their responsibility for dignity, and Lady Bird became Canus, a blend of "Canada" and "U.S."

20

Since the cranes came back to Aransas in the autumn of 1964, a number of things have happened that, joined to all that has gone before, will play a part in determining how many more journeys lie ahead of them. Will it be ten, twenty, fifty, or will they fly for many generations more? Some signs point toward a renewed future for them. Some indicate that the wild birds do not, indeed, have far to go.

As the returning cranes were counted in November 1964, it became clear they had again brought off one of their astonishing feats of last-ditch recovery. Not only did every one of the thirty-two birds that went north in the spring come back to Aransas, but the flock brought with them ten young birds—eight singles and one pair of twins. Including Canus, they had produced the record-breaking count of eleven young. The wild flock was thus forty-two. With eight cranes in captivity, the birds had at last reached that number whose roundness seems to give it some magic meaning: there were fifty whooping cranes on earth.

Meanwhile, there was another event that, taken purely from the point of view of the whooping cranes, was bound to be influential. On November 10, 1964, George Douglass died. He was fifty-seven years old. His obituary, carried throughout the nation by the Associated Press, identified him as the only man ever to raise whooping cranes in captivity—a fact that is indisputable, but double-edged. Taken either way, it will no doubt win him a place in the ornithological annals of the future. It is possible to guess, too, that the whooping cranes brought him some of his life's most glowing moments of satisfaction—and that there were other moments when he wished he had never heard the words *Grus americana*.

The New Orleans Park Commission filled Douglass' vacant post by appointing one of its number, a retired businessman named William Pohlmann, whose experience in breeding horses had led him to an interest in the zoo.

Pohlmann responded cordially to overtures from the Bureau of Sport Fisheries and Wildlife. He welcomed Mrs. Laybourne and Eugene Knoder to the zoo. Mrs. Laybourne made the important discovery that George, Georgette, and Pepper were males. Peewee, the third chick, who was born in 1958, was a female.

Mr. Pohlmann accepted an arrangement whereby new quarters for the cranes would be constructed at the expense of the Bureau and Eugene Knoder would supervise future nestings. The Bureau assured Pohlmann that it had no desire to move any of the present flock from New Orleans but that future offspring should be distributed "elsewhere" to guard against such catastrophes as disease, hurricane, fire, or flood. All the offspring of Rosie and half of the young of Peewee, should there be any, would be federal property.

During the winter of 1964–65, Knoder went to New Orleans several times. He found that Leo Buras, the diffident, soft-spoken keeper, had already successfully matched Rosie and George. Buras had always believed Peewee to be a female. Now, with Knoder's approval, he penned her with her brother, the former Georgette, renamed George II. For a time the two seemed to get along quite well, and even to be starting a courtship. Then, suddenly, an antagonism developed, and they had to be separated.

The new pens built during the winter were roofed with wire mesh at a height of ten feet, which allowed room for the leaps of the courting cranes, and provided fifty feet on each side. Bamboo curtains gave the birds privacy. In contrast to the weeds and dust that floored the old pens, there was now a ground cover of bluegrass and clover. The old tin water basins were scrapped. Water flowed continuously into concrete pools in each pen.

However, in spite of all the promise of the courtship dances and the improved accommodations, the spring of 1965 brought forth no young whooping cranes. Rosie and George mated, but they did not go so far as to build a nest. Only Josephine, that steady old grande dame, did her part, but less generously than in previous years. She laid two eggs that were taken from her and put under silky bantams provided by John Lynch, but both eggs were infertile. On May 13 she laid a third egg, which Lynch picked up and brought to Knoder for incubation at the Monte Vista laboratory. When it failed to hatch, Knoder opened it and found that the chick had died in the shell two days before hatching. Josephine did not lay again.

The previous fall there had been another important change in the cast of characters managing the cranes' future. Daniel Janzen, who had been the director of the Bureau of Sport Fisheries and Wildlife since its formation seven years earlier, retired, and his place was taken by John S. Gottschalk, who had been Northeast Regional Director at Boston.

The job of director of the Bureau came with limitations and frustrations firmly attached. The Fish and Wildlife Service's* purse strings are tightly tied by Congress. Each dime that is appropriated is earmarked by Congress for a specified purpose, and may be spent for no other. Thus Congress effectively controls the Service's actions. In the past, Congress has been greatly influenced by the views of the sportsmen's lobbies who watch jealously to see that major wildlife expenditures are to promote "sport," and not such frivolities as wild creatures in general or even whooping cranes in particular. In spite of these financial limitations, there were many things the Bureau director could do for the whooping cranes if he chose, beginning with a willingness to consider their existence a matter of importance. Mr. Gotts-

* In 1974 the Fish and Wildlife Service was reorganized and the Bureau of Sport Fisheries and Wildlife lost its separate identity.

chalk quite quickly convinced the whooping crane circle that his administration would have the cranes very much in mind.

Thereafter, at Aransas, there were changes helpful to the cranes.

For example, in the autumn of 1964 the cranes arrived to find a ninety-acre plot of land fenced to keep out four-footed intruders and seeded with grain crops. The whoopers came down off their high horses long enough to join hundreds of sandhills at the feast. As long as the grain held out, the cranes seldom wandered off the refuge. In 1965, the fenced area was doubled and planted with crops designed to last longer into the winter. In addition the manager was instructed to keep tabs on the marine food available. If it fails he will supply grain to tide the whoopers over a barren spell.

Steps were taken to protect the cranes from people. There was a better patrol of the waterway, and, as a small but important improvement, the warning signs were replaced. There was also an effort to stop the harassment of whooping cranes by low-flying aircraft. Texas is the land of the private airplane and more and more airborne cowboys buzzed the refuge. In 1965, the refuge manager wrote to the Federal Aviation Agency about the problem. The agency replied that the refuge could be put in the "restricted" category only if the birds were a danger to aircraft, not vice versa. However, the agency promised to warn pilots that there is a five-hundred-foot ceiling over the refuge.

If one asks why these protective steps, all simple in themselves, were not taken when Robert Allen suggested them more than ten years earlier, the primary answer is, of course, "money." In 1966 the annual budget for all the wildlife refuges was $13,000,000. This was a tenth of the sum allowed the Park Department. The difference is due to the fact that the parks serve people directly, and are thus vote-getters. Wildlife refuges, when they are doing their job best, keep people out of land reserved for the use of animals. To the public and its legislators the Fish and Wildlife Service's function often seems restrictive and negative.

21

In November 1964, Secretary Udall announced that the Bureau of Sport Fisheries and Wildlife wished to embark upon a project of research and protection designed to save from extinction a number of species of birds and mammals that were in imminent danger. He proposed a new laboratory at the Patuxent Wildlife Research Center in Maryland, including avicultural facilities to house the sandhill cranes that would be the pilot project for whooping crane propagation. In April 1965, Congress allotted the Bureau $350,000 to start the work. The buildings and staff were ready in early 1966. The initial sum was not large, but the start of the "Rare and Endangered Project" was tremendously significant not just for the whoopers but also as official recognition of a new attitude toward wildlife. The project, directed by Dr. Erickson, was the first in which creatures had been chosen for study because of their imperiled position rather than their economic value, and the Patuxent Center is the first research facility ever devoted to such an idealistic purpose.

The groundwork for whooping crane studies at Patuxent was laid by the work with sandhills begun by Erwin Boeker in 1961. The first phase was an effort to find out if it is possible to get a breeding stock of sandhills either by trapping wild birds or by taking eggs from the nests of wild birds and incubating them artificially: an experiment with obvious implications in the whooping crane controversy. Boeker experimented with three groups: greater and lesser sandhills trapped in the wild, and greater sandhills hatched from eggs stolen from the nests of wild birds. None of the methods of trapping worked out satisfactorily. "Walk-in" traps were unreliable and unselective; foot snares were ineffective; nets shot from cannons caused many injuries. The second stage of the sandhill experiment compared the survival of the different groups in captivity. The birds caught as yearlings remained wild and were difficult to handle; a number were killed in the same sort of unpredictable accidents that have so often attended the handling of whooping cranes. Hand-reared greater sandhills, on the other hand, did much better. Some were lost in infancy, but all of those that came through this critical period grew into healthy and tractable birds. By the end of 1963 it had been established that it would be far better to rear cranes, whoopers or sandhills, by taking their eggs than by attempting to capture them in the wild.

Late in 1963 Dr. Erickson at last was given funds to hire Eugene Knoder expressly to carry on the sandhill experiments. During 1964, Knoder, John Lynch, and others in the Bureau concentrated on solving the problems involved in picking up and hatching eggs taken from wild sandhills. The experimenters devised a portable incubator to carry eggs from the nests to the laboratory. It was an elaborate device, electrically powered by batteries, equipped with such refinements as sponges to maintain humidity and foam-rubber mounts to prevent jarring its precious contents. The experimenters compared different methods of incubation and tried out various diets on the growing chicks. In one experiment thirty eggs were collected. Of these, twenty-three hatched, but seven chicks died in their first six months. Each death provided a lesson of one sort or another. One four-month-old crane pecked at a shiny shovel hanging on a rack. The shovel fell and fractured its skull. Needless to say, there were no shovels in pens thereafter.

In the spring of 1964 the U.S. and Canadian wildlife services jointly announced their plan to take whooping crane eggs for propagation. The avicultural group was greatly pleased with it and the National Audubon Society decided to give its approval. The Society's biologists felt that the plan had been worked out with a care that not only gave it a reasonable chance of success, but also subjected the wild flock to a minimum of danger. The money appropriated for the "Rare and Endangered" program at last gave assurance that there would be facilities equal to the job. Thus, when the Bureau's whooping crane project began in 1967, the National Audubon Society was among those cheering it on—and for the first time in many years the whole whooping crane circle was united.

Now that it is possible to look back on the roles played by various members of that circle, it seems, paradoxically, that all the opponents in the controversy were right. Those who wanted whooping cranes captured were at least correct in their belief that aviculture had something to offer, and it was their pressure that forced the Bureau to make a start. The National Audubon Society was equally correct in its conviction that experiments with wild whoopers would have been worse than doing nothing. Its staunch defense of the wild flock prevented any premature meddling with them that would quite likely have been not only useless but fatal. And, finally, the Fish and Wildlife Service is to be thanked for having at last found a course that offers real hope of saving *Grus americana*.

22

On Thursday, September 9, 1965, a hurricane of extraordinary violence, which the Weather Bureau had named Hurricane Betsy, drove directly upon the city of New Orleans. As the barometer fell, the scene at the zoo was one of frantic battening down and shifting of animals to what, the men there hoped, would be safe quarters in the brick buildings. Oddly, most wild birds and animals become very tractable, almost as in the story of the Ark, when they are faced with natural catastrophe. In birds, hollow bones and body air sacs apparently act as "aneroid barometers," sensitive to outside atmospheric pressure. As pressure begins to drop, birds are at first very nervous, but as it falls to a hurricane low they become almost numb. Thus, Leo Buras with the help of other keepers was able to capture the whooping cranes in their large pens and move them into shelter. Each bird was walked across the grounds with one man holding the bill and a man on each side of it holding it by the wing.

By three-thirty in the afternoon, with the wind already rising in the huge live oaks surrounding the park, the whooping cranes were under cover. On Pohlmann's orders the two pairs and the four single birds were put in different areas of the zoo as a precaution against the demolition of any one building. Josephine and Crip found themselves in a corridor, closed by doors at either end, leading to the indoor cage of a giraffe. As the wind rose to the full thunder of hurricane force and trees began to crash, all the zoo's human inhabitants retreated to the Administration Building to spend the night.

The storm abated shortly after midnight. With flashlights the men ventured out to assess the damage, and found they would first have to hack paths through the tangled barriers of fallen trees. (In the end it took fifty men twelve days to clear the debris.) By dawn Friday, after the storm, Pohlmann and the keepers had reached the buildings in which the cranes were confined, and found that all of them had come through safely, as indeed had all the zoo's large animals. The only casualties were a number of small fowl housed in wooden buildings that had been demolished. All the brick buildings were intact, but the once lovely park landscape was a ghastly tangle of roots and branches of fallen trees.

The new crane pens, of sturdy wire mesh, had come through undamaged, and on Friday morning the whooping cranes were all returned to their regular quarters. If any of them were unduly excited by the unusual aspect of things and the crews of men with axes and saws working around them, no one noticed it.

Then, on Sunday, a helicopter hovered over the zoo. The flashing and noise of the whirling rotor blades were too much for the cranes. Several of the birds crouched in alarm and then dashed about their pens. Their whoops could be heard throughout the grounds. Leo Buras came running to quiet them. As he got there, Josephine gathered herself as though for a mighty effort of escape, and, half running, half flying, with all the remaining power of her pinioned wings, hurled herself into the air and hit the fence with the full weight of her hurtling body. It threw her back, but she rose and battered herself against it, until, by the time Leo reached her, her wing bones were rubbed raw. The helicopter moved on, and Josephine became quiet. She seemed not to have suffered any serious injury. The following morning, Monday, September 13, a keeper named Vincent Beals checked the crane pens when he came on duty at six o'clock. All was normal, except in the pen that contained Josephine and Crip. Josephine lay on the ground. Beals entered and picked her up. She was quite dead.

In November 1965, the refuge manager at Aransas counted the returning cranes and found that again they had had a good year. They had brought the fine crop of eight young birds with them. There were thirty-six adults and so the total was a new high-water mark of forty-four whooping cranes. On the other hand, six birds had vanished. One had died when it hit a high wire on the journey south. The fate of the others was as mysterious as ever and, as ever, an irreparable loss.

For me there is always a strange magic in knowing that once again the flock has completed another extraordinary journey. Somehow, mysteriously, from high in the air the birds sense the nearness beneath them of the small patches of sand and water that are theirs. They brake their flight, and descend, floating down in narrower and narrower spirals. For an instant before a whooping crane touches the ground, its huge wings seem to hold it in the air. Its legs stretch out, reaching for the earth, and then it settles. Its great tapered, shining white body comes down so softly it seems as though it could light upon an egg and not break it. Those who have seen this say it is a marvelous thing.

Postscript

It is fifteen years since I finished the whooping cranes' story. I spent two years working on it, and learned more from it and was more emotionally gripped by it than any other story I have done, but after it was published I heard news of the cranes only now and then. Recently when I checked up on them I felt excitement rising in me all over again; this time colored with much greater optimism. I found that there is still suspense in the cranes' situation and difficult problems remain, but in contrast to earlier days many more people are truly committed to solving them. There are greater resources of money and new biological skills to draw on.

The number of wild whooping cranes has increased; sixty-nine were counted in 1978. As always, they are vulnerable to disasters such as hurricanes and disease, but they are also more closely observed than they were fifteen or twenty years ago, so there is a better chance that some dangers can be averted or minimized.

The most interesting development has been the decade of experiments in the artificial propagation of whooping cranes. The project conceived and directed by Ray Erickson at the Patuxent Wildlife Research Center has had remarkable success. Eggs stolen from the nests of wild cranes have been incubated there and, despite high mortality among the chicks, there is now a flock of twenty-two birds. Eight of them are mature and form four breeding pairs that have in turn produced young. Thus it has been shown that whooping cranes can be perpetuated in cages for at least a few generations. In artificial conditions females can be induced to lay many more eggs in a season than is normal in the wild, so that the captive flock produces young at a greatly accelerated rate.

On the other hand, the most crucial part of this method of saving the cranes from extinction still lies ahead; the release of captive-bred cranes to the wild. The problem, of course, is that a captive-bred bird has not learned the social behavior and survival skills that wild birds pick up from their elders. No human being can teach a young whooping crane how to behave like a whooping crane; to mate and rear new generations. A number of techniques are being considered. One approach now being tested uses a strategy called "cross-fostering." Eggs taken from wild whooping cranes, as well as from captive birds at Patuxent, have been put in the nests of wild sandhill cranes at Grays Lake National Wildlife Refuge in eastern Idaho. Again, mortality has been high, but a few of these "ugly ducklings" have survived for over a year. Whether they can reach maturity and surmount the effects of their peculiar upbringing, and will mate with each other rather than with their stepbrothers and stepsisters, won't be known for another five or six years.

The importance of the zoo birds whose potential as parents meant so much in the 1960's has faded now that eggs can be gotten from wild birds and the captives at Patuxent. Nevertheless, I wanted to know what had become of them and telephoned the Audubon Park Zoo. I talked to John Allender, General Curator, a young man with a degree in zoology from Oklahoma State University, who said that in the last ten years the zoo has been much improved. Both he and the current director, L. Ronald Forman, are enthusiastic about cranes and eager to cooperate in their conservation. Allender told me that after Josephine's death Crip was sent to the San Antonio Zoo, where he mated with Rosie. They produced a daughter named Tex. Rosie died some years ago and Patuxent sent a female named Ektu to replace her as Crip's mate. In 1978, when Crip was over thirty years old, his mate produced a fertile egg. Unfortunately the embryo died. Crip died in 1979.

Josephine's offspring are of particular interest because they may carry a genetic trait for a sedentary rather than a migratory way of life. Her sons Peewee and Pepper are dead, but George and Georgette, both males and renamed Angus and Tony, have been lent to a breeding center established at Baraboo, Wisconsin, by a new organization, the International Crane Foundation. They are being mated, by artificial insemination, with their half sister Tex, also there on loan. If they produce offspring they will be Josephine's grandchildren and will carry a quarter of her genes. Allender and George Archibald, of the Foundation, are working on a plan to reestablish nonmigratory cranes on their ancestral marshes in western Louisiana and hope Tony and Angus will sire young birds as a nucleus.

I never met Robert Porter Allen, but while I was working on the cranes' story I was always aware of his presence at the center of it. He was the first to feel deeply about the birds and give all he could to the struggle to keep them on earth. His work, which I read and reread, transmitted his sense of their poetry and romance. He made me understand the moral and ecological logic behind his intense feeling.

At the time Allen died he felt deeply discouraged. The cranes' fortunes were at a low point. Rescue plans were at cross-purposes. The government's efforts were listless. The public seemed to feel only passing interest in the fate of the birds. It must have seemed to Allen that he had done his best several times over to little avail. Allen is now seldom mentioned in reports and stories about the cranes, but I believe it was his work, more than anything else, that was the inspiration and the basis of the efforts being made today.

Whooping cranes still fly free. There is reason to hope that they will continue to fly and to carry a message into the future. As I read that message it affirms that we can keep our heritage of wildness, beauty, and diversity of life forms if only we care enough.

THE EVER
HUNGRY JAY

In the winter we who live in the country owe a great debt to the birds that consent to come to our bird feeders. Everyone I know has a bird feeder and the action at the feeder is a major source of interest and conversation. Bird-feeding people employ various methods and devices. They have favorite birds and less favorite birds. The differing devices are feeders cleverly designed to let some birds get at the seed and exclude others. The bird most people want to exclude is the blue jay. A blue jay will sit in a bird feeder and swallow one sunflower seed after another as though his stomach were a bottomless pit. He swallows conspicuously. You can see the seed go down and hit bottom—thunk!— and then he gobbles another. While eating he looks rude and complacent—elbows on the table, no suggestion of gratitude. Sunflower seed is the blue jay's special delight—as it is for almost all birds—and it is the most expensive seed commonly fed to birds. I've heard people say they simply couldn't afford to be ripped off by blue jays and so they have bought elaborate contraptions to thwart them. Snowbound and watching birds wistfully, wishing I could sail over the white meadows instead of floundering, I began to think about the economics of bird feeding and social attitudes; to wonder if there is any parallel with some other public charities—a tendency to exclude some welfare cases on grounds of their ingratitude, lack of real need, or high cost, while we spend even more money to weed them out of the system. I decided to do a little local research with a view to answering such questions as these: Is the blue jay needy or greedy? Is it possible to fill up a blue jay? Do they have other resources, as some of my friends suspect, and simply prefer handouts? What is the cost of sunflower seed and how does this cost relate to the cost of a blue-jay-excluding device?

At the time of my investigation Damon's Hardware in Wakefield, Rhode Island, was selling twelve and a half pounds of sunflower seed for $4.50 and fifty pounds for $14.95. I took ten seeds to the drugstore and had them weighed on an apothecary's scale. With the help of my husband I computed that ten seeds weighing .92 grams equal 3/100 of an ounce. At this rate there are 4,969 seeds to the pound. At $14.95 for fifty pounds, a pound costs about thirty cents. Therefore each seed costs 6/1000 of a cent. In other words, I was able to buy 166 sunflower seeds for a penny.

Mr. Damon told me he sells only the best sunflower seed. They are fat and gray with a white stripe. Small, black sunflower seeds are cheaper, but have less meat. Most sunflower seed is grown, not in Kansas, but in North Dakota, and is a big business. For some reason the seed can't be harvested until after a frost, usually in November, so the seed on the market in October is last year's seed and Damon warns against it. Over the summer worms have hatched and eaten out the hearts. "This old inferior stuff is peddled," he said, "and you have to watch out. Also seed dries out. A bag that weighs fifty pounds in November weighs forty by summer."

Damon showed me his assorted bird feeders. One that is effective against jays has a plastic dome that can be lowered over the feeding tray to make the aperture so small a jay can't perch or get his head in. Another clever one has a counterbalance that works like a seesaw. If a heavy bird sits on the perch it sinks down, snapping shut a strip of metal across the feeding aperture. Since the feeder has a glass front the frustrated bird finds itself sitting there looking at the goodies inside.

While Damon and I were talking, a sunflower seed customer came in and bought four fifty-pound bags. Damon said this was this customer's second two-hundred-pound purchase this year. I asked the man if he excluded jays from his feeder. "They eat like hogs," he said, shouldering a bag, "but they've got to eat, too. I have a feeder just for small birds and feed the jays on the ground."

At home I telephoned a few friends for their views on bird feeding. I am happy to report that everyone I spoke to took a generous and liberal view of jays.

Elisabeth Keiffer, Ministerial Road: "Anyone can come to my feeder. We have no blue jay baffles. I have never understood this discrimination. Grosbeaks are just as fat and greedy but they're very popular."

Rita Lepper, Cherry Road: "We like blue jays. However, we have tried vainly to outfox squirrels. We hung a coconut from a very fine wire, but we have a squirrel who can hang by one toenail and get in."

William Innis, Rose Hill Road: "I think blue jays are very pushy, forward creatures, but I don't hate them. My favorite birds are chickadees and titmice."

Duncan Briggs, Old Post Road: "I have a feeder that keeps blue jays out, but I give them cracked corn on the ground. What the hell, I feed everything. I like nuthatches very much and I like chickadees. They do a terrific job hammering open those seeds."

Carol Mariner, Matunuck: "Don't ask about my bill. It's too awful. I like all the birds . . . everything but evening grosbeaks—they're so disagreeable to each other—and starlings, which are greasy, revolting birds that will eat anything. Blue jays I don't mind. I have a counterweighted feeder, but it doesn't have a glass front. I think that that kind of device is torture. If you're going to feed birds you should do it in a kind way. For a while I had a cage type of feeder with wire mesh that small birds could get through and big ones couldn't. It had a wooden plug in the top. A red squirrel chewed through and got in. Then he ate so much he was too fat to get out. We just had to wait—he and I—for him to get thin. I put in water, as I felt he might get quite dry. It took him forty-eight hours to shrink sufficiently. It was nerve-racking for us both."

C. DeWolf Gibson, Matunuck: "Blue jays are robbers! Absolute robbers! And they squawk a lot. But somehow I admire them just the same." Virginia Kittredge, Ministerial Road: "I adore blue jays. When a blue jay and a cardinal arrive together it's the most thrilling sight of winter." Betty Salomon, Bradford: "Blue jays pay their way. They warn me when something is going on. Sometimes it's a cat at the feeder. The other day the jays made a racket. I went out and saw a sharp-shinned hawk circling overhead. I said, "Thanks, jays, for letting me know." Barbara Davis, Matunuck: "I love blue jays. The bad birds we have are grackles. In the autumn they try to get in the house. They cluster on the sills and peer in at us. My grandmother hated them, too. At the age of eighty she picked up an old shotgun and fired into an apple tree and seven starlings fell dead. She was very pleased."

Having sampled local opinion, I telephoned Lee Gardener, the resident biologist at the Norman Bird Sanctuary in Middletown, Rhode Island, an expert witness on the habits of the blue jay. Members of the family Corvidae, jays are related to crows and are indeed smart and aggressive. They will even attack a person in defense of their young. "I've had a jay swoop and rake my head with its claws when I picked a baby up off the ground. They can lick almost any other bird except a mockingbird, which is even tougher. They live just about everywhere east of the Mississippi. It is hard to count them in a locality. They are casually migratory and move here and there with wind and weather. Their flocks are not due to comradeship but because when one jay finds food others follow, so a group will descend first on one bird feeder and then on another."

Gardener then confirmed the suspicion that blue jays are among the least needy of all the species in the bird breadline. "They are omnivorous and if seeds fail they can go to the beach and eat a clam or to the dump and eat a dead rat," Gardener said. I asked about their conspicuous gobbling, and he explained that, like crows, jays are hiders. They fill their crop with seeds, carry them away, and then cough them up. They husk and eat what they want and hide the rest under leaves or in nooks and crannies. Ecologically it is a valuable trait since jays plant seeds that they forget to dig up and thus help to start new growth, but the habit is indeed quite depleting to the sunflower seed supply at bird feeders. Gardener dismissed as unimportant the competition between jays and smaller birds at feeders, provided the seed supply is ample. If there is enough to go around, the small birds simply sit and wait their turn. Thus an alternative to the blue jay baffler is a sufficient supply of seed.

Gardener's information led me back to my financial calculations. After a half hour of watching jays swallow sunflower seeds, I arrived at a maximum of twenty-five seeds in one sitting. A jay flying away with twenty-five seeds is carrying off 15/100 of a penny's worth. A flock of ten jays is making off with one and a half cents' worth. If they do this three times a day, the cost is four and a half cents. Let's be generous and give them a nickel a day. I am happy that I have come upon this information. As I sit here by my window, aware that if I go out in the tempting, treacherous snow my feet will feel heavy and cold in no time, it is a great vicarious pleasure to watch a jay drift effortlessly from branch to branch—and thence to my offering of sunflower seeds, spread out on an open feeder available to all. I can watch him gobble his twenty-five-seed capacity with an easy mind. At 15/100 of a penny the sight is a real bargain. It gives me a feeling that is rare these days. It makes me feel terribly rich.

8

AND THE INDRI SANG
a visit to Madagascar

This chapter of my life belongs to the late Edward Steele, a remarkable man who lived in Tucson, Arizona, but met whomever he wished by telephone. He chose to meet me after I had published an article on the poisoning of predators and rodents by the Fish and Wildlife Service. Steele considered the practice abominable and, as one of the directors of an organization named Defenders of Wildlife, fought it for many years. He was gratified when *The New Yorker* published my article about it and by telephone he tracked me down in Rhode Island to tell me so. The call lasted twenty or thirty minutes while Steele interviewed me. Later, after a number of such calls, during which he deftly made us friends, I realized that in his skillful hands the telephone became a powerful instrument in the service of his campaigns.

The matter to which he devoted such intense feeling and so much telephone time was the defense of animals. Hearing of an encroachment here, an ecological outrage there, he consulted his huge list of friends and potential allies scattered everywhere and organized a counterattack on behalf of the animals. His work was carried out with craft, sensitivity, and perseverance. I had an opportunity to observe his strategy at first hand when he asked me to go to Madagascar and write a story on behalf of the lemurs that live there, and only there.

When the idea was first broached it seemed wildly impractical. To me, Madagascar was an island floating somewhere between the pages of *National Geographic* and I was not aware that lemurs are of greater interest than any other wildlife.

Steele, however, had learned a great deal about the island and its fauna and was dismayed by the terrible fact that its animal and botanical treasures are being quietly consumed while the rest of the world looks in other directions. He had no foolish hope that anything one organization could do might reverse the destruction, but he did have a passionate feeling that while anything remained to be done it should be done. Defenders of Wildlife might not be able to move mountains in Madagascar, but Steele believed that by documenting the island's situation in its magazine it might inspire other conservation organizations to launch rescue efforts before it is too late.

I accepted the assignment and was scared to death by the prospect. I had traveled in Europe and Mexico, but I had never tried to work in a foreign country. I could see how difficult it would be. French is spoken in the cities of Madagascar. I speak some French, but knew it wouldn't be enough.

All during the summer of 1974 Steele worked by phone on the problems of launching our expedition. Educated in France, he spoke perfect French. He talked to and charmed the Malagasy Ambassador in Washington. He stayed up all one night to put through a call to Tananarive, the capital of Madagascar, in order to enlist the sympathy of the minister in charge of Madagascar's Department of the Interior. Calls to Madagascar are routed through Paris, which multiplies the confusion of time zones and languages. In this case flying might have been easier, but Steele wouldn't give up and at 5 A.M. Arizona time he was suavely discussing lemurs with a surprised official in Tananarive who had never heard of Arizona, much less Defenders of Wildlife. The man was persuaded to give full cooperation to our expedition.

Before setting out I knew I had best learn all I could about the island. The experts I consulted told me that the situation in Madagascar, where interwoven strands of history form the present tangle of ecological problems, is typical of many situations in the Third World. The greatest wildlife catastrophes are taking place in the undeveloped countries since it is there that the greatest reservoirs of wildlife remain. These wildlife tragedies are heartbreaking, but it is useless to condemn the people and the practices responsible for them without understanding the forces behind current events. In this respect I found my visit to Madagascar tremendously enlightening.

Another thing I learned about the island is that it is a place full of mysticism and magic—sorcery's last stand. Whenever I think about Madagascar and the lemurs I wish the modern sor-

cery of money and the magic of ecological enlightenment might
somehow combine to save the fascinating and imperiled forms of
life found there. In this wish I do not forget its people, for if
their island becomes barren of life, they, too, will suffer.

Madagascar is a long, thin island that lies off the southeast
coast of Africa like a whale calf at its mother's side; and, in fact,
it once was part of that continent. Seventy million years ago,
Madagascar broke off from the mainland and began to drift,
millimeter by millimeter, on the imperceptibly slow currents of
the earth's moving surface. Today, two hundred and fifty miles
of water separate it from the coast of Mozambique. In its millions of years of isolation, Madagascar has become one of the
most peculiar places on earth. On it are plants and animals
whose ancestors separated from mainland relatives so long ago
that they evolved into distinct families, found nowhere else in
the world. Its human population, though more recently arrived,
is an amalgam of races and cultures that can also be called
unique.

In a certain part of the forest of Madagascar, there still lives a
creature whose scientific name is *Indri indri.* It wears a coat of
dark fur, patched here and there with white and beige as though
dappled by the sunlight piercing the thick tropical foliage. It has
long, slender arms and legs jointed in the same way as a man's.
Its hands, like ours, have flat fingernails. The hands and feet
have a long, strong thumb and big toe with which the indri grips
branches of the trees that are its home. Surprised by a human intruder, it may remain quiet, effortlessly holding itself against a
tree trunk, and stare down with wide golden eyes. Occasionally
the indri comes to the ground, where it stands almost upright, in
size and shape somewhat resembling a small person. To make the
resemblance more striking, the indri has no visible tail.

The Malagasy people have a number of legends about the
indri, whose native name is *babakoto,* which might be translated
as "little father." According to one legend, there was a time, long
ago, when a man and a woman lived serenely in the forest,
where they found enough fruits and nuts and tender leaves to

satisfy their wants. The couple had many children, and for a time the children, too, were content with this easy life. Then some of the children became more industrious. They cleared land and grew rice. These restless ones became the ancestors of men. The less ambitious children remained behind, preferring the ancestral life among the trees. In time they became *babakotos*. Since *babakotos* are the brothers of men, it was forbidden to kill them. Some forest-living Malagasy still honor the legend and do not kill the indri.

In this version of the Adam and Eve story, there is a sort of metaphor that eerily parallels the truth, though it has compressed the events of millions of years into a generation.

The indri is a lemur, the largest surviving species of a group of animals called prosimians, meaning early monkeys. They belong to a time when the offspring of the "ancestral primate" (the mysterious, little-known mammal to which so much is owed) first began to diverge from their forebears and develop simian characteristics. Yet they were not quite monkeys. Their body proportions, with long, agile arms and legs, and their hands and feet, with flexible fingers and toes, were like the primates of today, but their faces remained foxlike, presumably like those of their forebears. Their noses were long, like a dog's nose, and for the same purpose: to provide room for a highly developed sense of smell. Prosimians once flourished in all the forests of the world. The bones of an ancient lemur called *plesiadapis* have been found in France, and those of another species called *nothodectes* were found in North America. In fact, the North American continent once had lemurs similar to those living today.

For a long time, like the children of the forest-dwelling man and woman in the fable, these early lemurs must have lived happily in a world of plenty. They were the most highly evolved creatures on earth—lords of the forest. No big cats or other mammalian carnivores had yet evolved; only meat-eating reptiles and birds would have menaced them. They had few close competitors for the fruits of the jungles in which they lived.

But while the prosimians went on through the generations

without great variation in the pattern of their lives, other offspring of the ancestral primate were taking more ambitious steps. They began to depend more on their eyes than their sense of smell and to develop new brain areas. Their skulls became rounder, while their noses became shorter. Thus a branch of the prosimians became true monkeys. Some of them developed even further and produced, in time, the ancestors of apes and men. It is thought that the three great modern branches of the primates —the prosimians and the Old and New World primates—first diverged from each other during the Oligocene, or about 35 million years ago.

We do not know exactly why the early prosimians, so widespread and abundant, disappeared almost entirely from the face of the earth, but it was probably due to a variety of factors. In some regions they may have been unable to adapt to changes of climate and altered food supply, or the appearance of new and dangerous predators. In Africa and Asia, they found themselves in direct competition with their more clever and graceless kin, the monkeys. Monkeys are more capable than lemurs in a number of ways. Some monkeys are also predators, and it is possible they killed lemurs, as Cain slew Abel. In any case, monkeys ultimately took over the prosimians' niche in the trees.

In Asia and Africa the prosimians dwindled, species by species, until they now number only a very few. These are small, modest, nocturnal creatures that seem to have found refuge in an ecological niche the monkeys didn't care for. The African bush babies are modern representatives of these prosimians and so are the lorises of Asia.

The only other prosimians surviving today are those on Madagascar, where, in what was for so long an extraordinary sanctuary, lemurs found peace and plenty. On Madagascar, isolation from the mainland preserved the simpler world in which they had evolved. For the lemurs the island remained, age after age, a Garden of Eden, free of such evils as the carnivores and competitors that beset them in the world outside. On Madagascar, lemurs flourished and evolved into a rich variety of species. Including the beautiful indri, there are three families and nineteen species of lemurs on Madagascar. They range in size from the mouse lemur, small enough to fit in a teacup, to the indri, which stands a meter tall.

From the point of view of science, the existence of the lemurs on Madagascar is a marvelous piece of luck, the chance result of a giant geological accident that has preserved representatives of our earliest past in living flesh rather than mute and sterile bone. Lemurs are of value to science in many ways. Primatologists, anthropologists, ethologists, geneticists, and others can find in lemurs unique opportunities to examine and compare a line of evolution collateral to man's own. To the layman lemurs have another sort of importance more difficult to define, but easily felt by anyone fortunate enough to see a living lemur. One needn't be a scientist to look at a lemur's hand, for instance, and feel the thrill of recognition across a gap of 60 million years.

There is currently a great deal of scientific interest in all primates. Early researchers concentrated on apes and monkeys and it is only in the last ten years or so that lemurs have been discovered as an almost virgin field of study. Lemurologists form a small, select band united by concern that their study material is disappearing before their eyes. Before going to Madagascar I visited several of them in order to learn something of the scientific view of lemurs.

At Duke University, Dr. Peter Klopfer, a zoologist then working with captive lemurs, told me that lemurs offer a unique opportunity to study the origins of various kinds of behavior. Different species of lemurs eat different foods, have varied social arrangements, and care for their young in different ways, and yet they are closely related. "Madagascar is even more revealing than the Galápagos," Klopfer told me. "In both islands evolution followed a unique course, but Madagascar has been isolated much longer, so that whole families evolved rather than just species as in the Galápagos."

In Madagascar, he pointed out, a limited ancestral stock has developed a great diversity of species. On an island where resources are restricted, many animals must compete for each biological niche; that is, a particular way of making a living, of finding food, shelter, and security for its young. Dr. Klopfer used the analogy of shopkeepers in a town, all living at close quarters but earning their keep by different trades. In a town with too many bakers, some must switch to candlestick making or go out of business. The same is true of the struggle of animals for niches in which to live. It forces some to find new ways to earn their living, and thus become different species.

In Madagascar, the early prosimians found all sorts of niches empty and all sorts of opportunities to evolve. When nocturnal lemurs became crowded, some switched their activities to daytime. Still others foraged at dawn and dusk. They varied their body size through a range from very large to very small, and their dietary habits from omnivorous to eating only certain leaves. Some lemurs stuck to the rain forest while others learned to get along in swamp or semi-desert. Unhampered by monkeys or large carnivores, some even dared to live on the ground.

I asked Dr. Klopfer to explain why the animals of Madagascar had remained primitive, while on the continents evolution went on.

"Primitive," Dr. Klopfer said, "simply means prior. It doesn't mean simpler or less specialized. On the continents, a larger stock produced more mutations, and with more space the paths of development remained open. On Madagascar, the animals became specialized until all niches were filled by species that were highly efficient in that particular setting. There was no room for newcomers and no need for established species to change further. Things remained stable, with the result that animals could keep primitive characteristics that gradually disappeared elsewhere. That's why, when we look at the animals and plants of Madagascar, we really are looking back through the ages."

Lemurs, I learned, have many primitive characteristics. Their brains are small and narrow compared with the round monkey brain. Lemurs are in transition between dependence on smell and dependence on vision. They do poorly on intelligence tests involving objects. In the wild, lemurs don't play with things the way monkeys do. In the laboratory, they will play with them but seem witless about them. They will try to put big things into small holes. They haven't developed monkey cleverness but they have a rich and complicated social life with all the basics of primate society. They show that monkey-type society is possible without monkey intelligence.

In lemur social life the sense of smell plays an important role. Lemurs have a number of scent glands and use them in communication. No one has yet cracked the code, but it seems that different perfumes convey different meanings, perhaps such information as identity, sex, emotional states, treetop paths, and directions of travel. Lemurs mark tree limbs with scent, probably to keep troops from colliding with each other. A species whose scientific name is *Lemur catta* (one of the species I would see in Madagascar), is known to engage in what zoologists call "stink fights." Combatants rub scent from glands on their wrists onto their long, plumey tails which they wave in the direction of the enemy, presumably directing olfactory insults through the air.

The most distinguished French lemurologist is Dr. Jean Jacques Petter of the National Museum of Natural History, who maintains a collection of lemurs at the Museum's Ecology Laboratory in the Parisian suburb of Brunoy. I stopped there on my way to Madagascar.

Many of Dr. Petter's lemurs are nocturnal, and their cages are lit with red light during the daytime. Red light is invisible to nocturnal animals, and so, in what they take to be darkness, they go about their normal nighttime business. Dr. Petter has carefully reproduced the humidity, light intensity, and temperature of Madagascar inside the laboratory. Even the changing seasons must be duplicated in order to induce a natural breeding cycle.

We stopped first to look at a large cage containing a group of tiny *Microcebus coquereli*, a species of mouse lemur that is gravely endangered. These tiny primates are not much bigger than hamsters. They perched on fine twigs, staring with wide eyes. They had recently produced the first baby of their kind ever born in captivity. Quite a number of lemur species have such special needs in diet and surroundings, not yet fully understood, that they have never lived long in captivity. Dr. Petter talked of the reasons he felt lemurs are important to science. "The lemur is a fossil," he said, echoing Dr. Klopfer. "In Madagascar, you find the peak of perfection of adaptation. Lemurs have adapted to an extraordinary number of niches. The possibilities of study are endless.

"Consider the species *Lepilemur*, for instance. It eats leaves. If it is cold it curls up in a hole. It consumes very little energy to live. It is a fine example of economy of space and energy. Perhaps *Lepilemur* represents the best possible use of the forest to produce protein. It is rare to find such a biomass in such a small space.

"Lemurs have an extreme development of the senses. We are at the bottom of the scale in our ability to smell. Lemurs are at the top. Lemurs have complex ways of using scent; they can create odors that are both highly dispersed and long-lasting. These two characteristics are opposite and fascinating to study. Lemurs use scent in communication; yet they also use sight and sound as we do. They send different messages by different means. This has great bearing on the study of human communication.

"Lemur vocal communication should be studied. Some lemurs are especially fitted to signal through dense forest. Very high sounds are stopped by foliage. We have found that a sound between four thousand and six thousand hertz carries farthest in dense forest, and this is exactly the vocal range of some lemurs. The indri goes to a treetop to call. Its voice carries from treetop to distant treetop. Malagasy workers often use the same tone of voice and modulate it in the same way to call to each other through the forest. Mouse lemurs have ultrasonic communication. Not real sonar, but probably the beginning of sonar.

"*Lepilemur* not only can see in the dark, but has an extraordinary retina with special nerves so that it can see to leap from branch to branch. In other lemurs it is fascinating to see the evolution from nocturnal to diurnal. We are studying nocturnal lemurs with radio tracking. We used to think these nocturnals were solitary. Now we find that they are meeting and interacting much more than we thought."

Dr. Petter paused for a moment's thought. "There is very little material to study," he said finally. "We must be very careful with what we have. In ten years we may have many more research ideas. Then, if we have only bones, study will be impossible."

Madagascar is a large island; a thousand miles long and two to three hundred miles wide.

The northern part of Madagascar lies within the tropic zone. In early times it was shaken by eruptions and earthquakes. The center of the island rose to become a vast plateau dominated by mountain ranges. In places rolling hills cradle lakes, swamps, and marshes. Because of its elevation, the climate of the plateau is temperate, with neither intense heat nor cold, and there is a moderate rainy season. On the east coast, the plateau drops off sharply. This escarpment, facing the empty reaches of the Indian Ocean, catches the warm, wet trade winds blowing ceaselessly westward. Heavy rain has drenched this coastal strip for uncounted centuries, producing dense forests with an extraordinary variety of plant life—tall trees, trailing vines, delicate orchids, many in a fantastic richness and abundance, including species found nowhere else.

To the west of the high plateau, wide savannas slope gently to long, sandy beaches facing Africa. The west is hot—sometimes infernally hot. It has a dry season during the Madagascar winter, which corresponds to our summer, and its trees are deciduous. At the southern end of the island is yet a third zone of climate and vegetation. There is little rain, and the thin, arid soil is covered with desert plants the French call the *forêt épineuse*, the spiny forest, including many cactus-like plants unique to the island.

At the time Madagascar separated from the mainland none of the large mammals of modern times had yet evolved. There were no lions, leopards, or cheetahs; no elephants, monkeys, apes, or the hoofed animals that later populated the African mainland. When these did appear, the channel separating Madagascar from Africa was too wide for large creatures to cross; only a few small, early mammals were able to reach the island. They probably got there by riding on rafts. Large East African rivers drain into the Mozambique Channel and sometimes carry uprooted trees far out to sea. Small animals capable of clinging to branches could have made the journey across the channel in this way.

Possibly the first mammals to reach the island were primitive insectivores which evolved into a peculiar family called the *Tenrecidae,* which, like the lemurs, exists only in Madagascar. They are the most primitive non-marsupial mammals now alive. Like lemurs, tenrecs elsewhere lost out to stronger competitors, but the tenrecs of Madagascar developed into some two dozen species, adapted to different habitats. Some live in water, some on the ground, some partly in trees. One species is the size of a rabbit; another is only six inches long, has tiny eyes, long whiskers, and quills like a hedgehog. Still another tenrec has forty-seven vertebrae in its tail, providing it with the longest tail of any mammal. Tenrecs win the gold medal for motherhood, producing more babies in a single litter than any other mammal, usually fifteen but sometimes as many as twenty-four. The Malagasy people consider tenrecs good eating.

Small rodents and bats also made their way across the channel. There are now six families of bats on the island; one is a giant with a wingspread of three feet. The only hoofed animal to reach Madagascar was a pygmy hippopotamus that is now extinct. Huge land tortoises once lumbered about the island, but they, too, are gone. However, the unique radiated tortoise, small and handsomely colored, still lives, though precariously. Crocodiles and snakes reached Madagascar, but apparently the snakes came before the invention of the poisoned fang, for none of them has venom.

A rich assembly of chameleons evolved on the island. Madagascar has more species than anywhere else in the world. Many of them are of very curious form, with strange horns and spines, or leathery fringe, that makes them look like tiny dinosaurs. There is a huge chameleon two feet long that can capture mice and birds. Another, an inch and a half long, is the smallest living reptile.

Flying insects, of course, had no trouble reaching Madagascar. The island is noted for its butterflies. Eight hundred species have been counted. There are more species of spiders than biologists have yet been able to catalogue. Unlike the snakes, several spiders are poisonous, and one is said to be able to kill a cow.

Some of Madagascar's birds came from Africa, some from Asia, but at least three families are peculiar to the island. The most remarkable bird of all, the giant *Aepyornis,* is now extinct, but it survived into comparatively recent times. Arab travelers reported the existence of a bird so large it could lift an elephant into the air. This bird is probably the fabulous roc described in the tale of Sinbad the Sailor. No eyewitness report has survived, but intact eggs and complete skeletons have been found and testify that it was the largest bird ever known. Its eggs are a foot long with a contents of more than two gallons. *Aepyornis* stood almost ten feet tall and probably weighed a thousand pounds, three times the weight of an ostrich. Its wing bones were vestigial. It was a gentle vegetarian—too large to run with the speed of its cousin the ostrich. No one knows if *Aepyornis* evolved before Madagascar became an island or if it flew there and later became flightless, but it must have dwelt there for millions of peaceful years until the arrival of man. The great bird was undoubtedly alive when the first people settled on Madagascar around 500 A.D. *Aepyornis* eggs have been dated at least three hundred years later than that. The clear implication is that man exterminated *Aepyornis* as he did its relative the dodo, on the nearby island of Mauritius.

There must also have been a great variety of other birds in early Madagascar. There were large lakes and swamps ideal for water birds—ducks, spoonbills, herons, rails, and geese. Flamingos soared in pink clouds. A few flocks survive.

Among all these creatures there seems to have been none more formidable than the crocodiles that inhabited the marshes and lakes and a family of primitive carnivores called *Viverridae* that are related to mongooses and civets. Their modern descendants resemble undersized panthers and, like the lemurs, are forest dwellers in danger of extinction. For millions of years, while life on the continents produced larger, smarter, and more rapacious creatures, the inhabitants of Madagascar lived in a peaceful backwater of time.

Early Madagascar developed a profusion of plants as well as animals. It is probable that dense forests covered the entire island, including the mountains and what are now the treeless plains of the plateau. Even today, where patches of virgin forest survive they contain trees, shrubs, ferns, and vines in extraordinary variety. Orchids come in marvelous shapes and colors. Malagasy witch doctors use a large pharmacopoeia of wild plants for healing and sorcery. Since the island's plants have never been adequately catalogued, plants of potential use in modern life may vanish without having been recognized.

Madagascar was undisturbed by human beings far longer than most other parts of the world. No traces of prehistoric man have been found—no artifacts, no cave drawings or fossil bones. The first inhabitants are shadowy figures known only in legends. Malagasy folklore tells of a people called the Vazimba who were living on the island when the ancestors of the present Malagasy arrived. Their language, race, and culture have vanished; but their spirits still survive in the beliefs of the Malagasy.

The first people we know of to arrive in Madagascar came not from nearby Africa but from the far-off Malayo-Indonesian archipelago. They crossed the ocean in outrigger canoes, an exploit equal to the Polynesian voyages to Easter Island. They could have followed the trade winds and made the journey in stages, sailing first to India, thence to the Horn of Africa, and along the African coast to the island. The first of them probably arrived in the third or fourth century. Ashes from man-made fireplaces fifteen hundred years old have been discovered. Other voyagers followed until the migration stopped during the twelfth century. The language and culture of Madagascar appear to have become isolated from the main Indonesian culture at about that time. In later times Africans and a few Arabs also arrived and were absorbed. The present Malagasy are a racial mixture, but their language and culture remains predominantly Indonesian.

The first humans to come to Madagascar found the forests teeming with lemurs. As recently as a thousand years ago there were more than thirty species instead of the nineteen alive today. Among them were lemurs far larger than the indri. One form hung from the branches like orangutans. Another descended from the trees and browsed on the ground, where no hoofed animals competed for food. The memory of some of these vanished creatures lives on in Malagasy folklore. There is a legend of "the Kalanoro," little men with long hair, forest dwellers who moved among the trees with superhuman speed. We know there once existed a lemur the size of a baboon, called *Hadropithecus*. It was on the island when the first humans arrived, and this may have been the Kalanoro. Doubtless, the early Malagasy hunted and ate lemurs then as they do now. Scientists believe the early settlers brought about the extinction of *Hadropithecus*.

Another lemur called *Megaladapis*, which was almost as big as a gorilla and was the largest lemur we know of, probably survived into recent times. In the seventeenth century, a Frenchman, Sieur Etienne de Flacourt, spent some time in southern Madagascar and wrote a memoir entitled *Histoire de la Grande Isle Madagascar*. He left a description that could apply to *Megaladapis*:

"Tretretre, or tratratratra, an animal as big as a two-year-old calf, with a round head and the face of a man. It has woolly hair, a short tail and eyes like those of a man. . . . It can be seen near the Lipomani Lake, in the region which is its lair. It is a solitary animal; the local people fear it greatly, and flee from it as it does from them."

The bones of this creature are common near the town of Fort-Dauphin on the southeast coast. The skull of another large prosimian, *Archaeolemur*, has been found in the same area. This individual had apparently been killed with an ax. *Archaeolemur* and *Hadropithecus* had small faces and large brains. They represent the highest brain development of any lemur, perhaps analogous to anthropoid apes in relation to monkeys. Lemurologists deeply regret their loss. Dr. Petter has written: "As in the course of evolution which led from monkey to man, the way to 'humanization' was open for the lemurs. The arrival of the first men in Madagascar was certainly the cause of cutting it off, and . . . our contemporaries, by destroying the last living lemurs, will efface even the traces of that evolution."

Around lakes the first human settlers must have found an abundance of a species called *Hapalemur*, or gentle lemur, that browsed on the reeds among which it lived. A few of these still survive. Since their food is so close at hand, they have never learned to move fast. Modern Malagasy set fire to the reeds and drive the lemurs into the open where they are easily caught. Those not eaten make gentle pets.

Early Madagascar must have been a primitive hunter's paradise. After 50 million peaceful years undisturbed by large predators, most of the fauna of Madagascar were hopelessly unprepared to fight or flee or hide. The large forms succumbed first—the *Aepyornis*, the giant tortoise, the little hippos, and the lemurs that lived mainly on the ground. But it was not hunting that brought the most dire change to the island. The Malagasy were cultivators and herdsmen. Crops and cattle require open land. Generation after generation the people attacked the forest, and year by year it gave way. As the forest went so did the lemurs and much of the other fauna. Today more than three-quarters of the forest is gone and 90 percent of the lemurs are gone. Birds are no longer abundant. The primitive carnivores and insectivores hide in the remotest parts of the remaining jungle. Of the fauna of Madagascar, one scientist I spoke to said sadly,

"The fossil history of the island shows fantastic numbers of creatures, but they are long gone. What we see now is just the tail end. They are really no more than relics."

The first thing the arriving visitor in Madagascar becomes aware of is, naturally enough, not wildlife but people. Lots and lots of people. Dark-skinned people of a variety of shades, but few as dark as on the African mainland. Faces vary, too, from an African to an Asian cast. Clothes, at least those worn in the capital, are familiar Western clothes mingled with local touches—straw hats, printed shirts, or cloaks. But the language is strange to Western ears. It is Malagasy, a soft language full of vowels that stems from Polynesia. It is spoken by everyone. French, derived from eighty years of French rule, is the language of the government. It is spoken by many people in the capital and relatively few elsewhere.

There is a ten-mile drive from the airport to Tananarive. On the way one is quickly aware of the two principal factors in the ecology of Madagascar: rice and zebus. For centuries rice has been the staple food of Madagascar. On the plateau it is cultivated in paddies, just as in Indonesia. Tananarive is in a fertile area, and the paddies border the road right to the edge of the city. In years past, when the population grew slowly, Madagascar easily produced enough rice to feed the island. In 1902 the population was only two million. After World War II, the miracles of modern medicine and the Malagasy love of large families combined to produce a huge increase. Today the population is eight million and growing at the rate of 3 percent a year. This is more than the present agricultural system can keep up with, and the government is forced to import rice.

Zebus are humpbacked cattle with long, gracefully curved horns. They are central to the life of the rural people of Madagascar, and 90 percent of the Malagasy are rural. Zebus are used in religious ritual and as a form of currency. There are said to be ten million Zebus on the island, and it is partly for their sake that so much forest has been destroyed. Even as we drove through the outskirts of the capital, I saw zebus grazing by the roadside or drawing an occasional wagon.

Tananarive is an attractive city. It has clear air and warm sun. Distant mountains, purple bougainvillea cascading over walls, and jacaranda trees covered with violet blossoms made me think of Mexico. So did the traffic—small cars racing through narrow streets, avoiding disaster by inches. The streets are also crowded with pedestrians—people pulling carts, carrying bundles on their heads, or just trudging along to somewhere. The older buildings of the town are of soft, weathered brick, two or three stories high and relatively narrow, with steep roofs of red tile or corrugated tin. Balconies are common. In the center of the city, taller buildings whose architecture might be called "Western-universal" have taken over. There is a Hilton Hotel that looks like a Hilton Hotel. The city is built on the slopes of a series of hills, and the rooftops rise in terraces. On the highest hill stands the square palace of the last Malagasy queen, who was overthrown by the French in 1894.

As it is in every country, the history of Madagascar is part of its present. Though they speak a common language and share a religion based on ancestor worship, the Malagasy are divided into some eighteen tribes. The people of the plateau, the Merina, are more Asian in appearance than the tribes of the coast, particularly the west, where African influence is evident. Small-scale tribal wars divided the people for centuries. For some time the people of the west, the Sakalava, were dominant, but at the beginning of the nineteenth century the Merina conquered most of the island and established a kingdom. Although they were relatively advanced for their time and place, they enslaved other tribes, and this is not forgotten even now. Western influence did not penetrate Madagascar until the early 1800's when King Radama I allowed British advisors at his court and invited the London Missionary Society to invent a written script for the Malagasy language. For a considerable time, the Merina Kingdom managed to hang on to its sovereignty while the British and French took turns in their attempts to dominate trade with the island. Eventually, in 1894, the French invaded Madagascar, deposed the queen, and made the island a colony.

Under the French slavery was abolished and forced labor introduced. Catholic and Protestant missionaries brought medicine and Christianity into the hinterlands. Today there are about three million Malagasy who are Christians or combine Christian worship with their traditional religion. The life of the people of the plateau was considerably Westernized by French influence. In Tananarive the former ruling class survived as a sophisticated elite, but for the majority of the people, life went on much as before. They disliked French rule as they had Merina rule and continued to live by subsistence farming. World War II brought the beginning of the end of colonialism to Madagascar and in 1960 it became a republic, but the French managed to keep a tight grip on the island's finances, and virtually all the island's profits went into the pockets of foreigners.

Since 1972 a series of military rulers have struggled to rid the economy of foreign control. It is an understandable objective, but its side effects have been unfortunate for wildlife. Politics and conservation are closely connected. The present government, preoccupied with feeding its people, has no funds left over for wildlife and tends to view any outsiders, even scientific researchers or conservationists, with suspicion.

During the time my husband and I traveled about Madagascar our best friend and our window on the Malagasy world was a man named Emmanuel Folo (pronounced "Fooloo"), who had been lent to us as a guide by the Department of Tourism. Emmanuel has as much practical knowledge of wildlife as anyone in Madagascar and, what is more rare, a real love of it. We had also been lent an ancient Land-Rover, and in it the three of us rattled over more than two thousand miles of dirt roads on our way to see lemurs in different habitats.

On our first trip we hoped to see the indri, the *babakoto* of legend, which is found in the rain forest of the east coast escarpment. The forest is mostly without roads, but in one place the indri's home is easily accessible where a motor road intersects the railroad line that descends from the plateau to the coast.

At first the road from Tananarive descends slowly through grassy hills, rice paddies, and small settlements. Except for the rice paddies the hills are empty. The forest here was cut long ago, and the soil has degenerated, so that only coarse grass grows. At the time of our visit, in October, at the end of the dry season, the grass was a faded beige. Here and there patches of eucalyptus and pine have been planted. As the French did before them, the Malagasy authorities are using these two species in their reforestation projects. Pine and eucalyptus grow fast and provide lumber, pulp, and firewood. When eucalyptus is cut or burned, it sprouts again from the roots. Thus these species have short-term advantages. Unfortunately, eucalyptus also impoverishes the soil, and little else can grow in its vicinity. From the point of view of wildlife, particularly lemurs, eucalyptus is a disaster. Its pungent leaves are inedible, and there isn't an animal native to the island that can live in a forest of eucalyptus. There is no quicker way to destroy lemurs than to replace their native habitat with eucalyptus, as is being done.

As we descended the escarpment, the road became rougher and steeper and the endless curves sharper. We wound around abrupt, conical hills that seemed to go on forever, like hillocks in a sand dune. As we came to the level of heavy rainfall the hills were covered with second growth; a tangle of bushes and vines and giant ferns, dominated by the traveler palm, a curious palm whose fronds grow on a flat plane like a fan. The big trees are gone because for centuries the people of the east coast have lived by slash-and-burn agriculture, a primitive farming method that is common throughout the tropics. Unfortunately, the lush appearance of tropical forests gives a deceptive impression of the richness of the soil. In temperate climates falling leaves create protective mulch and rich topsoil, but in the tropics heat and humidity quickly decompose organic debris, so no humus forms. Nutrients are immediately reabsorbed by plants, creating a great luxuriance of leafy growth, while the soil remains poor and thin. To plant a crop the primitive farmer cuts the trees, and when they are dry, burns them. This puts nutrients into the soil and gives a good first crop. But the exposed soil will be leached by the tropical rains, and each subsequent crop is poorer. After a few seasons, the farmer must move on and clear another patch of forest. Given time, the forest will regenerate to some extent, but each time the process is repeated some species of trees do not return and the soil is ever more impoverished. Eventually nothing will grow but coarse grass.

When the population of Madagascar was small, attrition was slow, but the pace has accelerated. It has been estimated that forty to fifty square miles of forest are destroyed each year so that farmers can plant their crops of bananas, vegetables, and mountain rice (which can grow without irrigation). No one knows how much true rain forest remains. It has been reduced to a narrow strip on the steepest slopes of the east coast escarpment. What is perfectly clear is that this remnant is shrinking. Even the peasants who do the cutting are aware of it. "The people know they have to walk a long way to get to the forest," Emmanuel told me, "and that it once was close to their villages. But they say it is better to walk than to have nothing to eat."

The colonial government was aware of the destructive results of "tavy," as the practice is called in Madagascar, and tried to stop it, but laws prohibiting it were, naturally, unpopular. With independence the people demanded the right to cultivate in the traditional way. As long as any forest remains, tavy provides an easy subsistence living for the local population. It is less work to clear a new patch than to weed an old one. To replant the same patch of land year after year requires both machinery and fertilizer, which are not available to Malagasy farmers. It is hard to see any likelihood that tavy will cease while any forest remains.

The east coast forest is the home of the Betsimisáraka tribe, the second-largest of the Malagasy tribes. The name means "inseparable multitude." Emmanuel is a Betsimisáraka and he was happy to be home. He told us that the cash income of a family in this area might be around a hundred dollars a year, enough to cover candles, or oil for lamps, a few clothes and tools and utensils, or it might be nothing at all. By cutting a patch of forest and planting a crop a man could feed his family. If there was no money his wife could weave rough cloth out of raffia palm. Betsimisáraka traditionally do not kill indri, but they kill and eat any other lemurs they can catch. They kill them by blowgun, by snare, or, in the case of nocturnal lemurs, by locating their nests. Those with firearms use them, though cartridges are scarce just now. Killing lemurs is prohibited, but even gendarmes have been known to shoot lemurs. It is as natural for some Malagasy to kill lemurs as for rural Americans to kill rabbits or anything else they can find to hunt.

Once we stopped to eat and rest by a river that rushed down a steep gorge. The tangle of trees and shrubs clothing the hills around us looked impenetrably thick. Emmanuel stared across the ravine into the jungle and, as he opened a can of sardines, remarked that he could live in jungle like that for months without carrying any provisions. He would need only a machete.

"There are people who live in the forest even now and never leave it. They don't work, only live in the forest," he said. "When I was a boy I met a group of people who lived deep in the forest and paid no taxes. They came out only to buy salt. I made friends with them and went to live with them for a while. They used honey for sugar, raffia for clothes, sticks to dig out certain grubs that are good to eat. They ate birds. They killed lemurs with blowguns. There are eels in small pools in the forest. The forest people would grind up certain leaves and throw them in. The eels were intoxicated and came to the top. Today not many people live that way because the forest is disappearing, but there are still some who do. If you tell about it in Tananarive they don't believe it, but it is true."

A little further down the road we came to a clearing in which stood a few houses of the utmost simplicity. In our Deep South they would be called cabins, though these were made of split bamboo and had thatched roofs. We stopped to take a picture.

The place struck me as lonely and desolate. The children who had been playing in the bare earth around the cabins melted away. Through an open doorway I could see a woman peering at us from the shadows inside her house. The hills enclosed us. I felt that here the days must be steamy and monotonous, the nights very long. Emmanuel stood beside me and I saw that he was smiling with nostalgic recognition. "This is just like my home when I was a boy," he said. "My father grew rice and bananas and coffee. We had all we needed to eat. I had only one shirt at a time. Sometimes it was raffia. But I was perfectly free. I could do whatever I wanted. Life was very simple, very happy." He sighed as he turned away. "Life in Tananarive is very complicated," he said. "I sometimes think I would rather live like this. Perhaps I will come back someday." We got back into the Land-Rover. As we started again, I told him that an American had written a book entitled *You Can't Go Home Again.*

Halfway down the escarpment at the town of Andasibe (which the French called Perinet), we found an imposing Victorian railroad station of battered stucco with a great arched passageway to the platform, where travelers sat amidst bundles and sacks and suitcases. The railroad station also houses a hotel and restaurant, where meals are served on white damask tablecloths and the floors are of dark, beautiful hardwood boards that must have been cut long ago when virgin forest still covered the hills. The town itself is made up of small wooden houses with narrow streets of beaten earth. Here everything is tropical and damp. There are few tall trees, but the bush is all around. Flowers bloom in the grass by the roadside and there are bananas, palms, and bamboos.

The best time to see indri is early in the morning. We spent the night in the hotel and after breakfast drove down the road to the Réserve Forestière, where indri can be seen. A government department called Eaux et Forêts—Waters and Forests—manages natural resources and is also responsible for the reserves in which lemurs and other wildlife are supposedly protected. Unfortunately, this reserve is exploited in many ways. The process began long ago under the colonial government. The nearness of the road and the railroad encouraged woodcutting, graphite mining, and the planting of eucalyptus. Exploitation still goes on, and it is remarkable that there is any forest left. Because this is the one area in which tourists or scientific visitors can see indri without making a difficult jungle expedition, lemurologists are particularly anxious that the Malagasy government make an effort to save what remains of the forest.

We left the car near the highway and walked along a forest trail. The foliage glistened in the foggy dawn. The trees about us were tall and slender, and their bark was covered with lichen. Moss and fern grew along the path and the air was sweet. We came to a clearing on the brow of a hill from which we could see into a little valley and glimpse the peaks of countless, steep, forested hills around us. While we looked, the sun broke through the low clouds and touched the treetops. A moment later the indri began to sing. It was a wild and thrilling sound—a chorus of voices that held something of the human, something of the animal, and something unearthly. The whole valley was filled with it as the song first came from one hilltop and was answered from another. In this way, the indri, who spend the night in the treetops in small groups, greet the sun and signal their whereabouts to each other. The singing of the indri was a dawn-of-the-world sound, a sound from the youth of the family from which we come.

The indri sang at intervals for four or five minutes. Then there was silence. We waited for what seemed a long time; Emmanuel smoked several cigarettes and gazed back along the shadowy path. Finally, he pointed. I saw a tree sway, spotted a black-and-white creature clinging halfway up the trunk, in the manner of a man climbing a telephone pole. We walked quietly toward the indri, and it turned its head to stare at us. It had round, tufted ears that stood out on either side of its head like a teddy bear's. Its eyes were large and lemon yellow in a dark face, and its gaze was penetrating. Patches of white in its black fur mimicked the dappled sunlight coming through the leaves. Suddenly another

indri landed in a tree nearby. Indri vault from tree to tree in an upright position, like ski jumpers, and arrive feet first on vertical trunks, to which they cling easily with prehensile feet and hands. They seldom come to the ground, but when they do, they stand erect and bounce along, feet together, like a child on a pogo stick, except that their arms are held out for balance. The second indri began to pick leaves with its free hand and eat them, but the first continued to watch us with a hard, speculative look, until suddenly it made up its mind and, spring-propelled by its powerful hind legs, leaped effortlessly to a farther tree. It ricocheted to still another tree and vanished. When I looked back, its companion, too, was gone.

Indri are more often heard than seen. Emmanuel said that he had spent much of his boyhood in the forest, hearing indri often, but very rarely seeing them. Indri are not common even in unspoiled forest. Not only do they have a low birthrate, but the young face considerable risk. They must cling to their mother's fur from the moment of birth and hang on as she leaps from tree to tree. Dr. Petter believes there may be high mortality as new-born babies lose their grip and fall to their death. Indris are the heaviest lemurs, and their weight prevents prolonged flight. If they are pursued, the length and power of their leaps from tree to tree gradually diminish. When they are exhausted, they come to the ground to rest. As people become more sophisticated the taboos that protected indris are growing weaker. In some cases Christian churches, in their efforts to eliminate "superstition," have preached against taboos. A lemur scientist told me he had encountered a Catholic priest who, in order to convince his congregation that indris were merely beasts and not magic beings, killed several indris, roasted them, and served them as a meal for the congregation.

The east coast rain forest is also the home of the strangest and possibly the rarest lemur of all—the aye-aye. It is in a separate family from other lemurs, and it is the only member of that family to survive into modern times. Its scientific name is *Daubentonia madagascariensis*. Its popular name, aye-aye, is simply an expression of horror. Malagasy believe the aye-aye to be a sure harbinger of death.

The aye-aye has gone off on an evolutionary tangent all its own. One needn't be a zoologist to know that it is a peculiar creature, for the aye-aye looks as though it were made out of the spare parts of a number of other species of animals. It is the size of a large cat. Its coarse gray-black fur is of mixed short and long hair. Its long tail is bushy like that of a fox. Large ears stand out from its wide head. It has the chisel-like incisors of a rodent, and, like the teeth of rodents, they never stop growing. The aye-aye is nocturnal, and in daylight its wide, golden, light-reflective eyes, whose pupils contract to pinpoints, stare with what seems an inner glow. Strangest of all are the hands of the aye-aye. They are primate hands, but they are long and skeletal. The third finger has become a unique tool and feeding device. It is extra long, thin as a twig, and ends in a claw curved like a fishhook. The aye-aye uses it to extract grubs from deep hiding places in rotten wood.

Early zoologists thought the aye-aye to be a squirrel. Later it was classified as a tarsier, then a rodent. In 1863 Robert Owen, an English zoologist, showed that it was an aberrant and greatly specialized lemur. The aye-aye was scarce even then. What was thought to be the last aye-aye was a dead specimen reported in 1933. Zoologists laid the species to rest beside the dodo. Then, after more than twenty years, in 1957, Dr. Petter and his wife, Arlette, discovered two aye-ayes in a patch of forest south of Fenerive on the east coast of Madagascar. In the same locality, they heard distant cries that suggested the presence of others. The Petters were unable to return to the area until 1963. To their dismay they found that the building of a new road had destroyed much of the forest and the aye-ayes had disappeared. However, the next year Petter found two aye-ayes living near the village of Mahambo, where a few tall trees had been spared. Dr. Petter thinks that the older beliefs of the Malagasy forbade the killing of the aye-aye, but that these beliefs have recently changed. Other scientists disagree and think that the aye-aye has always been killed whenever it was found. It is certainly very much feared even now.

I asked Emmanuel what he knew about the magic of the aye-aye. He said, "It is different in different places. In some places people try to kill the aye-aye; in others they fear it so much they will move away if there is a chance of seeing one; for instance, if there is a rumor that one has been seen in the locality. The place where the aye-aye lives is the place where the bad spirit lives, and that makes the aye-aye very powerful. The aye-aye is not that spirit, but it is its messenger. It tells you that you are marked for death. Only a native doctor can save you. The doctor needs the finger of the aye-aye and that gives him great power. One way he may get the finger is to put medicine in his mouth and spit it in the face of the aye-aye and grab the finger and pull it off without killing the aye-aye. A doctor who has done this is a super doctor, but he must be very strong to dare to try it."

The aye-aye is a highly evolved creature and has the largest brain compared to body size of any lemur extant. Whether it is also the most intelligent is unknown. Dr. Petter, studying the few he was able to locate in the wild, made some observations on their habits. The aye-aye's nest is a complicated structure, and the aye-aye may spend twenty-four hours building it, but occupy it for only a few days and then build another. Why a nest is suddenly abandoned is unknown. The aye-aye sleeps all day and spends most of its night searching for food. With its extraordinary teeth, it can chew a hole in a coconut, then dig out the pulp with its third finger. It also searches branches for hidden larvae. Whether it smells them inside the wood or hears the crunching of their tiny mandibles cannot be determined. When it locates the prey the aye-aye gnaws a hole, inserts its finger and turns it about like a man using a pipe cleaner, pulling out pieces of the insect and flicking them into its mouth. It also eats the contents of an egg by this same method of scooping and flicking with its finger. Sometimes during its solitary wandering, the aye-aye utters a short, repeated call that Dr. Petter describes as sounding like metal sheets rubbed together. It may be answered by another aye-aye. Petter believes the call is the opposite of a friendly "hello"; rather, it is a warning of the aye-aye's presence so the two animals can avoid meeting.

Following his rediscovery of the aye-aye in 1964, Dr. Petter went to work to try to save at least a few. With help from the World Wildlife Fund, a young naturalist, André Peyrieras, was hired to make a survey and locate as many aye-ayes as possible. Aye-aye nests endure for a long time and are a help in locating aye-aye territory. Peyrieras began his survey in February 1965 and found signs of aye-ayes near several villages where they lived among coconut and litchi trees. Dr. Petter, meanwhile, had found a small, uninhabited island in the Bay of Antongil on the northeast coast. The island, called Nossi Mangabé, is about two square miles in size and some six miles offshore from the town of Maroantsetra. Dr. Petter found it had a rich variety of plants, including superb rain forest, and that several species of lemurs, *Cheirogalius major, Lemur macaco albifrons,* and *Varecia variegatus,* were flourishing there. He felt that it would serve as a safe refuge for aye-ayes, and with the help of Malagasy conservationists, the government was persuaded to declare the island a special reserve.

In the course of a year's work, Peyrieras had captured nine aye-ayes, four males and five females, and they were released on the island in 1966. Dr. Petter watched them as they made their way up the beach, walking on the crooked fingers of their strange hands, and climbed into the trees. Their fate since then is a mystery. No one has been back to search for them. When I talked to Dr. Petter, he said he felt that until the island could be properly guarded it is best left alone. At one time Dr. Petter dreamed of converting the island into a combination of research center and tourist attraction—as he put it, "a little paradise of lemuriens"—but there seems no way to realize that dream at present.

Meanwhile, it is known that at least a few aye-ayes survive on the mainland. During a trip to the northeast coast in 1974, Dr. Ian Tattersall, a British lemurologist, found an aye-aye dead on the road with a wire pulled tight around its neck.

The only aye-aye in captivity is a male at the zoo at Tzimbazaza Park in the center of Tananarive. Back in 1965 when André Peyrieras was capturing aye-ayes, he found an infant in a nest. Its mother had been killed by villagers. He bottle-fed it and raised it successfully. It was a male, and when, a little later, he captured an immature female, he decided to keep both in the hope of breeding them. He kept them at his home for a time and then turned them over to the zoo. Aye-ayes can adjust to a zoo diet and have lived a long time in captivity. They have survived eight or nine years in London and Paris, and the Amsterdam Zoo kept an aye-aye for twenty-three years. The pair at Tzimbazaza seemed healthy and normal, but no offspring resulted. Captive breeding of normally solitary animals is an especially tricky business. Recently the female aye-aye died. An autopsy showed chronic hepatitis and intestinal trouble. What with the frustration of all recent efforts to save this unlucky species, which is such an extraordinary fragment of our primate past, it seems that the aye-aye itself is the victim of the evil spirit that the Malagasy believe brings certain death.

In southern Madagascar, near the old port city of Fort-Dauphin, there is a unique sanctuary for lemurs on a private estate owned by M. Henry de Heaulme. M. de Heaulme and his son, Jean, have large business interests in Madagascar, including many acres planted in sisal. The de Heaulmes are French colonists of the old school. Their forebears left France in 1770 to settle on the French island of Réunion, which lies east of Madagascar, but in two hundred years the family has never lost touch with the homeland and the manner of life that is called "vieille France." The present family moved to Madagascar in 1928 and prospered there. As the largest landowner and employer of labor in the Fort-Dauphin area, the de Heaulme family has been in a position to set aside land for wildlife and to enforce its protection. The de Heaulmes are keenly interested in wildlife and are also aware of the ecological value of preserving some of the native forest. For some years the de Heaulme preserve has attracted scientific researchers, and the de Heaulmes have been most hospitable. There is a small guesthouse at the edge of the reserve that has been used by a series of lemur-watchers. At the time of our visit two researchers from Duke University, Jay Russell and Lee McGeorge, were working there and we arranged to visit them. It is seven hundred miles from Tananarive to Fort-Dauphin over a road that runs the length of the island's high plateau, a trip that takes three days. One morning my husband, Richard, Emmanuel, and I set off in the Land-Rover. Soon after leaving the city we found ourselves in a heavily farmed rural area, with terraced rice paddies tucked into every fertile nook among steep, treeless hills. Here and there I saw clusters of farmhouses that reminded me of rural France. On the plateau, houses are of adobe brick, and many are whitewashed. Most are two stories tall and have thatched roofs and no chimneys. Cooking is done on the second floor, and the smoke escapes through a window, blackening the eaves. It is cool on the plateau, and the men and women working in the fields or walking beside the road were swathed in striped or printed cotton robes.

On our second day of driving, the pavement ended and from then on it was a slow and bumpy ride over gravel. The land became drier with fewer streams to nourish rice paddies. Because of the prevailing winds off the Indian Ocean, rain comes first to the north and east of Madagascar and diminishes toward the south, so that the plateau becomes increasingly droughty. In this poor land, the villages are smaller and the houses simpler. Instead of rice the people grow drought-resistant crops such as manioc and tend their herds of zebus.

The zebus we saw at the roadside were handsome creatures, colored in variegated patterns of black and white or red and white. They are not raised for food in the usual sense, but for use as sacrificial offerings. A basic feature of the Malagasy religion is ancestor worship. To the Malagasy the spirits of their ancestors are an ever present force, dominating daily life. To maintain a satisfactory relationship with the unseen world requires numerous ceremonies which include, invariably, the sacrifice of zebus followed by a feast. An emergency, such as a sudden illness, can arise at any time. To be prepared to meet these needs, each family amasses as many zebus as it can. Zebus are seldom sold or eaten on ordinary occasions, but hoarded for future need.

"The worst thing that could happen to a family," Emmanuel explained, "is to have someone die and not have enough zebus to make a proper ceremony. And there are many other times when ceremonies are needed. If a baby boy is born and you are very glad, you might kill ten zebus to give proper thanks. If someone is sick, it may be because the ancestors are not happy and a sacrifice is needed. In some places a man may spend his whole life getting a great herd of zebus so that when he dies his sons can build him a proper tomb."

We passed these tombs standing alone on hilltops. They are rectangular stone piles, hung with the horns of the zebus that were sacrificed in the course of their construction, an effort which may have taken years.

Because zebus are so essential in everyone's life, they have become a form of wealth that rural Malagasy value more than cash. They invest in zebus rather than banks. Calves are comparable to interest. A large herd is a satisfaction to the owner and makes him a rich man in the eyes of the community. Large herds range from a hundred or so up to several hundred or even a thousand. The owner may live no differently than his neighbors, but he enjoys prestige and security.

The dark side of the zebu cult is its effect on the grassland and what is left of the forest. Zebus are kept all over the island, not only on the grasslands. In many places they overgraze, and the vegetation becomes constantly poorer. Worst of all is the Malagasy practice of burning the grasslands for the sake of their herds. This is done at the end of the dry season when the grass has turned yellow and lifeless and the cattle are growing thin. Then, if the grass is burned, the ashes provide a quick charge of fertilizer and new green shoots are coaxed out of the earth. Unfortunately, this is a short-term benefit with ultimately disastrous results. The fires destroy part of the root system of the grass, so that when rains come the grass cannot hold the soil and more erosion takes place. Wherever there are bushes or trees, the fires destroy their seedlings. Fires eat into the edges of the patches of forest that survive in valleys and along riverbanks. Little by little these patches shrink, and more and more land is laid bare. For years the French and now the Malagasy government have tried to deal with the problems of too many zebus and too many fires, but they have always been defeated by the combination of mystical belief, ancient custom, and short-term benefit.

Zebus and fire have combined diastrously with another element of Madagascar's ecology; lateritic soil. Most scholars believe that the great trees of the high plateau were cut many centuries ago. This cutting, followed by repeated fires, brought on the semi-desert conditions we see today. As the earth was laid bare, heavy tropical rains washed away the topsoil and exposed the lateritic clay beneath it. Lateritic clay, which has a high content of iron and other minerals, is the curse of Madagascar and many other countries near the equator. It has a particular potential for disastrous erosion. When it is exposed to the combination of water and sunlight, it becomes hard and bricklike. Few plants can penetrate it with their roots. Rain no longer sinks down, but runs along sloping surfaces in sheets, carrying away ever more soil until, eventually, nothing is left behind but stone and gravel. When it rains in Madagascar, the rivers run red with rusty particles of clay. Travelers arriving by air have commented that the rivers pouring into the ocean and staining it red seem to be carrying away the lifeblood of the island.

This damage is irreversible. Once the soil is gone, nothing within the reach of present technology can bring it back. In Madagascar the process began when the first tree was cut and the first fire set. Unlike the constantly rainy east coast, the highlands do not regenerate with new growth. As long as the population was small, tribes were able to move when an area became infertile. Probably the land seemed as inexhaustible to them as the American West did to us until quite recently. Now most of the population of Madagascar is crowded into the fertile strip along the east coast and in the areas of the pleateau that still produce rice. The rest of the island is empty or thinly peopled. Eighty percent of Madagascar's land has been described as "degraded savanna, grassland, and steppe."

As we drove the evidence of fire was everywhere. From the hilltops we could see across acres of blackened grass. Even sadder were the struggling trees with blackened trunks and withered leaves. Generations of fire have reduced Madagascar's highland landscape to barren mountains, stony hillsides, and plains covered by coarse grass—miles and miles of it extending to the far horizons. Sometimes eucalyptus or more rarely a grand old native tree shades the road. In places scattered trees and shrubs struggle against the hazards of drought and fire that now plague this land. Nevertheless, it is a rather grand and beautiful landscape, reminiscent of parts of Arizona and Nevada. "When you drive on the plateau," one friend had advised me, "try to imagine how it must have looked covered with forest." I tried to picture the tall trees and cool shade, the marshes and lakes, the birds, the little hippos and huge turtles, and, above all, the lemurs—all probably quite fearless and confiding as they met man for the first time. All I could see was empty distance. There was utter stillness, except where the wind blew the yellow grass. Not even a bird flew.

Rural people in Madagascar travel by "taxi brousse," or bush taxi; mostly Peugeot station wagons that speed from town to town in clouds of dust. Travelers are always glad of a lift from any passing car and after a while we picked up two hitchhikers—an old man and a young man. Emmanuel offered them cigarettes with elaborate courtesy, and the three began to chat easily, as though they were old friends. Courteous, friendly smiles and laughter seemed to be an essential part of rural manners. I asked what was being said, and Emmanuel told me that the two men were father and son. They had been to town but were hurrying home because the father's wife was having her eighth child. The son, Emmanuel told me, had said that he wasn't afraid of white people, the way some rustics were. He had ridden with white people in cars before, and had gotten used to them. Emmanuel explained that since colonial days many people believed that whites wanted to steal the blood of black men. When the two men got out at a cluster of small, thatched houses, they thanked us with smiles and handshakes. To have a large number of children is greatly desired everywhere in Madagascar. It is a terrible thing to have no children, Emmanuel told me. A barren wife can be divorced. There is no stigma to illegitimacy; in fact, trouble is likely to arise over which family will have the privilege of raising the child. As in all poor countries, a man's children are his social security system. Sons are of special importance, for it is sons who take care of their father's tomb, in preparation for the time when they, too, will be buried there. A man with no sons is out of luck, for daughters are buried in their husbands' tombs. If there is no male heir, the tomb is closed. Then, no one goes to visit it, and the ancestors are shamed. People believe that such things happen only to families that are somehow flawed.

Our next passengers were a man and his wife who had been sitting dejectedly at a crossroads with a few bags and bundles. The man was tall and thin and brownish, and was wearing a yellow sarong wrapped around his waist and a white shirt. He carried an ax. His wife was dark and pretty and had a gold tooth. Before long, the man was telling Emmanuel his story. His home was farther west. Years before, his wife's grandmother had married a man from the locality we were driving through. Recently, word that she had died five years ago had reached them. They had set off immediately to claim the body, but had met with nothing but frustration. No one in the town would tell them where the grandmother was buried. They had been sent on one fruitless search after another. They guessed that someone might have wrongfully claimed her estate and that the thief's neighbors were protecting him. But the man and his wife wanted not the grandmother's possessions but her bones; they could have no peace until she was properly buried. Now their savings were exhausted (they had spent sixteen thousand francs—about sixty-eight dollars—on the trip) and they were returning home to prepare for another effort.

The relationship between the dead and the living is very close in Madagascar. As Emmanuel explained, "The dead are like people living in another world. In Christianity, you believe the body is nothing; here we have respect for the body. If a man dies far away, his body must be brought back. You can be remembered among us for a hundred years. As soon as a baby starts to talk, he is told about his father's father, and so on. Some people have it in writing. Each tribe has its own form of showing respect for the dead. On the plateau, the bones are taken from the tomb every five years. There is a party. It is a happy thing. The dead person is told about family happenings since he died; then the bones are wrapped in new cloth and put back. Other tribes do not rewrap the body. In these tribes, there is a common tomb, but a man knows that his parents are there. The son will put things the old man liked on top of the tomb. He may leave a cigarette, or shoes, or an umbrella. When you drink liquor, you drop a bit on the ground for the ancestors. If a man dies far away and you can't bring him back, you must make a stone monument and put a cloth on it, and call, 'Joseph, you are dead in France. We call you to come into this cloth.' Then you sing a funeral song as though the man were inside the cloth, and bury it. Sometimes, a child of the man will wear the cloth. It will be made into a shirt and the child will wear it until it is gone."

I asked Emmanuel to tell me about other deities, and he said, "We have a god who is higher than the ancestors. There is a female god and a male god and also a bad god. We give the horns and the feet of the zebu to the bad god. If you forget to give the bad god his gift, there can be trouble at a ceremony. Perhaps a fight will break out. You put liquor in a glass and throw it to the east for the good god and throw it to the west for the bad god. Everybody jokes with the bad god, and taunts him, because he is not good enough to stay on the earth or to go to heaven, but is just stuck in between. Many people also believe in the Christian religion, yet feel closer to the ancestors."

On the morning of the third day, we entered the driest country so far. The grass was sparse, and sinister-looking termite hills rose up in endless ranks, like a disease of the earth. From time to time, we passed small villages, some of them consisting of only two or three houses. It was hard to imagine how people could survive, but Emmanuel said they had all they needed. Some of the men walking by the road carried spears, and we did not pick these men up, but when we encountered an old man leaning on a staff and wrapped in a toga, we stopped. He wore a rakish straw hat and had a rascally gleam in his eye. He immediately asked for money but settled agreeably for a drink of water. Then he took a flask made of a large, polished brown seed pod from under his robes and refreshed himself with a pinch of snuff. He told us that he was eighty years old and troubled by stiff knees, but otherwise was well. I asked if he found life better now than it was in his youth, and he replied that it was far better now. The French and the Merina before them had both been very terrible, he said, for both had forced people to work without pay. He told us that since a man could grow enough rice, manioc, and corn to live on, money was needed only to buy salt and oil for lamps, and rising prices therefore did not trouble him. I wanted to know how many zebus he had, but Emmanuel told me it would be rude to ask, so we discussed zebus in general. The old man said that four hundred was the maximum herd for this area, but that farther west a rich man might have a thousand zebus; that the price of a good zebu was forty thousand francs (about $171); and that the owner pays a herdsman two zebus a year and provides him with clothes. I asked why the old man was traveling, and he replied that he was going to visit his son, who had gone insane. The son, he said, had made the mistake of selling forty zebus for cash, and a neighbor, unable to resist the temptation, had placed him under a spell and driven him out of his mind, and then had stolen the cash, which was hidden in the house. Now the son was being cared for in another village. The practice of casting spells is common in Madagascar, Emmanuel told me. The work is usually performed by witch doctors, who also have a reputation for great skill as poisoners. They have developed poisons for all occasions and with all degrees of toxicity. They have a poison to stop the heart, a poison to cause illness, a poison to derange the mind, and a poison to kill. Not all native doctors are witch doctors, however. A good doctor will be insulted if he is asked to kill, for he believes that if he kills he will lose his power to cure. But a witch is trained to kill, and to make trouble. He is said to be possessed by an evil spirit, which can pass from father to son. There are ways to detect a witch. For one thing, a witch never helps when someone is dying. For another, at a moment of mishap, he laughs in a certain way. In addition to poison, witch doctors may employ lightning or magic. It is believed that a witch doctor has the power to send a bolt of lightning to kill a person; however, he must reckon with the fact that every person has a spiritual aura around him which may be strong enough to deflect the lightning bolt, or even send it back. A man's aura is said to be stronger than a woman's, and a woman's is said to be stronger than a child's. It sometimes happens that a bolt intended for a man is deflected and hits someone weaker nearby, perhaps his wife or child. A witch doctor may also kill by making use of symbols of death: it is said that a person can be killed by placing seven needles or bits of his clothing or hair along his path. Most witchcraft is inspired by revenge, and the danger is always present that the dead man's spirit will return to kill the killer. I had been hearing a good deal about witchcraft ever since I had arrived in Madagascar, and a question was bothering me. I now asked Emmanuel whether the person who hired a witch doctor to kill someone with lightning or magic paid in advance or afterward. "Afterward," he unhesitatingly replied, leaving me with a haunting inference.

In earlier days witches were sometimes stoned to death. The Christian missionaries put a stop to the practice. I recalled the fate of the Salem witches and told Emmanuel their story. His dark eyes widened with astonishment. "The Christians did *that?*" he asked, and chuckled with incredulous amusement.

Our next passengers were going to a fair. One was a man carrying a burlap bag full of empty bottles, and the other was a woman carrying a baby on her arm and a duck in a basket. She hoped to sell the duck for eight hundred francs, she said. Our new passengers told us that people were very satisfied with life at the moment, because the new government had abolished a personal tax which had forced everyone to acquire at least a small amount of cash. We passed a stretch of flaming grass that was singeing the few trees that stood alongside the road and gave it shade. The man with the bag of bottles said that the zebus were very thin now, and that the burning would help them. I asked what he thought about losing the trees, and he replied that it was too bad but could not be helped.

The fair, when we arrived there, was being held in the market square of a small village, beneath a roof of corrugated iron. Beans, corn, manioc, plastic pails, and printed cloth were on sale. One vendor was selling meatballs the size of marbles, which each customer ate from a spoon tied to the dish. I bought a freshly fried fritter spiced with pepper. It was very good.

After leaving the fair, we picked up a man walking barefoot on the highway and carrying a pair of shoes. Like so many of the people we had met, he was on business having to do with zebus: he was going to the next town to report the theft of some zebus. His herdsman had been taken for questioning by the police in connection with another incident of zebu stealing, and while he had been away his charges had been stolen. Zebu stealing is a serious problem in Madagascar. In fact, one tribe, the Antandroy, which inhabits the dry grasslands and semi-desert we were just approaching, has made zebu stealing a traditional part of life. In this tribe, when a boy is born, his parents will sometimes put a spell on him to make him steal when he grows up. "Because of the spell," Emmanuel told me, "he will have the idea in his head that he must steal or die."

By the end of the third day we had reached the true desert. In places the plant life was dense. Thorny scrub, with small grayish leaves, mingled with cactus-like growth in a great variety of peculiar shapes and forms. Now and then we saw a baobab tree, those weird giants with huge trunks crowned by a small cluster of twisted branches that look more like roots. The Malagasy say that at one time these trees were like any others, but God became displeased with them and turned them upside down.

This arid area of Madagascar is full of botanical curiosities. Among the strangest trees are the various species of *Didierea*, whose branches are studded with spines between which tiny green leaves grow. Remarkably, a few species of lemurs are adapted to live among them, feeding on the leaves. How they managed to leap from one spiny perch to the next without impaling their fingers is a mystery.

One would think that here, at least, in such inhospitable country, plants and animals might be left in peace; but alas, it isn't so. There are small settlements throughout the desert, and skinny zebus wander through the bush on sandy trails. Goats remove the spiny thickets. The bush is cleared for sisal and castor beans. For the lemur, it seems, there is no hiding place anywhere at all; no place so poor that it is not coveted by someone.

The de Heaulme estate is on the banks of the Mandrary River near the village of Berenty. Except along the riverbanks, the land is dry. We turned off the highway, entered a well-kept gravel road, and found the spiny forest replaced by a vast field of spiky sisal plants that stretched like a blue-green lake to the far distance. At one end of the field M. de Heaulme has preserved a few acres of virgin *Didierea*. We drove on and came to a wall of tall, leafy trees, where the gallery forest that borders the Mandrary River is stopped by the fields of sisal. This strip of forest is the lemur reserve. We passed an administration building and a hangar containing M. de Heaulme's private airplane and arrived at the edge of the forest. Jay Russell, the American biologist staying there, welcomed us to the guesthouse (a simple stucco building), gave us cold beers, and led us to the shade of a huge old tree in the yard. I was delighted to meet him and Lee McGeorge, a young woman also studying lemurs, but at that moment the thing that enchanted me most, even more than the beer, was meeting a tame lemur named Chico who was tethered to the tree. He leaped eagerly into Russell's arms and then into mine.

The lemur made interested, and interestingly expressive, snuffling sounds as he sat on my shoulder, smelling my face and neck and hair. He moved down to my bare arm, which he anointed with a few drops of urine as a friendly gesture. Then he gently groomed the back of my hand with his grooming comb. This is a dental arrangement peculiar to lemurs. Their lower front teeth are close together and narrow, just like the teeth of a fine comb, and project forward. The comb is used to groom their soft, thick fur and that of their comrades. Russell explained that Chico expected to be groomed in return. Lacking a comb, I did the best I could with my fingers.

Chico was dark brown with a slightly orangy ruff. He stood about two feet tall. He was a *Lemur fulvus collaris.* Russell said that the year before, a South African geologist had bought him from a Malagasy family that intended to eat him. He was weak and sick and had an eye infection and a broken leg. The geologist's wife nursed him, and he was now quite well. What was most remarkable about him was that though he had been an adult when caught and though he had suffered badly at human hands he had become utterly tame and confiding. When the South Africans left, they could find no place where he could be safely released and had given him to Russell.

Now I had a chance to examine a lemur's hands. The tips of the fingers are broad and padded to provide a sure grip on branches. The toes are also adapted for grasping, with a wide reach between the big toe and the others. One toe on each foot has a claw for grooming. Many animals avoid eye contact, but Chico's round copper-colored eyes met mine and were brimming with liveliness and feeling. While we drank our beer, Chico swallowed a glass of cold tea with appreciative murmurs. Russell said that Chico was extraordinarily gentle and affectionate, perhaps because he and Lee gave him a great deal of attention to compensate for the lack of his natural social life. As we talked, one or the other of us would groom Chico and play with him. He seemed to me to have none of the febrile, nervous jumpiness of true monkeys. When he looked into Russell's face it was with a sweet, trusting gaze that was more doglike than simian. The word "innocence" came to mind, and I wondered if it might have been a prosimian who ate the apple.

Lee McGeorge offered to show us a captive mouse lemur. The mouse lemur, or *Microcebus,* and the pygmy marmoset are the tiniest primates there are. An adult *Microcebus* weighs about two ounces. It occupies what is called the "fine-branch niche" because its small size allows it to go to the ends of slender twigs in order to capture insects. McGeorge went into the house and came back with a *Microcebus* between her cupped palms. It had soft brown fur and mouse-like ears that trembled. It seemed to me to be the hummingbird of the primates. *Microcebus* are nocturnal and this one, having been rudely awakened, stared at us with round, bewildered golden eyes. It was hard to believe that this fragile tiny being belonged within the order that included man, but the telltale signs were clearly visible: the eyes that looked forward, the elfin hands, and the flat fingernails, where claws would be in another beast.

The edge of the forest was within a few hundred feet of where we sat, and the air was filled with all sorts of birdcalls. One was the familiar sound of a dove; another, Russell identified as a *Coua gigas,* a bird unique to Madagascar, with a particularly melodic voice. A hawk, *Gymnogenys radiata,* sailed over us. The sun began to sink and Russell said this was a good time to walk into the forest and see the wild lemurs.

We walked along a sandy path under a canopy of enormous trees that reminded me of live oaks. They are tamarinds, locally called "kily," and produce a fruit that is eaten by lemurs. Their fallen leaves made a soft, tan carpet on the forest floor. The undergrowth was not thick; but here and there large vines trailed from high branches, and leafy shrubs made thickets. The forest didn't seem tropical, but more like a hardwood forest in the southern United States, perhaps the Carolinas.

A moment after we had entered the forest we came across a troop of *Lemur catta,* or "maki," as the Malagasy call them. They were coming down out of the trees and ambling along the path ahead of us, their tails waving gracefully. A few were already gathered at a water trough that had been put by the path for their benefit. One or two drank at a time while the others waited their turn. *Catta* spend more time on the ground than any other lemurs. The *catta's* fur is mostly gray with decorative touches of black and white. Its face is light-colored with black-ringed eyes and nose, and pointed, catlike ears. Its bushy tail is ringed in bands of black and white. Altogether the animal suggests a cross between a cat and a raccoon, although it is closer to a cat in size.

We stood still and the *cattas* gave us a brief glance and then went on about their business. Several females carried infants on their backs. They rode like tiny jockeys. The troop was extraordinarily pretty; their sharp markings, so bright and clean; their graceful way of bounding along on all fours with their backs a little arched, something like playful cats; their small encounters and jostlings as they maneuvered for a turn at the trough; all of it was a joy to watch. The setting was beautiful, too. The stately trees, the clean forest floor, the fading sunlight slanting through the glade made it an enchanting scene.

My husband wanted closer pictures. He began to move forward. When he came too close, the *cattas* looked up and suddenly bounded away in all directions, leaping effortlessly into the trees. A brave one stood its ground and, holding the edge of the trough with its hands, took a long drink. Then it, too, bounded into a tree and disappeared.

A few moments later we saw a family of *Propithecus;* a white-furred lemur the Malagasy call "sifaka." They are larger than *catta* and, like their cousins the indri, have long arms and legs that give a more nearly human body proportion. One sifaka sat on a branch and gazed at us while another hung by its feet, searching for fruit on an adjacent branch. Their fur was gleaming white with handsome touches of black on their faces and ears. Dr. Evelyn Hutchinson, professor emeritus of zoology at Yale, a distinguished authority on lemurs, once said that he thought the *Propithecus* to be the most beautiful mammal in the world. With so many contenders it is hard to say if I agree, but the *Propithecus* may be the most beautiful primate. It occurred to me that *Propithecus* and *catta* both are so much more beautiful than any monkey, ape, or human. It seems that primate looks have been going downhill ever since the monkeys took over from the lemurs.

The *Propithecus*, four of them, were lazing about in several tall trees, high above our heads. We craned our necks and watched. They were dining, in a leisurely way, picking kily pods off the trees. They moved with such ease from branch to branch that it seemed they must be light as feathers. In truth they are all fur and muscle. Their hind legs perform like powerful springs and can send them on soaring leaps of twenty feet or more. Like indri, they fly through the air standing upright and land feet first on the chosen tree trunk. We waited for a while and eventually one of the group decided to move on. It made a series of flying leaps from tree to tree, descending with each leap. Finally it hit the ground and bounced along standing upright with both feet together and its arms flung out for balance. Though it was a weird gait—like a man with his feet tied together—the *Propithecus* moved with astonishing speed. The rest of the troop followed the first through the trees, but didn't come to the ground. We lost sight of them and walked on.

Russell pointed out that the lemurs are remarkably adapted so that a great many can live in a small space. Thanks to this, the de Heaulme preserve, small as it is, may hold as many as three hundred *catta* and perhaps as many *Propithecus*. In addition, there are small nocturnal lemurs: *Lepilemur* and *Microcebus*. In tall trees the ranges of lemurs are stacked vertically, like those of apartment dwellers in a city. The *Propithecus* live at the tops of the trees. Large and peaceful, they eat mature leaves and don't have to go far for their meals. They are the big grazers of the treetops. Below them are the livelier *catta*. The *catta* live in bigger, busier troops than *Propithecus* and cover a larger range. They eat more fruit and buds and insects. At the bottom, near the ground, the small, more solitary insectivores, such as *Microcebus*, go high or low, wherever the vegetation has very small branches.

In a disappointingly short time we were at the edge of the reserve overlooking the Mandrary River. In flood the river is a quarter of a mile across, and every year it chews away chunks of the reserve. Now the riverbed was twenty feet below us, and the river itself was a peaceful ribbon in the center of a bed of clean sand. It was a lovely landscape. White herons stood on the sand by the water's edge or sailed upward to their roosts in the trees. In the distance, downriver, a herd of zebus filed across the sand to drink. Tall kily trees lined the banks as far as we could see. No houses were visible. It seemed a sylvan paradise. But as we stood there, Russell described the reality. The whole reserve is only forty acres. From where we stood it ran along the river a quarter of a mile downstream and a mere sixty or seventy yards upstream. There are people living in the forest on both banks of the river. Their cattle graze in the forest. The people cut trees for firewood and building. Lemurs straying from the protected area in which we stood are in dangerous territory.

As the government of Madagascar becomes more unfriendly to foreigners the future of the de Heaulme estate is increasingly precarious. In truth, the reserve is a very small fortress under siege. Its defenses are only as strong as the determination of the de Heaulme family and depend upon their continued presence.

After dinner we took head lamps and returned to the forest to look for *Lepilemur* and *Microcebus*. Russell explained that in order to see their eye reflection, a beam of light must be directed from the level of one's own eyes; hence, a headlight rather than a hand-held flashlight is necessary. Mouse lemurs are busy from dusk to dawn. They live in overlapping ranges with one male inside the range of several females, suggesting a harem arrangement. Several females may sleep together in a nest, with or without a male. Moving about their small domain, they keep in touch through scent and sound. *Lepilemur* are much bigger—the size of a large squirrel—and eat leaves, not insects. Like *Propithecus*, they make extraordinary leaps.

As our eyes adjusted to the dark, branches were silhouetted against the starlit sky. There was a strange, sweet smell in the air. Russell said it was the smell of bats. The forest was full of rustlings and stirrings; small squeaks and cries. Russell said that as darkness falls *Lepilemur* climb onto a perch and shout at their neighbors—insulting messages probably. Russell's current study is of *Lepilemur* physiology—their cycle of activity and what they eat and excrete. Since the earliest mammals were very small, like *Lepilemur*, such information can be used to reconstruct some aspects of evolution.

Our head lamps searched the dark masses of leaves above us. Suddenly I saw a star in a tree. It became two stars close together. They were the eyes of a *Lepilemur* sitting on a branch. Coming closer, I could make out its small, dark shape. Then a group of trees just beyond came to life. There were shrill calls and answers. A moment later, farther down the path, came the sounds of a *Lepilemur* quarrel. It sounded like a fight between squirrel-sized cats. As it died down there was a mighty flapping in the underbrush. Russell said we had disturbed an akanga, a bird something like a big guinea fowl.

We walked on, catching sight of twin stars on all sides. The smaller were *Microcebus*. Tiniest, and glowing with a reddish fire, were the eyes of a large moth. All about us the sounds of small, unseen beings, unidentifiable chirps and rustlings—birds, bats, insects, lemurs—made the forest as busy as a village square on market day. It seemed all the more marvelous since I had walked right through it in the daylight, unaware of the life hidden all around.

We left the lively dark and went into the house and the harsh, steady glare of the electric bulb. For a time it seemed very silent and dead inside the cement walls of the small room.

We talked of the lemurs' probable future. Russell said that he had traveled a good deal in Madagascar, trying to assess their status. He had found large patches of wild land left in Madagascar, but everywhere the forest is giving way to devouring fires, the farmer's ax, and the bulldozers of investors interested in developing land for cash crops.

Without trees there can be no lemurs, and the forest is under assault wherever it stands. The government is well aware that slash-and-burn agriculture gives a poor return at high cost in soil and future crops, but it knows, too, that the practice cannot be changed until an alternative is provided. The obvious alternative is large-scale agriculture with modern methods. When this is undertaken on already deforested land, it helps both the standard of living and the cause of conservation, but sadly often development is undertaken on forested tracts. In the south and west, the remnants of deciduous forests are being sacrificed to sisal, cotton, and other crops. In the east the rain forest is cleared for plantations of coffee, bananas, and so on, even when already cleared land stands idle in the same area. The valuable hardwoods in the forest are a tempting source of cash. Both foreign and Malagasy businessmen are exploiting them to some degree, and the pressure will increase. While the slash-and-burn method continues to do great damage, it is likely that it will be large-scale commercial exploitation that delivers the coup de grace. There are eleven natural reserves in Madagascar that are managed by the department of Eaux et Forêts. Unhappily the reserves are sanctuaries in name only. Some of them are quite large and contain good lemur habitat, but they are invaded by people who cut trees, clear land, and hunt lemurs. Eaux et Forêts has only limited funds and the most it can do to prevent these incursions is to provide one or two guards for each reserve. There is no money for motorcycles or other equipment; guards must patrol these large areas on foot —a more or less hopeless task.

To protect the parks adequately would be both expensive and politically inexpedient since it would be resented by the local people. Experience in African countries has shown that game reserves cannot succeed unless the people nearby somehow share in the benefits. It is not easy to find a way to do this in Madagascar where unlike Kenya, whose parks bring revenue from tourists, there would be no visible return. The great surge of interest in wildlife that has drawn millions of visitors to Africa has passed Madagascar by. Elephants and lions are dramatic. Lemurs are small and hard to see. They are thrilling only to an observer who is aware of what they represent.

Hunting lemurs, either in or out of a reserve, is illegal everywhere in Madagascar; nevertheless, a great many lemurs die at the hands of hunters. Some tribes spare certain species because of religious taboos, but as people move around increasingly, hunting is brought to areas where lemurs once were safe. Modern ideas, in general, are eroding the old protective taboos.

Lemurs are killed for sport and food. Lemur meat is a delicacy; something like squirrel to a Kentucky mountaineer. Hunters are hard to catch. Enforcement of hunting laws is unpopular with hunters and officials alike. Often people in forested areas have little idea that the forests don't extend indefinitely and that lemurs are not plentiful all over the world. Laws that prohibit hunting seem illogical and unfair. Only education can bring new concepts of conservation and such education will take a long time.

Guns and ammunition are expensive in Madagascar, so country people do most of their hunting by old-fashioned methods; but the idea of sport hunting is becoming fashionable with city people. Town dwellers take to the woods for a weekend of sport. One scientist I met told me of a hunter who had shot a dozen *Propithecus verreauxi* in a single afternoon.

The gap between country and town in Madagascar is another factor that works against the lemur. People raised in towns, particularly on the bare plateau, are apt to be unaware of the forest and its wildlife; yet these are the people most likely to enter government and make decisions affecting wildlife. Many highly educated people in Tananarive hardly know that lemurs exist. If lemurs are to be accorded any value in Madagascar, education is needed on all levels.

Russell summed up his assessment by saying that he believed some species of lemurs would outlast others, but that sooner or later all are doomed. Representatives of a few species may survive in zoos and research institutions, but there are many species no one has been able to keep alive in captivity. These will leave behind only stuffed skins to remind us of our loss. If wild lemurs become extinct it will bring to an end one entire branch of the primate family.

We left the reserve the following morning and started back to Tananarive. As we drove we talked of Russell's prediction, wondering helplessly if there is no way the lemurs might be redeemed. It was all too evident that the obstacles are large; a lot of money committed over a long period of time and the cooperation of the Malagasy government would be needed to set up and guard an adequate system of lemur sanctuaries.

Emmanuel mourned the likelihood that the Malagasy people would not learn the value of forests and soil and lemurs until it is too late. He found it difficult to understand why people in rich countries who have a greater comprehension and a greater capability than the Malagasy do not do more to save the lemurs.

Before I left home I had talked to a scientist who said, "Take a look at the plains of Madagascar and remember that what has happened there can happen in a lot of other countries. It tells us what may be in store for most of the world." His words haunted me now. It occurred to me that the people of Madagascar live by customs that served them well when their numbers were few and the land large, but are now lethal to the land, to plant and animal life, and ultimately to themselves. I thought of primitive Madagascar supporting a multitude of plants that converted sun and water and soil into nourishment for myriad other lives, man's included. Today the sun still shines and the rain falls, but there are huge areas of wastelands that the people and most of the animals and plants have abandoned. As in the tale of the goose that laid golden eggs, a bountiful ecosystem has been destroyed and replaced by a poverty-stricken landscape. I thought of what remains: of the indri singing from the hilltops in the golden dawn; of the gentle *Propithecus* and the busy *catta* in the tall, old kily trees communicating in the antique language of scent; of the *Lepilemur* and *Microcebus* and the aye-aye pursuing their mysterious nocturnal lives. I remembered Chico; the communicative little sounds he made and how, when he jumped into my arms, I felt the softness of his fur and his warm, living weight.

After a while we began to talk of other things. The sky had grown dark and a sudden rainstorm pelted the dry, red earth. When the storm had passed, a rainbow appeared and made a perfect arch between two distant mountain ranges. I asked Emmanuel if he believed that there was a pot of gold at the end of the rainbow. He looked startled. "Oh, no!" he exclaimed. "In Madagascar, we believe that if you find the end of the rainbow you die."

9

WOODCHUCK

If you live in woodchuck country, which in the East is almost everywhere, it is possible that someday you will find yourself holding a baby woodchuck and wondering what to do with it. In that case I hope these notes will be helpful. It happened to me on a recent spring day and as I picked it up my mind flashed back to another spring when I was ten years old. Then, any creature I encountered was an individual, as distinct, as worthy of life as myself and much more marvelous. This is a feeling that may be attacked as sentimental by those who see individual animals as interchangeable digits in a very large number and point out that while woodchucks come and go, only the existence of the species need concern us. This view has its validity. I have not spent my adult years putting up tombstones for deceased pets or holding funeral rites over fallen sparrows, and yet I have never divorced myself from the idea that individual worth in the animal kingdom is not restricted to human beings.

On May 29 there was a heavy rain. Our farm is in the midst of rolling fields. They were thoroughly soaked, and the new grass turned even more brilliant green. There were puddles in the driveway and on the low spots in our neighbor's potato field. The next day the sun came out beautifully hot. Driving back from the village, I decided that instead of going on another errand I would go home and get my bathing suit. I turned in and pulled the car up short, because a very small woodchuck was traveling along the road in front of me, its belly almost flat to the gravel.

I got out of the car, took off my sweater, threw it over the woodchuck and wrapped him in it, then put him on the floor of the car while I drove the short distance home. I surmised the rain had washed out his burrow and the young woodchucks had wandered off in different directions. If I hadn't come along this one—like his brothers—would have gone on in a hopeless search until he died of starvation. Rescuing him, I felt as powerful as Fate. It also occurred to me that by picking him up I was letting myself in for quite a lot of bother. I wondered if I really wanted to do it at my age. But by the time I thought of this, the woodchuck was already wrapped in my sweater and it was too late to reconsider.

At home I put him in the bathtub, where he valiantly scrabbled against the unyielding porcelain. My husband found a large carton. I put cat litter in the bottom and straw on top of that. I put the chuck in it. He did not try to bite. He gratefully burrowed into the straw.

I put the carton in the bathroom. This is where I always kept animals in my childhood. This also, I must admit, is where my first woodchuck met his end. He somehow climbed up and fell into the toilet, where he stayed for some time with his nose just above the surface. He died later, presumably of pneumonia, leaving me guilty and bereft. Now, faced with my new responsibility, I remembered other things about that first woodchuck. At that time we had a litter of kittens. We brought the mother and kittens into the bathroom. The little chuck shared their bed. The old cat licked him, and the kittens warmed him, but he could get no milk. His mouth was the wrong shape. We fed him with a bottle. He sat on his haunches like a bear and held the bottle in his paws. I remembered, too, that he followed me around making a sound like a tiny outboard motor. He also shared the cat's toilet pan, which was filled with sand. At the time I thought the mother cat had taught him, but I have since learned that this is innate in woodchucks.

In the old days there were doll nursing bottles with real rubber nipples to be had. Now the doll bottles are plastic and no use. Instead I tried a coarse medicine dropper. The chuck sucked noisily and greedily while I squeezed out a mixture of nonfat milk and baby cereal. He accepted me quickly. Within a day or two he was rushing into my hands and making a strange little noise when I came to feed him. Two ounces filled him to bulging. Then he slept, often on his back with legs flung out in an attitude of abandon. Awake, he began to play, rolling around and biting at the straw. If I put my hand in the carton, he nibbled my fingers and wrestled with them, kicking against my hand the way kittens do.

When I had first looked him over, I thought he was homely as a burlap bag. I felt sorry for him for being what he was—a mere woodchuck. He would never be graceful or very bright, never swift or surprising or beautiful. He would just be a chunky brown fellow with coarse fur and a taste for the depths of the earth. Now, as I held him, five or six times a day, I began to observe him closely and revise my perceptions.

I noticed his hands. They were black, with four very long fingers ending in long curved nails. The thumb was only a small projection. He could close these fingers to grasp something—the medicine dropper or my finger. With these expressive hands he was almost as dexterous as a squirrel and, of course, a woodchuck is in the squirrel family. It is the largest of the family Sciuridae, which includes the prairie dog, the squirrel, and the chipmunk. His coat, coarse against my hands as I held him, was a mixture of grays and tans and consisted of a thick undercoat interspersed with long, bristly guard hairs, banded in black and white, giving a tweedy appearance. His front and hind legs were very short but stout and strong. His shoulders, upper arms, and lower flanks were covered with red fur. His tail wasn't much, neither long nor short, and only slightly bushy. His belly was round and babyish, with rather sparse dark hair the color of coffee beans. I noted his ears. They were small, round squirrel ears, neat and pretty and appropriate to life spent partly in tunnels. His eyes were oval and set near the top of his skull to give good upward vision. They were dark as raisins and softly shiny. There were bristly whiskers by his nose and an additional set on his cheeks, I presume for checking the diameter of tunnels.

All of this, plus the energy and will emanating from him as he struggled mightily in my grasp to get every drop of milk despite the odd shape of the new teat, added up to the statement: "I am a woodchuck, and I want to live." And, while holding him and feeding him, I was receiving the added message: "I am *your* little brown woodchuck. My survival is up to you."

Very shortly the carton seemed too small. I let the woodchuck loose in the bathroom and offered him a nest made of a covered box, bedded with straw and with a round doorway cut in the front. He knew instantly that a hole spells home, and he dashed inside. I put the cat litter in a dishpan nearby. In the wild, woodchucks are fastidious, burying their excrement in a special chamber of the burrow. The woodchuck immediately used the pan for this purpose.

Now that he was free, his extreme wariness became evident. He was very sensitive to sound. Any sudden noise sent him flying into his house. At first the sight of me or my husband walking around scared him, too, but his fear wore off rapidly. He began to greet me by scrabbling at my ankles, trying to climb up my legs, a painful process. He often followed closely at my heels, making his funny, urgent little noise. If I offered my hand he nibbled it eagerly. He possessed four long, curved front teeth that could easily have punctured me, but his bite was always restrained. I guessed that wild woodchucks groom each other with these gentle bites. Together the nibbling and the chuckling sound were very expressive of emotion.

We have a dog, and a meeting was inevitable. The first few times the woodchuck fled at sight of the dog. Then he stood his ground. The dog, filled with curiosity, extended her nose, and the woodchuck's nose came up to meet it. As their noses met, the woodchuck turned, hissed as if he had tasted something disgusting, and withdrew. The dog's odor must advertise the meateater's lethal habits.

At this stage it occurred to me that I really knew little about the lives of woodchucks, and I turned to the library for some basic data. I found that there are woodchucks practically everywhere in the United States—including Alaska, but not the Deep South—and in Canada. The species that frequent the West and the high mountains are known as the yellowbellied marmot and the hoary marmot. The proper name of our woodchuck is *Marmota monax,* and there are nine subspecies. My particular wood-

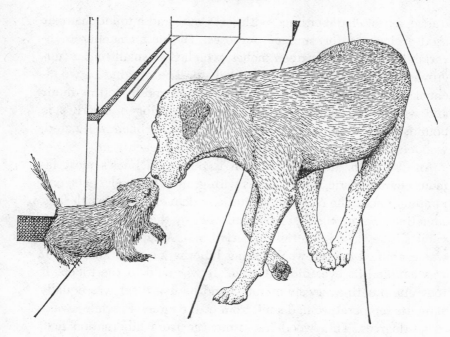

chuck is *Marmota monax preblorum,* and it must once have been
a forest dweller, since before our time dense forests covered the
East. With the cultivation of open fields *monax* has found an improved food supply and has prospered.

Woodchucks, the textbook says, have three white nipple-like
organs just inside the anus that emit a musky odor when the animal is excited and whose purpose probably is communication. (I
have smelled no musky odor on my woodchuck, however.) The
woodchuck also is said to whistle. I have not heard mine whistle,
either, but in addition to his chuckling plea for attention, I heard
an indignant yip when I dipped his front paws in water to wash
off spilled milk.

The life of a woodchuck revolves around its burrow. This is a
complicated structure that may be from twenty-five to thirty feet
long, with a front door that is obvious because of the dirt heaped
around it and a second plunge hole dug from beneath and thus
hard to see. Within the burrow there is a turnaround near the en-

trance, a nest chamber lined with soft grass, and a toilet chamber used exclusively for sanitary purposes. The nest chamber is invariably fourteen by sixteen inches, which is so small that a full-grown woodchuck must sleep curled up. The digging of woodchucks improves the soil by its mixing action and by letting in air and water. An average den requires the moving of nearly 400 pounds of dirt. In New York State, it has been estimated, woodchucks turn over 1.6 million tons of earth each year.

An ability for deep hibernation is the woodchuck's most famous characteristic, one it shares with ground squirrels, bats, and jumping mice. The older and fatter woodchucks go to earth first, sometimes before the first frost, followed by the yearlings and juveniles. They sleep in a tightly curled ball. A captive woodchuck was examined once a week during hibernation, and although it was handled its eyes did not open. It was cold to the touch. It took one breath every six minutes, and its heartbeat was equally slow. Its temperature had sunk from 96.8 degrees F. while awake to 50 degrees. Thin woodchucks emerge from hibernation first, sometimes even during winter. Wakening may be either slow or abrupt and accompanied by trembling. Woodchucks do not sleep in their summer dens but move to new dens in woods or brush, where leaves carpet the ground and the frost does not go deep. They prefer a slope safe from flooding. Their weight loss during hibernation ranges from one-third to one-half their body weight, but the newly awakened woodchucks are nonetheless in good condition. While they are asleep their teeth and toenails do not grow.

Woodchucks lead relatively unsocial lives. They live together only briefly during mating, though yearlings not yet ready to mate sometimes consort together and even occupy the same den. Chucks place their dens at a distance from each other whenever they can. They compete for food, but there is no real territoriality. Bigger woodchucks chase off smaller ones, which do not defend their home range. A woodchuck threatens by arching its back, flipping its erect tail up and down, and approaching the adversary with open mouth, but actual fights are few. Woodchucks are notorious eaters, and this is their main occupation. They eat selected succulent plants, particularly clover, chickweed, alfalfa, and dandelion when these are abundant. They love fruit and vegetables, and it is to this that they owe the great hostility of most farmers. Fat woodchucks weigh ten or twelve pounds, but a fifteen-pound specimen is not unheard of.

When the cycle of woodchuck life begins in the spring, the males immediately begin to wander, searching for dens occupied by females. The females stay at home, waiting to be courted. Thus in the spring it is possible to tell the sex of a woodchuck at a distance—a wanderer is a male, a stay-at-home is a female. Females also are warier, especially when pregnant.

Tails wagging, the males check each den to see if it is occupied by an agreeable female. If it is, and she accepts him, he usually moves in with her, though sometimes the two live in different burrows while the male visits his mate daily. During this period a mated pair is monogamous, something we tend to read of with approval, but the conjugal period is brief. The gestation of woodchucks is only about thirty days, and as the time of birth approaches, the female drives the male away. He is to be permitted no part in raising the young. It is one of nature's casual cruelties that the male remains sexually ardent after the female has rejected him, and so, for a while, the fields are full of frustrated males wandering lonesomely about. The arrangement, however, ensures that any female coming into heat later than the others will be mated nonetheless.

The young woodchucks are born in the early spring in litters that average four but may be larger. The newborn woodchuck is tiny: blind and hairless, it is only about four inches long and weighs an ounce. At four weeks its eyes are open and it weighs six and one-half ounces. At six weeks young chucks are active, weigh half a pound, and follow their mother into the open, but they don't go far. They sun themselves at the edge of the burrow and wrestle and play. The mother grooms them affectionately. It is at this stage, I was interested to read, that she begins to wean them by going farther from the burrow than they dare to follow, so they are forced to eat herbs to stay their hunger.

Sometime after the young are six weeks old their increasing size crowds the nest, and the mother separates them, leading each one to a new den dug nearby. There it must learn to do without the emotional support of the family and prepare for the solitary life that lies ahead. This preparation is gradual. The mother visits each one daily and spends time with it, grooming it and continuing its opportunity to learn from her such survival lessons as wariness and the selection of the proper herbs as food. Young woodchucks sometimes take food from a mother's mouth, and it is thought this is part of learning what is good to eat. They follow her example when she shows alarm and learn to respond to the sight or sound or smell of danger with a quick dive to safety. As the young woodchucks become more prepared physically and psychologically to face life alone, the mother's visits taper off. Then, sometime in midsummer, the young will feel an urge to move off and explore the world. They may go a long way or only a few hundred yards before they find new homes, but now they are on their own.

Once I had acquainted myself with the scenario of woodchuck life in the wild, it was clear how I must carry out my role as foster mother, but accomplishing it was not so easy. I brought my woodchuck all sorts of grasses and vegetables, but he merely tasted them and dropped them. I was happy when he consented to eat a cherry and a marigold, but he would go no further. I was also aware that life in my bathroom was not providing the proper lessons about growing plants, damp earth, and the sudden threat of a marauding dog, which would be the most important elements in his adult survival.

I took him outside and put him down on the lawn. He showed sheer terror at the sight of the open sky. I brought his box outside. He dashed in and refused to leave it. There seemed nothing to do but bring him back to the bathroom. I continued to leave offerings of grass and flowers, but he allowed them to wilt and clambered into my lap as eagerly as ever for each feeding.

At last I decided I must do what mother woodchucks do: put him in a new burrow. I searched along the wall of our orchard and found a small hole. I wasn't sure of its origin, or if it was occupied, but decided I must take a chance. I put the chuck, housed in his box, near the hole and left him, knowing that eventually hunger would drive him out. A few hours later, when his next feeding time came, I went out. The box was empty. I called, and within seconds my woodchuck emerged from the hole and flung himself on my ankle, chuckling gladly. I sat down and fed him. When I finished he tried persistently to follow me back to the house, but I put him on the far side of the wall and escaped.

I continued to visit him several times a day with his milk. Each time he greeted me joyfully and drank greedily, but I felt sure he must be finding food on his own. He also began to accept carrots and cherries and daisies. The final weaning came abruptly. Between breakfast and lunch he forgot how to suck. It was as if a switch had been flipped in his maturing nervous system. I offered milk a few more times, but he was quite unable to suck it in. Clearly, weaning had been accomplished.

Still the emotional ties persisted. I visited him every day bringing carrots. Sometimes he was quite far away, but he would always come at the sound of my voice. He showed more emotion about nibbling my fingers and climbing up my legs and into my arms than he did about the carrots. It is an odd feeling to be desperately embraced by a lonesome woodchuck. I always left him with a slight sense of guilt at rejecting him, and I wondered if wild woodchucks tried as hard to keep their mother's waning interest.

The parting came unexpectedly. I went away on a brief trip. When I came back there were days of rain and I didn't visit the burrow. In truth, it didn't seem as important as it once had. When I remembered and went out to call, no woodchuck came.

In the past weeks I have seen no sign of him, and I suppose he has moved away as the textbook said young woodchucks do. I hope he has found a safe, dry burrow. When autumn comes I will wish him deep sleep and happy dreams. In the spring when I see a large, handsome woodchuck ambling through the new grass, I will hope that it is he.

10

THE FALCONS OF
MORRO ROCK

On the central California coast, near the city of Morro Bay, there is a towering rock, almost six hundred feet high, that rises out of the water like a fortress or a castle. It is connected to the mainland by a causeway. There is just enough flat space bordering the rock for an encircling road and a shallow parking lot. Fishermen go there often. Cellophane wrappers and bait cans are scattered around on the gravel. The view toward land is also depressing; docks and industrial chimneys have eaten up the shore. But the rock itself—Morro Rock—is untouched. It stands above the litter with magnificence and faces the open sea, besieged, but not yet conquered.

I visited Morro Rock because I had been told that it was the scene of a curious struggle. A cleft high in its face was the nesting place of one of the very few pairs of peregrine falcons remaining in the state of California. Young falcons, because they are prized by people who pursue the sport of falconry, are worth a great deal of money, so the nestlings produced by the Morro Rock birds were in constant danger of being stolen. Had it not been for the remarkable determination of two citizens of Morro Bay, Mr. and Mrs. Vernon Davey, falconers might have spirited the young birds away undetected. But the Daveys had taken up the task of defending the nest and for several nesting seasons had maintained a vigil at the foot of the cliff, doing their utmost to guard the precious birds.

Falcons are close relatives of hawks and eagles. Among the many species of falcons, besides the peregrine, are the gyrfalcon, the lanner, the saker, and the merlin. Peregrines are about the size of a large crow, and they have a wingspread of three to four feet. They hunt other birds, swooping through the air at speeds of as much as 175 miles an hour and catching their prey in flight. Their aerial skill is thrilling to watch. Falconry—the sport of hunting wild quarry with trained falcons, hawks, or eagles—originated in China at least four thousand years ago. From the

East the sport drifted to medieval Europe, where it was practiced mainly by the elite. The Holy Roman Emperor Frederick II, for instance, was an ardent falconer, and he wrote the first treatise on the subject to be published in the West. For centuries, falconry has also flourished in the Middle East. Rich sheiks offer huge sums—sometimes thousands of dollars—for young falcons stolen from nests in the wild. Though many birds of prey can be used in falconry, the peregrine falcon is a favorite with falconers, because of its fierceness and beauty in the chase and its receptiveness in training. Unfortunately, the peregrine is in danger of becoming extinct in much of the world.

Until recently captive breeding of falcons was considered impossible. At the time of my visit to Morro Rock, in 1972, captive-bred birds had only recently been reared for the first time at the State University of New York. Since then Dr. Tom Cade of the Cornell University Laboratory of Ornithology has not only reared them but has succeeded in returning some to the wild. He is optimistic that, in time, falcons can be restored to their former range. But this goal is still many years in the future.

Falconry began to take hold in the United States in the 1930's, when the country still had a healthy population of peregrines. It was practiced by only a few people, who were, for the most part, skilled in the handling of birds and educated in the traditions of the sport. It was a rather precious pastime, associated with the lore of the Middle Ages. The spirit of falconry was captured by the British author T. H. White in his book *The Goshawk*, which described his struggle to tame a hawk—an endeavor he saw as a noble contest of wills. Since only a few Americans had ever heard of this esoteric and exacting sport, the effect of falconry on the falcon population in those days was negligible.

In the 1960's, the United States suddenly became aware of falconry. Sports and pastimes that had once been confined to small, special groups were being discovered by the disseminators of popular culture and turned into mass merchandise. The outdoors, nature, and animals proved to be marketable. Among other things, there was a tremendous demand for wildlife subjects suitable for films. One of those selected, by Walt Disney, was falconry. Walt Disney Productions made two television films dealing with hawks and eagles. Since the T. H. White medieval-mystique approach was hardly likely to go over with a general audience, Disney presented a sentimental picture of the taming of a bird of prey, suggesting that any twelve-year-old boy could turn one into a faithful pal—something like a collie with wings—and practice the sport of sheiks and princes. These films were shown several times on network television, and they had the same dire effect on the falcon population that Mrs. Kennedy's leopard coat had on spotted cats. Falconry, or what was thought to be falconry, caught on. Young would-be falconers robbed nests and bought and sold falcons. News that the birds brought prices in the hundreds of dollars inspired nest robbers whose only intent was to make a quick profit. Newspapers carried Sunday feature stories that glamorized falconry as a clean and romantic outdoor sport. Young men were photographed squinting into Marlboro Country with falcons perched on their leather-girt wrists. Because training a falcon to return is a long and difficult task, many of the captive falcons never flew; their owners simply carried them around to attract admiring attention. The birds became a cult emblem. Many falcon owners were unskilled at keeping birds, and many falcons died tethered to dirty perches in suburban backyards. Other birds—including some that were not falcons but had been mistaken for them by the uninitiated—were brought, half dead, to museums and zoos.

Although the falcon craze has had a serious effect on the peregrine population of the United States, it was not falconry that did the birds in. Rather, it was DDT. This chemical breaks down into a substance known as DDE, which causes a hormone disturbance in birds that prevents the formation of a normal egg-shell. The eggs of most species will hatch if their shells are as much as 80 percent of the normal thickness; any thinner than that, they usually break in the nest. Peregrine falcons were the first birds in this country to reach that fatal level. Owing to their feeding habits, they accumulated DDE more rapidly than other

birds. DDE moves up the food chain, being passed along by each organism to the one above, and it becomes increasingly concentrated in the process. Peregrines, preying on other birds, are at the top of the chain. During the 1950's and early 1960's, peregrines gradually vanished from all the agricultural areas of the United States. In addition, they no longer nest on the East Coast and are almost gone from the West Coast. Steven Herman, a naturalist from the University of California at Davis, who searched all known nesting places in California in 1969, found only ten peregrines, including two nesting pairs.

The Morro Bay falcons came to the attention of biologists in 1967, when Dr. Monte Kirven, of the San Diego Natural History Museum, heard of them. Dr. Kirven had a passionate interest in falconry, on the pre-Disney level, and kept in touch with people who had owned birds. He was surreptitiously tipped off by a falconer that a falcon nest on Morro Rock which had been inactive for years was now occupied. Dr. Kirven went to Morro Rock in the spring of that year and spotted two nestlings. Since these young birds seemed to represent one of the few hopes for the survival of peregrines in California, the biologist sought a way to guard the nest. He got in touch with the local Audubon Society, which asked its members to volunteer for guard duty. About twenty came forward—among them Vernon and May Davey, of Morro Bay, who thus entered upon what turned out to be one of the most extraordinary ordeals, emotional and physical, in the annals of bird-watching. Vernon Davey is a tall, thin man of sixty, not robust, who had retired after a lifetime of working as a marketing consultant for the Pillsbury Company. He is reserved, and seems gentle but resolute. His wife, a tall, pretty woman in her fifties, speaks quickly and openly, sometimes with rushes of feeling. Until they volunteered to help guard the falcons, neither had spent much time with birds; they had only recently joined the Audubon Society.

In 1967, the Morro Bay falcons nested on a ledge about three-quarters of the way up the face of the rock. From the parking lot below, it was possible to see the gleaming, gray-white breast feathers of the birds as they took turns sitting on the nest. The Audubon Society volunteers stationed themselves in the parking lot and watched the nest in shifts, day and night. It takes falcons three months to raise a brood, so the watchers were prepared for a long siege. There was already a state law against robbing a falcon nest, but, as further protection, the watchers succeeded in getting a State Park ordinance passed that prohibited the climbing of Morro Rock for any purpose. (Morro Rock is part of Morro Bay State Park, which was established to preserve the wetlands on that part of the coast.) During the weeks of the vigil, two birds hatched. The watchers turned away several climbers by threatening to call the police. Unhappily, one of the young birds died in the nest, but the other one lived and flew off into the world. All concerned felt that the effort had been worthwhile.

The next spring, the falcons returned and nested again. From their choice of the same nesting site and their appearance and habits, the Daveys assumed that they were the same pair. Again, a guard was organized. Mr. and Mrs. Davey, though they had begun as the novices of the group, became its most devoted members. Both began to have strong feelings about the importance of protecting the nest. What they saw as the birds' brave effort to carry on against overwhelming odds touched them deeply. Dr. Robert Risebrough, a biologist at the University of California at Berkeley, who had also become interested in the fate of the Morro Bay falcons, suggested that they watch the nest with binoculars and keep detailed notes of everything that went on as the birds incubated and then brooded their young. The Daveys found these observations fascinating, and they were stirred by the beauty of the birds. Dr. Risebrough came down from time to time to look over the notes. He urged the Daveys to keep on, pointing out that since this might be the last chance to observe peregrine falcons in the western states, the Daveys' records could have future scientific value. Dr. Risebrough told them that there was a chance—a very slim chance—that DDT levels would go down in California in time for peregrines to survive through these birds. The Daveys and their fellow watchers continued to guard the nest twenty-four hours a day.

In June 1968, three birds hatched. The Daveys were delighted. One of the young died several weeks after leaving the nest, of unknown causes, but the two remaining birds survived. Once the young were flying, Dr. Risebrough and Dr. Kirven climbed the rock and examined the nest. (The cliff, though it looks formidable, is not difficult for an experienced climber.) The expedition enabled them to solve the mystery of why this particular pair of peregrines was able to produce viable eggs. From the bones scattered on the ledge, they learned that these falcons were subsisting on doves rather than on seabirds. Doves, because they are seed-eaters, are less heavily contaminated with pesticides than fish-eating birds, so the peregrines had escaped the level of poisoning that causes fatally thin eggshells.

The next year, the pair of falcons returned to the rock in March and nested in the accustomed spot. The vigil was resumed. Mrs. Davey, in charge of arranging the schedule, found that the other club members were losing interest, and it became easier for her and her husband to do the whole job themselves than to round up others. Late one afternoon, while the eggs were still being laid, a bad storm blew up. Mr. and Mrs. Davey decided that no one would be likely to climb the rock in a gale and went home for the night. The next day, they couldn't get back to the rock. Local contractors had moved in and closed off the causeway. The Daveys learned, with dismay, that the city needed rock rubble to repair a road washout nearby, and the contractors were blasting from the face of the cliff, just below the falcon nest. With the help of searchlights, the blasting went on around the clock. Dr. Isaac Farfel, a retired dentist from New York City, who shared the Daveys' feeling about the birds, complained to the Department of State Parks and Recreation in Sacramento. He got nowhere. From their home, more than a mile from the rock, the Daveys could hear the incessant, rumbling detonations. After ten days, the contractors took down the barricades and went away. Mr. and Mrs. Davey hurried to the rock. The birds had left the nest and moved to a new site, on the opposite side of the rock. They seemed to be unharmed and to be nesting again. The Daveys resumed guard duty.

Within a few days, it became clear that the female peregrine was behaving strangely. "I could sense that there was something wrong," Mrs. Davey told me, recalling the scene. "You watch these birds and they become almost part of you, you know them so well. There was something different in the way the female behaved. I said to my husband, 'That bird isn't well.' The poor tiercel—that's the male—fretted at her. He kept trying to get her to eat, and she wouldn't." A day or two later, on Easter morning, Mrs. Davey arrived to hear the male screaming. She looked up and saw the female lying on the ledge. It was obvious from the way her body was sprawled, with the wind ruffling her feathers, that she was dead. Mrs. Davey wept.

The behavior of the male bird was dramatic, Vernon Davey said. "It seemed as if he didn't know what he was doing. He yelled and screamed and flew around. He attacked the cormorants, who also nest on the rock—something he had never done before, except in play. He would fly out over the ocean and attack gulls. And he kept calling to the female. It was terrible to watch." Davey called Dr. Risebrough, and he and Steven Herman hurried down to Morro Bay, arriving at three-thirty in the morning. At dawn, they all went to the cliff, and found that the dead bird had fallen from the ledge to the foot of the rock. Dr. Risebrough took the body back to his laboratory. An autopsy showed that the falcon had died of a rupture of the oviduct.

The male peregrine hung around the cliff through the fall, and the Daveys checked up on him from time to time. Sometimes he disappeared for a few days, and they surmised that he was searching for another mate—without success. He didn't leave the rock until December. The Daveys hoped that the male would find a female during his winter wandering, but when he reappeared, in the spring of 1970, he was still alone. He stayed at the rock all summer, in futile solitude, and left, according to falcon custom, in the fall.

The next spring, a pair of peregrines arrived and nested on the cliff. The Daveys were not sure whether it was the original male with a new mate or, perhaps, a pair formed from the young fledged in 1967 and 1968. In any case, the Daveys happily resumed their guard duty. The year before, after the nesting period had ended, they had bought a camper, and now they returned with it to the parking lot at the base of the cliff. They lived there during the week and returned to their house on the weekends, when three college boys from Los Angeles took over the vigil. Guard duty turned out to be very necessary. Although the Daveys had made every effort to keep the nest a secret, it was apparent that news of it was circulating among falconers. Falconry is in a strange twilight situation. It is illegal to capture a peregrine in this country, but it is not illegal to possess one. Falconers in California are registered with the State Fish and Game Department. The birds they keep are presumably taken from some place such as India or Spain, where the species still survives and capture is not illegal. Falconers profess to love falcons, and yet the scarcer they become, the more remorselessly the falconers pursue them. Mr. and Mrs. Davey find this hard to understand. As they had in 1967 and 1968, they frustrated a number of attempts to rob the nest. Davey got so he could smell a falconer, he says. Anyone who came and stood around looking up at the cliff was suspect. Davey took to glancing into parked cars. If he saw ropes or climbing gear, he would ask the owner about his intentions. Some climbers admitted what they were up to, and when Davey told them, in his mild way, that he would have to have them arrested, they gave up and went away. Other frustrated nest robbers grew abusive and drove away yelling curses and threats. The Daveys felt that robbers were most likely to strike on moonlit nights or just at dawn. Either Mr. or Mrs. Davey was always dressed and alert at those times.

Thanks to these precautions, the nesting proceeded as it should, and by late May the Daveys knew that there were three young birds. I arranged to visit the Daveys one day in early June. I drove across the causeway to the foot of the rock and found Davey sitting on a boulder near the camper with a spyglass and a notebook in his lap. He handed over the glass and showed me how to follow the seams in the rock until the nest came into view. Near the top of the cliff, in a shallow, cavelike recess, a bird with a dark head and dark wings could be seen sitting immobile. A strong onshore wind ruffled the silvery breast feathers. "That's the male," Davey said. "The female is off hunting."

Mrs. Davey came out of the camper, where she had been making coffee. "Listen," she said after a minute. "I hear the female. She's coming." Before the bird was visible there was a high, thin, eerie cry—a pure note, very urgent, repeated over and over. The cry became louder, and suddenly the bird was soaring round and round just above the parking lot. It rode the strong wind with terrific speed, gliding along the face of the cliff and then veering off, while continuing to call. After half a dozen passes, it landed on the ledge, and the male took off, launching himself into the wind and sailing away.

"Aren't they beautiful?" Davey asked, smiling proudly.

"I know we must seem like crazy people, sitting here for three months to protect a couple of birds," Mrs. Davey said. "But it seems so urgent. I've always been for the underdog, I guess, but the peregrine is more than that. Rationally, I know that the situation is hopeless. There are just too many things working against them—DDT, falconers, everything. But I can't give up. I think it has to do with my feeling that everything we love, everything beautiful and natural in the world, is being taken away. These birds are so wonderful. It's hard to explain, but anyone who watched them and really got to know them would feel the same. Vernon and I do sometimes think of giving up. Three months in a camper *is* a long time. But then we think of how we'd feel if something happened to them just because we weren't here, and we keep on."

On June 6, a few days after this visit, the young birds began to fly. The first of them to leave the nest gave the Daveys a bad scare. It fluttered along the cliff face, fell into a crevice, and disappeared. Davey called the Morro Bay State Park headquarters for help. The ranger there said he would be unable to come until the next day. The Daveys spent an unhappy night, but at dawn they found that the bird had somehow extricated itself. It was perching on the ledge, and the parents were feeding it. During the next few days, the two other young falcons launched themselves successfully. The Daveys guarded them for a week or so, while the young falcons gathered strength and daring. At first, the fledglings were clumsy and had to struggle to stay airborne. Their parents continued to feed and encourage them. Soon they were able to do acrobatics in the air and to take food from the parents' talons on the wing.

The following year, the pair of falcons returned to the rock in the middle of March and began nesting, but things had changed unhappily for the Daveys. Mr. Davey was not well. The all-night watches the year before had been exhausting, and he didn't feel able to take them up again. The Daveys appealed for volunteers to help out, but no one came forward. With many misgivings, they adopted a schedule of watching only during the daylight hours. All went well until Monday, May 8. By that time, two three-week-old birds were in the nest. The Daveys left the rock about 5 P.M. and went home. A man named Ronald Garret, who knew of the nest, was on the waterfront that evening, and just at dusk he saw a man's figure on top of the rock, silhouetted against the sky. "The man was holding out his arms like a cross, and the birds were swooping in a frenzy around him," Garret said later. Garret called Howard Martin, a Fish and Game Department warden, who called the police. They arrived within a few minutes, and found two young men descending the rock. They were from towns about thirty miles south of Morro Bay. Both denied having touched the falcons. They were charged with illegally climbing the rock and fined a hundred and fifty dollars apiece.

The next morning, Martin and a couple of colleagues climbed the rock to check on the two young birds. The nest was empty. On top of the rock were two climbing pitons and a litter of cigarette butts and candy wrappers. Since the two men descending the rock had been empty-handed when they were caught, the police suspected that a third man had slipped away in the darkness carrying the birds. The Fish and Game Department met with members of the California Hawking Club and asked them to get the word to whoever had the birds that they must be returned. At midnight, the Morro Bay police got an anonymous call informing them that the nestlings could be found in a bag near the rock. Martin and the police went to the rock and, after an hour's search, found the young birds. They brought them to the Daveys at two in the morning. The young birds were in good shape and accepted food. They looked like balls of white fluff with huge dark eyes. Early Wednesday morning, Martin and a Hawking Club member named Bryan Walton climbed the rock and put the two birds back in the nest. The Daveys waited below, wondering whether the parents would accept the young birds.

After a few hours, the female brought them a meal, and all seemed well.

Thursday passed uneventfully. The Daveys stayed at their post all day and left at dark. The next morning, the Daveys went to the rock at daybreak and encountered a man leaving the parking lot in a Volkswagen. As the morning wore on, they realized that the parent birds were not bringing food to the nest. They felt dreadfully afraid that something had gone wrong. At nightfall, they alerted Captain Hugh Thomas, the Fish and Game Department's supervisor for the central coast area. He climbed the rock and surprised a young man about to descend with climbing gear and a walkie-talkie. Waiting for him below in the Volkswagen was a friend with a matching walkie-talkie. Again, the nest was empty. The two young men denied having taken the birds. They were, however, charged with having attempted to do so, and with illegal climbing. At a later hearing they were convicted of illegal climbing, but acquitted on the charge of attempting to steal the birds. This time the baby peregrines were not returned.

I had been keeping in touch with the Daveys by telephone and they had told me about the nest robberies and the arrest of the two young men. Shortly after the suspects had been acquitted I called the Daveys again and found them feeling quite helpless and discouraged—at least during the first part of our talk, in which they described the events in court. Then we began to talk about the birds themselves. A note of new hope and determination came into May Davey's voice as she told me they were already making plans for yet another vigil the coming spring. "If only the falcons come back and nest . . . ," she said. "As long as the falcons keep trying, I think we have to keep trying, too."

11

DESERT FISH

In Death Valley, California, in the heart of a lunar land of bald rock and hard-baked sand, there is a salt flat where, astonishingly, water seeps to the surface and forms a network of interconnected puddles and ponds, some yards across, some just inches. Their sides are encrusted with salt, and in places deposits of salt roof over the connecting rivulets. The place is called Cottonball Marsh, but it has few of the life-sustaining attributes of an ordinary marsh. There is almost no vegetation, and in summer, when the surrounding sands shimmer with furious heat, it seems as if the thin layer of water must surely vanish into the thirsty air.

Five miles to the north there is a narrow gorge surrounded by bare dunes of coarse gravel where, with equal incongruity, a tiny stream a few inches deep and three or four feet across flows briskly for a few miles before it is finally sucked down and lost in the bone-dry earth. Its name is Salt Creek.

Eastward, across forty miles or so of desert, there is another anomalous spot where a mountain of jumbled rock, black from the volcanic furnace in which it was formed, rises above a desert plain thinly covered with mesquite and creosote bush. At the base of the mountain there is a narrow cleft struck like a mine shaft into the rock. Clear, sweet water rises in the shaft to within fifty feet of the rim. The place is called Devils Hole and is the opening of a deep artery of underground water that flows through tunnels and caves under the floor of the surrounding desert.

A few miles south, out on the desert flatland, the gravelly surface is suddenly broken by a round pool, its shape as symmetrical as if an ice-cream scoop had dipped into the earth. This is Big Spring. Limpid water pours from its stony depths and flows away in a little stream. For a few yards around its margins lush, green marsh grasses hold the desert vegetation at bay. In this part of the desert, which is called Ash Meadows, there are about twenty such outcroppings of water in clear, deep springs a few feet across. Big Spring, which is seventy-five feet across, is the largest. The smallest is Mexican Spring, which fills a basin not much bigger than a dishpan.

These bodies of water are miraculous oases, tiny lost worlds surviving the upheavals that dried their surroundings to dust and formed California's Mojave Desert of today. And, improbable as it seems, a remnant of the teeming water life of long ago, when vast lakes covered the region, has survived with them. In many of these remnant bodies of water—Cottonball Marsh, Salt Creek, Devils Hole, Big Spring, and others—there can still be found tiny fish whose ancestors were there through thousands of years and who are now isolated in these small, precariously surviving islands of water in a sea of sand. They are properly called cyprinodonts, members of the killifish family. Their popular name was given them by a scientist, Dr. Carl Hubbs, who did early studies on them and was struck by their lively way of leaping and darting about their small world. They reminded him of spunky little puppies, and so he named them desert pupfish. Their home is the deserts of California, Nevada, Arizona, New Mexico, Texas, and Mexico. Equally minuscule relatives are found in the tropics of both the New World and Eurasia.

Fifty thousand years ago the ancestors of today's Death Valley pupfish lived in the same area but in huge lakes and deep streams. Glaciers had crept down the continent, the climate was far wetter than today's, and water filled the hollows of what is now desert. Death Valley itself was filled by a lake 116 miles long and 600 feet deep. Then the glaciers receded, and the lakes and streams slowly vanished. With them went the succulent vegetation that had flourished on the lands around them and the animals it had supported. Mastodon, ground sloths, saber-toothed tigers, dire wolves, primitive camels, horses, elk, deer, and many smaller creatures failed to adapt to drier conditions and perished. The lakes had been populated with fish and most of these, of course, vanished as their habitat disappeared. But the pupfish, taking refuge in remnant pools and streams, managed somehow to adapt and go on spinning out their humble thread of life into the inhospitable twentieth century. Thus we are presented with the anomaly of a desert-dwelling fish.

To most laymen a desert fish must seem merely an interesting oddity; a small believe-it-or-not item of no apparent consequence. These were undoubtedly the feelings of a land developer named Francis Leo Cappaert, who, in the late sixties, cast a covetous eye on Ash Meadows and figured out a way to wring a profit from the store of underground water that sustains the springs in which several species of pupfish dwell. He bought a 12,000-acre tract adjoining Devils Hole and set to work, rearranging the landscape in order to grow alfalfa and raise beef cattle. The sagebrush was bulldozed away and wells sunk deep into the earth; seven of them within three and a half miles of Devils Hole. As pumping began the water in Devils Hole started to sink and its pupfish population was in immediate jeopardy. It was then that Cappaert first heard of the existence of pupfish and with even greater surprise learned of their importance. He found himself in a legal battle that ended only recently with a Supreme Court ruling in favor of the fish.

In 1973, while the outcome was still in doubt, *Audubon Magazine* asked me to look into the story of what was then our smallest endangered species. Scientists, I discovered, take pupfish seriously. To a biologist the desert pupfish is more than a curious relic; it is also a marvel of adaptation that offers an unusual range of possibilities for study. Thus the struggle over the survival of the desert pupfish involved not only legal principles but a valuable scientific resource.

Some of the strange characteristics of pupfish were discovered in 1936, when a student ichthyologist, Robert R. Miller, chose them for his Ph.D. thesis. This was a lucky break for pupfish because Dr. Miller, who went on to teach at the University of Michigan, remained interested in their fate and was a leader in organizing their rescue. In 1964 Dr. Miller began to wonder about the welfare of desert pupfish and wrote to Edwin P. Pister, a biologist in the California Department of Fish and Game, who was stationed at Bishop, California, in the Owens Valley, where Miller had studied pupfish thirty years before.

Owens Valley, on the edge of the Sierra Nevada northwest of Death Valley, was once part of the same water system, so that thousands of years ago pupfish could have swum from one place to the other. Now they are separated by seventy miles of desert. Pister searched the valley's streams and ponds and found only one small population of pupfish.

As it happened, Pister himself was worried about the survival of a number of native fish that were once abundant in the lakes and streams of California and Nevada. Draining, pumping, and alteration of springs and ponds were taking a heavy toll. Game fish planted in streams to provide sport were predators that the native fish were not equipped to cope with. For several years Pister wrote letters calling attention to the dangers besetting a number of species. Desert pupfish were at the head of the list. In 1969 he arranged a meeting of representatives of government agencies and university scientists to see what could be done. As they took inventory of the situation, they found that several species of pupfish had already been lost because no one at the scene had been aware of their value and bothered to save them. Now the most critical spot, they found, was at Ash Meadows. The group made a field trip there and were appalled by the destruction resulting from agricultural development. Ash Meadows' combination of bubbling springs arising in desert surroundings is unique in the United States. In Mexico the Cuatrociénegas Basin of Coahuila is comparable and it, too, is in danger. To biologists the loss of such unique biota for the sake of raising a few thousand head of cattle on land that is only marginally suited to that purpose seems a tragic mistake. At Devils Hole the survey party found that due to Cappaert's pumps the water was sinking and its tiny population of tiny fish was within an inch or two of being snuffed out. Thereupon a group called the Desert Fishes Council was formed and took up arms to save the fish.

Before going to Ash Meadows myself I arranged for a briefing on pupfish at the University of Nevada in Las Vegas from Dr.

James E. Deacon, who was working with Pister on the Desert
Fishes Council. We met in his campus office, whose shelves were
ornamented with all sorts of strange specimens, and I asked Deacon to begin at the beginning and explain what it was that gave
pupfish particular significance.

Deacon replied that one of the prime reasons pupfish are intriguing to scientists is simply that they have survived where so
many other forms of life have failed. Death Valley began to dry
up about 20,000 years ago, and by 4,000 years ago the lakes were
gone and the desert had been established. Living conditions in
the remaining marshes and springs, some volcanic, were often
quite uncongenial for fish; the water was either unusually warm
or saline or alkaline. One by one other kinds of fish gave up, but
the pupfish lived on, along with its close relative, the poolfish, of
which only one species remains. The pupfish not only adapted to
diffcult conditions, but did so in a very short space of evolutionary time.

Each of the habitats in which the pupfish found itself stranded
differed somewhat from the others, and as each population of fish
adapted to its situation, it came to differ from the ancestral stock;
in other words, new species or subspecies developed. In this respect, the pupfish, isolated in their islands of water, have been
compared to the species Darwin found in the Galápagos, which
provided such tremendous insight into genetic mechanisms.

There are at present five species of pupfish in the region of
Death Valley, and one of these species is further divided into
several subspecies. Four of the five pupfish species are within
Death Valley or adjacent to it in Ash Meadows. The fifth is the
Owens Valley species.

Most fish can survive only a limited range of temperatures and
salinity, but the tough little pupfish can stand the extraordinary
changes of temperature that occur when shallow marshes are
heated by the desert sun. They prosper in springs that range
from 72 to 93 degrees and have been found in water as hot as
112 degrees; and they can wait out freezing weather by hiber-
nating in mud. Their tolerance of salt is also remarkable. Cotton-

ball Marsh, in its most extreme reaches, is six times as salty as seawater. To survive in this water, pupfish have developed some highly efficient mechanisms to regulate the salt content of their tissues—or osmotic balance, as it is called; these mechanisms have interesting implications for human kidney research.

Dr. Deacon turned to the pupfish at Devils Hole, the species that had just had its successful day in court. The Devils Hole pupfish is a distinct species—*Cyprinodon diabolis*—that has been isolated in its stony prison for at least 2,000 years, and perhaps much longer. It is smaller than other pupfish—one inch compared to two. When in breeding condition, all pupfish males are a bright, iridescent blue; but Devils Hole males are bluer than any others. The females are a grayish tan. Males not in breeding condition may be as drab as females, an adaptation that spares them from attack by breeding males. All other pupfish are highly territorial, but the Devils Hole species is not; this behavioral difference holds interesting possibilities for research.

Devils Hole is virtually a bottomless pit. The shaft is known to go down several hundred feet into labyrinthine chambers. Divers from the National Park Service have explored part of the hole, and they say there is no darker place in the world. Three young scuba divers, exploring independently, lost their lives there.

The pupfish, however, do not use the depths of the shaft. They have been found wandering as far down as seventy feet, but most of their life cycle is acted out in one small area, over a sloping ledge that juts out just below the surface of the water. This ledge is the key to their existence. It produces their food supply and provides a nursery for their young. The few cubic feet of water above the ledge, which is only eight by sixteen feet, surely comprise the tiniest habitat possessed by any species in the world. The ledge provides a resting place for eggs which otherwise would drop into the dark, lifeless depths where young could not survive. Just as importantly, the ledge is the only area of the shaft that produces food.

The food chain for the desert pupfish begins with filamentous algae. These small, green water plants are the beginning of life in

Devils Hole as they transform water, sunlight, and dissolved minerals into living matter. Algae cannot grow on the steep walls of the shaft, which are hardly touched by the sun, but prosper on the shelf, in the direct rays of the summer sun. They in turn provide food and shelter for a variety of aquatic insects, snails, amphipods (which are freshwater shrimp only a few millimeters long), and other micro-animals. These are the foodstuffs on which the pupfish depend. In this miniature ecosystem, the pupfish is the top predator.

Deacon believes that the availability of their food supply, which varies with the season, explains the fluctuations of the pupfish population. In winter, because of the depth of the hole and the angle of the sun's rays, no direct sunshine reaches the water. There is little algae, and the population of pupfish declines to about two hundred. As the length of the day increases, more sunlight strikes the water and algae become more abundant, as do the microorganisms and the fish. A few pupfish begin to spawn in January. Most spawn in March and April. At two months the young can reproduce themselves, so several generations may be produced in a year. By midsummer there should be a thousand pupfish in the pool. That appears to be the limit that their food supply will sustain—or was, when things were normal, before development in Ash Meadows began to encroach on the Devils Hole water supply. In the autumn the algae begin to decline, and the numbers of fish dwindle accordingly. The life-span of a pupfish might be eight months to a year. Some die of starvation when the population reaches a peak. Major mortality is associated with the strain of spawning. All in all, though, the Devils Hole pupfish achieves a population balance that is just suited to its small world, and scientists would like to know more about the dynamics of that balance.

Devils Hole, it should be explained, is within a forty-acre tract that belongs to the National Park Service. It is in Nevada, but is administered as part of Death Valley National Monument, forty miles west in California. The rest of Ash Meadows, a valley approximately eleven miles north to south and six miles east to west, is a jumble of pieces in private ownership and under various public jurisdictions. A principal owner is the Bureau of Land Management. Cappaert acquired his holding by buying 7,000 acres from a private owner and, in addition, making a deal with BLM for 5,000 acres of public land in Ash Meadows in exchange for 5,000 acres in another county. This was a faux pas on the part of the Bureau that it later regretted.

When Cappaert moved in and began to pump, the water in Devils Hole started to sink; as it sank, the pupfish's already tiny cosmos began to shrink. In the spring of 1970 the water over the rocky shelf, once about three feet deep, dropped so low that more than half the shelf was exposed. With half their habitat destroyed it seemed the Devils Hole pupfish might become extinct at any moment. To provide first aid Deacon and the Park Service submerged an artificial shelf, made of plastic covered with pebbles, beside the real one. A sunlamp was hung over it to stimulate the growth of algae. For reasons that remain mysterious the pupfish refused to use the plastic shelf and stuck stubbornly to their dwindling ancestral home.

The Department of the Interior, which is responsible for endangered species, also took a hand. It tried to persuade Cappaert to halt the pumping. Negotiations failed. Therefore, in early 1971, the Department of Justice went to court asking for an injunction on the grounds that the public had a right to the water in Devils Hole in order to preserve the fish. In pleading the pupfish's cause the government argued that the species was needed for research to explain adaptation and survival in extreme environments, and that the species posed "intriguing problems in comparative physiology, population dynamics, ecology, genetics, behavior reactions, and other disciplines." These are heavy burdens to place on a species whose total population would fit in a shoe box, but Deacon, Miller, and others interested in *Cyprinodon diabolis* felt sure that if the species were spared it would be equal to them.

When things looked darkest for *diabolis* there naturally was thought given to keeping them in captivity in order to save their genes for at least a little while. It was obvious that captive breeding could not perpetuate the Devils Hole fish indefinitely, for under new conditions *C. diabolis*, with its great aptitude for change, would become something different from the parent stock. Nevertheless, it seemed better to save the Devils Hole pupfish even temporarily than not at all. Other pupfish had been kept and bred successfully, but for obscure reasons all efforts to keep *C. diabolis* in captivity through several generations failed. It was easy enough to keep the adults alive, but their eggs did not hatch. Attempts to transplant the fish to other desert springs were equally futile. Each time it was tried by the Nevada Department of Fish and Game the pupfish soon died out. Therefore, when the case of *diabolis* went to trial in Las Vegas, in July 1972, this was the last chance for the little fish.

While Federal Judge Roger D. Foley was pondering the decision, Cappaert continued to pump water and the level in Devils Hole continued to sink. The summer of 1972 was, in fact, almost fatal for *C. diabolis*, and for a while it looked as if a legal verdict would come too late. Rangers from the National Park Service headquarters at Death Valley monitored the water level each week and sent divers into the hole to count the fish. Instead of a summer population peak of 800 to 1,000, there were only 400 fish. Most of the shelf was out of water, so breeding potential of the pupfish was greatly reduced; they still rejected the artificial shelf.

On July 30, 1972, there occurred an event that at first seemed a disaster, but which in fact probably saved *C. diabolis*. An earthquake in Alaska caused an upwelling of water and a three-foot-high wave washed over the shelf, scouring out some of the gravel piled on it. This destroyed the algal growth and seemed a serious blow to the pupfish. Then on September 12, 1972, severe thunderstorms flooded the hole, washing in debris and destroying most of the algae then recovering from the earthquake. Dr. Miller, who took a census at the end of September, found that the population had been cut in half. The National Park Service, with help from other agencies, removed as much gravel as possible, thereby lowering the shelf so that once again most of it was under water. The fish began to spawn and spawned throughout the autumn, suggesting that when the population density is low they can spawn even at an abnormal time of year.

Diabolis got through the winter with a low though still viable population, but prospects for the summer of 1973 looked gloomy. The shelf was now at bedrock and could be lowered no farther or it would be below the reach of the sun's rays. Pupfish partisans were fairly certain that if Cappaert pumped water through the summer, as he evidently intended to do, it would spell the end for the species. At the eleventh hour, on April 18, Judge Foley handed down a decision that affirmed the right of *Cyprinodon diabolis* to survive. He announced that he had decided to appoint a "special master" with authority to limit Cappaert's pumping to whatever extent necessary to ensure survival of the pupfish. The judge acted on the legal theory that when the government set aside Devils Hole as a national monument and refuge for the pupfish it implicitly reserved sufficient water for that purpose. Thus Judge Foley's decision will have bearing in the many instances where there is a dispute over water rights on public land.

The defenders of Devils Hole pupfish were, of course, delighted with the judge's decision, but knew there would be an appeal. In fact, the case wasn't finally settled until three years later, when the Supreme Court agreed to consider the case of the pupfish. In 1976 the Court unanimously affirmed the right of the federal government to protect a water supply on public land for the sake of public interest.

After leaving Dr. Deacon, I drove to Bishop, California, to call on Edwin (Phil) Pister, chairman of the Desert Fishes Council, and to see the two pupfish refuges that have been built near there for *Cyprinodon radiosus,* the Owens pupfish. Pister told me that most of the Owens Valley water system had been diverted long ago to supply Los Angeles, leaving behind very little habitat for pupfish. Thereafter the Department of Fish and Game put bass and trout in the remaining streams and these predators just about finished off the remnants of Owens pupfish. They were, in fact, thought to be extinct until a few survivors were discovered in 1956 in a shallow pond. These were almost lost in the summer of 1969, when the pond became overgrown with weeds and nearly dried up. A student who was working with Pister that summer discovered the situation in the nick of time. He and Pister dug the pupfish out of the mud and kept them alive in a small spring. Now the Owens pupfish are safe in two refuges; one in a spring-fed pond at Fish Slough and a second in warm springs that gush from a mountainside south of Bishop.

Pister explained that since it was early April and the water at Fish Slough quite cold, the fish there would not be active. He drove me to the second refuge, which has warmer water, so that pupfish are visible all year. On the way Pister talked with tremendous enthusiasm and pride about the pupfish and its hard-won sanctuary; he made me feel that what we were about to see was fully as important as the vast lagoon that shelters gray whales in Baja California. We drove over a dirt track across a grassy valley and stopped at the foot of a steep rampart of rock.

Pister led the way to a clump of brush. He parted the branches and there was the pupfish refuge; a pool about the size of a backyard swimming pool, with natural banks and reeds at the edge. I looked into the shallow water at the edge and saw my first pupfish darting across the sandy bottom. Tiny, bright blue males were swimming busily about while the more modestly colored females seemed to go more quietly about their business. They were smaller and chunkier than any minnows I had ever seen, and their quick movements suggested the vitality of hummingbirds.

Pister regarded them with satisfaction. "Five Ph.D.'s are being written on the pupfish right now," he said, "and each bit of research opens up new possibilities. What we are attempting to do here is to save the unknown; to save this resource for future generations, which, we hope, will be more understanding." He quoted the nineteenth-century naturalist A. R. Wallace, who wrote that to the scientist the different species of animals and plants are like the letters in a sentence; if any are lost the message becomes unintelligible. "I am trying to save, along with the Death Valley fishes, my own self-respect and conscience," Pister added. "I feel that if this resource is destroyed it will be because I haven't worked hard enough to save it; and if I don't work hard enough, probably no one else will either."

At the small desert town of Shoshone, California, I joined Ben and Miriam Romero, two conservationists who had offered to conduct me on a pupfish tour in the Ash Meadows area. The Romeros live in Montrose, a suburb of Los Angeles, but they love the desert and spend a great deal of their spare time exploring it. Three years ago they chanced upon the pupfish in Big Spring in Ash Meadows. They were fascinated by the fish and indignant over the destruction accompanying development there. So the Romeros formed a Pupfish Habitat Preservation Committee, and their diligent work has helped make the pupfish famous throughout California. In some instances, Mrs. Romero told me, public feeling has been less than cordial. Bumper stickers with the leg-

end "Kill the Pupfish" were not uncommon, presumably expressing the feelings of people who resented the effort to stop development in Ash Meadows.

We headed first for Amargosa Canyon, which has a water system interrelated with that of Ash Meadows and Death Valley.
For most of its course the Amargosa River, which ends in
Death Valley, runs underground, and when it suddenly appears,
winding through the canyon at the foot of high, jagged crags, it
forms a marvelous green sanctuary where the air is fresh and
cool and full of the sound of birds. We walked along the river—a
small stream, at places only ankle-deep, bordered by coarse
reeds. Ben Romero bent over the water, where I could see the
darting shapes of pupfish skimming over the sand. He took a
small dip net from his pocket and caught one for his wife to photograph. For an instant it lay in his palm, a tiny, tannish fish,
quivering and surprised. It seemed extraordinary that such fragile entities could have clung to life through the ages.

All sorts of threats hang over the water system of the Amargosa. The Romeros told me that there are believed to be large
subterranean stores of water derived from the snow-clad mountains that lie just east and west. It has been suggested that these
reserves might be tapped to bring water to Las Vegas, or pumped
to the surface to irrigate the desert for agriculture. These proposals cause conservationists such as the Romeros to shudder.

From Amargosa Canyon we drove to Ash Meadows. Our first
stop was the battleground at Devils Hole, where a spire of rock,
with broken boulders at its base, rises like a fortress out of desert
sands. The Hole is an inconspicuous opening near the base of the
rock, about the size of an elevator shaft. We found it guarded by
barbed wire. Peering through, I was able to see only the stony
rim. The Romeros discouraged me from trying to go through the
wire, explaining that the water level is so far below the rim that
the fish are invisible from above.

We drove on across the level floor of Ash Meadows, whose
sandy soil is covered with a mixed growth of desert plants. A
thicket of trees marked the site of School Spring, one of the oases

that harbor pupfish. Here they are protected by the Bureau of Land Management, which has fenced off the spring and added a small pond outside the fence where visitors can see pupfish—in this case *Cyprinodon nevadensis pectoralis*—darting among the reeds. We moved on to Big Spring—which is big enough to be called a pond. There are no trees around it, but low desert brush and reeds where some of its water trickles off in a small stream. I stood and looked down into the clear depths, where water wells up from clefts in the rock. I could see male pupfish in bright blue breeding colors. They were vivid specks in constant motion, giving life and meaning to the scene.

A few miles further we came to what was, to me, the most extraordinary pupfish habitat, Mexican Spring. Together with School, Scruggs, and Indian springs, it holds the world's entire population of the subspecies *C. n. pectoralis*. We clambered over a rocky, desert slope, covered with prickly vegetation and dotted with desert flowers, to a low hilltop. Behind a fence we found a miniature spring that appeared to hold just a couple of hatfuls of water. Were it not for the fence, it seemed as if a wandering cow might drink it in one draft. Here, incredible as it seems, the pupfish have carried on for untold years, finding food and producing young in perfect proportion to their minute world. I knelt and watched them for quite a while. One tiny, tannish female, with delicate dark stripes and a silver eye, hung in the water in the shadow of a fallen blade of grass. She quivered with life and vitality. It struck me that, unlike ourselves, pupfish have no way of knowing that their world is very finite indeed.

12

THE GREAT WHALES

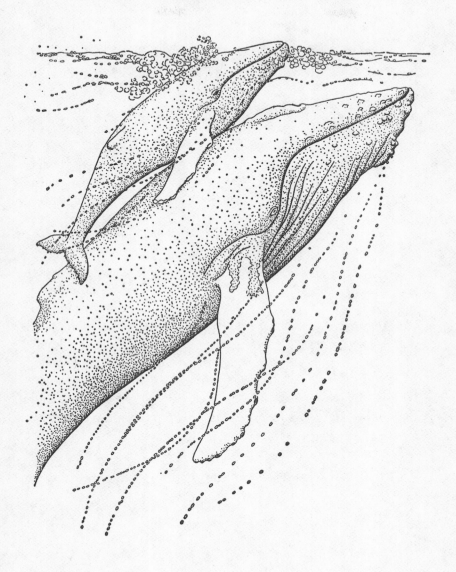

Of all our fellow mammals, the most remote and the most difficult to understand is the great whale. Its size and the alien element it inhabits cut it off from us both in imagination and as an object of study. It is more nearly possible to feel kinship with a mouse, and a mouse is also immeasurably easier for a scientist to observe. Men have pursued whales for centuries, and killed them with unbounded cruelty and in staggering numbers, without learning much more than the simplest facts about their anatomy and their habits. Most of our knowledge of whales, in fact, has been derived from dead whales. Their giant corpses have been dissected, and scientists have charted their astonishing insides: arteries with the circumference of stovepipes, hearts weighing a thousand pounds, and large, complex brains suggesting extraordinary mental powers. A mass of statistics records the location, the species, the size, the sex, and the reproductive state of virtually all the great whales killed over the last fifty years. If a female carried an unborn whale (and nearly half of the females killed have), sometimes it, too, has been measured before being shoveled into the cooking pots. From these data, cetologists have in recent years tried to figure out how many whales remain in the oceans and how many can be killed annually without destroying the various species for all time. Thus, while there is a large store of vital statistics on past generations of whales, long since converted into margarine and mink food, little is known of the living, breathing animals. This paradox exists partly because cetologists, many of them tied to the whaling industry, have been forced to consider whales primarily as a crop, but also because the great whales present the field biologist with one of the most baffling problems in nature. How do you study a living animal that is usually inaudible and is visible only in glimpses? With all the difficulties, some interesting items have been gathered just in the past few years. The fact that the great whales make sounds underwater, for instance, is a recent discovery, and biologists are now puzzling over its meaning. Also, in 1971, for the first time, a great whale was kept in captivity and carefully observed by scientists.

By now, most people are aware that the great whales have been hunted with such rapacity and improvidence that there is fear that some species may become extinct. The Japanese and the Russians are doing the major share of the killing. The British, the Norwegians, and the Dutch, who were once among the principal killers of whales, left the major hunting grounds—the Antarctic and the North Pacific—a few years ago, when the supply of whales fell so low that their expeditions became unprofitable. Though the United States killed more than its share in the last century, American whaling activities, which had been negligible for the previous forty years, ceased entirely in 1971, so, for once, we needn't feel guilty about an ecological outrage. On the other hand, we seem to be helpless to do anything about this one.

Whales, as prey, are prize packages, worth between ten and thirty thousand dollars apiece. Whaling "expeditions" (of which the Japanese and the Russians send out several each year) each consist of a factory ship almost as big as an aircraft carrier, attended by a fleet of small, fast catcher boats that roam in search of whales. Each catcher kills whales at an average rate of one or two a day with the utmost efficiency. The whales are run down and then killed by harpoons fired from cannons, which carry explosive charges that detonate inside the whales. The whales usually die within fifteen or twenty minutes, in gigantic, bloody flurries that churn the sea to red foam, but sometimes the death throes are more prolonged. (Humanitarians have pressed the whalers to devise less ghastly methods, but without success.) The catcher boat marks the corpse of a whale with a radio beacon so that it can be picked up by the factory ship while the catcher continues the hunt. When the factory ship arrives, huge winches haul the giant body of the dead whale up a ramp at the stern and onto a half acre of deck, where work gangs armed with flensing knives cut it into pieces. The bones and the blubber are boiled in great vats within the ship to extract the oil. The meat is frozen, some of it for human consumption (whale meat is eaten, though not in large quantities, by the Japanese and Russians), but much of it as food for dogs or ranch mink. In forty-five minutes, a whale eighty feet long and weighing a hundred tons can be converted into 96.66 long tons of raw material. Much whale oil is made into margarine, and that of sperm whales (which is inedible) makes an especially fine lubricant; all sorts of whale oil can be ingredients of cosmetics, shoe polish, paint, and soap. Whale products are used because they are the cheapest and most convenient raw material. In every case, a substitute can be found.

Though whales are diminishing in numbers, whaling goes on, partly because the equipment for it exists. Floating whale factories represent large investments of rubles and yen, and it is more profitable to use them even for a small catch than to scrap them. If the supply of large whales is finally exhausted, there will still be lesser species of Cetacea—pilot whales, beaked whales, and killer whales, for instance, and even the smaller dolphins—that can be exploited. The number of whales taken in modern whaling is huge. In the last fifty years, 2,000,000 have been killed. The high point of the massacre was 67,000, reached in 1962. Since then, the number has gone down drastically, but it is still very large. In the early 1970's the figure averaged about 37,000—a decline owing mainly to the fact that there were fewer whales to be killed.

Theoretically, whaling is regulated by the International Whaling Commission, representing both the active whaling nations and nations with an interest in whaling, the United States among them. (Several countries, including Iceland, Norway, and South Africa, have no factory ships but use smaller vessels to kill whales migrating off their shores and tow them to shore stations for processing.) The commission was founded after World War II with the laudable intent of restraining the excessive killing of whales. Unfortunately, the owners of whaling vessels (or, in the case of Russia, the officials governing the industry) have largely called the tune. In bargaining disguised as "conservation," the whaling nations have haggled over their share of the remaining whales, disputed scientific warnings that whales are dwindling, and piously agreed to stop killing endangered species only when there were so few individuals left that the commercial sacrifice was negligible.

In truth, the IWC, even if it means well (and apologists claim to see signs of reform), seems to be a toothless watchdog. Member nations are not bound to abide by its decisions; when the Russians and the Japanese are outvoted by more conservation-minded members, they may enter a formal objection and do as they please. The main argument for the continued existence of the commission is that it provides a framework for negotiation, and that the agreements it has reached are better than nothing. Should the commission collapse, the Russians and the Japanese might decide to race each other for the last whales and finish things then and there.

When I first became concerned with whales, I, like most people, had never seen a member of their order larger than a dolphin. In fact, I didn't know that there was any way to see a great whale short of shipping on a whaling vessel bound for the Antarctic. But the idea of seeing a whale, of trying to get some sense of the nature of this extraordinary beast, fascinated me, and when I learned that whales can easily be seen in several places close to our shores, I decided to go to two of them and try to see some. The places I planned to visit were the waters off Bermuda, where humpback whales migrating northward congregate in early spring, and Scammon Lagoon, in Baja California, where the great gray whales come to mate and give birth. Off Bermuda, the songs of the humpbacks have been studied by Dr. Roger S. Payne, a biologist on the staff of the New York Zoological Society; Scammon Lagoon is visited by tourist expeditions arranged by the Natural History Museum of San Diego. In the spring of 1971 I made arrangements to go to Bermuda with Dr. Payne and in 1972 I made the trip to Scammon. Meanwhile, I gathered some basic information about whales.

As most of us have learned at some time, there are two kinds—

those with teeth and those with a sieve-like arrangement of baleen, or whalebone, in their mouths which enables them to strain small organisms from the water. The baleen whales, of which there are ten species, constitute the suborder Mysticeti of the order Cetacea, and the toothed whales constitute the suborder Odontoceti. Toothed and baleen whales evolved separately from different land animals, which took to the sea independently of each other, and they are not believed to be closely related. The baleen whales are the most "whalelike." They make up the large majority of the so-called great whales—the leviathans. The blue whales, which may be a hundred feet long and weigh more than a hundred tons, and all the other huge whales except the sperm are baleen whales. The toothed whales, familiarly represented by the numerous kinds of dolphins and porpoises, are mostly small, the only really large toothed species being the sperm whale. (Moby Dick was, of course, a sperm whale.) Toothed whales make up a large and varied group, which includes the beluga, or white whale; the narwhal, which has a strange, twisted tusk; the friendly little pilot whale; and the killer whale, largest of the dolphins. Since both of the species I expected to see—humpback and gray—were baleen whales, I decided to concentrate more on this suborder.

Whales carry within them clear evidence of their origin on land. Fifty million years and more of life in the water has shaped and polished them like stones, gently rubbing away such externals as fur, outer ears, hind legs, and front toes, but the memory of all these things has not been quite erased from the genes. Whales no longer need a pelvis, but in the muscle tissue on either side of the genital opening is a small bone, only a foot long in the large whales, that is a relic of the pelvis they possessed when they were four-legged animals. The embryo whale is shaped very much like the embryo pig—or the embryo human being, for that matter—with a round head, a snout, a neck, ridges where ears might grow, and buds where hind legs should be. Usually, the vestigial hind legs disappear as the whale matures, but now and then the genes slip back an eon and legs are partially formed. Within the flipper are bones almost identical with those in human arms and hands. Most whales have five finger bones, though some lack a thumb. All the arm joints are rigid and buried within the flipper. Only the shoulders are workable.

Whales breathe through an aperture at or near the top of the head, the area closest to the surface of the water. Toothed whales have a single blowhole, and baleen whales have two. Embryos of either kind, however, have two nostrils at the tip of the snout, like any land animal; the nostrils migrate during fetal development. Every whale contains within its streamlined hide the usual liver and lights of a land animal. It takes seven strong men to drag the six-foot heart of a blue whale across the deck of a whaling ship. Nevertheless, its proportion to the animal's body weight is the same as that of a chimpanzee's or a rabbit's. The cetacean stomach is compartmented and resembles that of a cow. The whale's reproductive system is quite standard for mammals except that the external sex organs have moved inside, recessed within a slit in the whale's belly, with the mammary glands in two smaller slits, one on either side. All adult whales have only two teats, but the embryo porpoise has eight, indicating that long ago its young arrived in litters. All cetaceans now have only one offspring at a time. Whales have lost their body hair entirely, but whiskers survive on the chin and tip of the upper jaw of baleen whales. These are evidently tactile organs, for they are richly surrounded with blood and nerves. Their number varies from fifty to two hundred and fifty in different species. The feeding arrangement of baleen whales is unique. In place of teeth there is, growing from the upper jaw, a comb-like structure of flat strips of whalebone, half an inch or so apart, ending in a coarse fringe. (Whalebone is not bone but a substance akin to hair or fingernails.) When the baleen whale feeds, it simply engulfs a mouthful of water and whatever organisms the water contains; then, perhaps with the aid of its vast, cushiony tongue, it squirts the water out through the sieve of baleen and swallows whatever has been trapped and left behind. Differences in the embryos of toothed and baleen whales suggest that baleen whales are descended from short-tailed land animals and toothed whales from long-tailed land animals. The two suborders of whales resemble each other not because of common ancestry but because the demands of aquatic life have dictated similar adaptations. The earliest fossils of baleen whales date from the mid-Oligocene, twenty-seven million years ago. These early whales were small—about the size of dolphins. The embryos of certain baleen whales still have tooth buds hidden in the gums; it is only in the last few million years that baleen whales have lost their teeth and evolved to their enormous size. Blood tests indicate that the nearest living relatives of both baleen and toothed whales are, somewhat surprisingly, the Artiodactyla—the ungulates with an even number of toes, such as cattle, sheep, camels, and hippopotamuses.

Whales may once have walked into the sea on four legs, but they cannot be thought of as streamlined cows—or as air-breathing fish. They are unique in numerous ways, and difficult for zoologists to classify. Size, of course, is the whale's outstanding characteristic. Even a small whale is big by land standards. The size of land animals is limited by the ability of their legs to carry them, and this limit was reached by the prehistoric giant reptiles. Probably those reptiles were partly aquatic and regularly supported their bulk in the water of swamps. Whales, being totally waterborne, are not hampered by weight, but even in the sea there is a size limit beyond which organs cannot cope with physiological processes. Up to that point, great size is an advantage to a warm-blooded animal, since its foremost problem is how to keep warm. Water conducts heat twenty-seven times as rapidly as air, and the flow of water past a whale's skin robs it of heat just as a constant breeze would. The whale's great size is a defense against cold, and so is its streamlined shape, which reduces its surface and thus its contact with the water. There can be no small warm-blooded creatures in the sea—no sea mice or sea rabbits.

From the eternal chill of its world the whale has no hiding place. It cannot curl up or take shelter to keep warm, and so it has developed protective devices. It has a high metabolism—an internal heating plant operating at top draft—that allows it to move ceaselessly. (Whales are said to sleep mostly when they are in the warmer latitudes to which most of them move in winter.) The whale has an extraordinary layer of insulation—a coat of blubber that holds in heat like asbestos around a stove. There may be twenty tons of blubber on a ninety-foot blue whale, and the blubber of a Greenland whale may constitute almost half its weight, wrapping its internal organs in a layer two feet thick. This permanent insulation presents the whale with problems similiar to those of a man with only one coat for all occasions. The whale cannot sweat or pant to cool off, so it would seem that, with exertion, it might fatally overheat. Cetologists believe that its fins, which are without blubber and have a rich blood supply, may act as devices to liberate excess heat. Fortunately for the whale, temperatures in the sea don't reach great extremes and don't fluctuate sharply. There is only a forty-five-degree difference between the waters of the tropics and the poles. The distribution of food also works out neatly to the baleen whale's advantage. It is plentiful in cold water, where it is most needed, and scarcer in warm water, where the whale can do without it.

The whale's great body is covered with a skin designed to aid its swift passage through the water. It is extremely thin and as smooth as glass, and the outer layer is ordinarily highly sensitive. The only portion of the skin of most whales that is thick enough for use as leather is that of the penis, which whalers have been known to convert into golf bags. The whale's skin is often marked with scars where the whale has bumped into ice floes. The mouths of lampreys leave round scars on whales, and various small crustaceans attach themselves to them; a humpback may carry a thousand pounds of barnacles. Killer whales attack and scar the large baleen whales.

The skeleton of the whale is designed not to bear weight but to anchor a giant musculature. There are forty tons of muscle in a hundred-ton blue whale, a great mass of it in the lower back to move the tail and its flukes. The bones are light and spongy, with a fatty marrow, which produces a great deal of oil when they are boiled by whalers. Stripped of flesh, the skeleton of a whale has a profile quite different from the living animal. The huge head disappears, and the skull becomes recognizably mammalian. The baleen whales have immense jawbones, curved like the tusks of elephants. In Norway, they are used as arched gateways by whalers who cherish souvenirs. Like most mammals, from mice to giraffes, whales have seven neck vertebrae. These are compressed and relatively rigid, although whales can nod and shake their heads. The body is made supple by extra vertebrae, cushioned by pads of cartilage, and though whales cannot quite bend to touch their tails, they are astonishingly flexible. Whales swim differently from fish, which move by swishing their tails from side to side. A whale beats its flukes up and down, like a frogman swimming with feet tied together. Some whales have a small dorsal fin and some no fin at all. They use their flippers not for swimming but to add balance and to help steer.

Whales solve the problem of breathing in a very special way. Moving the nostrils to the top of the head has required rearrangement of the bones of the skull. The nostrils, or blowholes, of baleen whales are two slits whose highly elastic sides normally seal out water. From the blowhole a nasal passage leads to the opening of the throat, just as in any mammal. Land mammals, however, cannot breathe and swallow at the same time. Whales can. The nasal passages of land beasts have specialized cells that filter out dust and moisten air, but since sea air is clean and moist, whales have dispensed with them. Whales have a larynx, or voice box, in the same place as other mammals, but they have no vocal cords. One of the mysteries of cetology is how baleen whales make their diverse sounds.

When a whale surfaces and exhales, there is a visible spout, and the spout of each species has a characteristic size and shape, enabling whalers to tell the various species apart. The spout of the blue whale is a plume twenty feet high. Right whales, another baleen species, blow two spouts, which form a V. The spout is visible not because the whale has inhaled water but because when gas under pressure escapes it becomes cool and moist and turns to droplets; thus, vapor from the lungs of the whale condenses in the air like a man's breath on a cold day. The lungs of a blue whale weigh as much as a ton, but relative to the size of the whale's body they are rather small. The whale makes up for this, to some extent, by emptying and refilling its lungs almost completely with each breath. The small lung capacity is also compensated for by large oxygen-storage capacity in the bloodstream and muscles and by an ability the whale possesses to divert circulation on occasion from the parts of the body that can endure lack of oxygen and to send the oxygen directly to the heart and brain, which must be continuously supplied.

Most of the food of baleen whales is concentrated in the upper layers of water, but sometimes the whales may go down a thousand feet or more. A fin whale, the second-largest of the baleen species, has been struck by a harpoon with a pressure gauge attached and, in the subsequent dive, has carried harpoon and instrument to a recorded depth of 194 fathoms (1,164 feet). A humpback has been found entangled in an underwater cable at 60 fathoms. (360 feet). Baleen whales usually stay underwater for four to seven minutes between breaths, but, naturally, a whale's breathing rhythm changes with exertion. A whale that is being chased pants like a running horse and must surface more often, and thus fast catcher boats are able to force the creatures to the surface to be shot.

Any animal's body is 70 percent water, and that water's salinity is far lower than seawater's. Fish get rid of extra salt through their gills. It is something of a mystery how whales manage, but the probability is that they excrete the salt with the help of very large kidneys. Whales do not drink water but absorb it from their food.

The senses of baleen whales have not been studied, but much can be inferred from investigations of dolphins. In both sorts of whale, toothed and baleen, hearing is believed to be the sense on which they rely the most. Water is an excellent medium for sound, which travels four and a half times as fast there as in air.

Whalers have long been aware that whales have acute hearing, but this faculty was not studied scientifically until the 1950's, when dolphins were shown to have an acuteness of hearing second only to that of bats. Like bats, dolphins and other toothed whales have the ability to perceive objects by echolocation; that is, by bouncing vibrations off the objects and picking up the returning sound waves, in the manner of sonar. Dolphins can perform astonishing feats through echolocation, such as finding a nickel on the bottom of a pool or discriminating between two sorts of metal. There is no evidence so far that baleen whales also echolocate; neither is there any evidence that they do not.

The cetacean ear is hardly visible. The external ear has disappeared, leaving simply a hole about the diameter of pencil lead; the aural canal is the size of a piece of string. In order for any creature to tell the direction of a sound, each ear must receive it independently, with the brain noting the fractional difference in arrival time and intensity. A man underwater can hear sound, but, because his skull bones conduct vibrations, it seems to come from everywhere at once. To obviate this, acoustic isolation of the ear is needed, and whales have achieved it with cavities, filled with albuminous foam, that isolate the middle ear from the surrounding bones. Dolphins, and probably all whales, have excellent directional hearing. A mystery of the whale's ear is that the semicircular canals, which provide a sense of balance, are remarkably small—no larger in a dolphin than in a hamster.

In the progressively greater darkness under the surface of the sea, eyes are far less useful than ears. Only 10 percent of the light striking the surface penetrates as far down as thirty feet; at that depth a big whale could not see its fluke before its face. Below 215 fathoms (1,290 feet) there is a total darkness. The eyes of whales are adapted to enhance vision in dim light. They have a well-developed tapetum lucidum, or reflective backing to the eye, which makes the eye shine in the dark, and they have more, and longer, light receptors, or rods, than most mammals. Whales have no need for eyebrows, eyelashes, or tears to protect their eyes from dust and sweat, but they do have eyelids for protection; the outer layer of the cornea is made of tough cells and is bathed in an oily secretion. The vision of baleen whales has not been tested, but dolphins, for instance, can catch food flung to them and perform other tricks which show that, out of water at least, they see very well.

Fish can smell underwater, but if whales inhaled water they would drown. Consequently, their smelling apparatus has atrophied and all but disappeared. It is possible that baleen whales, which have vestiges of olfactory structures, can detect smells when their blowholes are out of water, but smell probably has little function in their lives.

There has been a great deal of speculation about the brain of the whale, which is strikingly large and convoluted. The brains of toothed whales are relatively larger than those of baleen whales. The largest brain on record is that of a sperm whale. It weighed 19.6 pounds. A hundred-ton blue whale had a brain weighing 15.25 pounds. Large animals have large brains, but intelligence as we think of it does not necessarily rise proportionately. Next to the whale, the elephant possesses the largest brain. It averages eleven pounds. A human brain weighs three pounds. Most biologists believe that the brains of whales are primarily devoted to acoustic perception rather than to deep thought. In the 1960's, a neurologist, Dr. John C. Lilly, created quite a popular stir with his theories about the marvelous mental faculties of dolphins and the possibility of meaningful communication between whales and men. Dolphins do indeed exhibit remarkable capacities, but Dr. Lilly's ideas are not taken seriously by most of the scientific community.

Whales are herd animals. The social life of dolphins seems to be intense and complicated. Far less is known about that of baleen whales, but it is clear that they communicate with and respond to each other, though they are spread out over wide stretches of water. Blue whales and several other species of baleen whales are thought to be monogamous. Females defend their calves fiercely. It is well established that toothed whales sometimes come to the aid of a wounded comrade, lifting it with their heads and supporting it in the water. Baleen whales, too, have been recorded as trying to help each other in moments of distress. These episodes are among the rare moments in which a whale reacts in a way that we can identify and sympathize with —though, unfortunately, it is usually done in response to human ferocity.

Of the ten species of baleen whales, six are grouped together in a family commonly known as the rorquals—from the Norwegian *rørhval,* or "tubed whale." The "tubes" are a series of deep pleats or grooves that mark their undersides from chin to navel. Most of the rorquals are long, graceful whales, streamlined from snout to flukes. Each of the species has a small, crescent dorsal fin and a powerful tail, which propels it at speeds that can exceed twenty miles an hour. The lower jaw is undershot, with the hard lower lip embracing the upper, which seems to fit into it as a lid fits into a teapot. A small brown eye is set near each corner of the mouth, where an upward groove suggests a smile. The species of rorquals descend in size from the gigantic blue whale to the middle-sized fin whale, and then to three smaller whales—the sei, Bryde's whale, and the minke. The humpback, which has a few pleats, is somewhere in the middle, although, being chunkier, it doesn't look like the other rorquals.

The rorquals range worldwide. All are deep-water whales, feeding in the polar seas, north and south, and migrating to warmer waters to give birth and mate. In earlier times, the rorquals were not hunted because they were too fast for sailors rowing whaleboats. Also, in death their corpses sink, so they could not be "harvested" until modern technology provided fast boats and a method of inflating a dead whale with compressed air to keep it afloat. The modern age of whaling dawned in the 1860's with the perfection, by Svend Foyn, a Norwegian whaler, of the explosive harpoon fired by a gun. The Norwegians first used it to harvest the blue whales and fin whales in the North Atlantic. As these became scarce, the hunters shifted their attention to the gold mine of whales in the Antarctic. Starting in 1904, the destruction of rorquals began.

An ancient Phoenician word for whale meant "lord of the fish," and this surely applies to the largest rorqual, the blue whale. Longer than a railroad passenger car and twenty feet high at the midsection, it is by far the largest living creature, and perhaps the largest creature that has ever lived. (In size, the blue whale easily outclasses even the greatest of the dinosaurs, but it may have been equaled by an extinct shark whose fossilized teeth indicate a monumental size.) The largest blue whale on record was 110.8 feet long, and until twenty or thirty years ago such a size was more common than it is today. In the recent twilight of the species, though, few blue whales have lived long enough to grow anywhere near that big. Weighing a blue whale is a herculean task that can be accomplished only by cutting up the whale and weighing the pieces, and this has not been done often. The heaviest one weighed came to 134.25 tons. However, blue whales gain and lose gigantic amounts of weight according to the season. In their polar summer, they eat constantly and may gain thirty or forty tons, which is metabolized during a subsequent period of fasting. Blue whales generally cruise at six to eight miles per hour, but they can steam along at more than twice this speed for several hours. If they are frightened, they can surge forward at more than twenty miles an hour. A harpooned blue whale has pulled a ninety-foot boat, with its engines going full speed astern, for seven hours over fifty miles of ocean.

Blue whales are actually a mottled slate color, paler underneath. They sometimes turn yellow when a film of algae blooms on their skin; hence they have been called sulphur-bottom whales. They like deep water and seldom approach shore, but occasionally one is stranded. In 1922, a huge blue whale entered the Panama Canal, where it was machine-gunned by a military vessel. Blue whales sometimes assemble in groups of five or six, but there are no large herds. When whalers find a pair of blue whales, they try to shoot the female first, because the male will not desert her, but the female may leave the wounded male. Young blue whales are inquisitive, and when a catcher boat approaches them they often swim toward their executioners.

There may have been 200,000 blue whales in the Antarctic when whaling there began to achieve its peak, in the 1920's. The catch of blues rose annually, to a high point of 29,410 in the 1930–31 season, and declined thereafter, until in the 1964–65 season whalers found only twenty blue whales to kill. At that point, the International Whaling Commission decided that protection was in order. The present number of blue whales is unknown. They are occasionally sighted in all oceans, and optimists estimate that there are several thousand—enough to keep the species alive—but pessimists suggest that the remnant may dwindle to zero. No one can say whether the blue whale will ever return to its former abundance, or, if it does, how many hundreds of years that might take.

The humpback is a great, chunky beast, around fifty feet long, with a huge head and a small, rounded dorsal fin, which gives the whale a humpbacked appearance when it dives. The humpback usually has a black back and various piebald patches of white on its underside—a gaily parti-colored whale, with no two quite alike. A so far inexplicable feature of the humpback is a series of knobs or bumps on its head and jaws and on the edge of its flippers. Each knob sprouts one or two coarse bristles, and it is possible that these function in some way as sense organs. The humpback has winglike flippers, which are sometimes as long as fifteen feet—far longer than those of any other whale. There are humpbacks in both the northern and the southern oceans, and they migrate from the poles to the equator, occasionally following the shorelines of the continents. The humpback is a slow swimmer and can easily be caught by primitive methods; consequently, humpbacks have been hunted not only in their polar feeding grounds but from shore stations along their routes. With these whales attacked everywhere, their stocks all over the world have been reduced to a remnant. As recently as 1963, whalers killed 2,339 humpbacks in the North Pacific and, in the 1962–63 season, 270 in the Antarctic. Then, in 1963, when there were few left to kill, the whaling nations agreed to stop the slaughter in the Antarctic. The killing in the North Pacific was not stopped until

1966. By rough estimate, a species whose numbers may have originally been more than 100,000 has been reduced to 5,000 or so.

The humpback is the most athletic and playful of the giants. It leaps and falls flat on its side or back, smacking the water with a gargantuan splash. Sometimes it swims on its back or turns a whole somersault above the water. A whaling captain, Charles Scammon, writing of experiences in the mid-nineteenth century, when humpbacks were plentiful, described their behavior thus: "In the mating season they are noted for their amorous antics. At such times their caresses are of the most amusing and novel character. . . . When lying by the side of each other, the *megapteras* [humpbacks] frequently administer alternate blows with their long fins, which love-pats may, on a still day, be heard at a distance of miles. They also rub each other with these same huge and flexible arms, rolling occasionally from side to side, and indulging in other gambols which can easier be imagined than described." It is perhaps not surprising that such a lively whale also emits the most musical sounds of any whale so far recorded. Scientists listening with hydrophones have discovered that humpbacks sing long, complicated songs that have some of the qualities of slightly mad orchestral music and some of the qualities of a gigantic bird singing in a gigantic birdbath.

My quest for a glimpse of great whales first took me to Bermuda, where Dr. Payne and his wife, Katy, were recording the sounds of humpbacks from a forty-four-foot motor sailer named the *Rockfish*, which had been lent them by Dr. Henry Clay Frick, a New York surgeon, who is a grandson of the steel millionaire, is a trustee of the New York Zoological Society, and has a home in Bermuda. On a choppy, windy April day, we set off from a harbor on the east end of the island, heading down along the south shore toward Challenger Bank, where the Paynes had had good luck finding humpback whales on previous trips. On board were the captain, a ruddy-faced Bermudian named Campbell O'Connor; the Paynes; Jane Frick, Dr. Frick's daughter, who likes to take underwater photographs and hope to get some of whales; and Oliver Brazier, a quiet Bostonian who is an expert on electronic equipment. Roger Payne is a tall, dark-eyed, boyish-looking man then in his late thirties, with the ability to alternate intense seriousness with easy and graceful humor. He has passionate personal feelings about whales, and writes and talks of them with a romantic eloquence that raises the hackles of some of his fellow biologists. Most cetologists have started out as fishery men. Haddock and herring are not such stuff as dreams are made on, and these men have viewed whales primarily as a problem in population dynamics. They have wished to save whales only to make the maximum "use" of them. Payne, who has been crusading to save whales for the sake of whales, rather than having them used as a cheap food for mink—or even for men, since he considers it wicked to encourage the further overpopulation that menaces the globe—has a quite different point of view. His initial interest, after his graduation from Harvard, was in animal behavior, and he began by doing research on the hearing of bats, insects, and owls. He was diverted to whales by an emotional experience that occurred early in his career when he was on the staff of Tufts University. Late one sleety March night when he was working in his laboratory, he heard on the radio that a dead whale had washed ashore on Revere Beach. On an impulse, he drove out to see it. Later, he wrote about standing on the deserted beach at the water's edge, looking at the whale in the beam of a flashlight:

> It was a small whale—a porpoise about eight feet long, with lovely, subtle curves glistening in the cold rain. It had been mutilated. Someone had hacked off its flukes for a souvenir and two other people had carved their initials deeply into its side. Someone else had stuck a cigar butt into its blowhole. I removed the cigar and I stood there for a long time with feelings I can't describe. Everybody has some such experience that affects him for life, probably several. That night was one of mine. At some point the flashlight went out, but as the tide came in I could periodically see the graceful outline of the whale against the white foam cast up by the waves. Although it is more typical

than not of what happens to whales when they encounter man, that experience was somehow the last straw, and I decided to use the first possible opportunity to learn enough about whales so I might have some effect on their future.

When Payne found that humpback whales congregate off Bermuda in winter and early spring, he and his wife made a trip there in 1967. They met Frank Watlington, then an engineer with the Columbia University Geophysical Field Station at Bermuda. Some time before, hydrophones had been installed in the ocean offshore from Watlington's office, which is on a rocky headland, to record whatever sounds came along. He had been startled to find that these included medleys of a sort of unearthly singing, grunting, wailing, and rumbling, which he could attribute only to the humpbacks that were to be seen breaching and spouting offshore at the time the sounds were recorded.

When Roger Payne, who plays the cello and loves music, heard Watlington's recordings of whale sounds, he was deeply stirred. As he later described it: "Katy and I first heard humpback sounds over the roar of a generator and blower. Even so, what we experienced in that crowded, noisy compartment were the most fascinating and beautiful sounds of the wild world I had ever heard." Watlington gave the Paynes copies of the tapes, and back home in New York they played them over and over. What impressed and fascinated Payne particularly was the variety of the sounds. At first, they seemed to come in random sequence, but after many hearings he realized that there were definite patterns, repeated from time to time. It occurred to him that these patterns—which could be called songs in the same sense that the characteristic sound sequences of birds are called songs—offered a valuable tool for the study of whale behavior. The study of the humpback songs thus united Dr. Payne's two main interests: the use of sound in animal communication and the behavior of whales.

The next year, the Paynes went to Bermuda again, and, hoping to get close to the whales without frightening them, Payne put out to sea in a plywood rowboat. There were humpbacks surfacing around him, but he could only get about fifty feet from them. When a pair of whales that he had been vainly chasing went down for a long dive, Payne shipped his oars and waited for them to reappear. As he sat there, he suddenly heard whale music emanating eerily from the hull of the boat. Because of the different densities of air and water, very little sound from the depths can escape into the air, but wood is of an intermediate density and can act as a transducer. (Payne points out that whaling literature includes accounts of strange, ethereal music reverberating through quiet ships at night, and thinks that these accounts can be explained as whale sounds transmitted through wooden hulls.) The sounds that Payne heard in his rowboat were not only clear but startlingly similar to Watlington's tapes. "This blew my mind," Payne says. "It was confirmation that not only do individual humpbacks repeat their songs but other humpbacks may sing the same song at a different time and place." His conclusion that there are definite, recurring sequences in whale song was later confirmed by spectrographic analysis. Payne lent Watlington's tapes to Scott McVay, who was then a Princeton University administrator and who undertook to work with him on their analysis. This involved the use of a spectrograph machine, which produces a chart that shows both frequency over a period of time and amplitude, and resembles musical notation. Thus printed out, the separate whale songs are as recognizable as, say, "The Star-Spangled Banner."

Katy Payne, an attractive blue-eyed young woman, is, like her husband, an accomplished musician, and she has become deeply involved in analyzing the tapes of whale music they have collected. She has even learned to sing like a whale, imitating the sounds in a high, silvery voice, and even reproducing the rude Bronx cheers and ratchet sounds that break into the lyrical passages.

When I joined the Paynes on their Bermuda expedition, they warned me that whale-watching can be a frustrating business. Whales appear briefly and unpredictably, they said, and moments of excitement are followed by long stretches of nothing but rough water. My notes on the trip follow, beginning in the morning as the six of us, in the cockpit of the *Rockfish*, braced ourselves against the surging roll of the waves en route to the banks where the whales are most often found.

Roger explains that his immediate goal is to find out how loud the whale sounds are and how far they can carry—fundamental information that would help explain the function of the sounds. He speculates that the sounds could be a means of recognition between individuals or could proclaim territory, provide contact between migrant groups, or be involved in sex recognition and attraction. Or perhaps some components of the whale's sounds could be used in echolocation, like the sonar clicks of porpoises. Is the song the whale's altimeter, telling it where it is in relation to the surface in the course of a dive? Roger suggests still another theory: "A whale herd is like a convoy of boats, and the whales can't afford to collide. Their skins are very delicate. Maneuvering such a bulk must be like trying to drive a giant trailer truck in traffic. I figure whales have to be alert and communicate rapidly and precisely."

Katy asks, "Is there a sound for left and one for right?"

Roger grins and says, "I wish I knew." He would love to know how complex the communications are, he continues. Can whales convey as much information as a honeybee, which can tell other bees precisely where to find a certain supply of food? Are different components of the whale sounds used for different purposes? Is there, perhaps, one sound for close maneuvering and another that, like bird song, simply says, "I am a healthy male and I would like to meet you"?

A little later, Roger says, "Whales have the most acoustically complex life possible." He wants to know how whales get around in a nonvisual world. The more wide-ranging and unpredictable the life of a whale is, the more need it has to communicate over long distances. The food of whales drifts randomly over featureless ocean, and in order not to compete with each other they must stay far apart while feeding. Roger theorizes that sound frees individuals from the need for close contact, so they can spread out and make the most of the food supply. But, as nomads wandering over vast distances, unable to leave a track or a scent for others to follow, they have the problem of getting back together. "If they can shout information on where they are," Roger says, "then the whole sea becomes an enormous room."

Roger explains that there is something called "the deep sound channel"—a layer of water that confines sound so that it can carry as far as halfway around the world. The sound of a dynamite blast near Australia, for instance, was once picked up by a listening device off Bermuda several hours later. Roger speculates that whales may send their signals over hundreds of miles through the deep sound channel. He is distressed because the multitude of ships churning through the ocean nowadays—there are fourteen hundred in the North Atlantic on any given day— are polluting the seas with noise. The whir of their propellers is on the same sound wavelength as the whales' noises and may mess up whale communications.

I ask Roger what other aspect of whales' lives he wants to investigate. He says he wants to know everything—where they go, what they do at each stage of their lives, and why. "A biologist wants to become part of an animal's life. I would like to be a flea on the shoulder of a bat. That's impossible, but maybe somebody will invent a little capsule in which you could attach yourself to a whale. What I want is to be *with* whales as much as possible." He says that close observations are very difficult around Bermuda, where the water is rough and the whales are rather widely dispersed, but that he has found a place off the South American coast where southern right whales gather in calm water behind a barrier reef and can be watched at close quarters. He thinks that, with enough patience, a human being will be able to get as close to whales as George Schaller and Jane Goodall have got to apes. He thinks that if you hang around whales long enough the older ones will come to ignore you, and you can take advantage of the curiosity of the young. But if you chase, injure, or frighten an animal, he says, you're finished. He has resolved to pursue his studies by methods that don't risk hurting his subjects.

Katy says that one of her objectives in analyzing whale songs is to find out whether individuals can be recognized by their songs—or, if not individuals, then groups. If so, they could be tracked by their songs, and their travels charted. She compares whale song to bird song, pointing out that because birds are so small their lives are speeded up. A bird song lasts only a few seconds—or, at most, a few minutes—and the notes are very close together. She thinks whales sing huge, slow songs appropriate to their size, and that is why each note is so distinct. It sounds to human ears like a record slowed down.

We are chugging along into rising swells, and the horizon is turbulent with whitecaps. Campbell O'Connor, our captain, says it is going to get rougher and now might be a good time to eat. Katy goes below and gets us crackers, cheese, and soup. While we eat, Roger explains how he hopes to gather information on the loudness of whale sounds. He wants to record a whale's voice on tape and then, when the whale surfaces, measure its distance from the boat. There are three things to be measured at the same time: the intensity of the sound as it reaches the hydrophones, the distance to the whale, and the temperature of the water, which influences sound conductivity. Measuring the distance to a singing whale is not easy. First, the whale must be identified as the one that is being heard through the earphones, and then its position must be fixed at a moment coinciding with a certain segment of the tape recording of its song. Roger has thought of various ways to measure the distance to the whale, but fears that some of them would frighten the whale into silence and flight. He has decided to try taking simultaneous pictures from two cameras fixed a certain distance apart, and calculating the angle between the two images. As he snaps the shutter, he will record an identifying number on the tape. The camera rig is lying on top of the deckhouse.

Katy shouts, "Whale!" Roger asks O'Connor to turn off the engine. The boat drifts and rolls in the choppy waves, which whisper and splash against its sides. Only the jib steadies us. Off to one side, there is a round slick, as if a ship had sunk. This is characteristic of a spot where a whale has gone down. Oliver Brazier, the sound expert, puts the hydrophones over the side. Roger, in bathing trunks and earphones, stands tensely in the heaving cockpit, listening, but reports that he is hearing only strumming interference.

"What direction was he going?" he asks.

"East," says O'Connor, pointing ahead. We are about two miles offshore.

Roger says, "I hear a very distant whale."

I picture a vast, green chamber beneath us, and wonder if any person will ever be able to move in it as freely as the whales do. Roger and Oliver are fiddling with the equipment. When they finally decide that the machinery is working right, there is no whale.

O'Connor says, "That whale's got no time to mess with you people. He's gone to sing to his girlfriend."

We raise the mainsail and go to look for other whales. We plow through the waves with white foam at our bow. We are all getting impatient, but see nothing except gray waves hurrying past us. Then O'Connor says, "There's one!" and points off the port bow. A second later, I see a whale spout. The spout is like a puff of smoke. It hangs in the air, then disintegrates. It comes again. We lower the mainsail, and Katy throws the hydrophones over. The whale stays under for what seems a long time—actually, it's only a few minutes—and then suddenly rises a stone's throw away. I see a gleaming black back and patches of brilliant white. Then it is gone, in a surge of foam. Roger is on top of the boom struggling with the cameras. Katy says, "I'm getting great sound, but it can't be this whale. It's too far away." She hands me the earphones. They are filled with sound. Mixed with the gurgle and wash of water I hear something like a baby crying very far away. Then the cry turns into a medley of ethereal calls such as tiny translucent fairies might make. Katy thinks we are hearing two or three whales at once. There is an impression, impossible to confirm, of calls and answers. The whale we saw doesn't appear again. What we are hearing *must* be far away. We settle down to wait for another strolling singer. In spite of the jib, we roll and slat as the gray seas come past like rolling mountains. Not far beneath us, there are real mountains, rising from a tremendous depth. They have flattened, mesa-like tops that form banks a hundred and eighty feet below the surface. At the moment, I learn, we are over the saddle between Challenger and Plantagenet banks. The valley floor is three or four thousand feet below the mountaintops, and the slopes are so steep, O'Connor says, that he once dropped bow and stern anchors in this area and found his bow in a hundred and eighty feet of water and his stern in five hundred. I wonder if the whales slide down the sides of the mountains, coasting like kids on snow, and then laze along the valley floor.

I ask how close we might get to a whale. Katy says that one year three whales headed straight for the boat. She jumped in the water with a mask on and, looking down, could see their giant forms and white-banded flippers gleaming right below her. She says she felt awfully small. And once, at the South American whale grounds, she and Brazier were in a small outboard motorboat when a whale came up, raised its head out of the water to peer at them, turned tail and flurried the water in threat, then thrust its flukes under the boat, lifted it into the air, and put it down. As they hit the surface, Oliver started the motor, and they scooted away. Katy noticed that there were two mother whales with calves nearby, and wondered if the whale that threatened them was a bull protecting females. It escorted them from the area. Roger says he had a similar experience when a whale followed his skiff and nudged the stern with its head. "My first reaction was ecstasy," he recalls. "My next was terror."

After an hour, no whale has appeared. We pull in the hydrophones and move on. Half an hour later, we haul the mainsail down again and put the hydrophones over. Katy listens, and immediately her face brightens. She says the whale sounds are very loud. Roger begins recording. I listen for a moment. There is a sound like the hinge on a creaky iron door. Then we hear what sounds like a high-low operatic duet. Is it really a duet or one whale talking to itself? Roger would give a lot to know. All at once, O'Connor sees a whale swimming parallel to us. It is surprisingly hard to estimate the distance of a whale from a boat, but this one looks huge and seems close—perhaps only a couple of hundred yards away. It blows. The great, gleaming black back surges out with a swift roll. There is a glimpse of the little fin near the tail, and then the whale is gone. The few moments the whale is visible are intensely exciting and tantalizing. To be so close to something so enormous and so transient! There is a longing to detain it, explore it, touch it, make some contact—to say or do something that the whale will respond to.

Now there are four whales off the bow, blowing as they move away from us, while closer at hand two black torpedoes cut the water in front of us. The black backs roll out and under. Then three more whales appear, even closer, and they blow twice and make a leisurely turn around our stern. They are visible for a count of twelve. I can see the small eye and the smile at the corner of the mouth. Over the white bands on the flippers the water takes on a turquoise hue, as it does over white sand in the tropics. While these three are circling us, Roger thinks, they are within a hundred feet. We are up to our ears in whales—so many that there is no way to tell which are singing. Katy reports a great medley of sounds. I listen briefly, and hear groans, bleats, moos, even motorcycles starting up and receding into the distance.

It is afternoon now, and we have been hearing continuous song for an hour without seeing a whale. This indicates to Roger that either the sound comes from very far off or the whales are staying down a very long time. Katy lends me her earphones. I hear a slightly daft siren song. The sweetest, most poetic notes, pure and piercing, are followed by low ratchet sounds—haunted-house sounds—Cathy calling Heathcliff. Then a switch to a rural scene —somebody blowing into a jug, beagles yipping, cattle lowing.

I contemplate the endless motion of whales. They go through the water like perpetually turning wheels, doomed never to rest or to form any attachment to a single place. They are Flying Dutchmen. I mention this to Roger. He says that at the South American site the whales loll along the shore, circling there and resting on the current. Sometimes they lie on their backs and wave their gigantic flippers. He says it is a marvelous place to observe whale behavior, because you can stand on a cliff and look right down on the whales. He often saw contact between them—heads touching, bodies sliding over each other. In greeting each other, the whales arch their backs in a peculiar way. He saw a mating. The female, with a calf beside her, lay in the water. The male slid smoothly beneath her, turned belly up, and arched his back. It lasted only a second. There are old reports of whales mating in a vertical position, rising out of the water belly to belly, but Roger thinks that this is unlikely.

Roger's South American whales are right whales. Humpbacks apparently cease to sing when they move to their northern feeding grounds, where they stay from May to December; sounds have been recorded, but they have not been found to be "song." This summer silence is puzzling to Roger, but he notes that the whales are particularly scattered then, and it is harder to pick up their sounds. He wonders if perhaps they have been silenced by fear of the large, noisy vessels from which recording has been attempted. He thinks it very important to approach whales in a sailboat.

Since whales have a larynx but no vocal cords, we discuss the mystery of how they make their sounds. People emit air to cause sound vibration, but there are other possible techniques— stridulation, for instance. The whale might strum a taut membrane inside itself. Roger, however, thinks it most likely that whales use air, because an air-filled cavity produces a harmonic series similar to whale sounds; namely, even multiples of the fun-

damental. This theory assumes that the whale transfers air inside it from one cavity to another, and implies the use of some sort of plumbing, probably in the head, for the purpose. Whales have a number of cavities associated with the larynx and the nasal passage which might serve to produce sound—and the sound need not necessarily come *out* of any particular aperture. It could simply emerge through the blubber and skin.

We've just seen a black back wheel out of the water. It is coming toward us, with a smaller one just behind—a mother and a calf. They are so close that as they submerge we again see the water turn turquoise over the gleaming white on their flippers. Their skins shine like divers' wet suits. There is a wake of champagne-like bubbles, and smooth eddies behind it. The whales blow a deep, long, sighing exhalation, quite loud—first the mother and then the baby—and sink. They surface three more times, moving slowly away. Roger photographs them, but Katy hears nothing on the earphones.

We raise the sail and start for Challenger Bank. When we reach it, we haul down the sail and drop the hydrophones over.

Bermuda is barely visible. There is a whale half a mile ahead. Katy hears a distant whale sound over the earphones. On the horizon behind us I suddenly see a cigar-shaped cylinder thrust out of the water to an incredible height, like the lift-off of a rocket. It is a whale standing on its tail. I yell, and everybody sees the giant splash as it topples and hits the water. Katy says the singing she was hearing in the earphones stopped about that time, and Roger thinks perhaps we have seen Katy's singing whale. He has a theory that whales sing when they are near the surface, rising and falling in shallow dives and not traveling fast. He thinks that they lie in the water and sing, and that the sound resembling a ratchet occurs when the whale is coming to the surface for a breath.

After a while, we start moving again. O'Connor says there are fish pots ahead, and predicts that we'll find whales among them. He says the whales like to rub their backs on the fish pots, which sometimes damages the pots' little marker flags and angers the fishermen, who often shoot at the whales. We approach a fish pot marked by a staff flying a pennant, which seems a strange touch of civilization in this empty wilderness of water. Suddenly we are in the midst of whales. A pair, with a third whale behind them, surge alongside and blow—one, two, three great sighing, steamy sounds, like those made by a steam locomotive settling down on a siding. I see an open blowhole quivering and vibrating. It is a couple of inches across. Jane Frick has jumped overboard in her blue jeans and is paddling around like a seal, upright in the choppy water, wet hair streaming over her eyes, as she tries to adjust her camera. There is excited activity on board, with Katy and Oliver working the sound equipment and Roger taking pictures. The whales surge by. They surface and sink, surface and sink, with a rhythmic, easy roll that has a wonderful grace.

These whales go by very fast. I am reminded of being at the rail of a racetrack when the horses come swiftly toward you. For an extraordinary instant, they are right beside you, so that you smell the sweat and hear the panting and the creak of leather. Then they are going away. For just such an instant, the whales surface beside the boat and they hurry on past the bow, and abruptly decide to sound. They rise, then dive steeply, seeming to stand on their heads. Their huge flukes wave above the surface like the wings of giant black butterflies; then they sink smoothly into the sea and are gone. The waving flukes are a sign that they are heading for the depths. Everybody seems to feel very frustrated. Jane climbs back in the boat, having failed to get a picture. The deck is a tangle of wires, but the sounds that Katy heard over the earphones were distant ones and could not have been from these whales. Roger has good pictures but no whale sounds to match them.

After a dismal, letdown hour of sloshing around, we motor to a spot near another bunch of fish traps. Roger puts on earphones. He reports that he has briefly heard a whale singing, but it has quit. "I'm afraid we shut it up with the motor," he says. After a minute, his face brightens. "Watch for a blow," he says. "There's somebody close." We watch in vain. Though the sounds are tantalizingly clear, an hour or so passes and we see nothing. Now it seems miraculous that we saw the other whales so close.

We move again, and as soon as the hydrophones are down Katy reports that she hears some beautiful grunts. She passes me the earphones, and I hear sounds exactly like water chugging out of a bottle. Then comes the siren song. Now I picture dark green corridors lined with mirrors, and sirens in diaphanous white garments drifting through them. Jane yells, "Breach!" and I turn my head in time to see a giant splash a few hundred yards astern. The whale rises again, and almost its entire body is visible. It hangs above the water for an instant and falls with a loud report, amid geysers of water. It vanishes. We wait hopefully, but it doesn't reappear. Apparently, it is also silent. The sounds on the hydrophones are coming from a distance. I hand the earphones back to Katy, who sits watching the water and listening. At intervals, she says, "It's so beautiful!"

My notes on the trip end there, but I remember, perhaps best of all, what came afterward.

For several hours, we drifted over the banks, rolling steadily but less furiously than in the early afternoon. An evening calm was settling on the water. Now and then, we saw a distant spout —nothing close. (Roger suspects that a whale can exhale invisibly underwater and then surface just long enough to take a breath without being seen.) Katy sat in the stern, resting against a pile of life jackets, listening. The sun sank, and the sky and water turned mauve and gray. O'Connor planned to let us drift through the night. He lit the running lights and went below to get some supper. Oliver and Roger went down to work with the recording equipment. They wanted to run the recorder all night.

I sat in the cockpit, watching the light soften and turn silver, watching the ceaseless movement of the water, and becoming aware that our boat was shrinking—that it had become a very small platform to rest on in this endless ocean. As I gazed at the metallic surface of the waves, it occurred to me that in the fifty million years that whales have existed the land has changed beyond recognition but the sea has remained a primeval landscape, and may have looked just like this at the beginning of creation. The sky was empty. There were no clouds to keep us company, and no birds.

Katy put down the earphones and went below. After a moment, I moved to her place and put them on. Whale songs were coming through beautifully. They were lovely and fascinating, but what struck me most of all was that they had the warmth of life. The cold, empty world of the surface dropped away as I slipped into the populated depths. Far from being empty, the great chamber below was filled with life. I relaxed as I listened to its lively hum. It was like looking through a pane of glass, watching busy activities on the other side, yet not being quite able to enter. I thought about the various speculations as to why whales make their strange sounds, and the answer suddenly seemed clear: they sing their songs so that they won't be alone.

The key element in the existence of the great whales is, of course, their food supply. In certain regions of the ocean, plankton, made up of a variety of small, drifting plants and of tiny animals, the most common of which is krill, grows with fantastic speed and abundance. The other very large sea creatures—the forty-foot basking shark, the fifty-foot whale shark, and the huge manta ray—also depend on plankton. Since plankton is so abundant—two hundred million tons of krill alone are produced annually, or nearly three times the tonnage of sea creatures that human beings harvest—it has been suggested that we might harvest plankton and eat it ourselves, but so far no one has produced an acceptable food made of krill. All life in the sea, as on land, depends on plants, which alone can synthesize organic matter from carbonic acid, sunlight, and water. But whereas the tropical land areas produce the most luxuriant plant life, things are reversed in the sea, and cold waters are the richest. This is because cold water holds more dissolved oxygen and carbonic acid than warm water does, and also because the surface water near the poles contains an especially rich supply of plant nutrients, derived from the bodies of dead organisms and other waste products. Normally, this debris sinks to the bottom, but in the polar regions there are vast areas of upwelling water—currents from the deep rising abruptly to the surface—which endlessly bring up supplies of food for the tiny plants floating in the sunlit surface layer. Thus, the cold, gray polar seas are in fact bubbling springs of life, thousands of times as productive as the transparent blue waters of the tropical oceans. The sea plants, thriving in the almost endless sunshine of the polar summer, provide pasture for a host of small grazing organisms: worms, snails, jellyfish, and shrimp. One of the most abundant, particularly in the Antarctic, is the shrimplike crustacean *Euphausia superba* Dana—otherwise, krill. In the high latitudes, krill can occur in fantastic concentrations, forming a rusty-red carpet thirty feet thick over several square miles of ocean. Krill is the staple food of baleen whales, and the amounts of it they consume are enormous. It is not unusual for the stomach of a blue whale to contain a ton of krill.

The seasonal cycle of the rorqual is tied to the summer harvest

of krill and other plankton in polar waters. For three months or
so, the whales graze through the long polar days, storing up
riches in the form of fat. Females with young wean them in the
midst of this abundance. Pregnant females are able to nourish
the unborn young at a rate that permits tremendous growth
within the womb. As autumn darkness falls and the pastures of
plankton wither, the whales move toward the equator in a migration of thousands of miles. Though they eat little or nothing,
they are still fat and strong as they approach the equator—in
prime condition for the great physiological demands of mating
and nursing that lie ahead. When they reach warm water, the females that have weaned calves during the summer mate again
and begin gestation. Pregnant females give birth in the warm
water.

No one has yet seen the birth of a baleen whale, but it is generally believed that the calf is born tail first, so that there is no
risk of its taking a lungful of water during birth. Dolphin
mothers quickly push the newborn to the surface, and probably
baleen whales do, too. The nipples of the female whale, recessed
in openings on either side of the genital slit, are equipped with
muscles that squirt milk into the mouth of the calf. The calf,
which lacks soft lips, seizes the teat between tongue and palate.
Whale milk is creamy white, slightly fishy in taste, and very rich
—three or four times as concentrated as cow's milk. It has been
guessed that a big whale gives more than a hundred and thirty
gallons a day. Infant whales are huge babies by any standard. A
newborn blue whale weighs two tons and is twenty-five feet long
—almost a third the length of its mother. Every day while it is
nursing, it grows two inches and gains two hundred pounds. It
can swim capably from birth, and during the nursing period
sticks close to its mother's side.

The age at which the great whales reach sexual maturity is not
definitely known; it is thought that blue whales and fin whales
reach puberty when they are six years old, at which time they
have completed 85 percent of their growth. The rate at which
females produce young is likewise uncertain. Species probably

differ; some may give birth every year, some every two years, and some every three years. Examination of dead females has revealed scars on the ovaries which are thought to correspond to the number of times the whales have ovulated, but the scars do not indicate over what period of time the ovulations have taken place. The only clue to the age of a mature baleen whale is found in a waxy earplug that appears to add layers throughout the whale's lifetime. But how often a layer is added—whether every six, twelve, or eighteen months, or every two years—has not been established. Also unknown is the natural life-span of whales. In most mammals, childhood occupies an eighth to a sixth of the total life expectancy. This would indicate an age of thirty-five or forty years for whales. An old harpoon found in a right whale has been identified after forty years and one in a sperm whale has been identified after thirty-two years, but, naturally, these findings do not indicate how much longer the whales might have lived.

The birth rate of whales is of paramount interest to cetologists, because therein lies the key to the numbers of individuals that whalers can kill without exterminating the species. In all animal populations, more individuals are born than the environment can sustain. Thus, a certain percentage of each species is a surplus that can be killed (or "harvested," as those in the trade prefer to call it) without affecting the crop of young the following year. This possible crop, year after year, is called the sustainable yield. If it is exceeded, the remaining breeding stock cannot make up the loss, and the population shrinks. This smaller population has an even smaller sustainable yield, and so on. If the latter number continues to be exceeded, the population inevitably sinks to zero. To find the magic number—sustainable yield—it is necessary to know the number of animals at a given time in the basic stock, the death rate, and the birth rate. In dealing with whales, scientists are sure of only one of these factors—the death rate. It can be safely assumed that very few great whales of the hunted species escape the hunters to die of old age; therefore, the number recorded as killed by the whalers is near the actual death rate.

Neither of the other figures essential for an accurate estimate of sustainable yield has been established. The total population of each species is roughly estimated from the number of sightings. The birth rate is guessed at from examination of the ovaries of females, but the interpretation of these data is open to dispute. It can thus be fairly said that the men who annually set the quota of whales that can be killed "safely," without jeopardizing the stock, actually have very little idea of what they are doing. For almost twenty years, disinterested scientists have warned that the rate of killing was quite likely more than the stocks could sustain, and year after year their predictions of shrinking stocks of whales have been confirmed. The industry has ignored the warnings, on the ground that "proof" of overkilling was still lacking. In the case of the Japanese, the industry maintains captive scientists who regularly provide optimistic interpretations of the data to bolster the view that there are still plenty of whales left to kill.

The rarest of all the great whales—so rare that it is seldom seen, and is seldom even mentioned except in scientific papers now and then—is the right whale. The North Atlantic right whale and its close relative the Greenland right whale were the first to be hunted to near extinction. The right whale is massive and slow, and easy to catch from an open boat, and hence it was the earliest to be attacked by primitive hunters everywhere. The right whale is short and stocky—a sixty-foot specimen may be forty feet around the waist—with a huge head, which makes up almost a third of the body length. When it is dead, its carcass floats, and for this reason, as well as its slowness and high oil content, it became known as the "right" whale to catch.

Right whales once swam by the thousands in the temperate waters of both the Atlantic and the Pacific. The Japanese hunted them from shore from the earliest times. In Europe, major commercial whaling began in the eleventh century in the Bay of Biscay, which then teemed with right whales. The Basques were the first whalers, but other Europeans soon joined in, and by the sixteenth century they had destroyed the stock on their coasts of the Atlantic. A couple of hundred years later, American whalers did the same on our coasts. On the other side of the world, the rights were given a little more time, but in the nineteenth century a great fleet of whaling ships of many nations swept the Pacific, both north and south, and polished off the right whales there within fifty years. The fact that the right whale is so rare and yet still exists poses an interesting question for biologists. Why is it that although it has not been hunted in a hundred years it has multiplied so little? Or, on the other hand, why has it not gone under entirely? If the other baleen whales follow its example, the stocks may never regenerate.

Now, with the blue whale almost gone and the fin whale greatly reduced, the whalers are turning to the small rorquals for their harvest. The sei and Bryde's whale are much alike. Both are about fifty feet long and look like small fin whales; Bryde's whale, which is rarer, is found mainly off the coast of South Africa. The sei, so named by the Norwegians because it appeared along the coast at the same time as a kind of fish called the seje, ranges from pole to pole but avoids the coldest water. It is equipped with baleen that ends in fringe as soft and fine as fleece, with which it can strain very small creatures out of the water. In the Pacific, however, it often eats small fish. It twists and turns its lithe body as it pursues its prey. For short sprints, the sei is the fastest whale, and when it is harpooned it thrashes mightily, which has given it a bad name among whalers.

Because seis yield less oil than bigger whales, they were not heavily hunted in earlier days. The world catch from 1909 to 1949 was 35,908—only a small fraction of the number of blues and fins killed in that time. Most of the seis were killed off the coasts of Japan and Korea. The Chinese think the sei is the best eating of all whales. Intensive killing of seis began in the early 1960's, and perhaps half the original stock in the Antarctic, estimated at 150,000, has been killed. Seis have also been hunted heavily in the North Pacific. The International Whaling Commission finally set a quota for the killing—7,500 for 1973–74—but many experts believed that this ran true to IWC form and was too high.

The smallest rorqual is called the little piked whale, or minke, the latter name immortalizing, derisively, a Norwegian gunner who shot one he mistook for a blue—a mistake his shipmates found amusing, since the little piked whale is only thirty feet long. It looks like a diminutive fin whale, but it has a distinguishing white band across the flippers. It ranges high latitudes around the world and goes deeper into the Antarctic than any other whale. In 1908, Sir Ernest Henry Shackleton, a British explorer, named the Bay of Whales after discovering vast numbers of minkes gamboling among the ice floes there. Assemblages of a thousand have been seen.

In the Northern Hemisphere, the minke visits the coast of Europe, and some have even swum up the Thames to London. It is the whale most frequently stranded on the British coast. When bigger whales were plentiful, minkes were not heavily hunted except off Norway and Japan. Between 1938 and 1954, the Norwegians killed 37,716. It is believed that there is still a sizable population in the Antarctic, where a quota of 5,000 has now been set by the IWC. Thus, these small whales provide economic insurance for continued voyages in the course of which the remnants of the bigger species are taken.

Of all the baleen whales, the one that is most easily seen and studied is the gray whale, which parades along the California coast on its migrations between its summer pasture in the Bering Sea and its winter quarters on the coast of Baja California. En route, the gray can be watched from shore or counted from airplanes, and a fairly accurate tally of its numbers is possible. The gray whale constitutes a family in itself. It has more hair (one gray whale had sixty hairs on its head and a hundred and twenty on its lower jaw) and a slightly more flexible body. Overall, the gray is a slim whale, forty or so feet long and rather cigar-shaped, with a small head. The mouth neatly divides the head into two equal parts. Gray whales have from two to four pleats on the throat, and so are intermediate between right whales, which lack pleats, and the rorquals, which have from forty to a hundred. Gray whales occur only in the Pacific, and there are, or were, two stocks—those seen on the California coast and a separate group that migrated between Korea and the Sea of Okhotsk —which the Japanese have to all intents and purposes destroyed.

The California gray whales, too, were nearly exterminated, but they have made a remarkable recovery. It has been estimated that between 25,000 and 50,000 gray whales originally frequented the California coast. As settlers reached the area, they opened shore stations and fell upon the whales. Beginning in the 1850's, thousands were killed each year, including nursing mothers and young. With the discovery of their breeding grounds, in Baja California, the slaughter intensified. Within forty years, the gray whales had very nearly disappeared, and the industry collapsed. But gray whales have displayed an unusual power to regenerate the species, perhaps because they stay relatively close together and so have no difficulty finding each other even when their numbers are small. By the 1920's, gray whales were again to be found off the California coast. The hunting was resumed, and again the whales were nearly exterminated. In 1938, when there were only a few hundred left, they were protected by an international agreement. In the years since, they have once more recovered remarkably. In recent years, the Russians are known to have resumed the killing during the whales' northern sojourn, in what they claim are moderate numbers.

Midway down the dry, rocky west coast of Baja California, there is a great, shallow lagoon known as Scammon Lagoon, after its discoverer, the same Captain Charles Scammon who described the humpbacks' "amorous antics." In 1857, the captain had set forth from San Francisco to go whaling and "elephanting" (killing the huge, preposterous-looking, and helpless elephant seals that inhabited the rocks along the coast). Three hundred and fifty miles south of San Diego, off Sebastián Vizcaíno Bay, he steered his bark past rolling surf and through a narrow channel, and found himself in a vast, tranquil inland lake surrounded by desert and filled with great gray whales. He had discovered the grays' major breeding ground, where, as he reported in his memoirs, they "gathered in large numbers, passing and repassing into and out of the estuaries, or slowly raising their colossal forms midway above the surface, falling over on their sides as if by accident and dashing the water into foam and spray about them."

The captain sent out his whaleboats, and two large cows were easily killed. But the next morning, as a boat pursued a whale, the whale smashed it with its flukes, spilling the crew in all directions and injuring many of them. A relief boat was staved by another whale. The crew members were so demoralized by these attacks that when next they attempted to harpoon a whale most of them jumped overboard the moment it appeared beside them. The captain found his position peculiar, his vessel safe in smooth water, with countless whales nearby, but the men so panic-stricken that he couldn't man a boat. He had brought along a primitive type of explosive harpoon (or "bomb lance"), which he now decided to try out. With this weapon, his men safely killed all the whales the ship could handle and returned to San Francisco "so deeply laden that her scuppers were washed by the rippling tide."

Scammon's success soon brought other whalers down the coast. He described the scene in the lagoon the next season, when nine vessels and twenty or thirty whaleboats were there:

> The scene of slaughter was exceedingly picturesque and unusually exciting, especially on a calm morning, when the mirage would transform not only the boats and their crews into fantastic imagery, but the whales, as they sent forth their towering spouts of aqueous vapor, frequently tinted with blood, would appear greatly distorted. . . . The boats . . . would be seen gliding over the molten-looking surface of the water, with a . . . colossal form of the whale appearing for an instant, like a spectre . . . while the report of the bomb-guns would sound like the sudden discharge of musketry; but one cannot fully realize, unless he be an eyewitness, the intense and boisterous excitement of the reckless

pursuit. . . . Numbers of [boats] will be fast to whales at the same time, and the stricken animals, in their efforts to escape, can be seen darting in every direction through the water, or breaching headlong clear of its surface, coming down with a splash that sends columns of foam in every direction. . . . The men in the boats shout and yell . . . it is one continually changing aquatic battle scene.

During the 1850's, the hunting of gray whales extended along the coast of Upper and Lower California. "Every navigable lagoon of the region was discovered and explored, and the animals were hunted in every winding and intricate estuary. . . . In the seasons of 1858 and 1859, not only the bays and lagoons were teeming [with whalers], but the outside coast was lined with ships, from San Diego southward to Cape St. Lucas," wrote Captain Scammon. The captain wondered if the killing hadn't been overdone:

> The large bays and lagoons, where these animals once congregated, brought forth and nurtured their young, are already nearly deserted. The mammoth bones . . . lie bleaching on the shores of those silvery waters, and are scattered along the broken coasts, from Siberia to the Gulf of California; and ere long it may be questioned whether this mammal will not be numbered among the extinct species of the Pacific.

The captain's prophecy was twice almost fulfilled, but now there are estimated to be from 8,000 to 14,000 gray whales— enough to make them a major tourist attraction. On their migratory journey, hundreds can be seen from the California shore, and people gather at vantage points or go out in small boats to watch them pass. In the sixties the San Diego Natural History Museum began to offer whale-watching trips, chartering a large excursion fishing boat to take people 350 miles down the coast to Scammon Lagoon for a closer look, and a year after my trip to Bermuda I signed up for the voyage. For two days, our boat—the *HM 85*, eighty-five feet long, with forty of us aboard, including the crew—sailed down the coast, stopping for brief, fascinating shore excursions at the rocky islets of San Benito and San Martín, which are part of Mexico and are inhabited only by seasonal fishermen, elephant seals, sea lions, and birds. In the evenings, in the crowded cabin, I talked with Dr. William A. Burns, the museum director, about gray whales. Burns is not a biologist, but he is thoroughly acquainted with the subject. He is a former New Yorker—a squarely built man with warm blue eyes, great enthusiasm, and a large repertoire of entertaining stories. In discussing the whales, he gave credit for his information to the museum's whale specialist, Dr. Raymond M. Gilmore, whose title is Research Associate in Marine Mammals, who has made many trips to Scammon.

The California gray whale makes the longest migration of any mammal. The trip from its summer pasture in the northern seas to Baja California covers between four thousand and six thousand miles, depending on the route, and takes about three months of steady swimming. The gray whale cruises at four knots and covers from sixty to eighty nautical miles in twenty-four hours. Gray whales have been seen pegging along even on the darkest nights. How the whale navigates is not definitely known, but it is believed to use the position of the sun and, since it follows the coast for long stretches (the southward-migrating whales first come near shore in numbers off Oregon), underwater landmarks as well. Dr. Gilmore thinks that it is also guided by the remembered taste of sediment in the water that flows out of lagoons and estuaries.

When the whales start south, they are on a tight schedule. Pregnant females are in the van of the migration, for babies born in the cold, rough water of the open sea might die. Mating, gestation, and birth are all neatly arranged so that they happen in the right place and at the right time. The gestation period is thirteen months. After giving birth, a female spends eleven months nursing and resting. She mates during her next stay in the lagoon and carries the baby through the rich summer months, and it is born in the south the second winter after the previous birth. On the wintering grounds, then, half the mature females are giving birth or nursing and half are mating.

On our third morning, after an early breakfast, we rounded a buoy at the entrance to Scammon Lagoon. Ahead of us were high white sand dunes. On the right, breakers extended half a mile offshore. I admired Captain Scammon's nerve at taking his bark into these waters, and I wondered if this was where he had seen whales playing in the surf, as he described them in his memoirs:

> About the shoals at the mouth of one of the lagoons, in 1860, we saw large numbers of the monsters. It was at the low stage of the tide, and the shoal places were plainly marked by the constantly foaming breakers. To our surprise we saw many of the whales going through the surf where the depth of water was barely sufficient to float them. . . . One in particular lay for a half hour in the breakers, playing, as seals often do . . . turning from side to side with half-extended fins . . . at times making a playful spring with its bending flukes, throwing its body clear of the water, coming down with a heavy splash . . . with the heavy swell the animal would roll over in a listless manner, to all appearance enjoying the sport intensely.

I wished that I could witness intense enjoyment in a whale, but our captain did not take us close to the breakers. As we entered the channel, the dark green seas became violently choppy and we were warned by the crew to hang on tight. Black-backed gulls flapped along beside us. Then I saw ahead a white plume rise from the surface of the water, hang, and vanish. Shortly after that, we overtook a whale surging along, its broad back awash and gleaming; it was heading purposefully for the entrance to the lagoon, as we were. Ten minutes later, we were out of the chop and inside the lagoon. There was sudden calm. On one side of us were sculptured mountains of white sand; on the other, rippling water reached to the horizon. The main lagoon is a long, irregular crescent varying from five to ten miles in width and extending into the desert for almost thirty miles. There are many shallows, islands, and sand flats. Here and there, smaller tributary lagoons branch off. All around is one of the world's most desolate deserts—the Vizcaíno, which matches the Sahara for dryness. There is only one natural source of fresh water within hundreds of square miles—Ojo de Liebre, or Jack Rabbit Spring, where there was once a small settlement. The shores surrounding us were roadless and totally uninhabited.

A rusty fishing boat, at anchor, now came into view. It was serving as a base ship for outboard-engine skiffs we would use for following whales in the lagoon. We anchored. The skiffs were brought alongside, and the tourists, wearing orange life jackets, climbed into them. I found a seat beside Dr. Burns. The sailor at the tiller of our boat steered us toward the center of the lagoon, where several whales had spouted, and we buzzed over the water. I regretted the motor, for I would rather have drifted and waited for whales to appear, but Dr. Burns explained that chasing the whales in this fashion gave the tourists a better chance of getting pictures, and that was what most of them wanted.

Within five minutes, we were coming up on a whale. First, its head appeared. I saw the long slit of its mouth, a small eye, and a pattern of barnacles. It exhaled, with a sound like a steam pants presser, and then its huge back rolled out, ridged toward the tail with a series of small knobs, like the back of a prehistoric beast. We were so close that I felt my heart lurch. Being on the same level with a whale was quite different from viewing one from the deck of a big boat. The whale rose, blew, sank, rose again, blew another sighing, steamy breath, and disappeared with a wave of its flukes, leaving a swirling slick on the surface. The flukes, Dr. Burns said, are about ten feet across, weigh several hundred pounds, and can deliver a blow like that of a rubber sledgehammer. A couple of years ago, a diver swimming off La Jolla met a whale underwater and made the mistake of touching its tail as it glided by. The startled whale gave a mighty swish of its flukes, grazing the diver and knocking his mask off while the barnacles on its skin cut a gash in his forehead. He was lucky to survive. The flukes are a formidable means of defense for the whale, as Captain Scammon discovered. He also reported that sometimes the whales overturned boats by "rooting" them with their snouts, like pigs overturning a trough.

For the next hour, we motored here and there, seeing whales now close, now far off. Dr. Burns said he had heard it estimated that there were two or three thousand of them within the lagoon at this time. (Meanwhile, other groups of grays were wintering in other lagoons.) Every minute or so, a spout rose somewhere. We often saw whales performing what are called "spy hops"— sticking their heads eight or ten feet out of the water and hanging there for a few seconds, apparently intent on seeing what is going on. The most startling displays were the whales' extraordinary breaches, usually performed by the males. A forty-foot whale on end towers as high as a three-story building. This incredible length shoots out of the water at terrific speed, hangs in the air, and falls amid fountains of spray. The whales may breach out of sheer exuberance, or the breaching may be primarily a display of strength by males, or possibly slapping against the water allays an itch from barnacles; occasionally mothers and calves also breach.

A number of times, we came upon mothers and young swimming side by side, the baby whale rising and falling in a rhythm that exactly matched that of its parent. These calves were a few weeks old. A newborn gray is from twelve to seventeen feet long and weighs from fifteen hundred to three thousand pounds. Captain Scammon wrote that as birth time arrived the pregnant whales collected in the remote reaches of the lagoon and "huddled together so thickly that it was difficult for a boat to cross the waters without coming in contact with them." He also wrote of the whales' strong maternal feelings: "This species of whale manifests the greatest affection for its young, and seeks the sheltered estuaries lying under a tropical sun, as if to warm its offspring." He described how a whale struck with a harpoon would attempt to escape by running along the bottom, and noted that if a mother was harpooned and lost sight of her calf she would instantly "stop and 'sweep' around in search." He added, "If the boat comes in contact with her, it is quite sure to be staved." In the case of the wounding of a calf, he wrote, "the parent animal, in her frenzy, will chase the boats, and . . . overturn them with her head, or dash them in pieces with a stroke of her ponderous flukes." Whalers sometimes deliberately shot a calf and towed it into shallow water, because the mother would follow and could be more easily killed there.

We came across several sleeping whales, lying awash like logs. Having slept so little on migration, the gray whales catch up in the lagoons. We saw a sleeping mother whose calf was apparently trying to wake her by splashing and nudging as we approached. She seemed to wake with a start, and both of them dived out of sight.

What caused the greatest sensation in our skiff was coming across whales courting. This activity often involves not two animals but a trio. Since half the females are pregnant or nursing, only half are in breeding condition, so there are two males to every available female. The exact role of the second male— whether he is a bystander or a participant, perhaps assisting by lying across the female to stabilize her—is debated by cetologists. Whatever is happening, the three of them make a tremendous flurry in the water, rising, falling, splashing, and revolving, with giant flippers waving above the surface. We came on several such scenes, but nothing was explicit until, quite close to our boat, a whale revolved in the water, turning belly up on the surface, and there was a brief but distinct glimpse of its long, pink, erect penis. Our boatload was divided between the happy photographers who had caught this memorable view and the chagrined photographers who had missed it. Dr. Burns was jubilant, since both winners and losers had had a fair chance, and the trip was now undeniably a success.

When we got back to the *HM 85*, two people who were living aboard the rusty anchored fishing boat had come over to visit. They were Peter Paul Ott, a wildlife painter and photographer from Laguna Beach, and his wife, Holly. They had been living on the boat for two months, and had found the beauty and the solitude marvelous. Ott described some of their experiences with whales. He said that when the boat was quiet, with the auxiliary engine for generating electricity turned off, the whales seemed to become curious, and made closer and closer passes. One evening after dark, he had heard a whale blow very close. A large baby whale and a huge mother were coming straight for the boat. Ott shone a light on them and saw the calf dive under the boat. Then the mother dove underneath, looking like a blimp outlined in phosphorescence. The calf emerged, rolled over on its side, and looked up at Ott with its ridiculously small eye. Ott tried to scratch its back, but couldn't reach it. He said that sleeping whales sometimes collided with the boat as they drifted with the tide, hitting with a dull thud. In the calm of night, a whale's blow could be heard for miles, and a breach sounded like a cannon as it echoed among the dunes.

Ott's most distressing experience, he said, was with an orphaned and injured calf. He saw it swimming alone, listing to one side. It became stranded on a beach. With an oar, Ott was able to heave it back in the water. There were two large whales nearby, but they offered no help. The next day, the orphan was stranded again, higher on the beach, and there was nothing that Ott could do for it. It rolled its eyes, watching him, and winced as he touched it. Its skin was so delicate that it broke at the touch of a fingernail. Gulls settled on it and tore it. The whale waved its tail as the gulls pecked, but it made no cry. Ott concealed himself and watched. Coyotes came and circled. It was very gruesome, Ott said, and he could think of no way to help or to administer a coup de grace. He was greatly relieved when the whale died.

When I woke the next morning, a soft gray haze hung over the lagoon, and the water was like a dark mirror. The whales seemed to be moving more slowly or resting with their whole length on the surface. The *HM 85* coasted deeper into the lagoon, across shallows where weeds grew. I went ashore with a small group and walked alone on a beach bordered by strange rocks and twisted, thorny desert shrubs. The solitude seemed boundless; Captain Scammon and his bomb lances and cooking pots had left no trace. It was perhaps the most beautiful meeting place of land and sea that I had ever seen. Once in a while, as I walked along the silent, endless beach, a whale would rise just offshore, and I would hear its soft, sighing breath. It was a companionable sound.

In the 1950's, Dr. Paul Dudley White, the heart specialist, in the course of attempts to measure the heartbeat of a gray whale, pursued several in Scammon Lagoon, trying to implant a harpoon carrying electrocardiographic equipment. After various difficulties, he at last connected with a whale, but the resulting data were far from clear, and he gave up. In 1965, Dr. Robert Elsner, a physiologist from the Scripps Institution, and Dr. David Kenney, a veterinarian who was also a vice-president of a marine park in San Diego called Sea World, decided to try their luck. They hired a Japanese whale gunner and went to Scammon, where they harpooned a baby whale and lifted it to the deck in a net. When the heart recordings were finished, it seemed useless to put the little whale back in the water, since it could only die of its wound, so they lashed it to the deck of their boat and took it back to San Diego. The trip lasted three days, but the whale lived, and was put in a pool at Sea World. Dr. Kenney patched it up, and, in spite of a collapsed lung, the whale amazed its captors by surviving for almost two months.

This episode convinced Kenney that, with gentle handling, a baby whale could be captured and kept indefinitely. He was fascinated by the possibility of raising such animals in captivity, and the other Sea World directors agreed to the project. In March 1971, Kenney again went to Scammon Lagoon. After a number of chases in a small boat, he maneuvered a mother and her calf under the bow of the boat, slipped a noose around the calf, and hauled it to the beach. The mother left as darkness fell. In the morning, the calf was worked onto a stretcher and floated out to a larger vessel, where it was put in a converted fish well for the trip to San Diego. The calf, an eighteen-foot female, arrived in good health and was put in a large, round tank. She was weighed in a sling and tipped the scale at forty-three hundred pounds. Now Dr. Kenney tried to fabricate whale milk from its known ingredients. The resulting mixture had the consistency of cooling fudge and would not go through a feeding tube, so he improvised a concoction of heavy cream, ground squid and fish, cod-liver oil, yeast, vitamins, and water. The whale, who had been named Gigi, reluctantly partook of it. Kenney's laboratory-animal manager, a tall, kindly Nebraskan named Bud N. Dona-hoo, was in charge of the feedings, for which the water in the whale's tank was lowered. To get the tube into Gigi's esophagus, Donahoo had to thrust his arm into her mouth, parting the bristles of baleen that hung like curtains from her jaw. This was apparently somewhat painful at first, but after a while there was a permanent gap and no further pain. In her first two weeks in the tank, Gigi lost a hundred and fifty pounds. Then she began to gain and grow, at the rate of twenty-seven pounds and a third of an inch a day. She was moved to a larger tank. The only abnormal thing about Gigi was that she seemed exceptionally fond of sleeping, even for an infant. A dolphin was put in with her for company, and girl swimmers from Sea World's corps of performing Sea Maids were employed to swim beside her, poking at her to keep her awake. After a while, Gigi came to life and began to tear around the tank, jumping, flopping, rolling, and waving her flippers like a normal whale.

An important factor in the successful captivity of Gigi was the relationship that developed between her and Donahoo. He thought of her as a lonely, confused being, imprisoned in her great sensitive bulk of flesh and isolated by lack of communication. He also realized that she was only a baby and must long for reassurance. He searched for some way to make contact with her. By accident, when he was cleaning the tank one day, he sprayed a hose on her flukes, and she lifted them to hold them in the spray. It was a clue that she might enjoy being rubbed. He began touching her gently. At first, she shuddered and twitched, but soon he was rubbing her from nose to tail, and she relaxed under his hands. His next problem was to find a means of communication. He talked to her constantly, but it didn't seem likely that she would understand words, so he decided on a system of pats as signals—one pat for attention, two pats to open her mouth, three firm pats for "No" or "Be quiet." The whale learned these commands. Now Donahoo was able to move her about in the tank, and this was a tremendous help in handling her. With the water lowered, he could stand by her head, signaling to her, and she would wiggle her great bulk to follow him.

Gigi's weaning took place when Donahoo felt her sucking on his hand while he was putting the tube in her throat. He put a squid in her mouth, and she swallowed it gratefully. Soon she was eating squid by the handful, and then sucking them up from the floor of her tank. This was a development that fascinated scientific observers, for never before had the mechanics of a gray whale eating been directly observed. The cetologist William E. Schevill, of Harvard, watched as she scooped in the squid—turning on her side, opening one side of her mouth and sucking like a giant vacuum cleaner, and then ramming her tongue forward to squirt out the water. Once weaned, Gigi learned to take food from the hands of people swimming beside her or to come to the side of the tank at the sight of a bucket. When Donahoo dropped the water level and approached her, she would come over to him eagerly, with her mouth open.

One of the things that greatly puzzled Donahoo was how Gigi could distinguish him from anyone else. When other handlers tried to do things with her—often in connection with the numerous scientific tests she was undergoing—she frequently raised such a ruckus that they were forced to stop and send for Donahoo. As soon as he arrived, no matter what he was wearing —and in a wet suit identity is well hidden—Gigi calmed down. Donahoo never figured out how Gigi recognized him, but it seemed clear that he had become her parental figure. Mutual affection also sprang up between the whale and one of the Sea Maids, a girl named Sue Bailey, who was deft at feeding Gigi.

By the end of Gigi's first year in the tank at Sea World, she had grown to nearly seven tons and was twenty-seven feet long. Scientists from numerous institutions had made a great variety of physiological tests, and Dr. Kenney had filing cabinets full of new whale data. Her rate of growth, food consumption, blood composition, and respiratory function had been recorded. But, to Dr. Kenney's regret, the managers of Sea World, which by now was spending two hundred dollars a day just on her food, felt that the upkeep expense was prohibitive, and they decided that soon they would have to put her back in the sea, before she got too big to be moved. When I heard about this, and having visited Gigi's birthplace at Scammon Lagoon, I decided to go to Sea World to see her.

At the gate of the park, I was met by Bud Donahoo, a tall, athletic-looking man in his late thirties with kind blue eyes and a boyish face, and Sue Bailey, a pretty girl with long brown hair. They led me to a circular tank, fifty feet across. A huge gray cylinder rested at the bottom of the tank. "That's her favorite place —by the water inlet," Sue said. After a minute or two, Gigi slowly pumped her flukes, rose, and began to glide majestically in a slow circle on the surface, blowing leisurely spouts. I said I thought she was lovely, and Donahoo and Sue beamed. Gigi sank peacefully to the bottom and went to sleep.

I went back the next morning, at the suggestion of Donahoo, who had told me that the water in the tank would be lowered then so that Gigi could be fed and Sue could attempt to ride her. First, Sue, in a wet suit, approached the whale, splashing water ahead of her as though to announce her coming. She splashed Gigi's head, and then put her hands on her back and rubbed her vigorously. Donahoo, carrying a bucket of squid, approached and also patted her. "She's talking!" he shouted up at me. "Can you hear it?" Water splashing loudly over the rim of an adjoining tank drowned out any sound from the whale, but, as I watched, her whole body swelled and heaved in response to Donahoo's caress. Her huge, rubbery person seemed to emanate feeling. Sue took a handful of squid and began stuffing them into Gigi's mouth, her arm disappearing to the elbow. As Donahoo and Sue went on rubbing and patting vigorously, and stuffing in squid, the huge cylinder of flesh vibrated with responsive animation.

Then Sue put her hands on Gigi's back and leaped astride. Gigi's tail fluttered, and, ponderously, she began to move. As they slowly circled the tank, Donahoo climbed out and joined me. "If Gigi didn't like being ridden, she'd roll Sue off any time she liked," he said. The whale and the girl went around and around, Sue sitting astride her like a mahout aboard an elephant, and the whale's flukes pumping rhythmically. Then Gigi came to a halt. Sue patted her head and she moved again. Donahoo said that she was responding to signals from Sue. Sue stopped her, dismounted, and resumed caressing Gigi around the head and stuffing her mouth with squid.

Donahoo said it amazed him how Gigi could discriminate between different kinds of food. Given twenty pounds of squid with a few mackerel mixed in, she would swallow the squid and spit out the mackerel. "She's usually a docile animal," he said. "But she can be aggressive. She bobs her head up and down and shakes her whole body from side to side when she's perturbed. She's knocked me across the tank many times. But I can always calm her down. The signal to be quiet is three firm pats. She may start right up again, but then I quiet her again until she gets over whatever it is that's disturbing her." Next, Donahoo told me about talking to the whale. He said Gigi made deep interior noises that he couldn't describe. One day, early in their relationship, he tapped out a peculiar rhythm on her head and was astonished to hear the whale repeat the sequence. He tried another rhythm, and she repeated that, too. He concluded that Gigi was trying to talk to him. Thereafter, throughout her babyhood, he had daily conversations with her, tapping and getting answers. Now her answers had tapered off, perhaps in discouragement at getting no whale sounds back, but she still talked on occasion. "I believe that this animal can be communicated with by sound," Donahoo said. To his regret, none of the visiting scientists had been interested in the phenomenon, because they did not regard it as part of the whale's natural behavior. Donahoo told me that he had learned to distinguish at least four different sounds made by Gigi. When she uttered them, he said, the whole tank vibrated. "The vibrations hit your legs," he continued. "When she's happy, there's one big grunt. Her whole body swells up. Sometimes she makes other sounds before or after, but the happy sound is just one."

Sue had mounted again, and she and Gigi were again making stately circles. Then the whale gave a leisurely roll and Sue fell off. She remounted and was dumped again. Leaving Gigi, she climbed the ladder and joined us.

Plans for releasing Gigi were made by Dr. William Evans, a marine biologist at the Naval Undersea Center, in San Diego, who had been studying her. He felt that she would have the best chance of survival if she was released in spring, when the gray whales were migrating north to the feeding grounds. Even so, he suspected that release would be a shock to her; the sudden change to the darkness of the sea's depths, the noise of ships' propellers, and the need to find food would be "harrowing," he told a newspaper reporter. He worked out a way to attach an instrument package, which could store and transmit data, to her back, in order to keep track of her after her release. A few weeks ahead of time, large stitches of nylon thread were sewn through the blubber of her back, with loops sticking up to hold the equipment.

Before dawn on a cool March day, Gigi was wrapped in a sling and hoisted from the tank by a crane. She was put down on a six-teen-inch-thick foam-rubber mattress on a thirty-two-foot Navy flatbed truck and covered with wet blankets. Donahoo and Sue rode with her, patting and reassuring her. She breathed quickly, indicating apprehension, but gave no signs of serious distress. The truck drove six miles through dark city streets to a Navy pier, and there Gigi was transferred to a barge, which carried her four and a half miles out to sea. Then, a few minutes before ten, a crane lowered the sling into the water. As it touched the surface, Donahoo dived over the side and, when the sling was released, pulled the canvas clear. The whale gave a graceful wave of her flukes and swam free. Donahoo swam beside her for twenty or thirty yards, and then she dived. She surfaced two or three hundred yards away, made a wide sweep around the boat, as through orienting herself, and started north. There were other northbound whales in the area, and their spouts were visible, a half mile away. For several days, Evans tracked her in a small research vessel, picking up signals from the transmitter on her back. This was more difficult than he had expected. The transmitter sent its signals by means of a two-foot-tall antenna, which operated only when it was out of water. Evans had failed to allow for the fact that yearling whales do not roll as far out of the water as adults do, and so the signals were relatively brief and infrequent. When Evans left Gigi, a Navy plane picked up her signal, and her northward progress was recorded. She covered eighty miles in the first four days. The instruments indicated that she was diving to maximum depths of two and three hundred feet. From the plane, observers saw signs in the water that she had found something to eat. At one point, to Evans' dismay, she lingered to play in a kelp bed and bent the antenna, reducing the range of the signals from twenty-five or thirty miles to five or ten. Nevertheless, her progress was followed by plane for more than two weeks longer. At that point, the funds allotted for the project were exhausted and the Navy ceased to follow her. At the last report, early in May, she was with other gray whales north of Monterey. She had covered more than five hundred miles. The transmitter was designed to work for months, and there was a remote hope that a ship or a plane would pick up her signals during the summer or on her return journey south, but this didn't occur. In any event, for the first time in all the eons of human and whale existence a great whale had been in the power of human beings and had escaped with its life.

Epilogue
... AND THE SONG ENDS

There are scientists who predict that during the next twenty-five or thirty years almost all wild animals—perhaps three-quarters of the species living today—will become extinct. I find this almost impossible to believe—it is too much for me to comprehend—and yet sober and competent men, possessed of information I do not have, do not find it incredible. Therefore I, too, must accept it as possible. If this prediction is fulfilled, two or three generations from now there will be few people who have seen a living creature in the wild. Will these future people find this as inexpressibly sad as we do, contemplating it now? Can one miss what one has never had? By definition, one cannot. And yet a person robbed of his inheritance is the poorer whether he knows it or not. The death of the animals will be the end of a long and intimate association. If one consults Genesis, one finds that man's relationship with the animals began shortly after the fifth day, when God gave him dominion over every living thing. Or, if one consults the scientists, one is told that in early times the progenitors of men were indistinguishable from the rest of the animal kingdom, becoming altered and estranged only a few million years ago. Even after that, the relationship remained close. Besides hunting animals and eating them, as is normal for a predator, people lived closely with animals, deriving from them material for art, poetry, folklore, fable, philosophy, science, and much of the imagery of their language. It is difficult to say how the people born fifty or sixty years from now, into a world that is barren of almost any life except that which human beings husband or control, will feel about it. Quite likely they will adapt adequately, but they may find some of the past meaningless and puzzling. What, for instance, can it mean to such a person of the future to read of the lion lying down with the lamb, or the way of the serpent upon the rock, the tiger burning bright, the sly fox, the prudent ant, the wolf at the door, or the Owl and the Pussycat going to sea? Will this future reader, leafing through an old book, experience a strange, intuitive twinge of longing as he wonders what it means to be "happy as a lark"?